HENRY J. KAISER

Builder in the Modern American West

American Studies Series
WILLIAM H. GOETZMANN, EDITOR

Henry J. KAISER

Builder in the Modern American West

BY MARK S. FOSTER
FOREWORD BY WILLIAM H. GOETZMANN

UNIVERSITY OF TEXAS PRESS
AUSTIN

Grateful acknowledgment is made to the Bancroft Library, University of California, Berkeley, and to Edgar F. Kaiser, Jr., for permission to use materials from the Henry J. Kaiser Papers, the Edgar F. Kaiser, Sr., Papers, and the Six Companies Papers, and to the original publishers for permission to reprint material from the following articles by Mark S. Foster: "Giant of the West: Henry J. Kaiser and Regional Industrialization, 1930–1950," *Business History Review* 59 (Spring 1985): 1–23, "Challenger from the West: Henry J. Kaiser and the Detroit Automobile Industry, 1945–1955," *Michigan History* 70 (January–February 1986): 30–39; "Prosperity's Prophet: Henry J. Kaiser and the Consumer/Suburban Culture, 1930–1950," *Western Historical Quarterly* 17 (April 1986): 165–184.

FIRST EDITION, 1989

Requests for permission to reproduce material
from this work should be sent to:
Permissions, University of Texas Press
Box 7819   Austin, Texas 78713-7819

LIBRARY OF CONGRESS
CATALOGING-IN-PUBLICATION DATA

Foster, Mark S.
  Henry J. Kaiser : builder in the modern American West / by Mark S. Foster.—1st ed.
    p.   cm.—(American studies series)
  Bibliography: p.
  Includes index.
  ISBN: 978-0-292-74226-0
  1. Kaiser, Henry J., 1882–   . 2. Businessmen—United States—Biography. I. Title. II. Series.
  HC102.5.K3F67   1989
  338.092—dc20
  [B]   89-33275
                                                                 CIP

First paperback printing, 2012

CONTENTS

FOREWORD
BY WILLIAM H. GOETZMANN

To the generation of Americans who remember the World War II home front, Henry J. Kaiser is the unforgettable "can do" industrialist whose Liberty Ships, built at an incredible rate, were a major factor in defeating the Axis powers. To latter-day business historians, he is a one-of-a-kind eccentric whose operations defied all the logic of scientific management. For cultural historians, Kaiser is a Horatio Alger story—that of the boy, born of modest parents, who quit school after the eighth grade and began a seemingly endless success story with his skill in marketing cameras, including an ever-increasing series of cheap photographic products just then being produced for the first time by Kodak. From the beginning he seemed to grasp the broader implications of twentieth-century technologies and engineering developments. As an industrialist he became a national legend—one not always admired by his fellow industrialists, who resented Kaiser's boldness and ability to attact media attention. Because he became, in himself, such a many-sided phenomenon—master builder of huge dams, like the Hoover and the Grand Coulee, producer of instant Liberty Ships, a steel producer, a cement maker, a man who understood and even admired organized labor, and, finally, a man who revolutionized medical care with his Kaiser Permanente Medical Care Program—Henry J. Kaiser is a fitting figure for inclusion in a series devoted to interdisciplinary studies of American life.

Like American Studies students, he doesn't fit easily into one disciplinary or theoretical framework. He was bold enough to transcend the normal specialties of an increasingly specializing American industrial structure. He had so few bureaucrats on his managerial team that it often appeared to rivals that he did not know what he was doing whenever he entered an unfamiliar field. Needless to say, Kaiser was a fast learner with an empathic personality. Indeed, with respect to the latter quality, some said that his success in building massive public works during the New Deal was entirely due to the fact that he was the only contractor who could get along with Secretary of the Interior Harold Ickes, FDR's official curmudgeon. Certainly Kaiser was an important figure in providing massive WPA employment during the Depression, in part because he offered a private industrial alternative to the Army Corps of Engineers, which Ickes detested so much that he even wrote a book denouncing it for the boondoggle institution that he considered it to be. Better than most businessmen, Kaiser knew Washington's corridors of power in the 1930s. At almost the same time, but with different goals, another young man was also learning about the power structure in Washington. Thanks to this knowledge, Lyndon B. Johnson became one of the capital's leading brokers of power, and eventually president of the United States.

Besides their understanding of power and their ability to empathize with the masses of ordinary men and women workers, the two men had one other thing in common. They were at heart western men. Indeed, one of the things that is so striking about Kaiser is his western way of doing things. Like the early oil mogul, Bet-A-Million Gates, Kaiser was a wildcatter who loved to take a chance on new projects. He gambled on his intuition, his charm, his public relations skills, his persistence, and he usually won. As the shadows of the twentieth century lengthen over the American West, it behooves policy-makers, as well as scholars and writers, to understand the often perverse western maverick mentality. Millions of television viewers around the world now identify the typical western man not as the cowboy (including the Marlboro Man), but as the wheeler-dealer J. R. Ewing of *Dallas*.

One of the fascinating things about Kaiser is how he seems to be characteristic of at least one of the benign Ewing wheeler-dealer archetypes. He thought big. He was flexible and pragmatic. He got things done on a grand scale. Even more fascinating, however, than the comparison with the Ewings (one with which his conservative rivals would have happily agreed), is just how much Henry J. Kaiser represents continuity and tradition in the winning of the West. He liked to think of himself as a rugged individualist, a self-made man who, taking Horace Greeley's advice, went West and "grew up with the country." The truth is that, like virtually all of the early western entrepreneurs, Kaiser succeeded only with the help of a federal government which, as a rugged westerner, he was supposed to despise. However, Kaiser, whether building dams or constructing Liberty Ships, resembled nothing so much as the old-time western entrepreneur who existed on purveying supplies to the frontier army, or who traveled in stagecoaches and wagon trains often protected by the U.S. cavalry. As the Corps of Topographical Engineers mapped the West, laid the main wagon roads, and inventoried the potential riches of the country, they made it possible for pioneers to better survive and prosper. The great Powell, King, Hayden, and Wheeler geographical and geological surveys after the Civil War represented even more substantial federal aid to the western entrepreneur. Then there were the land-grant colleges that began to turn out legions of men and women who, thanks to the federal government, were able to aid in the development of the West. Finally, too, the federal creation of national parks and monuments knitted together the West's most characteristic industry—one in which Kaiser participated in his latter days as he developed hotels and resorts in far western Hawaii—tourism.

Thus, though Henry J. Kaiser appeared in many roles, the one that perhaps fits him best and sets him aside from the old-money "enterprising elite" of the conservative East and the Midwest, is his role as the descendant of the typical western entrepreneur—whether cattleman, sodbuster, city-builder, or transcontinental railroad mogul. Perhaps he didn't realize it, though many who knew him sensed it, but Kaiser took on his real lineage from the Old West. He became a more modern part of the legend. In this respect, as well as any number of others, his story is a fascinating one as told by Mark Foster in this book.

May 16, 1989

ACKNOWLEDGMENTS

It is ironic that many books, including this one, bear a single author's name; without support from numerous institutions and hundreds of other people, most volumes would never be written and published. Many others played key roles in guiding this work.

Financial support and release time from other professional tasks were indispensable. Daniel Fallon, former dean of liberal arts at the University of Colorado at Denver, helped me obtain a year-long fellowship; his successor, John Ostheimer, provided important follow-up institutional support. My history department colleagues have tolerated my prolonged absences; Mary Conroy, John S. Haller, Jr., Tom Noel, and others have patiently endured endless discussions of my subject. Henry J. Kaiser could hardly have imagined an author taking six years to finish his biography; he would likely have been looking for results after six weeks. But his grandson, Edgar F. Kaiser, Jr., shared my vision of a scholarly book. Knowing that a non-controlled biography of his grandfather would meet with the disfavor of many former and present Kaiser executives, Edgar Kaiser, Jr., still believed this book should be written. He not only read two versions of my manuscript but also was instrumental in arranging a generous "no-strings-attached" research support grant. The Herbert C. Hoover and Harry S. Truman presidential libraries also provided financial support. Robert Litchard of the University of Colorado Foundation efficiently transferred these funds to me when I was running short.

I spent five months at the Bancroft Library, where patient staff members endured thousands of requests for assistance. I am grateful for the guidance of Dr. Bonnie Hardwick, Estelle Rebec, Malca Chall, Richard Ogar, Ollin Blue, Peter Hanff, Ellen Jones, Franz Enciso, Irene Moran, Larry Dinnean, Mairi McFall, and Melissa Riley. Another important visit was to the National Archives, where René M. Jassaud, Daniel T. Goggin,

George P. Perros, John E. Taylor, Jerry N. Hess, Gary Ryan, Georgia Stamas, and Janet Hargett provided expert guidance through bewildering thickets of Record Groups. In Washington, Paul T. Heffron and others at the Library of Congress provided helpful assistance, as did Don Post through the U.S. Maritime Commission collections.

I visited four presidential libraries. At the Eisenhower Library, Rod Soubers helped me turn a brief stop into a profitable visit; the same was true of Frances M. Seeber and the staff at the Roosevelt Library. My visits to the Hoover and Truman libraries were longer. At the Hoover Library, John Fawcett, Dale Mayer, Robert Wood, Cora F. Pedersen, Mildred Mather, Shirley Sondergard, and R. Lawrence Angove went out of their way to draw my attention to collections I had not considered using. At the Truman Library, Benedict K. Zobrist, Dennis Bilger, Erwin Mueller, and Nell Cleveland Flanagan directed me toward very useful oral history tapes.

I used the resources of many more research libraries. I would like to thank the following individuals: James Wrenn of the Motor Vehicle Manufacturers Association Library in Detroit; Warner Pflug and Dione Miles of the Walter Reuther Library at Wayne State University; Charles A. Sherrill and James B. Casey of the Western Reserve Historical Society in Cleveland; Mary Jo Pugh, Bentley Library, University of Michigan; Collin B. Hamer, Jr., New Orleans Public Library; Erika Chadbourn, Harvard University Law School Library; Judith A. Schiff, Manuscripts and Archives, Yale University Libraries; Janet Ness, University of Washington Libraries; Nicholas B. Scheetz, Manuscript Division, Georgetown University Library; and Harold L. Miller, State Historical Society of Wisconsin.

Many people performed crucial research tasks in archives I was unable to visit personally. In West Germany, Dr. Norbert Finzsch and Martina Sprengel of the Anglo-American Institute, University of Cologne, conducted rigorous genealogical research in parish records. In upstate New York, Irina Clark of the Canajoharie Art Museum and Library dug out information about Kaiser family activities in the late nineteenth century. Dr. John C. Shideler, President of Futurepast, a historical consulting firm, helped me uncover many of Kaiser's activities in Spokane. Ric Fergeson, a Ph.D. candidate in history at the University of California, Berkeley, located several of Kaiser's homes in Oakland. Meg Sondey, a doctoral candidate in business history at the Ohio State University, enlightened me about the important technological advances in heavy construction equipment attributable to Robert Le Tourneau. Brian Taves, a Ph.D. candidate in cinema history and criticism at the University of Southern California, helped unravel details of Hollywood's interest during World War II in making a movie based on Kaiser's life. Other scholars shared their research on Kaiser and closely related subjects. Dr. Elizabeth A. Cobbs allowed me to read a chapter of her Ph.D. dissertation on Kaiser's and Rockefeller's activities in South America. Dr. Mimi Stein, president of Oral History Associates in San Francisco, generously allowed me access to transcripts of several Kaiser executives I was unable to interview.

Several dozen former Kaiser executives and individuals who had other connections with him provided useful information in personal interviews and/or extensive correspondence. They include Stephen D. Bechtel, Tim A. Bedford, Mario Bermudez, Richard C. Block, Walston S. Brown, Edward A. Carlson, Cecil C. Cutting (M.D.), Fred Drewes, Theodore A. Dungan, Milton D. Eisele, Scott Fleming, Sidney R. Garfield (M.D.), The Honorable Arthur Goldberg, Sherlock D. Hackley, C. E. Harper, Peter S. Hass, Clifton F. Haughey, Philip Haughey, Stanley Hiller, Jr., Ward C. Humphreys, Frank E. Justice, Raymond M. Kay (M.D.), Clifford H. Keene (M.D.), David Lamoreaux, Leighton S. C. Louis, Thomas K. McCarthy, John A. McCone, Ken and Blanche Mericle, John J. Motley, James T. Nolan, Carl A. Olson, Louis H. Oppenheim, Edward R. Ordway, Gerard Piel, Mrs. Thomas Price, Thomas J. Ready, Jr., George and Ruth Scheer, David C. Slipher, Bud Smyser, William Soule, James E. Toomey, Alex Troffey, Tudor A. Wall, Todd Woodell, Mrs. George Woods, and James A. Vohs.

Several individuals associated with Kaiser went far out of their way to provide useful guidance. Donald A. Duffy, Vice President of Public and Community Relations for the Kaiser Foundation Health Plan, has been enthusiastic and supportive since I first approached the organization eight years ago. Lambreth Hancock, long-time personal aide to Kaiser, allowed me to examine his unpublished memoirs of his years with the boss. Both of these men provided useful criticisms of portions of my manuscript. James F. McCloud, former President of Industrias Kaiser Argentina, answered my letter of inquiry with a probing twenty-page analysis of Kaiser's association with Juan Perón and his business ties to South America. McCloud also provided a useful critique of my chapters on Kaiser Aluminum and the South America venture. Eugene E. Trefethen, Jr., perhaps Kaiser's closest business associate for forty years, submitted to three separate interviews and read an early version of the entire manuscript. He patiently helped me unravel many complicated facets of Kaiser's business career. His secretary, Brunla Van Cleve, tracked down missing addresses of dozens of former Kaiser personnel. K. Tim Yee, former Vice Chairman of the Kaiser Development Company, provided many hours of thoughtful commentary on Kaiser's development of Hawaii; he and his son Kevin royally entertained me and my wife when we visited Hawaii in 1984. These wise, generous people are more than professional contacts; they are friends.

Kaiser family members offered insights into Henry Kaiser's personal life. Edgar F. Kaiser, Jr., recalled many hours of guidance his grandfather passed along in his last years. Alyce Kaiser willingly submitted to two long interviews and fed me two splendid lunches in New York. Gretchen Gudgell, Henry Kaiser III, Henry M. Kaiser, and Carlyn Stark provided revealing personal accounts of their interaction with their grandfather.

A number of scholars provided additional guidance and advice; they include Carl Abbott, Jack S. Ballard, Paul Barrett, Elizabeth A. Cobbs, Peter L. Grant, George R. Inger, Frederick C. Luebke, Albro Martin, Elliot A. Rosen, H. Lee Scamehorn, Bruce E. Seely, Paul Smith, Peter C. Stewart, and William M. Tuttle, Jr. Several intrepid souls plowed through early versions of the manuscript; John G. Clark, Donald Hinchey, and Edward A. White provided much needed criticism and encouragement. With Mark H. Rose, I tested the limits of our long professional association and warm friendship; he endured both early and late versions of the whole manuscript.

Finally, my immediate family has been closest to this project over the past six years. My stepdaughters, Adrienne and Abby Whitelaw, have been too busy growing up to take much notice; yet they have provided crucial relief from total absorption in this project. My wife, Rickey Lynn Hendricks, has been deeply involved from the start. She became my partner in this project in far more than a conventional spousal sense. A historian herself, she became so fascinated with Kaiser that she completed a Ph.D. dissertation on the Kaiser Health Plan. In addition, she read portions of this work and provided trenchant criticism. For her love, counsel and all other types of support, I dedicate this book to her.

M.S.F., March 1989

HENRY J. KAISER

Builder in the Modern American West

INTRODUCTION

Shortly before 1942 Henry J. Kaiser had become widely known; that summer he became a national celebrity. In 1941 Kaiser-managed shipyards on the West Coast turned out hundreds of cargo vessels, but Axis submarines were sinking the slow-moving targets as fast as they were launched. So in a speech to shipyard workers in Portland, Oregon, on July 19, 1942, Kaiser unveiled a novel idea. He proposed to convert some shipyards into aircraft plants; he would build a fleet of five thousand large cargo planes to fly critically needed troops and materiel over the submarines. According to Kaiser, if the government authorized the proposal, he would finish the job by the end of 1943.

Some believed the idea was preposterous. But by then, Kaiser had done the "impossible" so often that even his most outrageous proposals could not be easily dismissed. He deliberately presented the Portland speech on Sunday morning, allowing reporters time to provide full accounts in Monday morning editions of eastern papers. The press took the bait; several national columnists urged President Roosevelt to try Kaiser's idea. Before the month was out, the irrepressible western industrialist unveiled the details of the plan in the Oval Office. Like many of Roosevelt's visitors, Kaiser misinterpreted the President's frequent smiles and nods as enthusiastic support. Having heard what he wanted, he pressured government officials to bend bureaucratic rules and provide required authorizations promptly.

But established aircraft manufacturers quickly countered. War or no war, they had no intention of permitting the upstart shipbuilder to join their industry. War Production Board (WPB) chief Donald M. Nelson felt the pressure. He sincerely believed that Kaiser's initiative would interfere with aircraft production, yet he knew that if the WPB turned Kaiser down flat, his agency would face a public relations disaster. The war effort was not yet going well, and government officials were prime targets for sniping journalists. The upshot was that although the government denied Kaiser's bid to build conventional cargo planes, the WPB authorized three prototypes for huge experimental cargo planes in the one-to-two-hundred-ton range. The catch was that Kaiser could not interfere with ongoing aircraft production, nor could he raid established contractors for experienced personnel.

Many other men would have recognized such a "runaround" for what it was and would have given up. Not Kaiser. Two of his most remarkable qualities were enthusiasm and perseverance. As soon as he had authorization letters in hand, Kaiser demonstrated these qualities by working his magic on Howard Hughes. The movie mogul and aircraft designer was only beginning to gain a reputation as an eccentric. But he had alienated important military officials and did not have much war work. Hughes was recuperating from an illness at the Fairmont Hotel in San Francisco. Kaiser bounced into Hughes' suite and laid out a complete program; if Hughes designed the prototypes, Kaiser would build planes. Even Hughes' biographers were impressed by how Kaiser won him over: "[Kaiser] turned on all his considerable charm and powers of persuasion. . . . Against his better judgment and swept up by Kaiser's appeal [Hughes] agreed to the collaboration."[1] The episode was vintage Kaiser. Once he made up his mind, he moved quickly and forcefully. Throughout his life, Kaiser dominated men who usually dominated others.

Just who was Henry J. Kaiser, this enigmatic public figure who achieved prominence so suddenly and dramatically that reporters dubbed him "The Miracle Man"? To admirers, Kaiser's achievements seemed unprecedented, his business practices audacious and bold, his relations with others direct and magnanimous. To critics, Kaiser's "triumphs" were costly boondoggles, his ethics suspect, and his interpersonal dealings furtive and self-serving. By V-J Day, he had become one of the nation's most controversial public figures; most held strong opinions about him. Like a handful of American entrepreneurs, such as Andrew Carnegie, Henry Ford, and Thomas Edison, Kaiser partly fit the Horatio Alger mold. As with his predecessors, myth-makers exaggerated Kaiser's virtues and faults and stamped them into the public consciousness. To contemporaries, Kaiser was larger than life.

The first enterprises bearing Kaiser's name—photography studios—appeared on the East Coast; when he died in 1967 he controlled a large multinational organization. But his most important works were concentrated in the American West.[2] When Kaiser arrived in Spokane in 1907, the West was unquestionably ripe for industrialization; had he not stepped in to play a leading role in this development, others would have. Between the world wars, his contributions paralleled those of his nineteenth-century predecessors in emphasizing development of the regional infrastructure. He and various partners helped set the stage for an increased pace of economic development by constructing hundreds of miles of paved roads and pipelines, dozens of bridges and tunnels, and several of the huge dams authorized by the federal government during the Depression. From 1939 on, Kaiser entered an ever-widening circle of industries, including cement, magnesium, shipbuilding, steel, aluminum, housing, building materials, and nuclear power plants. His medical program eventually spread east, but when he died it served mainly the West. Kaiser hoped to begin a West Coast automobile industry, but logistical and other problems persuaded him to center operations in Detroit; the automobile endeavor was his single, obvious failure. Kaiser's contributions to western development reached far beyond the Golden Gate Bridge. After he "retired" to Hawaii in 1954, he promoted tourism, built hotels and a new city, and entered radio and television on Oahu.

Kaiser achieved his greatest successes late in life, after his sixtieth birthday. His ascent was slow and steady for nearly half a century; he reached the summit in a dramatic rush. Government support was central to his success before and during World War II; even after V-J Day, it played an important role in the expansion of some enterprises. Kaiser eventually competed effectively in the private arena; but many business leaders viewed him with distaste, and it took years to shake off his parasite image.

The basis of rivals' irritation with Kaiser appears rooted in two factors. First, although Kaiser was a newcomer among industrialists—and many questioned whether he belonged there—it was he rather than any longtime "member of the club" who became the nation's foremost symbol of the "can-do" entrepreneur in World War II. Kaiser was in the background when business leaders absorbed much of the blame for the nation's ills during the Depression, but he attracted much of the glory when public attitudes toward enterpreneurs improved dramatically in 1941 and 1942. Even more irritating was Kaiser's proclivity for lecturing rival enterpreneurs about their shortcomings. For example, he warned of impending steel shortages in mid-1940, a full year before federal officials saw the light and pressured Big Steel to expand production. Not only was Kaiser right, but he entered the steelmakers' own bailiwick—once again with government support. Then, in December 1942, just as most businesses were finally gearing up for all-out war production, the enfant terrible urged them in a highly visible public address to start thinking about reconversion for peace.

Kaiser was not trying to embarrass rival entrepreneurs; his suggestions were based on conviction and sheer enthusiasm. In the postwar period he continued to take controversial stands on many important issues. Organized medicine, represented by the American Medical Association (AMA), tolerated the Kaiser Permanente Medical Care Program as a temporary expedient to treat shipyard workers through World War II. But when Kaiser offered the program to the general public in 1945, the AMA charged that he was advocating "socialized medicine." Kaiser's dealings with unions bothered many tradition-bound business executives. Not only did he usually offer generous settlements in wage disputes, but he also frequently chided his business rivals for their short-sighted, intransigent opposition to legitimate workers' requests.

Most criticism of Kaiser came from a narrow segment of American business. In fact, Kaiser may have held a more profound belief in the soundness of American capitalism than many of his critics. His message to Americans—and to the world—changed little during the last quarter-century of his life. Kaiser was not simply a material positivist, but he repeatedly stated that he would best serve mankind by producing "more things for more people." Those close to Kaiser sensed the urgency and conviction of his words, and they believed his effort matched his rhetoric. They, too, were inspired by his example. Throughout his career, Kaiser stressed that his success was due to his ability to hire men smarter than he was and give them opportunities to grow. But even his ablest subordinates looked to him for direction. Together, they tackled thousands of problems—which Kaiser renamed "opportunities in work-clothes." Kaiser's qualities included a vivid imagination, phenomenal foresight, and an enormous capacity for hard work; they comprised his genius.

Although Henry Kaiser loved his family and enjoyed their company, available evidence sheds little light on his life away from the public arena. Considering his gargantuan appetite for work, the weeks and months he traveled every year, and his manifold operations, he devoted very little time exclusively to his family. Even in his early years, most family activities revolved around one or another of his business ventures. This study stresses Kaiser's public career, but I believe it captures his essence. It is no exaggeration to claim that Kaiser was all business.

Even so, Kaiser provides a formidable challenge to the biographer and business historian. A few words about my approach are in order here. Much of the pathbreaking work in business history, inspired by Alfred D. Chandler, Jr., Louis Galambos, and others, focuses on the "modernization" of business systems.[3] Galambos and others perceive modernization in business-government alliances, technology-driven innovations in business practices, and many other areas. One might convincingly argue that in forming an important multinational conglomerate, Kaiser Industries, in 1956, Henry Kaiser logically fits into the "organizational-synthesis" framework. Perhaps so, but I leave that work to others. Kaiser left the creation of Kaiser Industries in the hands of financial advisors and highly capable administrators. As an entrepreneur and "business thinker," Kaiser was essentially an old-school, "seat-of-his-pants" operator. He lived in the realm of big ideas and long-range future possibilities. He was very gifted at delegating authority to subordinates; "detail work" in Kaiser's companies usually represented significant challenges for even the most gifted individuals.

Kaiser exerted so much influence on twentieth-century American enterprise that attempting a "definitive" work in one volume would be an unrealistic objective. Obviously, many important questions are not addressed here. I expect that other writers will probe Kaiser's influence in particular industries and realms of social endeavor in greater depth, and I encourage these efforts.[4]

1
Roots

On May 9, 1882, in a small, unpretentious farmhouse in upstate New York, Henry John Kaiser was born. There was nothing extraordinary about the times, the place, or the circumstances surrounding his birth. The weather that day was typical for spring: windy and rainy, with a high temperature about sixty degrees. There were no earthshaking news stories. The convicted assassin of the late President Garfield, Charles G. Guiteau, and his lawyers were due in court to appeal his conviction. In Albany, a freshman assemblyman named Theodore Roosevelt made headlines by calling for the resignation of state supreme court justice T. R. Westbrook. New Yorkers speculated about when the incredible Brooklyn Bridge would be finished. In Madison Square, the five-story-high arm of what would become the Statue of Liberty stood open for public viewing; the rest of the monument was being assembled in France. In terms of concern for larger world events, Americans generally appeared extremely insular.

Certainly such was the case for Henry Kaiser's immediate family. His parents were German immigrants who arrived in central New York state a century after pioneers settled the region. The Kaisers were not risk-takers; they seemed determined to re-create as much of their former lives in Germany as possible. Henry's father bequeathed to his son little beyond good genes; the elder Kaiser lived to be eighty-seven, and Henry reached eighty-five. Henry's mother, Mary, provided attention and love, and she helped channel his restless, striving spirit. As the sole male offspring and youngest of four children, Henry lived in a female-dominated household. His mother fueled his driving ambition. Kaiser fulfilled the ideal so prevalent in the United States a century ago: the son of European immigrants would become famous and wealthy in the new country.

Kaiser's forebears going back three generations lived in a small town, Steinheim, situated close to Frankfurt in what is now the southwestern region in West Germany. At the outset of the nineteenth century Steinheim was 450 years old, still essentially a late medieval village, steeped in Gemeinschaft traditions. Not until 1808 were feudal services abolished, and serfdom was practiced until 1811.[1] A peasant village with a stable population of roughly 1,000, Steinheim was entering decades of uncertainty and upheaval.

A generation before Germany's unification crisis in the late 1860s, severe economic problems jolted the Steinheim region. The Grand Duchy of Hesse-Darmstadt's population grew steadily, from 627,000 at the end of the Napoleonic Wars to nearly 850,000 in 1850. The 1840s were marked by poor crops and near-famine conditions. The government encouraged emigration; between 1841 and 1847 almost 16,500 people departed, all but 1,000 to the United States.[2]

Henry Kaiser's ancestors did not join the first wave of emigrants; until mid-century both his parents' families appeared reasonably well situated in Steinheim. Public records reveal that although neither parent's family was wealthy, they included property-owning farmers, who often supplemented their incomes as skilled craftsmen. Kaiser's mother, Anna Marie Jobst, was born in 1847, the year of Steinheim's worst hunger crisis. She was reared amidst economic hardship; her early memories of life in Germany probably included worried discussions between her parents over their financial plight. Parish records in Steinheim reveal that in the early 1850s her father owed seven hundred gulden; there is no record of this debt ever being repaid, and he evidently forfeited title to his land.[3]

Anna Marie's parents emigrated under a dark cloud. Losing a family estate was a crushing defeat for a newly landed former peasant. They decided in 1853 to try their luck in the United States. The family arrived in New York two years before the Castle Gardens immigration center opened. An official Americanized the family name; he entered it on the books as "Yops," and they adopted that spelling. Johann became John. The family probably had a prearranged destination; they moved directly to Canajoharie, a community of just under two thousand people with a heavy concentration of German immigrants. They traveled either by railroad or by steamship to Albany, then by barge over the Erie Canal. John's first job was as a day laborer on the canal. To six-year-old Anna Marie, the month-long trek from Steinheim to the small American town must have been an amazing adventure.[4]

The Yops and Kaiser families were almost certainly acquaintances in Steinheim. Henry Kaiser's father, Franz, was born in 1842, just six months after his parents' marriage. Franz's mother died eight months after he was born, and his father remarried nine months later. More children followed; by 1851 young Franz had two half-brothers and a half-sister.[5]

Franz spent his youth and early manhood as a shoemaker. When his father died in 1871, Franz decided to emigrate to the United States. The reasons seem clear. He was twenty-nine and faced a bleak future in Steinheim. His stepmother and half-siblings still lived in the village; Franz would inherit little, if any, of his father's estate. In 1872 he sailed alone for the United States; he went directly to the Canajoharie home of former townsman John Yops. There he found room and board, along with companionship and a familiar tongue while he acquainted himself with his adopted land.[6]

Franz, soon known as Frank, moved into the home of a reasonably prosperous countryman. By 1872 Yops had been in the United States almost two decades and owned a medium-sized farm. Frank received shelter and advice; in return, he helped out with chores. Anna Marie Yops was now called Mary; a dutiful daughter, she still lived at home and worked as a practical nurse to help support the family. She probably gave little thought to the idea of a boarder moving into the house; such arrangements were very common.

The situation was ripe for romance, and a courtship quickly developed. Frank and Mary married in 1873 and settled in the tiny crossroads town of Sprout Brook, located about eight miles from Canajoharie. Frank set up a cobbler shop in an old barn, then built a wood frame house for his wife and future family.[7]

But Frank Kaiser seemed destined for failure. Consciously or otherwise, he tried to re-create his backward-looking German lifestyle in an industrializing region in the United States. Sprout Brook was a rural backwater: one hotel, a general store, a post office, a one-room school, and a few houses. But close by, in Utica, in Schenectady, and even in the small town of Canajoharie, industrial plants were mass-producing consumer items. Perhaps the thought of working in a local factory frightened him; more likely, he perceived such work as alien to his skills as a craftsman. His business methods reflected his peasant roots. Frank made leather boots by hand for local customers. He frequently loaded a large leather bag and hiked eight miles into Canajoharie to make deliveries.[8] Even a century ago, such business methods may have appeared primitive to neighbors, let alone to Kaiser's competitors operating large shops and factories nearby. By the 1870s, American shoe manufacturers sold and distributed goods through far more sophisticated delivery networks.

Frank Kaiser was not much of a businessman, but he and Mary lost little time establishing a family. Three girls, Elizabeth, Anna, and Augusta, were born between 1873 and 1878. Four years later Henry John Kaiser arrived. In later years, Henry recalled little about his early upbringing; perhaps he subconsciously buried some unhappy memories. According to sketchy recollections of family members, his parents' marriage experienced some tough times. After the children were born, a Catholic priest somehow convinced Frank that his marriage was invalid. He briefly abandoned Mary and the children, and they returned to her family for shelter. Town gossip in Canajoharie held that Frank Kaiser was an alcoholic.[9]

Frank Kaiser may simply have sought temporary refuge in the bottle and in Catholic attitudes toward intermarriage with Protestants. By 1889, when Henry was seven, his father and mother were back together at Sprout Brook. But the shoe repair business provided a precarious income. Frank finally realized that if he desired higher volume, he needed a larger, more centrally located facility. Mary's prospects of working outside the home to supplement Frank's meager income may also have influenced their decision to move. In 1889, they moved fifty miles west to Whitesboro. This village had 1,663 residents in 1890. The family rented a modest two-story wood frame house within walking distance of a rented cobbler shop downtown.[10]

Whitesboro was a fascinating environment in shaping influences for youths. The Kaiser home was within blocks of the Erie Canal; when they were not doing chores, young Henry and his sisters spent hours watching barges slip by. When the canal was frozen, children and adults used it for skating. Most boys in town, and perhaps some girls too, probably fantasized about being boat captains, or engineers on the New York Central, which also passed directly through town. There were ample opportunities for mischief. Mothers admonished their charges not to hang around the Central Hotel or the Park House; too many "drummers" of questionable moral character lurked in wait for innocent children. The stable and blacksmith shops similarly fascinated youngsters whiling away time on drowsy summer afternoons. The Kaiser girls were warned in no uncertain terms to stay away from the riffraff operating barges along the canal. Frank and Mary Kaiser undoubtedly had firm ideas about how young girls without proper guidance might misuse their leisure time.[11]

Young Henry was a bubbly, gregarious child. As the family baby and the only male, he was "fussed over" shamelessly by his sisters. Henry's sisters recalled some of his shenanigans. He once hid under the house in Sprout Brook for hours while the family searched for him with mounting concern. Although he was only seven when he moved from Sprout Brook, former playmates recalled him as an agreeable and high-spirited companion.[12] After Kaiser became famous, boyhood chum Harry McFee speculated that Frank Kaiser's lack of success indirectly provided valuable lessons to his son. The laborious hand craftsmanship and the time-consuming deliveries of Frank Kaiser's goods "may have unconsciously so strongly impressed young Kaiser that it made him naturally turn to the easier, quicker, greater measures which have made him America's No. 1 production miracle man." Circumstantial evidence hints that the bond between Henry and his father was quite tenuous. During three decades as a public figure,

Kaiser's few references to his father were perfunctory and were usually issued indirectly, through his public relations staff. Deliberately or otherwise, Kaiser later confused inquirers concerning the reasons for his father's decision to emigrate. In a 1944 interview he told a reporter that his father had fled tyranny; vagueness about his father's past suggested distance between father and son.[13]

Myths about Kaiser's childhood and early years abounded. As late as 1961, noted social critic and novelist William J. Lederer wrote that when Kaiser was an adolescent, he was a "shy, stumbling youth" who "fouled up everything he tried." Even more revealing than the myths was the casual, even perfunctory manner in which Kaiser and his public relations personnel responded. In 1946 the Kaiser organization compiled a detailed history, justifying in elaborate detail all government loans, contracts, etc. There was an extensive section on Kaiser's personal life; the few pages dealing with his youth supplied terse answers to only the most obvious questions.[14]

A persistent mystery was why he quit school at thirteen. One well-worn version was that the family income was so low that his mother had to work. According to Kaiser's second wife, Alyce, Henry begged to quit school to help support the family. His mother was opposed, so Henry persuaded his teacher to help convince her. By this account, Mary agreed, on the condition that Henry would continue his studies at night.[15]

This account possesses a ring of truth in that by 1895, when Kaiser was thirteen, the nation was in the throes of a deep national depression; times were hard in Whitesboro, and Kaiser's parents may have experienced more hardship than usual. Kaiser usually told this version throughout his life. However, conflicting evidence raises doubts. When a reporter submitted a manuscript to Kaiser's public relations department for a factual check in 1944, a top-ranking executive answered that Mr. Kaiser had examined it and had singled out specific errors: "[Mr. Kaiser's] family was not poor and could have given him the educational advantages which were then available. His decision to leave school was entirely his own . . ." In an interview late in 1948, Kaiser provided yet another version, informing a reporter: "I thought I was ready to lick the world single-handed, so I dropped out."[16] Unfortunately, no local school records from the 1880s and early 1890s survive, so Kaiser's academic record remains a mystery. But his striving for independence reflected typical dreams of youths reared on *McGuffey's Reader* and Horatio Alger stories.

Henry sought his first formal employment during hard times. He had plenty of experience with household chores and odd jobs for neighbors. In addition, he had already experienced at least one reversal. He recalled pitching hay for a farmer to earn money for a bicycle. But the farmer refused to pay him, and Henry, heartbroken, did not get his bicycle. However, when he left school, the adolescent had big dreams of instantly becoming a man. According to one account, he immediately journeyed to New York and spent three weeks tramping the streets looking for a job. This story is almost certainly apocryphal. Alyce Kaiser recalled her husband telling her that he searched for work in that city, but only when he was sixteen or seventeen. It is hard to imagine his deeply concerned mother permitting a thirteen-year-old to venture alone to the big city in the midst of a frightening depression.[17]

The version of Kaiser's first job hunt set forth by John Gunther in his famous book *Inside U.S.A.* is close to the mark. According to Gunther, Kaiser originally sought work in Utica, only four miles from the family house in Whitesboro, but already a thriving commercial city of 44,000 in 1890; it gained another 12,400 residents the following decade. Years later Henry vividly recalled the trauma of his first job search. He paced up and down a commercial street for hours before summoning the courage to peddle his own services. In later years he made thousands of sales calls; in all likelihood, none was as difficult as his first.[18]

Henry lost count of his inquiries but recalled that it took three weeks to find a job. His first employer was the J. B. Wells dry goods store in Utica. For full-time work, he earned $1.50 per week. At such low wages he could not afford the electric trolley, a new form of public transportation that had recently come to Utica. At first he walked the four miles between the store and his home. He soon bought a bicycle, and some of his fondest memories were the joyful ride from home to work and back again.[19]

Henry's work for J. B. Wells was not glamorous; he was a stockroom and delivery boy. Other duties included straightening up the store after harried salesmen strewed samples of goods about the counters in showing their wares to exacting and capricious patrons. More than fifty years later Kaiser remembered an early business lesson from owner Ed Wells. On one occasion Henry neglected to return curtains to a shelf after a salesman displayed them. Wells asked why he hadn't put them back. The young clerk replied that there was no need; another customer would want to see them, and they'd be unfolded again. Wells kindly suggested that he ask his mother not to make his bed because he'd just mess it up again. Henry remembered that the older man "taught an unforgettable lesson in orderliness."[20]

In later life, Henry fondly recalled lessons learned from his mother. No matter how late he returned, she would be waiting for him, anxious to hear about his day. Often they read aloud to each other, as she insisted that he informally continue learning. A favorite book was an early work about Theodore Roosevelt, published before he became president. Kaiser was inspired by "the courage, daring, and adventurous spirit of the future president of the United States."[21] Perhaps this book influenced Henry's decision to seek his own fortune in the West a decade later.

Despite Henry's contretemps with Ed Wells over the care of curtains, he was soon promoted to sales clerk. Signing up for a correspondence course on salesmanship, Kaiser studied his craft after regular business hours. Evidently, he learned rapidly. By sixteen, he was a traveling salesman for J. B. Wells. The young man had already learned a good deal about the world of business and had demonstrated persistence by remaining at one job for three years. However, he began to feel restless, in search of bigger things. It was probably in about 1898 that he went to New York. Evidently, the job search in New York was unsuccessful; he returned to his parents' house in Whitesboro a few weeks later.[22]

Henry was a hard-working adolescent, intent upon helping ease the burden of strained family finances; but according to recollections of friends, he was also an exuberant youth with a healthy penchant for fun and adventure. He enjoyed vigorous exercise, as he frequently bicycled to his relatives' farms in Canajoharie, fifty miles from Whitesboro. Given old-fashioned, cumbersome bicycles and primitive late-nineteenth-century roads, this was a more formidable jaunt then than it would be today.

Years later, one Katherine Moerschler, a former friend of Kaiser's Canajoharie relatives, recalled a visit to his uncle's farm. Even as an adolescent, Kaiser came across as something of a city slicker to the rural youths in the region. As Moerschler recalled,

> I was invited to a party your aunt had for you one afternoon. . . . At the time
> I remember you were about fourteen or fifteen years of age or younger. . . .
> I remember you were about a year or more older than I, and you were show-
> ing us some tricks, such as putting a bean or pea in your nostril and taking
> it out of your ear, which surprised us farmer girls and boys. I have always
> thought of you as a witty boy . . .[23]

His older sisters had taught Henry to be comfortable around girls, and he had some pocket money. By several accounts, he was a natty dresser. A photograph of Henry in his teens reveals a handsome, square-jawed young man with a full head of dark hair parted neatly in the middle. With a full-time job and improving prospects, he attracted admiring glances from young ladies in Utica and Whitesboro. But he had little opportunity to socialize with the "best" youths in town. Many of them still attended school; a few went to Hamilton College in Clinton, nine miles south of Utica. Such ambitions and dreams were far beyond the world of Kaiser, but there is no indication he regretted it.

By sixteen Henry was clearly tiring of the dry goods business. He had been fascinated by photography from the age of twelve, when he acquired his own camera. It was probably the Kodak pocket camera, a marvelous invention recently mass-marketed by George Eastman. Soon after he began work at the Wells store, he began moonlighting. He took photographs by "flashlight" at parties, then developed them at home. Mary Kaiser's hours grew increasingly late, as she waited up for her son. Photography became Henry's consuming passion. He quit his job at Wells in 1898 and worked briefly at two photography stores in Utica. First he clerked for E. E. Colwell Company, a wholesaler and retailer of photography supplies; he left in March 1899 to work for Colwell's competitor W. A. Semple as a traveling salesman in a major regional territory. Kaiser sold photography supplies across central and eastern New York state; his stops included Albany, Binghamton, Rochester, and other large towns.[24]

By 1899, Henry was deeply involved in what he then believed would be his life's work, when a crisis occurred which exerted a profound impact on his future. For months, Mary Kaiser's health had deteriorated, and she gave up nursing and remained at home. With the loss of her income, the family could not afford private medical care. As a practical nurse, she may have sensed that her illness was grave; if any doctor visited her, there is no record of a diagnosis. Mary Kaiser died on December 1, 1899, aged fifty-two.[25] On hundreds of occasions throughout his life, Henry claimed that his mother died in his arms, and that the inability of his family to afford proper medical care fueled his determination to build what eventually became the Kaiser Permanente Medical Care Program.

The tale of Mary Kaiser's death in her son's arms is probably a fabrication. Although the family knew that she was ill, her death was sudden, on a Friday morning. Young Henry was seventeen and worked long hours on the road. Henry told the story so often in later years that he probably believed it. He was very close to his mother, and his sense of loss was deep. One important effect of her death was that it severed the strongest cord tying him to the family home in Whitesboro. Frank Kaiser was fifty-seven and also had health problems; he was going blind, which further impaired his ability to earn a living. Henry's three sisters, all in their twenties, still lived at home. Anna was twenty-three and was employed locally as a milliner.[26] But the family's financial picture was grim as the twentieth century opened.

Shortly after Mary's death, Henry permanently left Whitesboro. The 1900 census listed him as residing at the family home, but it is almost certain that he only visited occasionally. By then he was acquiring as much experience as possible in his chosen profession—photography. In later years, he claimed that he left home to earn money to support his father and sisters. Henry had no way of knowing that Frank would outlive Mary by thirty years, and that his sisters would carry the primary responsibility for looking after him. Frank Kaiser remained in Whitesboro with the oldest daughter, Lizzie, through World War I and then, in his eighties, moved to Daytona Beach, Florida, where he lived until his death in 1928 with Augusta (Gussie) and her husband.[27]

Henry was not quite ready to become an independent entrepreneur. For about a year he worked for the Hyatt Photography Studio in Cortland, a town of nine thousand residents about a hundred miles southwest of Utica. The eighteen-year-old boarded in the home of Charles Hulbert. Young Henry enjoyed certain social advantages by choosing this particular home, as another boarder was house mother at the Alpha Delta sorority at Cortland Teachers College (now SUNY–Cortland). One may well imagine that the working photographer parlayed the acquaintance into both business and social opportunities; he would meet his first bride in a photography studio a few years later.

Henry quickly mastered the photography business; as a salesman for Hyatt he traveled extensively, meeting others in the business. In the spring of 1901 he learned of an opportunity to obtain a share of a photography studio in Lake Placid, a tiny resort community of perhaps 750 souls at the peak of the tourist season. Henry ventured there to look up the owner; he had little to offer except energy and a passion for work. Certainly he had no capital; he later recalled borrowing five dollars from his sister Lizzie for train fare to Lake Placid. Eager to become self-employed, to have a direct financial stake in the business he loved, Kaiser made an irresistible offer to the owner. By twenty, Kaiser was launched as a photographic entrepreneur, and his break from home was final.[28]

2

Launching a Career

During the first years of the new century Henry Kaiser led a nomadic existence. In fact, he never truly developed a strong sense of attachment to place, not even when he and his second wife, Alyce, semi-retired to Hawaii in 1954. Between 1901, when the nineteen-year-old entered the photography business in Lake Placid, and 1921, when he set up modest company headquarters in Oakland, California, Kaiser was constantly on the move.

His train ride north from Albany to Lake Placid took him through some of the most notable resort areas in America, such as Saratoga Springs and Glens Falls. These communities were already well established and teeming with wealthy New Yorkers and Bostonians seeking relief from summer's heat and humidity. Henry must have marveled at rich carriages and handsome teams of horses, as liveried servants greeted some of his fellow passengers. Farther north, beyond Glens Falls, settlement thinned out quickly, but the lush mountain scenery remained breathtaking. When he arrived in Lake Placid, Henry probably sensed why tourists enjoyed the area. The lake itself was lovely, aptly named. Due north of town loomed Whiteface Mountain. There were, of course, no ski trails yet; the sport was virtually unknown outside of Scandinavia in 1901. The town was a small, rustic resort community which relied heavily upon the tourist trade. Urbanities jaded by overdoses of civilization engaged in boating, fishing, swimming, hiking, and other vigorous activities. Lake Placid had not yet become fashionable. Summertime population in 1900 reached about one thousand; in winter, human habitation almost vanished. [1]

The young man who descended from the train had reason to be anxious. Gazing up and down a dusty street, he realized that the place was even smaller than Whitesboro. How could he make his fortune in such an outpost? But Kaiser was optimistic, and he decided to make the best of his situation. He promptly found W. W. Brownell's studio and encountered another shock. The shop was a ramshackle, one-story wooden structure adjacent to a dilapidated three-story building with a brick and stone façade. On the other side of Brownell's was a vacant, weed-infested lot.

Kaiser had come to Lake Placid for adventure, but mainly for business. He had a very complimentary letter of introduction from W. A. Semple, and he probably had other testimonials. With six years of practical business training, he confidently approached Brownell. According to some accounts, probably embellished by publicists in later years, Kaiser offered to work with no pay for a year and triple the volume of business, in return for room and board and an equal share of the partnership if he succeeded. [2]

Whatever the actual terms, Kaiser's proposal suited Brownell. He was looking forwarded to semi-retirement, and here was an appealing young man with both technical and merchandising experience. Kaiser waited on customers, sold film, and developed proofs after hours or when business was slow. An occasional customer sat for formal photographs, and the young man became adept in touching up prints to please even the most exacting patrons.

Henry worked long hours, but he also enjoyed the ambience of the lovely resort. There were scores of young people in town, mostly the offspring of well-heeled parents "taking the cure" of rest from worldly concerns. Kaiser got along well with the Brownells and their pretty daughter, Flo. A surviving photograph shows an attractive, laughing teenager sitting with Kaiser in a remarkably intimate pose. Perhaps the snapshot was simply a prank, or possibly the Brownells believed they were in partnership with a future son-in-law. Henry thoroughly enjoyed female companionship. Decades later one long-lost acquaintance, Mrs. H. G. (Jill) Seim, sent him a photograph showing the handsome young man in a boat with two lovely young ladies and a male chum. She couldn't resist needling her old friend: "Thought you would like to look at yourself when you were a handsome chap. But how you have changed. How did you let yourself get so fat?" [3]

However enjoyable the summers in Lake Placid, tourists vanished with the glorious bronze foliage of the fall. Winter brought numbing cold and little business. Whether or not Kaiser ever spent a winter in Lake Placid is uncertain. Within a year, he fulfilled his pledge to Brownell and received half of the enterprise. The pace of business may have been too fast for Brownell, who turned over most of the work to his partner. By Kaiser's account, a year after he acquired half of the business, he bought out Brownell. With full control, he promptly expanded the scope of his operations. Kaiser refurbished the store and hung up a shingle reading: "Henry J. Kaiser: the Man With the Smile." Business may have been good in the North, but it was strictly seasonal, so Kaiser followed the tourists. According to a public relations man many years later, "Florida beaches had begun to flourish and those who could afford the luxury of play went south with the birds. The lure of opportunity was irresistible to Henry, and he presently found himself in Daytona Beach scouting business prospects in the area."[4]

Kaiser took several employees to Florida and initially fell upon hard times. He found no facility suitable for rent or purchase, and he possessed insufficient capital to build the type he desired. He remembered glumly walking the streets, absorbed in his problems, when a heaven-sent stranger stopped him and inquired into the nature of his distress. Upon learning of the young photographer's plans, he allegedly loaned Kaiser sufficient funds to help him get started.[5]

Kaiser never explained his strategy for developing photography markets in Florida, but he clearly attempted to establish a chain of retail sales and service stores. He had worked for others, then purchased his own business; owning several stores and hiring others to run them offered the potential of multiplying profits. Raised in central New York state, he had witnessed firsthand the phenomenally rapid rise of Eastman-Kodak, and he intended to get in on the ground floor.

The story about the stranger lending him money was probably apocryphal. One of the roles he most cherished late in life was serving as mentor for bright young protégés, and he may have conjured up similar images of older men helping him. On another occasion, Kaiser told a different story: just one year after he bought out Brownell in Lake Placid, he allegedly sold most of his business there for $5,000 and "with this capital . . . went to Florida." The probability that the young man possessed a modest bankroll and was prepared to invest in local property may have opened bankers' doors in the Sunshine State. In any event, he soon had a Daytona Beach store and additional shops in Jacksonville, St. Augustine, and Palm Beach. His decision to expand into other cities may have been influenced by a disagreement with his supplier, Eastman-Kodak. Soon after the Daytona Beach store opened, he felt important enough to demand an exclusive distributorship for their products in that city. But the Eastman-Kodak people recognized an expanding market when they saw one. In response to Kaiser's initiative, they permitted thirteen other dealers to compete with him. As owner-investor in several shops, the young entrepreneur spent much of his time on the road, checking up on business. Nights frequently found him fitfully napping on the hard, rattan-covered seats on railroad coaches en route from one Florida city to another: "I used to shuttle between those locations," recalled Kaiser half a century later. "I haven't liked railroads since then."[6]

Despite its promise, Kaiser discovered that the photography business was no easy road to instant riches. Although he sold most of his interest in the Lake Placid store, he evidently retained at least part of it, since he returned to the northern resort for several summers. However, he remained in Florida for one off-season. During that time, he strained his limited investment capital: "It was a wretched summer in Florida, then, no tourist business at all." He worked as a guide on a sight-seeing boat on the Tumoka River near Daytona Beach. He sold film to the few tourists who showed up and encouraged them to use up at least one roll during the boat ride. As they departed, he collected their film. At night he developed pictures and placed their prints in their hotel room mailboxes before breakfast next morning. It was hard work, and Kaiser put in long hours. But the job had its exciting moments. On one occasion he dropped a lens overboard while demonstrating a camera to a tourist. Either the lens was a long-time favorite or it was expensive, as he leaped into the water after it without a thought. He quickly realized that the river was infested with alligators and scrambled back on board. His publicists claimed that he retrieved the lens. Years later he admitted that he had lost it.[7]

Apparently Henry spent only one summer as a tour guide in Florida, usually returning to Lake Placid for summers. In 1905, he fell in love. One day, a dark-haired, round-faced, attractive, and well-dressed young woman wandered into the Lake Placid store to buy film. Her name was Bess Fosburgh, and she was vacationing with her father, a well-to-do lumberman from Virginia. Bess was a shy, sheltered nineteen-year-old, who had been raised in eminently proper circumstances. Only a week earlier, she had graduated from Dana Hall, a fashionable finishing school near Boston. Obviously, she moved in very different circles from those of the young man who waited on her.[8]

By the summer of 1905 the twenty-three-year-old Kaiser was well known in Lake Placid. He was outgoing, confident, and popular. With a background so varied and with so many experiences and so much travel, Henry fascinated Bess. He was easy to talk to, and he soon persuaded her to sit for a formal photo session. Yet Bess probably never considered making any overt move to turn their relationship into anything more than a chance acquaintanceship.[9]

To Henry, Bess appeared totally beyond reach initially because of her social class. It would be hard to imagine Bess sharing anything more than pleasantries during their first few encounters. But they began a courtship. They undoubtedly spent a good deal of time out of doors on strolls, boating, perhaps an occasional picnic. Henry owned his first motorboat at Lake Placid, a hobby he would pursue with mounting passion in succeeding decades.

As the courtship ripened and Bess talked more openly about herself, Henry sensed that, for all her apparent advantages, she had experienced a lonely childhood. He probably did not learn the full extent of her unhappiness until they were married, and perhaps only years after that. Bess was born on April 9, 1886; her mother, Bessie, died just two weeks later. Her father, Edgar Charles Fosburgh, was grief-stricken; as a busy executive, he felt unable to raise the infant himself. Three weeks after her birth, Bess was taken to Wilkes-Barre, Pennsylvania, to live with her grandmother and an uncle.[10]

Thus commenced a series of temporary living arrangements lasting thirteen years which provided the youngster sustenance, but no meaningful bonding. In a remarkably candid, deeply revealing conversation with a close friend late in life, Bess recalled childhood experiences revealing the depths of her torment and low self-esteem. However generous he was in supporting her, even Bess's father exacerbated her misery. When she was thirteen, he decided she needed more prestigious schooling and enrolled her in the Howard Seminary in West Bridgewater, Massachusetts. Before leaving for boarding school, Bess visited him in Norfolk. She never forgot his greeting as she got off the train. "How he sighed when he saw this poor ugly duckling." Forty years later, she remembered his words: "Oh, Bess, your mother was so tiny, dainty, and lovely, and you are so fat, with such hands and feet, and oh, such clothes." His words, undoubtedly simple thoughtlessness, were devastating. Although her stepmother usually rejected Bess, for once she came to the rescue. Bess remembered how she "outfitted me with clothes, room and all for those school experiences. I will always remember with gratitude her interest and generosity."[11]

Edgar Fosburgh delivered the thirteen-year-old to Howard Seminary in the fall of 1899. After the unstable living situations Bess had confronted up to that point, adjusting to life at boarding school was easy. She spent six enjoyable years within this highly protected environment, first at Howard, later at Dana Hall. Due to her unstable home life, Bess's school work had been neglected, so she studied with girls a year or two younger than herself. Bess was nineteen when she graduated from Dana Hall in 1905. Undoubtedly she had gone to carefully chaperoned social functions. Bess spent summers away from Boston, home of most of her classmates and their male acquaintances. It is unlikely she had opportunities to pursue even the most innocent relationship, had she been so inclined. A week after graduation, she met the ardent young photographer. The blossoming relationship with Kaiser was probably her first serious romance.

Having ignored Bess for so long, Edgar Fosburgh overcompensated for previous neglect. He demonstrated love by subjecting her suitor to intense scrutiny. The young people went separate ways after the summer of 1905; Bess returned to West Newton to study music, Henry to Florida and the photography studios. They wrote often, Kaiser sending retouched studio postcards that the stores sold to tourists. Distance increased their ardor; when Kaiser returned north following the 1905–1906 winter season, he forthrightly asked Edgar Fosburgh for his daughter's hand in marriage.

Evidently the meeting occurred in April or May 1906, just after Bess turned twenty. Fosburgh had intense feelings about his prospective son-in-law. He, too had lower-middle-class roots and had worked at an early age; by Bess's account, he admired Kaiser's initiative. But he had inchoate feelings of guilt for having never provided a good home for his daughter. A traveling man, he sensed that marriage to an itinerant photographer would subject Bess to similar neglect.

Had Kaiser been the untested scion of one of Boston's blue-blood families, he would have endured less rigorous scrutiny. Since Kaiser had neither a distinguished family background nor formal education, Fosburgh imposed stiff terms. He considered photography an inconsequential business. As a lumberman, he perceived real enterprise as creation of a solid, tangible product. He urged Kaiser to go west and establish himself in a "substantial" business. In addition, he demanded that Kaiser build a home for Bess, save $1,000, and earn $125 per month before any marriage would take place.[12]

Such imperious demands by prospective fathers-in-law were common eighty years ago, and Kaiser evidently took no offense at the conditions. Other than the fact that the suggestion to "go west" was conventional advice to young men starting careers, it is uncertain why Fosburgh urged him in that direction. Although his lumber firm owned warehouses in the Pacific Northwest, Fosburgh offered Kaiser no assistance in that enterprise. Perhaps he believed that by creating distance between the lovers, he might quell their passion.

Kaiser apparently accepted Fosburgh's terms with alacrity. Since Fosburgh demanded that he abandon his trade and begin anew at something else, one may wonder why Henry agreed. Perhaps his love for Bess was so intense that he would accept any humiliation; certainly feelings between the young lovers were genuine and deep. Yet another factor played an important role. Kaiser was tiring of the photography business and, consciously or unconsciously, he sought an escape. Years later he discussed his feelings about the enterprise. He detested being urged to alter proofs to obscure truth. He did not mind doing so with formal portraits; after all, blemishes were usually temporary annoyances. But he disliked promotional work for hotels and travel agencies, especially in Florida. He was often required to alter photographs of beautiful natural scenery in grotesque ways to satisfy the whims of paying clients. Commercialization of his work drained much of the joy he had originally derived from his creative endeavors.[13] When Edgar Fosburgh urged him to abandon photography, Kaiser knew that the lumberman was thinking of his own interests. But he apparently approached Kaiser at the right moment to effect a profound influence upon his future. The photographer had just finished a season in Florida and was en route north for the summer season. It was a "natural" break.

Henry accepted Fosburgh's challenge, and he and Bess became engaged. Bess's stepmother reverted to her former attitude toward her. Bess claimed that she tried to hide the fact that Edgar had been married previously; thus, no engagement announcements or parties took place. When Henry went west, Bess was probably the only member of the family hoping for his return.

Kaiser had little idea where he was headed. When he boarded a train on a summer day in 1906, he may have had no plan beyond getting off at the first town that looked promising from the window. He marveled at the nation's scenery as his train headed west, across the endless prairies of North Dakota and Montana, and through the rugged Northern Rockies. Even if his destination was uncertain, he went directly to Spokane. Associates and family members had little idea why he settled there; sketchy references to the issue are inconclusive. One account in the *Spokesman-Review* held that Kaiser first looked for work in Lewiston, Idaho, before trying Spokane.[14]

Spokane was as good a choice as any other small city in the Pacific Northwest at that time. During the first decade of the twentieth century, the "Capital of the Inland Empire" was a boomtown, as its population almost tripled from 36,848 to 104,402. There were several causes for this growth, most related to development of the adjacent region. The federal government had reneged on recent "eternal" promises to Native Americans and had opened several nearby reservations to exploitation by whites. The land was cheap, and over 300,000 prospective farmers filed claims. Wheat and apples grown in eastern Washington gained reputations on world markets. Spokane directly benefited as the major service center for agriculture. Large amounts of water power were being developed, and boosters predicted an industrial bonanza. The latter would be assured if the city won its appeal under the recently passed Hepburn Act and forced the Great Northern to end rate discrimination favoring Portland and Seattle.[15]

When Kaiser arrived in 1906, Spokane still had many rough edges of a frontier town. Nearby silver lodes, particularly at Coeur D'Alene, Idaho, brought profitable business to Spokane. City boosters loved the quick pace of investment in downtown property, an upswing in the wholesale provisions trade, and brisk banking activity. Privately, they deplored the inevitable mix of human flotsam accompanying the boom: luckless miners, ne'er-do-well drifters, and prostitutes. Spokane was a wide-open town; vice and gambling were rampant in 1906. Blue-noses formed a Good Citizens League to battle moral corruption.[16]

However promising prospects in Spokane appeared in the summer of

1906, Kaiser had trouble getting started. Four decades later, when trying desperately to revive spirits of a moribund dealer organization at Kaiser-Frazer, he recounted one of the low points in his own life. A vivid memory was calling on over one hundred businesses in Spokane before being hired. Kaiser recalled changing his thinking from negative to positive: "Prospects looked as black as possible. One day as I stood on a street corner I decided to pick one fellow I wanted most to work for and concentrate on him." [17]

His target was McGowan Brothers Hardware. Having chosen his objective, Kaiser gave the owner no rest. Four decades later, James C. McGowan recalled that the persistent easterner called on him repeatedly, only to be refused each time. His store had just suffered a serious fire, and he had no intention of increasing the payroll. But Kaiser perceived opportunity in the ashes. Several thousand dollars' worth of hardware had seemingly been destroyed. Even if insurance covered the loss, recovery would take months. Kaiser finally persuaded McGowan to let him try to salvage something from the mess. He hired about two dozen women, who polished the damaged goods until they looked new, or at least salable. Kaiser proudly told McGowan the job was finished and asked him what he should do next. According to one account, the partner replied, "You've finished your job; you're fired." [18]

McGowan promptly reconsidered and hired Kaiser as a clerk at a base salary of seven dollars per week. It seemed that Kaiser was back where he had been ten years earlier: a retail clerk. However, he was determined to move up quickly, and it has been claimed that within weeks he had memorized the price of every item in the store. Clerks who had worked there for years soon started calling out, "Henry, what's the price of this? What's the price of that?" McGowan was so impressed that within a couple of months Henry received a promotion. McGowan stated years later, "Mr. Kaiser speedily showed at that time that he was not a $7 a week man." [19]

McGowan recalled promoting him to store manager, but Kaiser remembered moving first into sporting goods as assistant buyer and later becoming city sales manager. McGowan Brothers was not the typical neighborhood hardware store emphasizing small retail transactions. The firm did a far larger volume of regional wholesale business, including northern Idaho and western Montana. Kaiser recalled that they had between sixty and seventy salesmen; some called on local businesses, while others worked in outlying areas. Kaiser was promoted to city sales manager when John T. Little took over sales in rural areas. Kaiser quickly received several raises. [20]

In later years, Kaiser recalled that his primary objective of meeting Edgar Fosburgh's conditions for marrying Bess was always uppermost in his mind. In fact, he fulfilled the terms ten months after he left the East. In later years, Kaiser's public relations department did nothing to counteract the image of a nearly penniless young man arriving in Spokane, but simple logic suggests that this is probably another myth. He may have been able to live off his meager salary, but he could hardly have acquired a house without having established a bank account and a credit rating almost immediately upon his arrival. When he left the photography business, he had turned over the Daytona Beach studio to his sister Gussie; she and her husband Richard LaSesne managed it for many years. Kaiser sold all or part of his interest in the other Florida shops to employees or other investors. Thus he probably arrived in Spokane with a decent bankroll. He rented a room at 1618 Riverside Avenue for several months, then purchased a small house at 418 Fourth Avenue.[21] In April 1907 he took a train back East to claim his bride.

Although Edgar Fosburgh had agreed to the marriage, Bess's stepmother remained nervous about the entire affair. According to Bess, she was still hiding the fact of Edgar's earlier marriage, so the festivities were moved far from Norfolk. The Fosburghs held the ceremony at the Hotel Touraine, in Boston. The "official" explanation may have been that Bess had lived and been educated in Boston, and her friends resided there. Hence, that location was more convenient for bridesmaids and guests, presumably including members of Henry's family in central New York. Unfortunately, a terse announcement in one Boston newspaper provided no guest list; it revealed only that the Reverend Edward H. Rudd of Dedham performed the ceremony on April 8, 1907.[22] If Frank Kaiser and Henry's sisters attended, they probably felt uncomfortable amid the Fosburghs and Bess's elegant friends from finishing school.

If family tensions bothered the newlyweds, they didn't show it. After a night in the bridal suite at the Touraine, Henry and his bride departed for Spokane. Bess remembered that they traveled in style in a drawing room. A week after they were married, Henry was back on the job. Long-time sales associate John T. Little remembered his return: "When I arrived at the store Monday, just two weeks since the day of his departure, there was Henry shaking hands with the help and passing out cigars and candy."[23]

Henry and Bess initially moved into the house at 418 Fourth Avenue, only a few blocks from the store, between two busy streets. The couple soon made plans to build a new home in a more secluded part of town. On February 20, 1908, Kaiser borrowed $5,000 from one Anna Roemer at 8 percent interest; two months later he purchased three elevated lots in the prestigious southeast portion of town. The property, situated at 1115 South Grand Avenue, offered a spectacular view of downtown, the Spokane River, and the picturesque falls. Henry hired W. W. Hyslop, one of Spokane's most noted architects, to draw up plans, then spent every available free moment supervising construction. Less than two months after he purchased the lots, a new home stood completed and furnished.[24] Speed in construction was critical, for Bess was almost eight months pregnant when they moved in.

It is uncertain whether Edgar Fosburgh ever visited the young couple in Spokane, as he died suddenly in 1910. However, he would have approved his son-in-law's fulfillment of his side of the bargain. The house was spectacular for its time, architecturally daring and well planned. Solidly constructed, its cement walls conveyed a feeling that it was built for the ages. Its total cost was about $6,500.[25]

For the first time in his life, Kaiser may have lived beyond his means. The exclusive design, the location of the lots, and the attention the house attracted from local realty concerns suggested that it was no typical dwelling for a twenty-six-year-old hardware salesman. It seemed more appropriate for a bank vice president and labeled its owner as upper middle class, if not among the city's social and economic elite.

But Kaiser was confident about his future income. He was unquestionably working very hard to earn it, spending twelve-to-fifteen-hour days managing hardware sales. If Bess resented his long hours, she hid her feelings well. Henry brought home large paychecks, and she always knew where he was. He spent free time around the house installing other gadgets. Bess, in turn, was very much interested in his business. According to John Little, McGowan encouraged wives' involvement in their spouses' work. Saturday was a very busy day; the store opened early and closed late. It became a company tradition for employees' families to come down in mid-evening and help close up. Often the socializing lasted into Sunday morning. As Little remembered, "Bess seldom missed a Saturday night at the store. She was the affable type. She was agreeable and talked to everyone."[26]

Her young husband was a workaholic. Why didn't Bess object? Undoubtedly, she understood his need to work hard to pay off their splendid home and make their way in the world. But she fit comfortably into a supportive role for deeper reasons. Having never experienced emotional security in her youth, she reveled in their nest. Equally important, the time they spent together was rich in meaning for both. Many people who either caught glimpses of them together or spent time with the couple over many years recalled how well they suited each other. Unlike many husbands of that time, Kaiser frequently asked his wife for advice; more important, he often followed it. From the first years of their marriage until her death forty-three years later, Bess's thoughts and instincts played a larger part in corporate history than many realized. According to one of Bess's most intimate friends, Henry particularly valued her advice on personnel moves; she had acute instincts for sensing character and integrity in Kaiser's associates.[27]

Another factor helps explain why Bess adjusted so well to Henry's lifestyle. He was the first important man in her life who did not abandon her, at least in the psychological and emotional sense. Her father and step-mother shunted her aside on several occasions. Her uncle permitted another woman to create a wedge between himself and Bess. Hence, early in her life, threatening women shattered intimate connections with two important men in her life. Years later, when her two sons married, Bess's childhood scars would be reopened.

In the summer of 1908, however, all was serene in the Kaiser household. On July 29, Bess gave birth to a healthy baby boy, Edgar Fosburgh Kaiser. John Little remembered how pleased Henry was. The proud father greeted Little in front of the store and chortled, "He's a boy—get in the car. Let's go up and see him." Kaiser's brand new Model-T Ford chugged up Grand Avenue to the house. Bess greeted the two warmly at the front door, and soon a nurse wheeled out the newborn for one of his first public appearances. For young Edgar, there would be many thousands more.[28]

By the end of Henry's second year with McGowan, he set his own pace with the firm. He zipped about Spokane's newly paved streets in his company car, little realizing that he would soon enter the paving business himself. However, he was tiring of a sales territory limited to the confines of Spokane; he sought more challenges. As city sales manager he sold a good deal of heavy hardware, and he soon knew every important contractor in the region. After he achieved fame, one of Kaiser's renowned strengths was an ability to sense opportunities and move quickly. That trait was readily apparent in Spokane. When a large school building project opened south of the city, Kaiser wanted to go after the business. McGowan demurred, telling Kaiser, "If they want our hardware, they'll come in. Nobody goes out after orders." Perhaps McGowan was observing local etiquette concerning school business, as he pursued orders aggressively elsewhere. However, Kaiser would not be swayed; he insisted on seeking the order. McGowan told him that he'd have to pay his own expenses, that he was off on a wild goose chase. The admonition fell on deaf ears, as Kaiser was out the door as soon as he heard something sounding like "OK." Two days later, Henry bounced back in with orders for all the hardware equipment for the big job.

Kaiser was landing many large orders for heavy-construction hardware items. When a big order was at stake, McGowan often sent Kaiser. Years later McGowan recalled that Kaiser won a $10,000 contract against tough competition to supply reinforcing steel for a bridge across the Spokane River. He also got a $12,000 order for construction supplies at the National Bank Building. By 1910, Kaiser earned $250 per month and probably received quite a bit extra in commissions.[29]

But Kaiser would soon end his comfortable association with McGowan. According to Kaiser's public relations department, he remained with McGowan Brothers until 1912, when he joined Hawkeye Fuel Company in

Spokane. In fact, Kaiser changed jobs in 1910. According to long-time associate Clay P. Bedford, Kaiser had sold Hawkeye some shaker screens, used for sorting rock into various sizes. The buyer could not get them to work and complained to McGowan. The boss called in Henry, who believed that Hawkeye just needed training to work them properly. To retain the good will of a valued client, McGowan "loaned" Kaiser to Hawkeye for a couple of weeks.[30]

Kaiser never returned. Evidently, the hardware man bore no rancor toward Hawkeye for hiring away his star salesman. Henry had been growing restless for some time, and McGowan probably sensed that it was but a matter of time until he left. Kaiser joined Hawkeye primarily for a steady income while learning the construction business, and he stayed for a year. One of Hawkeye's large customers was J. F. Hill Company, a paving and road contractor with extensive operations in and near Spokane. Kaiser joined Hill in 1911. With Hill, he acquired what he most desired: a wealth of useful experience with the opportunities and hazards challenging general contractors. After a year working in and around Spokane, Hill placed him in charge of jobs as far away as British Columbia.[31]

Kaiser's years with Hill provided a critical learning experience. The company gained a $1 million contract for paving Browne's addition in Spokane. In 1911, this was a big job, and Kaiser supervised the work. Many of Hill's jobs were city paving. Governments were not yet spending significant sums paving roads between cities and towns. Another major job Kaiser ran for Hill was construction of sand and gravel facilities in Spokane. Kaiser also gained a crash course in local politics involved in awarding contracts. In the summer of 1911 company officials publicized corruption within the Spokane city council. Hill's president charged that a councilman had offered to steer a large contract his way in return for "rebates." The councilman denied the allegation, and the matter evidently ended there. But Kaiser was learning the hazards of the trade.[32]

By 1913, Kaiser was doing very well with Hill. He went to Canada to drum up additional contracts for one of Hill's subsidiaries, Canadian Mineral and Rubber Company. He earned $8,000 a year, which allowed him to bring Bess and young Edgar on some of his lengthier stays away from Spokane. The Kaisers thus commenced a vagabond lifestyle which they followed until they settled down, after a fashion, in Oakland in about 1920. Business was good for Hill in 1913. Kaiser had authority to submit bids for the company, and he brought in numerous profitable contracts.[33]

This comfortable state of affairs ended abruptly. Two factions engaged in a power struggle for control of the Hill Company. One group gained the upper hand and summoned Kaiser. They suggested that if he was smart, he'd line up with the winners. They also urged him to "doctor" his reports to make the competing faction look bad. This roused Henry's ire;

he said that there wasn't enough money in the world to make him do it. His supervisors advised him to cooperate, or he would be fired.[34]

Kaiser ignored incoming management's threat to fire him and returned to the field. His paychecks stopped immediately. Kaiser proved his basic integrity then and there, spending four months meeting unfinished contracts. He could have walked off these jobs, and few would have faulted him; Kaiser's conduct won him warm admirers and future customers.[35]

But construction success was measured largely in dollars, and in 1914 Kaiser's immediate prospects looked bleak. He had just been fired, and he was marooned far from home with his wife and child. Becoming a contractor required considerable capital; he had some money in the bank, and he and Bess had a home, but they still owed several thousand dollars on the mortgage. Years later, Edgar Kaiser recalled a frightening Christmas season in 1913. He was only five, but he remembered his mother having been hospitalized after losing a stillborn daughter.[36] But Kaiser possessed experience, boundless energy, and optimism. There were some jobs opening up in British Columbia, and the thirty-two-year-old salesman was ready to strike out on his own.

3

Taming the Wilderness—Roads

The year 1914 marked the outbreak of World War I, which transformed the political, social, and economic fortunes of many of the world's nations. That same year, in Vancouver, British Columbia, Henry Kaiser launched a career in general construction that profoundly changed the Pacific Coast region. Over the next thirty years he constructed dams, laid pipelines, built sand and gravel facilities, dug tunnels, erected jetties, and participated in many other projects. He spent most of the years between 1914 and 1931 building roads. Kaiser had demonstrated his enormous drive and energy in earlier endeavors. His experience in road building provided many basic business lessons which served him well when he created an industrial empire.

During these years Kaiser developed the core of his corporate organization. By the 1920s he had earned a reputation for completing contracts with remarkable speed. One reason was that he developed an uncanny skill at coordinating the flow of workers and materials. He also adapted new technology to his construction techniques, pioneered several inventions, and formed important professional associations with men who aided his career. By comparison with later achievements, his road building during the 1910s and 1920s might appear insignificant. A few of the roads are still used; most are obsolete or have disappeared. But Kaiser always considered the road-building years the bedrock of his maturation as a businessman.

Kaiser was hardly so philosophical after being fired by Hill. He was without income; a wife and six-year-old son depended on him. He needed immediate income, but he confronted the dilemma facing all contractors: to make money, one had to spend money first. He confronted three major obstacles. Two of them he could easily surmount. He had neither an organization nor machinery, but he knew how to acquire them. In Vancouver he had formed a high regard for a young construction supervisor named Alonzo B. Ordway; Henry quickly hired "Ord" and several of his best men. When Hill's subsidiary, Canadian Mineral Rubber Company, went bankrupt following the management shakeup at the parent company, Kaiser knew where to buy cheap equipment. He didn't need much machinery: shovels, wheelbarrows, a few horse-drawn scrapers.

The big hurdle, of course, was capital. By 1914 Kaiser had been negotiating bids for two years; his skills were highly developed. His problem was gaining access to sufficient funds to accept contracts he won. Local government units letting contracts generally required performance bonds of 10 percent of contract value. In 1914, Vancouver officials opened bidding for a paving job on Victoria Avenue. Kaiser submitted the lowest bid and won the contract. But he somehow had to create major new lines of credit. He possessed little collateral other than three years of construction experience, willingness to work twenty-hour days, and unbounded enthusiasm.

The young contractor had one key contact. Sir William McKenzie of Toronto, a director of the Canadian Bank of Commerce, had been involved in the management struggle at the Hill Company. By finishing Hill's contracts, Kaiser had earned McKenzie's respect. He undoubtedly used McKenzie's name when he visited the Vancouver branch of the bank.

He gained an interview with the branch president. Kaiser later recalled walking across the thickest green carpet he had ever felt under his feet. He outlined his plans and asked for $25,000. The astonished banker sat silently for a few moments, then leaned over his desk and said, "You mean to sit there and inform me, young man, you want me to loan you $25,000 and you don't even have a company, you don't even have any equipment, you don't have any men?" He continued, ". . . all you have is a contract and an idea that you think might work, and . . . it might make a profit and you want me, on that sort of a basis to loan you this sum of money?" Kaiser looked the president straight in the eye and replied, "Yes, that's what I'm here for." The banker said nothing for several more moments, then reached for a pad of paper and wrote a brief note. He told Kaiser, "Go down and hand this to the head cashier." The contractor stumbled out of the room, thinking the note might instruct the cashier to throw him out of the building. It stated: "Honor Henry J. Kaiser's signature for $25,000." This may have been the most important loan he ever received.[1] Kaiser was in business.

During his first year as a contractor, Kaiser paved streets in Vancouver and Victoria. He earned $19,000 for ten months' work on Victoria Avenue, and the *Daily Building Record,* a Vancouver business journal, reported that he won several other paving contracts. One job was resurfacing a mile of Bodwell Road in Vancouver. Kaiser bid $39,057.25, beating out the closest of six competitors by $882.75.[2] He spent his days overseeing work on several jobs. After hours, he kept a sharp eye for job announcements from the city engineer's office and those in nearby towns.

Kaiser went to unusual lengths to develop a reputation for quality work. One early associate recalled that when bidding on a contract in Victoria, he persuaded city council members to visit a previous job. To their amazement, he revealed sections that had washed into the gutter and asked for their suggestions for improving work on future contracts. Whether an artfully contrived gesture or evidence of a sincere desire for help, Kaiser's action impressed the politicians.[3] Equally important, his work improved, and Kaiser occasionally gained contracts even when not the lowest bidder.

Kaiser was uninterested in paper work, and legal technicalities bored him. But for legal and tax purposes he filed legal documents creating his first company on December 14, 1914. Kaiser was either prescient concerning the variety of businesses he would pursue, or he simply wished to avoid the bother of filing additional papers should he decide later to enter new fields in Canada. In addition to his immediate aim, paving, he listed production of cement and steel, home construction, and the development of water and power resources.[4]

Even before striking out on his own, Kaiser had made friends with numerous construction men. One of North America's best-known and most respected companies, Warren Brothers, headquartered in Massachusetts, did construction work across the United States and Canada. Although Warren family ancestors had been involved in general construction and paving for a century, the company did not incorporate until 1899; the reason was to patent and market the "bitulithic all-weather" paving technique. Kaiser was fascinated with new methods and searched tirelessly for ways to trim costs. In 1911 he became friendly with Ralph Warren, then responsible for the firm's western interests. Kaiser used the Warren product on several jobs completed for Hill and Canadian Mineral Rubber. In bidding on new jobs, however, Kaiser and Warren frequently competed. In 1913, Warren Brothers bid on a major paving contract in Nanaimo, located on Vancouver Island, directly west of Vancouver. The eastern outfit lost the bid to Canadian Mineral Rubber. After Canadian Mineral Rubber went out of business, Kaiser took over the Nanaimo contract. He needed help and turned to Warren Brothers.[5]

This was an astute move, as Warren provided both short- and long-term guidance. Kaiser's long association with the firm was crucial in advancing his career. Even though he gained initial access to bank loans in Vancouver by early 1915, few construction projects were completed, and his collections were slow. In February 1915, Kaiser needed more money to finish the Nanaimo jobs. Warren Brothers provided it by underwriting the Nanaimo Paving Company; the easterners furnished the funding, Kaiser the labor, equipment, and management. This was not philanthropy on the part of Warren Brothers; Kaiser used their bitulithic asphalt and gave it wider western exposure. Warren Brothers controlled a majority of stock in Kaiser's second company. The Nanaimo jobs were small: thirteen scattered street improvements, totaling only two miles of paving. Warren Brothers underwrote many additional Kaiser contracts in subsequent years and steered some lucrative jobs his way. In return, when Kaiser became a national figure, he invited Warren Brothers to share some of his most profitable work.[6]

Through 1915 Kaiser concentrated on city streets in Vancouver and Nanaimo. His operations were comparatively simple. In some cases he could take in the entire scope of a job at a glance; if not, he could drive from one end to the other in minutes. His men stored tools and machinery overnight in convenient sheds and garages. Hiring was usually very casual and simple. A good foreman could manage the work of a dozen or so unskilled or semi-skilled workers. Although Kaiser never claimed to have done much work with his hands, the young contractor ruined many pairs of shoes and pants lending a hand in a pinch. When workers were injured, co-workers might apply first aid; when wounds were serious, the boss sometimes transported victims to local hospitals in his own vehicle. Kaiser was not stingy, but compensation was sporadic. Long-time associates remembered that Kaiser often became so wrapped up in jobs that he forgot scheduled paydays.[7]

The concentration of Kaiser's work in urban areas was about to change, primarily because of larger societal trends and government policy. By World War I, the potential for mass-produced automobiles to revolutionize both urban and rural transportation was obvious. In 1916 the United States government passed an epochal highway bill, initiating construction of the national highway system. Commitment to improving public roads had far broader implications. Until then, almost all paved roads were in urban areas; primitive, rutted dirt roads challenged intrepid drivers venturing beyond town limits. During the 1910s state and local officials followed the federal lead and provided a bonanza of funding for road improvements, many in remote rural areas.[8]

It was probably the United States' rapid acceptance of the automobile that diverted Kaiser's attention from Canadian projects by the end of 1916. Between 1916 and 1921 he gradually moved his headquarters farther south, including brief periods in Seattle and Portland. In 1921 he permanently located his growing organization in Oakland. Beginning in 1916 in the state of Washington, he was awarded a series of ever-larger contracts, some in very isolated areas. The changing nature of his road-building tasks induced gradual adjustments in his business methods.

After moving south into Washington, the contractor formed Kaiser

Paving Company under U.S. laws. Once again, Warren Brothers provided over half the capital. Kaiser Paving built several roads, mostly east of Everett in Snohomish County. Both the number and the size of his contracts were increasing. Between 1916 and 1920, Kaiser Paving finished $2.5 million in road building, primarily in Washington and Idaho.[9]

In April 1916 the company struck a bonanza by obtaining a $2.76 million contract for work on the Paradise Irrigation project near Stanfield, Oregon, and another $1.1 million for irrigation near Echo, Oregon. These jobs dwarfed everything Kaiser had done previously. The Paradise project embraced forty-seven thousand acres and included almost one hundred miles of main canal, many additional miles of side canals, and two reservoirs, one to retain seven thousand acre-feet, the other thirty thousand.[10]

But most of Kaiser's contracts were considerably smaller; the more modest projects were the company's bread and butter. Most wartime jobs were county roads in rural areas. One contract called for a 6.7-mile stretch of two-lane paved road in Skagit County, Washington, near the town of Avon; it was typical of the better rural roads built during this period. The width was sixteen feet, and the paving was only five inches deep. Recalling this 1918 project thirty-three years later, the county engineer commented that the person awarding the contract needed only "a thermometer and a beautiful faith in Mr. Kaiser and the asphalt industry." He observed that by mid-century standards the specifications had been "extremely simple and loose." Although the road was built for light vehicles, the engineer marveled that the surface had stood the test of time remarkably well. The job had cost only $96,475.[11]

As most of Kaiser's jobs were in rural mountain or desert areas, the nature of work shifted constantly. In some cases, jobs were far enough from civilization that daily travel between quarters in town and the work site was not feasible. Kaiser experimented with converting offices and other facilities to mobile units. Workers often slept in tents or on the ground. Early associates recalled road building as "a scrambling business, with the Kaisers living out of a car as often as not." When they had several jobs under way, the boss and his family would drive from job to job after hours. On some nights all four Kaisers slept in the car. Fortunately, Henry, Jr., born in 1917, needed little room. But one night in the desert the car seemed crowded or was too hot. Henry, Sr., crawled under the car to catch a nap. He awakened in the presence of a very large snake. That cured him of sleeping on open ground. Other dangers were ever-present. Young Edgar grew up with the contracting business, and his father put him to work very early. At age twelve, his job was filling out dispatch tickets which kept track of truckloads of aggregates. A driver forgot his ticket, so Edgar ran after his rumbling truck. He caught up to the vehicle but slipped and fell under the rear wheel. His foot was crushed. Ordway and Tom Price, who were supervising the job, rushed Edgar to a distant hospital. Doctors wanted to amputate, but Ordway wouldn't allow it until the boy's father arrived. It was a wise decision, as surgeons eventually saved his foot.[12]

The World War I years and those immediately following were rough financially. Kaiser did a large volume of business, but earnings were low. He remembered in later years that profits were high on rural jobs, but on those near cities he often lost money: "Everybody could go home at night; maybe that was the reason." In a more insightful moment, Kaiser provided a better explanation. World War I brought rampant inflation. Costs doubled between 1914 and 1920. He remembered, "although I raised my bids trying to ancitipate the constantly increasing wages and prices of materials, I never quite caught up with the soaring costs. The result was that for five years I made no money."[13]

The first years in road building may have been desperate times. Kaiser remembered fondly the camaraderie of life in the tent camps and nights spent in the car. But camping out also saved time and travel costs, and a lot of money in hotel bills. Although he no doubt exaggerated their poverty, Kaiser claimed that one Christmas he had only a nickel to spend on presents for the boys.[14]

Even in slack periods, Kaiser demonstrated loyalty to key associates by retaining them when jobs were scarce. In return, he attracted men who reciprocated his loyalty and stayed with him for decades. His first employee, Ordway, remained in the organization for more than half a century. In 1912 Ordway was a foreman for a rival contractor in Vancouver. About eight o'clock on a cold, rainy night he was alone at a job site, cleaning up a mess left by another foreman. He was almost blinded by the lights of an approaching vehicle. Thinking it was the other foreman, Ordway prepared to vent his anger. Instead, Kaiser's head popped out the window, and he introduced himself. Typically, both men were working long after usual hours, and Kaiser sensed a kindred spirit. He invited Ordway to his hotel room for a "little lunch." Ordway never forgot that meeting; Kaiser "applied his vacuum cleaner and learned more about me in the next hour than I knew about myself. That was my first meeting and I went away amazed and starry-eyed." When Kaiser took over Hill's contracts, he immediately hired Ordway. As Ordway put it, Kaiser managed "by indirect needling [to] . . . get more out of me and everyone else."[15]

Another early Kaiser employee was James Arnold "Totem" Shaw. A huge, gregarious black man, Shaw never achieved managerial status. His race and nocturnal diversions accounted for that. He had an affinity for the bottle and a crap game, and Kaiser personally bailed him out of several jails, at least in the early years. Years later, Kaiser fondly remembered Shaw: In the early 1920s, crews were laying a mountain road and had to maintain a detour. Kaiser put six different men on the job, but nobody got it done. Finally, he turned the job over to Shaw. Almost immediately, the detour became a decent road. Impressed, Kaiser asked "Totem" how he had done it. Shaw replied, "Mr. Kaiser, I'm mixing mud with brains." Kaiser loved the phrase; it became a company slogan. Shaw worked for Kaiser through World War II.[16]

In the early 1920s Kaiser added three men who made more publicized contributions to his corporate empire. Tom Price, a master at locating and handling raw materials, later played a leading role at Kaiser Steel. George G. "Sherry" Sherwood served as corporate treasurer for many years. Joaquin F. "Joe" Reis started as a time-keeper in highway construction and became a key figure in dam building, ship building, and many other Kaiser ventures.[17]

In the 1940s Kaiser gained a reputation as a friend of blue-collar workers, but he experienced some problems earlier. During and immediately following World War I, the Pacific Northwest was a hotbed of conflict between management and labor. The Seattle general strike in February 1919 set the tone for the hysteria that quickly developed into a "Red Scare." Many employers used violence to weed out the Industrial Workers of the World (IWW, nicknamed "Wobblies"). Some victims of brutal management thugs, or actual troublemakers, drifted into and through Kaiser's construction camps.

By all accounts, Kaiser and his foremen treated road construction workers well. The nature of the work camps helps explain generally good relations. Management and labor teams were small; on most jobs there were only a few dozen workers; Kaiser knew them by name. He was no absentee boss; that helped too. Ordway, Price, and even Kaiser would get hands and feet dirty helping out with tough jobs. Yet Kaiser could be domineering, occasionally chewing out subordinates; everyone knew who was boss.

Confrontations in Kaiser's camps occasionally took on a farcical, even humorous tone. On one job, several shovels were lost, and Tom Price, suspecting theft, "branded" the rest with the initials H.J.K. Nevertheless, several more disappeared, so Price decided to take a discreet look about workers' homes in town. He soon found a branded shovel in one worker's yard. Asked where he got the shovel, the worker alleged he'd purchased it. Asked what "H.J.K." stood for, the culprit blurted, "H.J.K.—H.J.K.—H.J.K.—Holy Jesus K-rist, how do I know—that must be it." Much as Kaiser appreciated quick thinking and wit, he despised dishonesty; the worker was summarily fired.[18]

By 1920 opportunities in road building were virtually unlimited. Ever-cheaper Model-T Fords rolled off assembly lines in record numbers. The public developed an insatiable appetite for highway travel. Governments at various levels quickly increased funding for new and improved roads. This created a contractor's dream, but business was very competitive. Aggressive firms constantly sought to expand operations. Although Kaiser built many roads in Washington and Oregon, he also looked farther south. Even in the 1920s Californians showed a particular affinity for the automobile culture. Kaiser found an opening into the Golden State by accident in February 1921. Ordway had not vacationed since he joined Kaiser. He and his wife finally visited San Francisco. During their return, they stopped at a hotel in either Redding or Red Bluff; accounts vary. Ordway overheard two men discussing a large job for the road connecting Redding and Red Bluff. He artfully extracted the details, which they supplied because they assumed he already knew about it. Ordway immediately wired Kaiser in Seattle. Roads through the northern California mountains were primitive; two days of driving got the Ordways only to Roseburg, Oregon. When they registered at the Umpquah Hotel, the clerk handed Ordway a telegram. It was from Kaiser, instructing Ordway to meet him in Portland. They were returning to California to get that job.[19]

Ordway was surprised at Kaiser's ability to find him, but his boss claimed it was simple. He figured that since he was with his wife, they'd stay in good hotels. The two men caught a train to San Francisco, which passed through Redding. Once aboard, they learned that it did not stop at Redding, but that it slowed down just enough for the engineer to grab a satchel of orders from a pole. According to Ordway, Kaiser decided they'd jump off the train, which was still moving about thirty miles per hour. Almost thirty-nine, Kaiser was already corpulent. But the intrepid contractor allegedly leaped off, became a human bowling ball, and wound up under a clump of trees. Ordway, who claimed to have done some hoboing, followed. Their suits were torn, hands and knees badly skinned. But the two men patched themselves up, visited the job site, and figured their bid. They submitted the lowest bid and won a $500,000 job.[20]

In later years, this escapade became a chestnut in corporate lore. The Redding job was an important contract, a key factor persuading Kaiser to center corporate activities in California. Over the years, Kaiser, Ordway, and other key company officials told the story so many times that they must have believed it. They probably invented the part about leaping from a moving train. It is difficult to believe that the train did not stop in Redding, the largest town in far northern California. Even if the train was a special "flyer," two well-dressed men with their renowned powers of persuasion could probably have induced the conductor to stop a few seconds. True or not, the tale became part of the emerging Kaiser legend.

Between 1916 and 1921 Kaiser Paving had laid roughly eighty miles of roads in Washington state. The company matched that figure during the first two years in California. The Redding to Red Bluff job traversed relatively flat terrain, at least compared to the mountainous area north of Redding. The road was to be a heavily used U.S. highway. As such, it was considerably wider and had to be far more durable than the county roads Kaiser usually built. Kaiser and his men promptly established new records for speed. According to Ordway, no contractor in California had ever laid more than two miles of such highway per month. However, Kaiser Paving was soon sending reports to Sacramento about progressing at the unheard-of rate of a mile per week. Kaiser had a good reputation in Washington and Oregon but was unknown in California. His reports to Sacramento aroused suspicion; his men worked so fast that state engineers assumed that they must be doing a sloppy job. By company accounts, "spies" from state offices visited the work site, making sure that specifications were met. When the chief engineer failed to unearth discrepancies, the newcomers attracted favorable publicity.[21]

Kaiser's road builders maintained a record-setting pace through the spring and summer of 1921, but wet weather slowed progress in the fall. Kaiser earned several other contracts on U.S. Highway 99 during 1921 and 1922. In 1921 the company began work on a 10-mile stretch north from Redding, and the following year saw them complete a 15-mile section from Dunsmuir to Weed. The latter job provided their first experience with mountain roads; naturally, progress was much slower than on earlier work. All told, during the 1920s, Kaiser Paving constructed over 150 miles of highway in northern California, most of it on U.S. 99 and U.S. 40. Even more satisfying to the boss, the jobs were bigger too. During World War I typical contracts had been under $100,000. In California in the early 1920s, many projects ranged between $250,000 and $500,000.[22]

With the stepped-up pace of road building and the challenges posed by mountainous terrain, Kaiser introduced more sophisticated construction techniques. On early jobs, he had used comparatively primitive equipment: shovels, horse-drawn scrapers, etc. Throughout his life, Kaiser was fascinated with new technology, and he constantly tried to speed up work and make it less physically demanding. On one road job, he had observed that pushing old-fashioned wheelbarrows with iron-rimmed wheels through mud or rocky ground was very tiring. He equipped wheelbarrows with rubber tires and used ball bearings to lessen friction between the wheel and axle. Kaiser experimented with Caterpillar tractors; they pulled five scrapers, while horses were limited to one. Simple adjustments in equipment saved much needless effort and reduced careless errors and accidents caused by fatigue. The health and safety of his men was important, but it was obviously not Kaiser's only concern. He learned quickly that wasted time was a big "money-eater" in construction. Devices facilitating work and enhancing speed often made the difference between profit and loss. He dreamed of tackling jobs far larger than those he had finished, but he needed more sophisticated and powerful machinery.[23]

In the early 1920s Kaiser met an engineer who helped him realize these goals. Robert G. Le Tourneau was experimenting with a variety of mechanized construction devices in a shop in Stockton, California. Le Tourneau produced power shovels, mechanized dump trucks, and an ingenious power scraper. The latter device was very new in both concept and design; the inventor aptly labeled it the "earth mover." It was basically a large tractor mounted on caterpillar tracks, with five large buckets telescoping into and out of its frame. In one minute, the earth mover could scrape up about ten cubic yards of earth. When Kaiser saw this device, his eyes bulged. He immediately sensed how it would speed up his work. He offered to buy out Le Tourneau's patents on the spot. Le Tourneau was dazzled by Kaiser's vision and stunned by the offer. As he recalled, "[Kaiser] was the first contractor I had ever met who didn't look upon my machines as trick instruments to do small jobs faster. He saw them as instruments to make big jobs small." The two men eventually agreed on $50,000 for patent rights and Kaiser's exclusive use of Le Tourneau's machines.[24] With these devices, Kaiser undertook many additional projects in the late 1920s and 1930s. They helped construct Kaiser's first earthen dam, the Philbrook, on the Feather River roughly thirty miles northeast of Chico, California.

Even before the new machines proved their worth on the dam job, Kaiser hired Le Tourneau to build a larger shop near Oakland. With patent rights on new equipment, Kaiser kept close tabs on new ideas emanating from the shop. Kaiser personally initiated several improvements in heavy equipment.[25]

Philbrook Dam was another major step for Kaiser. Having never built a dam, Kaiser was challenged to figure a competitive bid that yielded a profit. He could not predict how well Le Tourneau's equipment would work on this job, since the two men were pioneers in heavy construction equipment. Years later Le Tourneau remembered that the dam site looked very different from typical mid-1920s construction projects. Machinery, not men and animals, dominated the scene. Kaiser's managerial skills played an important, if less dramatic role in the success of the dam project. He possessed an uncanny ability to integrate men and machines smoothly. Although there were a thousand men on the site with teams performing many different tasks, Le Tourneau recalled that Kaiser "had that big job timed to perfection. More, he knew how to get along with men when men didn't know how to get along with each other."[26]

Kaiser had a highly developed instinct for perceiving potential new opportunities. In September 1923 he won a contract for ten miles of county highways near Livermore. It was his first significant contract in the Bay Area. He had to construct a gravel plant to last the duration of the project. Kaiser built a plant much larger than required; it was more expensive, but he saw the chance to sell gravel permanently in a major marketing area. Initially the plant produced two hundred tons per hour; capacity later expanded to five hundred tons. Between 1923 and depletion of deposits eight years later, it yielded five million tons of material and profits of $1,375,000. By 1931 Kaiser was deeply committed to the Hoover Dam project, but he stayed in the gravel business. In fact, he wanted to expand production of aggregates. Longtime associates recalled that he loved the Livermore plant; it was a steady money-maker, and several of his bright young men started work there, including Donald A. "Dusty" Rhoades and Eugene E. Trefethen, Jr.[27]

When the Livermore sources neared exhaustion, Kaiser bought even larger deposits nearby. The negotiations reflected Kaiser's integrity. He asked Tom Price to scout for gravel, and Price discovered substantial deposits near Pleasanton. The gravel was several inches under topsoil, and Price knew that Kaiser could probably purchase the land at a low price, since the owners were unaware of the value of the deposits. Price explained the options to his boss. Kaiser refused to take advantage of the situation; he instructed Price to inform the owners of his geological findings. Impressed with Kaiser's honesty, they sold the land to him at a reasonable price. The new facility, called the Radum plant, was still producing when Kaiser died in 1967. In addition to gravel plants, Kaiser soon opened sand and crushed rock facilities in the Bay Area.[28]

Kaiser's decision to locate corporate offices in Oakland was a sound move. Oakland was ideally located, near the state capital and in the middle of a major marketing area. Even before he arrived in Oakland, he began to establish useful California connections. Shortly after he won the Redding to Red Bluff road contract in 1921, Warren A. "Dad" Bechtel, an influential western contractor, visited the job site and urged the younger man to join a contractors' organization. After briefly hesitating, Kaiser paid his dues.[29] Thus began another friendship as important to Kaiser's career as his ties to Ralph Warren. Bechtel, a founder of the Northern California chapter of the Associated General Contractors (AGC), a national booster organization, particularly valued early supporters of the regional chapter. He developed warm feelings for the younger man, and they eventually shared many construction projects. Their first joint ventures in the 1920s were regional; by the 1950s the Kaiser and Bechtel organizations shared huge projects scattered about the globe. Kaiser succeeded Bechtel as president of the Northern California chapter, and later (in 1932) as national president of AGC.

As an officer of the local chapter, Kaiser actively lobbied in Sacramento. By the mid-1920s, bond issues for original county and state roads were largely depleted, and highway construction languished. Kaiser helped promote the first Gas Tax Act in California, gaining valuable experience in "interest" politics.[30] These lessons were useful a few years later when he was chosen by another group of contractors to protect their interests in Washington, D.C., during the Hoover Dam job.

By the late 1920s Kaiser's professional associations led him into several projects outside of California. Warren Brothers invited him to share levee maintenance work on the Mississippi River. Kaiser experimented with Le Tourneau's machines under very different conditions; they did not perform up to previous levels, as Mississippi mud stuck to the big shovels like glue. The levee work, in response to devastating floods in 1927, took place between 1928 and 1930. Kaiser's share was minor, amounting to $185,000.[31] The experience in the swampy land along the river was frustrating, but the men learned lessons which proved invaluable when they built a road under similar conditions in Cuba.

Kaiser's ties to Bechtel soon led him into ventures outside California. By the late 1920s the natural gas business was booming in the southern Great Plains, the Panhandle sections of Oklahoma and Texas, and as far north and west as Montana and Idaho. Bechtel and Kaiser won contracts for almost one thousand miles of pipeline between 1930 and 1933. Most pipeline work occurred between 1931 and 1933; during those three years, contracts were worth $3,961,000. As late as 1939 the two firms continued laying pipeline; the latter year the joint operations realized a profit of $60,000.[32] By then, however, Kaiser's major interests had shifted elsewhere.

Kaiser had no inkling in the late 1920s that he was about to start his final road project; but it was to be a major challenge. From the time Kaiser began paving operations until 1927, his contracts totaled about $8 million. He was well known in the West, but was by no means nationally prominent. That would soon change. Warren Brothers landed a juicy contract for a 750-mile highway construction job in Cuba. The firm would build the Central Highway, traversing the length of the island. In March 1927, Ralph Warren offered Kaiser a major subcontract for 200 miles of road and about five hundred small bridges. According to Clay Bedford, Warren's offer was not simple generosity. The easterners could not find adequate sources of aggregates, but the Californians were experts in that area. The size of the proffered job—almost $20 million—clearly represented Kaiser's greatest opportunity yet. Public relations men claimed later that he accepted on the spot, but evidence suggests otherwise. According to Dr. Paul F. Cadman, a close friend and advisor, Henry took Bess and A. B. Ordway to Cuba before committing himself. Reaching the job site required a long ride on a rickety train, plus a day-long trek on horseback. The heat was oppressive, and there was no ice, so they drank warm Coca Colas. Ignoring first impressions, Kaiser accepted the challenge.[33]

The potential benefits outweighed the risks. Having formed his first company in Canada, he was not afraid of business in foreign countries, and

Cuba appeared to be relatively stable under President Gerardo Machado, in power since 1925. In the spring and early summer of 1927 most of Kaiser's attention was directed toward mobilizing machinery and men for the tremendous challenge ahead. In the Oakland machine shop, Le Tourneau prepared equipment for shipment through the Panama Canal: concrete mixers, power shovels, and diesel tractors. Kaiser sent several of his most capable foremen to Cuba; most manual workers would be native Cubans. His "boys" would show the Cubans a thing or two about building highways. They might even teach Warren Brothers a few new wrinkles.

Kaiser learned valuable lessons in Cuba. Perhaps the most beneficial was that, in foreign lands, American techniques were not always best. For the first few months, his foremen experienced constant frustration trying to teach Cuban workers to use sophisticated equipment. They simple did not develop rhythm, a sense of how Kaiser's heavy machinery could be integrated into an efficient, smooth-flowing operation. It took a week to assemble aggregates that one big machine used in a day. Ordway noted that Cuban machine operators were fascinated with carburetors, which they evidently perceived as the source of any and all mechanical breakdowns. Regardless of the problem, they invariably applied a wrench to the carburetor. The eventual solution was to mount all carburetors beyond reach of a wrench.[34]

Other problems included the Cubans' failure to differentiate between grease and oil, which they applied interchangeably on machines, and their habit of releasing the clutches of their vehicles and coasting down hills. The Cubans figured that using gears simply wore them out and wasted fuel. Fortunately, most of the work was on comparatively flat, marshy terrain, and few serious accidents occurred. Kaiser's foremen learned the hard way how best to deal with Cuban workers. At first they occasionally berated stubborn workers—in the style generally tolerated on American jobs. But public chastisement seldom improved work habits; it created sullen, glowering workers. Foremen eventually learned that Cubans delivered and received criticism indirectly, through a third party and in private. Thus, an erring worker avoided humiliation before his peers.[35]

Eventually the Americans grew to admire Cuban workers and learned to work with them. When management permitted an unusually long lunch hour, workers got the job done. Kaiser's men discovered that the Cubans did some jobs faster with their hands, oxen, and burros than with his twentieth-century equipment. Cubans worked long hours in hot, humid conditions with little complaint. The two thousand workers chopped through miles of jungle and mango swamps, and they overcame malaria, dysentery, and pests.

Kaiser's biggest problems in Cuba were with government officials and suppliers. Bedford recalled that Cuban contractors claimed that they were hauling in quantities of sand over long distances, and they charged mileage. In fact, they often extracted the sand from nearby river banks. Some suppliers raided existing stockpiles of materials at night, then tried to resell them the next day. But company lore holds that Kaiser and his managers experienced their most acute distress in dealing with corruption, and that the boss was so offended by bribery that he refused to pursue foreign ventures for a quarter-century after the Cuban job. According to one publicist, Kaiser said in effect, "If that's the way it works, we'll never go overseas again."[36]

Over the years, Kaiser's high ethical standards were evident to most; however, it is hard to believe that he was suprised or unduly offended by the corruption in Cuba. When Kaiser accepted that subcontract he was forty-five years old and had been an independent entrepreneur for thirteen years. Certainly he had been around enough county courthouses and state legislatures to realize that Americans were experts at "kickbacks" and other forms of graft. There is little question that Kaiser was approached for bribes. When he came to Cuba, he spent a good deal of his time dealing with "misunderstandings" between his managers and President Machado's top men.

The Cuban job marked a significant departure from Kaiser's normal way of conducting business. Until 1927, most of his jobs were close to each other. He might have several road-building jobs going at once, along with a dam project here and a gravel facility there. Basically, Kaiser was a troubleshooter; when problems arose on one job, he might remain at the location for several days. Although company officers were in Oakland, Kaiser used them to collect mail and store field reports; he spent many nights and days in the field. The Cuban job, however, was exceedingly remote, several days' hard travel from California. Between 1927 and 1930, the years of the Cuban job, he was also engaged in road and dam building in California, levee work on the Mississippi River, and pipeline operations throughout the West.

During his visits to Cuba, Kaiser occasionally dropped in on his sister Gussie and her husband, Richard LaSesne, and checked up on their photography business at the old shop at Daytona Beach. Kaiser's father was over eighty and was living out the last years of his life with Gussie and Richard.

Kaiser only went to Cuba three or four times. These visits were brief, usually lasting a week or two. Kaiser trusted his subordinates; Ordway and Bedford supervised the work. Fortunately, his managers were up to the challenge; those who were not quickly fell by the wayside. Kaiser later recalled that Cuba had taught him the value of developing young men and of hiring and training talented local people.[37]

Kaiser recruited one of his most brilliant men in Cuba. George Havas, a twenty-five-year-old native of Budapest, Hungary, was supervising a banana plantation when the Kaiser team arrived. Before he knew it he was working in road construction and was launched on a dazzling career in the Kaiser organization. The German-trained engineer came on board at a key moment. According to publicist Robert C. Elliott, "Havas also contributed some caution to balance Henry Kaiser's daring. He made it the modus-operandi that every bid was to be solidly based on carefully worked out reports. No longer did Kaiser bid low and then figure out how to do the job lower than bid." [38]

With help from Cuban workers, Bedford, Ordway, and Havas laid out Kaiser's portion of the road. In certain respects, it resembled jobs they had completed a decade earlier. The road was only twenty feet wide, consisting of five or six inches of concrete topped with two inches of Warren Brothers' bitulithic asphalt. However, there were some unique challenges. Bedford recalled that poor drainage was the primary reason they had to construct five hundred bridges. In some marshy areas they built solid islands, then directed standing water into channels flowing under the bridges. Another obstacle was the poor quality of local clay, which formed the base for the roads. Crews packed rock into the clay so that it would not crack when surface paving dried. Bedford claimed that Kaiser's roads lasted many years longer than those of other contractors. [39]

Ordway recalled that they worked around the clock to finish the job ahead of schedule; Kaiser wanted to be sure they got paid. President Machado was simultaneously spending $10 million on a sumptuous palace in Havana, and the Californians planned to be at the head of the line when it came time to collect. Apparently, this was a wise move. Although Kaiser exaggerated the plight of slower contractors, he claimed, "We got paid in cash. Some of the other outfits got paper that wasn't worth a damn." [40]

According to leaders in the Kaiser organization, the Cuban job was a key turning point in corporate history. Kaiser stressed that the job matured his young men very quickly and provided valuable experience. "It was rough pioneering, really tough. . . . It was only by marshaling the utmost abilities among the young fellows . . . that we were able to finish the Cuban highway . . . three years [?] ahead of time and make a profit." Perhaps Ordway analyzed the significance of the Cuban job even more aptly: ". . . our determination to go into Cuba gave us that one large job we had never had and always wanted. We finished the job a year ahead of schedule to enhance our reputation, and it provided the money that allowed us to go into big dam building and beyond." Kaiser Paving Company earned a net profit of $2.1 million. [41]

The Cuban job was finished in 1930, and it was a good thing that Kaiser and his men were full of enthusiasm. The United States had lost faith in

President Hoover's assurances of imminent economic recovery from the stock market crash of the preceding year. Unlike most of their compatriots, Kaiser and his key men were accutely attuned to the possibilities of grand new ventures. Fortunately for Kaiser, even greater opportunity *was* just around the corner.

4

Taming the Wilderness—Dams

The Cuban road-building expedition was Kaiser's largest contract to date, but by 1930 he was anxious to move on to other jobs. For three full years it had been his primary concern, largely because of the size of the contract. But after Kaiser and his foremen organized the workers' tasks and obtained steady sources of supplies, the Cuban job presented a few new managerial and engineering challenges. Kaiser felt an urge to explore new opportunities, and he faced far more worrisome responsibilities in the United States.

A very real concern was the survival of his companies. As the Cuba job neared completion, the United States entered the Depression; construction firms were among the first victims of the economic collapse. Road-building contracts were canceled or reduced in size. Government agencies cut back wherever they could, ordered cheaper materials, and delayed payments. Private clients defaulted in frightening numbers; so did a few city and local governments. Contractors held large inventories of machines, materials, and other tangible assets; bankers, desperate for cash themselves, hounded them for payments on loans.

By 1930 contractors sensed the chill of potential disaster; Kaiser was no exception. He had an excellent reputation on the West Coast, but most previous work had been for local governments, or as subcontracts for larger firms. A large project spread over years and sponsored by the federal government would obviously provide Kaiser and his employees a degree of security. Just as important, it would elevate them to a higher echelon among big-time firms. But there were many large contractors, and all needed work.

By the early 1930s, bids on large federal projects were highly competitive. One of the biggest plums was a massive job on the Colorado River.[1] Even before the turn of the century engineers had dreamed of someday taming the capricious Colorado. In its natural state, the river was of little economic use. It provided breathtaking scenery and water for a few thousand acres of adjacent farmland, but during flood season it caused havoc. In 1905 high water broke through dikes in the Imperial Valley of California; coaxing the river back into its former channel cost over a million dollars. Four years later it broke through the levees again and changed its course through Mexico to the Gulf of California. In addition, with a maximum flow of 210,000 second-feet of water, the Colorado River brought upland silt into California's gardens. Not only did it represent a serious loss for upland states, but silt removal in California cost over a million dollars annually.[2]

Reclamation engineers envisioned turning a liability into an economic asset for the entire Southwest. Controlling and storing the flow of the 1,500-mile-long river would create enormous sources of cheap water and power, along with flood control. In the eyes of enthusiastic promoters, a huge federal dam would be the linchpin to future urbanization and industrialization of the region. Vast irrigation projects in conjunction with the dam could convert two million acres of desert into valuable farmland.[3]

In 1901, engineers studied sections of the Colorado between Needles, California, and Yuma, Arizona; they identified five potential locations for a dam. Political controversy slowed progress for twenty years, but by the early 1920s government engineers had narrowed potential dam sites to two—Boulder Canyon and Black Canyon. In 1923 decisionmakers accepted recommendations for the Black Canyon site, where the dam was built. Political maneuvering over naming of the dam confused the public for thirty years.[4]

The physical dimensions of the project were staggering. Engineers estimated that 4.5 million cubic yards of concrete were needed for the dam and its immediate appurtenances alone; this was more concrete than the Bureau of Reclamation had used in all previous federal projects to date. In addition, 19 million pounds of reinforcing steel were required. The completed dam would create a reservoir 115 miles long, with an area of 193 square miles and a shoreline of 550 miles. The power plant would possess a capacity of 1.0–1.2 million horsepower, half again the total output at Niagara Falls and Muscle Shoals combined.[5]

Because of sharply conflicting interests in a seven-state region, it had taken decades for progressives in Congress to develop a fragile coalition favoring a dam. A major stumbling block was fears of representatives of thinly settled states that rapidly growing California would grab most of the water. By dividing water equally between Upper Basin states (Utah, New Mexico, Colorado, and Wyoming) and Lower Basin states (Arizona, California, and Nevada), the Boulder Canyon Act of 1922 had satisfied everyone except representatives from Arizona.[6] Just before the onset of the

Depression in 1929, the Bureau of Reclamation overcame the last obstacles. On December 21, 1928, President Coolidge finally signed the Boulder Canyon Project Act into law, authorizing $165 million for the project. In 1930 federal agencies finally opened bidding for the enormous job.[7]

As eager as contractors were to submit bids, they faced two formidable problems. First, the job was huge, and even the largest contractors would be stretched to their limits meeting the $5 million performance bond requirement. Second, no dam this large had ever been built, and even experienced engineers were uncertain about how to figure bids. Specifications called for 119 separate bid items. Even the soundest company faced potential disaster if it miscalculated a bid. Consequently, no single company bid alone. When Interior Secretary Ray Lyman Wilbur formally opened bidding, his department sent engineering specifications to over one hundred contractors. In the end, three groups of construction companies combined to submit legitimate bids. The consortiums drew upon members' strengths and—most important—spread risks.[8]

Although still involved in Cuba, Kaiser kept abreast of developments through Bechtel. The two men had teamed together in numerous projects, but Kaiser may have considered submitting a proposal by himself. One factor in Kaiser's decision to find partners was that, although respected as a western contractor, he was still the "junior" member in dealings with Bechtel and Warren Brothers. Warren had favored him in Cuba, and he returned the favor by including the firm among his partners in Hoover Dam bidding. Kaiser ached to be kingpin on a massive job of his own. However, sober judgment convinced him that the job required far more expertise than he yet possessed.[9]

Forming consortiums became a fascinating ritual. Most construction men possess large egos; concerns about who asked and who would be courted, which engineers supervised the job, and whose friends in law, banking, and insurance handled paper work all had to be settled before serious work on bids began. In later years several individuals claimed credit for founding Kaiser's group, Six Companies. Kaiser never claimed that role. According to most accounts, Bechtel invited Kaiser to join him in bidding on the Hoover Dam job; they formed Bechtel-Kaiser and sought other partners.[10]

The Hoover Dam bid was so huge, and so much preliminary work was required that rumors about who might bid circulated freely. The bonding glue of the Six Companies partnership was a mixture of mutual respect and need, along with personal friendships.[11] Kaiser shared a good deal in common with his future Six Companies partners, several of whom fit the Horatio Alger pattern. Brothers Edmund O. and William H. Wattis began their careers as teamsters on railroad jobs in the Pacific Northwest before founding a highly successful firm, Utah Construction Company. Bechtel was the son of a Kansas farmer. As a young man, he went broke in the cattle business before heading west into "Indian Territory." There, he worked as a manual laborer on railroads and in construction for over a decade before finally becoming a contractor. Harry W. Morrison, of Morrison-Knudsen, started work at fifteen as a water boy for a Chicago construction company; several years later, he joined the U.S. Bureau of Reclamation as a foreman in field operations. In 1907 he was transferred to Boise, Idaho, where he later formed a partnership with Morris Knudsen, specializing in railroads, highways, irrigation dams and canals, power plants, and tunnels. Charles A. Shea was the son of a plumber in Los Angeles. He and his father founded J. F. Shea Company in 1914, and the firm thrived with the land boom in southern California during the 1920s. The only "college boy" among the Six Companies operators, Alan MacDonald, was such an independent thinker that he allegedly was fired from fifteen jobs after graduating in engineering from Cornell University in 1905. Original thinking was an enormous asset when he joined Felix Kahn in 1911. In his willingness to assume hair-raising risks, he closely resembled Kaiser, and his brilliant engineering decisions ultimately helped his partners stay ahead of schedule on the Hoover Dam project.[12]

There was nothing inevitable about the final makeup of Six Companies. In fact, membership and percentages of participation on the Hoover Dam project remained fluid even after bids were made and work begun. Six Companies incorporated in Delaware on February 18, 1931, barely two weeks before formal bids were opened in Denver. Kaiser was elected chairman of the executive committee. The partners had to raise $5 million for bonding, and their investments were unequal. The original percentages were:

MacDonald and Kahn	20
Utah Construction	20
Kaiser Paving Co. and W. A. Bechtel	30
Morrison-Knudson Co., Inc.	10
J. F. Shea Co.	10
Pacific Bridge	10

The latter two organizations were headquartered in Portland, Oregon.[13]

In forming bids, all the operators were flying blind. Engineering specifications were precise, but the job was so immense that nobody could predict confidently the materiel and labor required for each phase. The government allowed seven years for completion, and anything could happen to wage scales and prices for materials. Could available technology do the job? Getting machinery to the job site and providing fuel and electricity were formidable challenges. Answers to many problems would never be found in engineering textbooks. The builders had to combine knowledge with bold imagination, intuitive timing, and highly developed powers of persuasion.

Nobody worked harder studying the Hoover Dam job than Kaiser. In the weeks before bids were submitted, his frantic dashes between company headquarters in Oakland and the remote dam site became the stuff of company lore. Kaiser would work a full day, then pile into his yellow Marmon automobile at 5 P.M. and drive all night at seventy miles an hour. After an hour or two napping in the front seat of his car, he was a bright-eyed, inquisitive visitor wanting to study every crack in the canyon walls.[14] By the spring of 1931 Kaiser probably knew the canyon better than anyone but job superintendent Frank T. Crowe.

When the Six Companies partners gathered in San Francisco to finalize their bid, Kaiser's estimate was well thought out. After lengthy discussion, the partners agreed to present separate figures, then average the estimates. They came up with a figure of $48,890,995.50, submitted it to the Department of Interior, and headed for Denver, where the bids would be opened. Upon their arrival at Denver's Brown Palace Hotel, they learned that there were only two other serious competitors. Woods Brothers Construction Company of Nebraska had teamed with A. Guthrie and Company of Portland, Oregon; and the Arundel Company of Baltimore had joined Lynn Atkinson of Los Angeles.

The tension prior to opening the bids in the Bureau of Reclamation Office on March 4, 1931, was palpable. It was the depths of the Depression, and the winning companies would be busy for several years. The fateful moment finally arrived. The Woods-Guthrie team had bid $58.6 million; the Arundel-Atkinson combine came in at $53.9 million. Six Companies, with a bid $5 million lower than the closest competitor, had won the job.[15]

Joyous as the occasion was for the partners, there was no time for celebration. Few contractors ever began jobs under less favorable circumstances. The work site was one of the least hospitable locations on the planet, roughly thirty miles south of Las Vegas, Nevada. Daytime temperatures in the canyon often reached 120, even 130 degrees during summers, which stretched endlessly from May through September. Although winters were short, temperatures dropped to 20 degrees and winds created uncomfortably chilly conditions.[16] Moderate weather was infrequent. Since the dam site was remote from transportation networks, urban areas, and sources of power, virtually all supplies for maintenance of a large work force had to be hauled in over long distances at great expense.

In the 1920s there was little to attract people to southern Nevada. The region's economy was precarious. The tourist industry barely existed; gambling and entertainment did not thrive until after World War II. Easy fortunes made in nearby precious-metals operations had largely vanished. Intrepid farmers had tried to establish agriculture in the region, but except for eight thousand acres of irrigated land in Moapa Valley, fifty miles northeast of Las Vegas, only a few scraggly farms and ranches were nearby.[17]

Old-time residents of Las Vegas initially reacted with delight when the misnamed Boulder Canyon Project Act became law. Unfortunately, its first fruits tasted bitter; during nearly two years between the signing of the act and the awarding of the contract to Six Companies, the much-ballyhooed project brought only headaches to local residents and public officials. The initial result was as predictable as it was unhealthy: an overnight speculative land boom. In 1928, developed sections of Las Vegas covered 1.5 square miles and contained a population of 8,000. By 1931, land developers had subdivided enough lots to accommodate a city of between 350,000 and 400,000. One could only pity gullible investors who purchased parcels of land sight unseen. A ten-mile drive from town over rutted, dusty roads brought luckless plungers to windswept subdivisions featuring a couple of tarpaper shacks and faded signs reading "Fairview Heights," "Country Club," "Woodland Park," and "Grandview."[18]

Land speculation didn't bother the locals much; they knew the desert and weren't likely to be taken in by slick salesmen. What concerned them was the increasing number of vagrants. From 1928 forward, rumors of the imminent start-up of work on the dam attracted prospective workers to the region. With the stock market crash late in 1929 and sickening rises in unemployment through 1930, a trickle of a few dozen Americans with visions of El Dorado in the desert became a torrent of hundreds of desperate families. All too often the breadwinners were unskilled and in bad health, unprepared for the harsh environment awaiting them in the desert.[19]

Much has been made of the alleged heartlessness of Herbert Hoover and his advisors concerning unemployed Americans, but this image has been overdrawn. To his credit, Secretary of Interior Wilbur warned prospective workers that it would be months between bidding the project and actual hiring. But frantic job-seekers ignored advice to stay at home. What Wilbur and his colleagues failed to comprehend fully was that many had no homes and had staked their last dollar on the hope of finding work in Las Vegas. At the local level, initial compassion for the itinerant unemployed was soon replaced by fear and cynicism. A reporter observed that so many men slept in front of the train station that the scene resembled a Civil War battlefield each morning. By early 1931, police routinely rounded up suspected vagrants, drove them twenty miles out into the desert, and dumped them off with the warning to "keep moving."[20]

In normal times, the contractors might have taken their time lining up skilled workers, materials, and machinery. Under ideal circumstances, they would have first hired a small cadre of skilled technicians for start-up operations and recruited unskilled workers after the job was organized and living quarters set up. But these were hardly normal times; politicians and bureaucrats felt enormous pressure to begin work immediately, regardless of logistical and technical problems. Six Companies had chosen a seasoned forty-eighty-year-old civil engineer, Frank T. Crowe, to head up field operations. Crowe had a quarter-century of experience on major construction projects, first with the Bureau of Reclamation, and later with Morrison-Knudsen.[21] No time was lost. Within minutes of the official awarding of the contract on March 11, Crowe and a skeleton crew of engineers began work.

In human terms, the situation they confronted at the dam site was pitiful. For months, potential workers had drifted into a campsite, nicknamed "ragtown," located along the river, close to the construction site. Estimates of the number of persons in "ragtown" ranged from 500 to 1,500. Living conditions were primitive. The fanciest "dwellings" were tarpaper shacks, and some people slept on open ground, covered only by thin blankets. Food supplies were nonexistent; once or twice a week, men thumbed rides into Las Vegas to buy or beg for food for starving families. The only plentiful commodity was river water, used for bathing, washing, and drinking. Local health officials were amazed that the camp had escaped a serious epidemic.[22]

Even before Six Companies had signed the contract, Crowe had encountered problems coordinating the hiring of hundreds of workers. Hiring was done through the U.S. Employment Service, which began screening potential workers several months before actual construction of the dam commenced. First, four diversionary tunnels fifty feet in diameter and nearly four thousand feet long had to be blasted through the nearly vertical walls of the narrow canyon, and the river turned. This work required highly skilled workers, most of whom were brought in from outside. Only then could inexperienced and unskilled workers be used effectively. But government authorities pressured the contractors to hire unskilled workers promptly. Crowe reluctantly compromised normal standards of efficiency. A month before Secretary Wilbur's pen sealed the contract, 106 men were on the payroll; on the date of the signing, 208; two months later, 598; by December 1931, 2,745.[23]

On construction projects near large towns, contractors did not provide housing; workers usually made their own arrangements. In such a remote and inhospitable setting, however, this approach was not feasible. The contract called for a permanent town close to the construction site. Although the government paid the bills and Bureau of Reclamation officials planned the town layout, Six Companies built it. Planning was remarkably thorough. Bearing in mind the stifling summer heat, planners searched for the coolest possible location. They chose a high plain site in Nevada, seven miles from and almost two thousand feet above the canyon floor. Mean daily temperatures there were nine degrees cooler than those at river level. Publicists claimed that living facilities in Boulder City would be as close to ideal as the harsh environment would permit.[24]

However, it took several months to built the town. Six Companies erected a temporary barracks near the canyon floor that housed 480 men. Without shade or breezes, the quarters were oven-like. There were no showers, electric lights, or treated water. In the meantime, other workers shifted for themselves. Unfortunately, the summer of 1931 was one of the hottest on record in southern Nevada. Thermometers recorded 128 degrees in the shade, and during the hottest months daily highs averaged 119. Even at night temperatures seldom dropped below 90. In an effort to guarantee work for as many men as possible, the government insisted that Six Companies work three shifts, around the clock. Working conditions were brutal enough for men on the day shift; those who toiled at night and tried to sleep in stifling barracks or tents during the heat of day experienced living hell.[25]

The situation demanded speed in building Boulder City, along with interim relief. The government hired renowned planner Saco R. DeBoer to design the permanent town. In the meantime, "ragtown" was replaced by another temporary construction camp, nicknamed "tent city."[26] Workers loathed the tents, but they noted one significant improvement: the contractors set up a mess hall. Employees and their families finally enjoyed sufficient and nourishing meals. A few unfortunate people went berserk when they saw all the food they could eat and gorged themselves to the point of violent illness.[27]

Complaints about working conditions were infrequent early in 1931. Many workers had been unemployed for two years; steady work as unskilled laborers at four dollars per day was a godsend. Workers fit every description and came from across the nation. Of 3,371 employees at the end of 1931, the largest numbers came from California (886) and Nevada (440); all states but North Dakota and Vermont were represented. No women were hired, at least for field work. The men averaged thirty-four years of age, and 51.5 percent were married. Fitness requirements were low; of 3,544 men examined medically by U.S. Employment Service doctors, only 173 were rejected.[28]

The thrill of gainful employment quickly passed, however; full bellies alone did not prevent mounting worker frustration. Workers complained that $1.60 per day for room and board was excessive, since it consumed almost half the paycheck of unskilled men. Working conditions in the canyon were beyond imagination. The men complained that management did not supply enough ice water, making the searing heat almost unbearable. The collapse of workers from heat prostration became a daily occurrence; that cause alone killed fourteen men between June 25 and July 26, 1931. In addition to severe hazards from heat, the work was extremely dangerous. Before tunnel bores could be started and access roads carved in the cliffs, canyon walls had to be cleared of debris and loose rocks. In performing this arduous task, men dangled by rope from the top of the canyon, several hundred feet above the riverbed. Even after the walls were cleaned, rockfalls sent men scurrying for cover. Stones the size of an olive could injure workers severely. If left exposed to midday sun for more than a few minutes, gasoline cans became combustible. Hoover Dam was more dangerous than ordinary construction jobs, and dozens of lives were lost.[29]

Workers had outside assistance focusing their discontent. The Industrial Workers of the World (IWW), renowned for its revolutionary objectives during the 1910s, had fallen upon hard times in the 1920s. Union organizers hoped to revive their sagging fortunes as the Depression deepened, and they believed that their vision of a worker's commonwealth would appeal to desperate workers. The Hoover Dam job was one of the most highly publicized projects in the nation; a successful organizing effort there would enhance the IWW's power and prestige. The first organizers showed up in May 1931 and surreptitiously distributed their literature in the camps.[30]

Local law enforcement officers cracked down hard; IWW organizers openly handing out leaflets on the streets of Las Vegas were arrested and held on trumped-up vagrancy charges. A remarkably even-handed municipal judge ordered them released, and they continued organizing efforts. They were particularly critical of working conditions at Hoover Dam and claimed that Six Companies could do much more to ensure the workers' safety and comfort. The contractors finally provided fresh water and water coolers at the barracks on the river and eliminated some of the worst safety hazards. But neither the employers nor union organizers could do anything about the primary cause of discontent, the stifling summer heat.[31]

Worker discontent came to a head in the summer heat in early August 1931. At the start of the afternoon shift on August 7, about 175 men struck. The primary issue was working conditions, not wages. The strike spread quickly, and by the next day over 1,000 workers had gone out. Crowe, a tough, no-nonsense boss who firmly believed in the open shop, spent little time negotiating. He called in several dozen "security personnel," who arrived under cover of darkness. Union leaders called them corporate thugs. The U.S. Employment Service cooperated with management at least in promising to hire replacement workers as quickly as possible. Eventually, 1,400 workers either quit or were fired. The strike failed, and work resumed on a limited scale a week later. Several hundred disaffected workers returned to their jobs.[32]

Accounts of the strike varied widely. Labor newspapers vilified the operators in general and presented a very unflattering portrait of Crowe. Militant labor papers charged that management's indifference had resulted in hideous accidents and explosions costing up to a hundred lives. The objectivity of their reporters was suspect. The operators answered the charges in a less sensational manner, but their rebuttals were equally dubious. From San Francisco, the Wattis brothers argued that conditions in the camps were nearly ideal and claimed that "agitation" had been perpetrated by "Communists and Wobblies."[33]

Six Companies executives had labor views typical of most businessmen of the time. Henry Kaiser's enterprises were open shop, as were those of his associates. Their contracts with the government included inflexible deadlines for completion of work; portions finished ahead of schedule meant quicker collections and larger net profits. Equally important, if the contractors could not drill diversionary tunnels and "turn" the Colorado River by October 1, 1933, they would pay a fine of $3,000 per day until the task was finished. In addition, the Hoover Dam job was highly visible; their reputations for fast, efficient work were on the line. For these reasons, the contractors stoutly resisted work stoppages.[34]

An authoritative account of the construction of Hoover Dam paints basically unflattering pictures of the treatment of labor organizers and workers by both the Bureau of Reclamation and the Six Companies, at least during the early years. Although Boulder City provided life's necessities, it was a tightly controlled company town, run by a bureau-appointed city manager with almost dictatorial authority. In their haste to beat deadlines and improve profits, Six Companies officials knowingly risked workers' lives. To speed up blasting, foremen instructed workers to store dynamite boxes much too close to explosion sites. The boxes could explode prematurely if direct sunlight melted nitroglycerin fuses and falling debris jarred the contents. In November 1931 the state mine inspector ordered Six Companies to stop using gasoline-powered trucks to haul materials into and out of the diversionary tunnels. Carbon monoxide fumes were slowly poisoning men working eight-hour shifts in the tunnels. Company lawyers successfully obstructed Nevada laws for the duration of the project. In the summer of 1933 several workers who allegedly had suffered long-term health damage because of gas fumes sued Six Companies. Directors agreed to fight back aggressively and hired high-powered San Francisco attorneys to argue the cases. At the conclusion of the trials, a careful student of the construction project concluded,

> It appeared that . . . Six Companies investigators had engaged in pimping, criminal conspiracy, intimidation of witnesses, and jury tampering in their effort to dispose of the gas cases and protect the company's treasury and business reputation. Their tactics had been ruthless, their methods heavy-handed, but instead of scaring Austin [the plaintiff's attorney] off, they had only goaded him on. Now the higher ups had to decide whether the game was worth the candle. With its money and clout, Six Companies could win the battles, but it might lose the war if Austin persisted, as he showed every sign of doing, in a long campaign of attrition.

By August 1935 there were forty-eight separate gas suits against Six Companies; the plaintiffs sought a total of $4.8 million in damages. The companies decided to negotiate, in January 1936 an out-of-court settlement was reached; checks for undisclosed amounts were sent by company officials to fifty plaintiffs.[35]

Unfortunately, available evidence sheds little light on the roles of individual directors in determining Six Companies' strategy; neither board minutes nor surviving correspondence provide such sensitive information. Among the key Six Companies executives, Henry Kaiser was probably the farthest removed from decisions at the construction site. Yet as chairman of the executive committee, it is almost inconceivable that he was not at least consulted by telephone before crucial decisions were made. There is no evidence that Kaiser ever objected to his associates' tactics. Only after completion of Hoover Dam was there evidence that Kaiser took a more compassionate, enlightened view toward labor in general, including unions. In later years, Kaiser's publicists stressed his sympathetic identification with the "little guy." There is truth to this, but he was also keenly aware of larger social and political trends. By the mid-1930s, New Dealers were solidly behind organized labor; Kaiser's "enlightened" labor views attracted support not only from workers, but from key decisionmakers in Washington as well.

Though Kaiser was far removed from day-to-day operations, he was not immune from labor's resentment. The summer of 1931 was not quickly forgotten by workers. Although weakened by the Depression, organized labor had enough clout to force Congress to investigate conditions at the dam site. Thus, in the spring of 1932, Kaiser was called before a congressional subcommittee to defend the partners' position. A representative from the American Federation of Labor (AFL) testified that Six Companies paid only $.75 per hour even for skilled labor, amounting to between $2 and $4 per day less than prevailing wages. Kaiser blamed bureaucratic complexity: confusion wrought by the recently enacted Davis-Bacon wage law made it extremely difficult for contractors to determine legally "prevailing wages." Large contractors faced mountains of paper work if they made hundreds of adjustments in pay scales for separate tasks at every job site. Kaiser claimed that his partners would pay a reasonable wage scale when told what it was, but a union spokesman angrily stated that Kaiser was avoiding more basic issues. He bitterly disputed Kaiser's claim that decent working conditions existed at the dam site:

> The wage scale is probably satisfactory as far as Mr. Kaiser is concerned but so far as organized labor is concerned it is not . . . . [Mr. Kaiser], you have been in Washington for the past two summers, and certainly last summer you appreciated the heat that prevails here in that season. Now I venture to say that

if you had to work at Boulder Dam for $4 per day, you would not last fifteen minutes. You would have to go to the hospital.[36]

Kaiser later earned a well-deserved reputation as an enlightened entrepreneur in labor relations, but these qualities were not evident at least publicly in the early 1930s.

The IWW strike in August 1931 was the most serious management-labor conflict at Hoover Dam. Occasional confrontations threatened operations: a second IWW attempt to organize the workers in 1933, the gas suits, and close corporate and government control of the work site created sporadic tensions. But after 1931 relations generally improved. Once Boulder City opened and families moved into decent, if Spartan, facilities, management and labor leaders conferred in more civil tones. Most important, both sides concentrated on building the dam.

By the end of 1932 most preliminary tasks were completed. The most challenging was building the diversionary tunnels. Realizing the need for speed, workers devised an ingenious solution. Drillers boring holes for dynamite normally lifted and operated heavy diamond drills manually. It was back-breaking, dangerous work. In a careless split second, a hot, fatigued worker might let a drill slip and mangle his foot. A foreman, Bernard F. "Woody" Williams, rigged a dozen or so diamond drills on the rear of a huge truck, backed the contraption, called a "drilling jumbo," into the tunnel and up against the wall to be drilled, and told the men to start their equipment. A dozen drills simultaneously clawed holes, with far less effort by the men. Out came the truck from the tunnel, and in went the powder men with dynamite. A huge explosion sent tons of rock toward the opening. The experiment was a rousing success. In one day Williams' crew made more progress than others made in a week. Several more "jumbos" were built; they were crucial in speeding up the process of boring the tunnels. By November 13, 1932, the last tunnel had been blasted through; tunnel walls on the Arizona side had been lined and were ready for use. The river was turned, just before the rainy season and potential flooding.[37]

Work on the dam could finally begin. While drillers finished the tunnels, other teams built plants yielding two different types of concrete. Still other crews crisscrossed the site with roads, railroad tracks, power lines, and gigantic cables supporting a variety of heavy cranes. Temporary cofferdams were erected, and the foundation for the dam was carefully prepared. Finally, evidence of the massive amount of work already performed became visible to the untrained eye. Never had so much concrete been poured at one location. The base of the dam was 660 feet wide; it would be 726 feet high and 45 feet across at the top. Engineers calculated that it would contain four million cubic yards of concrete.[38]

In early 1933 the immense dam began to creep up the sheer walls of the canyon. Even experienced construction men were awed at the human engineering and conquest of nature which it symbolized. At dusk, workers from the day shift sometimes returned from Boulder City to sit on the rim of the canyon and gaze in wonder at what they were making.[39]

By then, life in Boulder City was settling down. Public schools had opened in September 1932; sanitation facilities were completed; and the dormitories were fitted with air heating and cooling. Life in Boulder City was hardly luxurious. Single rooms in dormitories were cramped, measuring seven by ten feet. Family houses were small; a cottage with two rooms, shower, and a large sleeping porch rented for $19 a month. A similar unit with three bedrooms cost $30 per month. Workers still grumbled about $1.60 per day for room and board. Six Companies built a commissary run by a private concessionaire offering necessary staples, including clothing, furniture, and a few luxuries such as radios and phonographs. But workers complained that prices compared unfavorably to those of large outlets in Las Vegas.[40]

Decades later, former residents of Boulder City recalled those years with mixtures of nostalgia and humor. Tim A. Bedford, who later enjoyed a distinguished career in the Kaiser organization, went to Hoover Dam in 1932 as a young engineer. Although a college graduate and younger brother of Clay Bedford, a leader in the Kaiser organization, he got no special treatment. Young Bedford started as a manual laborer and lived in a dormitory. He claimed that the bedbugs were so bad that the best defense was placing all four iron bedposts in cans filled with kerosene. Even then, the bugs sometimes parachuted from the ceilings and scored direct hits. If one did not kill them promptly, they'd start a family. In Boulder City's early months, there were no street signs, and houses were identical. One worker supposedly knew where his house was in the last row. Returning home after the "swing" shift, he located his house, kicked off his boots, and called out, "Woman, let me in." A strange woman opened the door, pointed a gun at him, and said, "Run, or I'll fire!" During his shift, builders had set up an entire row of houses. Workers made frequent jokes about the alleged infidelity of night shift workers' wives. One night, a new worker returning to Boulder City noted a veteran seated next to him with a powder tamping stick in his hand. The greenhorn asked what it was for, and the veteran claimed, with a straight face, that when he got home he banged on the front door to announce his return, then raced to the back of the house to club any Lothario making a hasty exit. The joke was on the seasoned worker, as a voice piped out of the back of the bus, "That's right, and he's knocked out a different man every night for the past twenty years!"[41]

If life in Boulder City was tolerable by 1932, it was tedious, particularly for two thousand or so single men in the dormitories. Though the labor was strenuous, they worked eight-hour shifts. Bored, lonely, and with spare cash, they craved excitement. Federal officials had created a reservation more than a hundred square miles in area, which included the dam site and Boulder City. Hard liquor was prohibited; only "near beer" was allowed. At a checkpoint at the reservation entrance, authorites searched cars for illegal liquor and weapons.[42]

Predictably, few single men adhered to the "good life" prescribed by moralistic bureaucrats. On payday, lines of dusty Model-T Fords chugged toward southern Nevada's Gomorrah, Las Vegas. Some eager revelers couldn't wait, getting sidetracked by cheaply tinseled bars and gambling joints just outside the reservation gates. In Las Vegas, sleek bartenders, wisecracking card sharpers, and bejeweled madams awaited their prey. An hour after the paymaster handed wages to the last men in line, a thousand pleasure-starved men might be sampling the delights of the tempting oasis. Friday night's revelry began about 6 P.M. and reached its climax around 2 A.M. Saturday morning.[43]

As dawn's first light crept over the low rim of the desert, the last cars weaved slowly southward. Seasoned veterans, who had departed under cover of full darkness, might pull over a mile or so north of the reservation checkpoint. One or two men might alight unsteadily from the car clutching bottles of rye or bourbon, which they smuggled in through "Bootleg Canyon." Stragglers got back to Boulder City just in time to stumble, bleary-eyed, onto the last truck carrying the day shift to work. Survivors never forgot the horror of sweating out a quart of gin over a shift in 125-degree heat, without benefit of sleep. But next payday, the cycle was repeated.[44] Management and bureau officials tolerated such revelry on the grounds that the men worked hard and needed the release.

Progress on the huge new dam naturally received the most publicity. But to keep the job moving on schedule, other key tasks had to be done behind the scenes. Many different types of heavy machinery had to be leased or purchased; delivery schedules for hundreds of different supplies had to be coordinated; and complicated insurance policies had to be negotiated. One of Kaiser's responsibilities was to coordinate the flow of materials; Clay Bedford and Tom Price helped with that. But perhaps the most critical and delicate job of all was that of liaison between government officials and the contractors. As work began in the spring of 1931, Six Companies named Kaiser their "point man" in Washington.[45]

Among many pivotal events in his career, this seemingly casual decision was one of the most critical. From that point forward, Kaiser became increasingly immersed in political and bureaucratic machinations in the nation's capital. His constant attention to opportunities for government contracts and his intimate knowledge of operations of Congress and bureaucrats helped him initiate many important future ventures. In the spring of 1931, however, his chief task was to keep government funding flowing into Six Companies coffers.

This was no easy task. During Hoover's last two years, lawmakers, believing that a balanced budget was sacrosanct, economized wherever possible. The Hoover Dam benefits were exceedingly long-range, and politicians worried about the most visible, short-range problems first. The dam, with its huge price tag, was a tempting target for budget-cutters. Kaiser's first mission for Six Companies was to shepherd through Congress appropriations which had already been approved in principle. His partners assumed that he would limit his work to quietly lining up support for the project, but they soon learned that he perceived his role in far broader terms. According to the biographer of one associate, Kaiser became "a fertile-minded publicist, [who] generated a steady flow of news stories, information kits, progress reports and special 'briefings' which built a national and international reputation for the Six Companies." Kaiser also demonstrated a more sophisticated grasp of public relations than did his partners. When he recommended spending $25,000 on a guest house at Boulder City for visiting dignitaries, other directors balked. Several men thought that a few weeks in Washington had distorted his priorities. But Kaiser persisted and finally got his way. A luxurious Spanish-style hacienda was built, with room for six overnight guests and staffed with servants and an excellent cook. As Kaiser had predicted, the guest house was used often. Critics might justifiably argue that Kaiser was too solicitous of decisionmakers' physical comfort, especially in hard times. But his astute gamesmanship helped the dam gain an image as the Bureau of Reclamation's most glamorous project.[46]

Such triumphs were not easily achieved. In the summer of 1932, suspension of funding for the dam became a real possibility. The Depression neared its trough, and President Hoover's inability to handle the crisis was painfully evident. All summer, growing numbers of World War I veterans gathered in the capital, demanding immediate payment of benefits not legally due for several more years. The "Bonus Army" generated considerable public sympathy. Lawmakers debated their request all summer, as tensions rose. Finally, Hoover's patience snapped; according to widely circulated news reports, Hoover ordered the Army, under General Douglas MacArthur, to remove the veterans' encampment at nearby Anacostia Flats. The administration "won" the uneven contest, but Hoover probably sacrificed any remote chance he may have had for reelection.[47]

This was the atmosphere in which Kaiser had to persuade Congress to release funds for Hoover Dam. If funds were withheld, work would obviously stop. Kaiser and his partners were very concerned about the timing of the job. On June 27, 1932, Kaiser testified that a critical priority was turning the river in the fall and winter, when water flow was minimal. If this were not done, construction might be delayed for a year. Kaiser claimed that if $7 million were not immediately forthcoming, Six Companies would lose $6 million by failing to meet deadlines. To members of Congress unmoved by the prospect of business losses, Kaiser provided a more persuasive consideration: if Six Companies closed down, three thousand workers would lose their jobs and seven thousand dependents would be destitute.[48]

Through the remainder of Hoover's term, funding for the dam remained problematic. Kaiser shuttled by train between Oakland and Washington. He spent weeks going hat-in-hand to bureaucratic offices and wheedling funds from parsimonious legislators. Congress sometimes resisted funding basic services at Boulder City. Even after completion of the mess hall, several hundred family dwellings, and nine dormitories for single men, Congress initially refused funding for schools. A few parents pooled resources and tried to hire teachers for the children. Their only other option was sending them to public schools in Las Vegas. To their credit, Six Companies directors pushed hard for schools at Boulder City. The government finally authorized $70,000 on the condition that Six Companies agreed to carry a negotiated percentage of the burden.[49] This typified the tight funding for the dam during the Hoover years. After Roosevelt assumed office, money flowed more freely.

Dividing his time between Oakland and Washington, with hurried visits to other projects, Kaiser worked at a furious pace. Clearly the work in Washington broadened his perspective. With few exceptions, Kaiser developed cordial working relations with public officials, particularly New Dealers. He proved equally adept at obtaining funding and at explaining developments which might otherwise have embarrassed the contractors. He formed a close association with Harold L. Ickes, Roosevelt's Interior Secretary, whose support would be critical in Kaiser's future career.

But Kaiser's apprenticeship in Washington had rough spots, and he occasionally irritated Ickes. Early in 1935 several newspapers reported that living conditions at Boulder City remained primitive and that concessionaires were reaping inordinate profits. These stories resembled earlier accounts; Ickes, a political veteran, initially discounted them. Six Companies was ahead of schedule and within its budget. However, when several public officials called for an investigation, Kaiser reacted with a stream of multi-page telegrams protesting the contractors' innocence. Ickes, annoyed, confided to Senator Key Pittman of Nevada:

> I may say to you frankly . . . that Mr. Kaiser's telegraphic bombardment has not made a favorable impression upon me. If there has been no violation of the law, there is nothing to cause apprehension in the breast of Mr. Kaiser. . . . Mr.

Kaiser has telegraphed to me, he has telegraphed to the President, he has telegraphed to you, and he has telegraphed to others, who have telegraphed to me, to what purpose I do not know, since obviously an investigation once begun cannot be called off until completed. . . . Frankly, he is doing himself and his company no good by his lack of composure.

Pittman acknowledged that Kaiser had, indeed, developed "jitters."[50]

Kaiser learned from mistakes. In a deferential reply to Ickes, Kaiser wrote, "Your personal assistant, Mr. Slattery, suggested that I be patient. I have recognized that perhaps this constructive suggestion was well made." But he reminded Ickes that after later testimony revealed the innocence of his partners, the public would remember the charges, not subsequent retractions.[51]

Kaiser also learned that Ickes was a tenacious watchdog over his department's expenditures. The Interior chief was convinced that Six Companies wasted money on overtime, performed in other than "emergency" situations. As Six Companies' work wound down in the summer of 1935, Ickes counted more than seventy thousand separate violations of the letter of the contract and authorized a payroll audit. Ickes suspected no criminal intent but was a stickler for detail. He was irritated by Six Companies' casual interpretation of the rules, and he considered a $350,000 fine.[52] Rather than challenge Ickes' charges directly, Kaiser devised a masterful response. Several weeks later, as the dam superstructure neared completion, Kaiser arranged for publication of a handsome illustrated booklet, *So Hoover Was Built,* by Six Companies publicist George Pettit. Copies of the booklet were to be mailed to influential opinion-makers across the country, thus presenting the Six Companies' perspective before any headline-seeking investigations or negative assessments could surface. In keeping with his determination not to alienate Ickes, Kaiser mailed copies to him before general distribution. The secretary backed down part way and lowered the fine to $100,000.[53]

Ickes was renowned for his prickly personality; his nickname was "Old Curmudgeon." Kaiser learned one secret of getting along with him, consistently flattering Ickes and keeping him informed of developments at Hoover Dam. In March 1936, Ickes wrote to Kaiser, "Your company has made a remarkable engineering record in overcoming the obstacles incident to constructing such a difficult project and in advancing the time of completion so materially. . . . I have been very impressed with the fair attitude of you and other officials, which resulted in a satisfactory working relationship."[54] This was probably as close to sentiment as the dour Ickes got, at least in correspondence with those other than President Roosevelt.

Kaiser's cordial relationships with public officials would yield personal benefits for many years. They brought direct benefits for Six Companies almost immediately. In June 1936, Louis Glavis, Director of Investigation for the Department of Interior, claimed that he had "confidential information" that the partners had a slush fund of $100,000. According to Glavis, the money was "disbursed for some unknown purpose." The implication was obvious; Six Companies partners might have used it for bribery.[55]

A month after informing Ickes of his suspicions, Glavis resigned. He had a distinguished thirty-year career as watchdog in the department, including a role in the Pinchot-Ballinger controversy during the Taft administration. He had several "old Progressive" friends in Congress, and Ickes shared many of their views. The secretary decided to investigate Six Companies. Kaiser spent weeks testifying before congressional subcommittee hearings and convincing public officials that the Six Companies record was clean.[56] The investigation yielded no evidence of a slush fund, but the experience steeled Kaiser against sensational charges directed his way in later years.

Even before this investigation, Kaiser's partners wrapped up the project. On September 30, 1935, President Roosevelt made a pilgrimage to dedicate the dam. (On May 8, 1933, Ickes had arbitrarily renamed it "Boulder Dam," so Roosevelt avoided the embarrassment of christening a dam named for his predecessor.) Only the superstructure was finished. Considerable work remained to be done on the power plant, transmission lines, and channels for diversion of water and irrigation. That mattered little to the governors of six states, dozens of bureaucrats, and twelve thousand visitors who applauded the President's speech and marveled at the latest triumph of human genius.[57]

Long before the dedication, Kaiser was helping maneuver Six Companies into position to win bids for other federal dams. His liaison activities, their reputation for fast and effective work, and intelligent bidding by shifting groups of Six Companies partners soon brought more work their way. Since the turn of the century, engineers had dreamed of harnessing the far-flung network of rivers forming the Columbia River Basin. The region, five times the size of England, included portions of seven western states: Idaho, Montana, Nevada, Oregon, Utah, Washington, and Wyoming. The Columbia River's powerful flow had cut a deep valley through a plateau much of which was 500 feet or more above the river. Windmills could pump water only 150 feet. Farmers and ranchers who could see the river from parched fields gazed in frustration as millions of gallons of water flowed, beyond their reach, into the Pacific Ocean.[58]

In the 1890s, when railroads opened up the Pacific Northwest for economic development, lack of control over the untamed river did not appear important. The land near the rapidly growing cities of Portland, Tacoma, and Seattle was drenched with rainfall, and little irrigation was needed. However, settlement quickly spread east, and prospective farmers and ranchers soon occupied hundreds of thousands of acres of land far removed from the fertile, humid coastal plains. Few worried that inland regions averaged only eight inches of rain annually. Crops thrived at first, largely by drawing up moisture stored beneath a mat of grass and other vegetation. In a few years, that resource was depleted. Wheat failed, and range grass dried up; starving cattle searched in vain for fodder. Inevitably, creditors took over the land. In 1937 one perceptive observer wrote: "Today, more than a generation later, crumbling barns, rotting farmhouses, and decaying wagon-wheels still tell the story of expectations that exceeded the rainfall."[59]

The task of harnessing the Columbia River mirrored that of the Colorado River in decades of effort. There was one important difference: unlike the nearly deserted Colorado River Basin, the Columbia River Basin had tens of thousands of inhabitants; thus, when a "Columbia River Development League" was formed at the end of World War I, more local initiative was involved. At the national level, Secretary of Commerce Herbert Hoover warmly endorsed the concept in 1926, and President Coolidge observed that the project was "not too far distant." Once elected president, Hoover changed his mind. Although a westerner, he believed that the federal government should not begin another expensive dam in the region.[60]

President Roosevelt had no such qualms; he promptly signed bills authorizing the Bonneville and Grand Coulee dams. The Bonneville contracts were opened for bidding late in 1933. The site was forty miles east of Portland and offered a different challenge from Hoover Dam. Canyon walls were soft and far apart; no diversionary tunnels were needed, only a temporary cofferdam to divert the river while sections of the main dam were built. Even so, the river posed serious problems. With a maximum flow of one million feet per second, it was potentially five times as powerful as the Colorado.

Kaiser hoped to bring in Six Companies as a unit, but several partners balked at his initiative. The contract amounted to a mere $16 million, small by Hoover Dam standards, and they saw little room for profit. Six Companies temporarily separated, setting an amoeba-like pattern which prevailed for years. In numerous future situations, a single firm sponsored and managed the job, while the others were invited to join as financial, or "silent," partners. On other occasions they went their own ways. In fact, the Bonneville job marked open competition between several partners. Kaiser sponsored one bid, bringing in "Dad" Bechtel, Felix Kahn, and Harry Morrison. Charlie Shea and Jack McEachern, the latter from Seattle, bid against them. Both teams got work at Bonneville. Kaiser's combine won the construction job and the Shea-McEachern group gained the powerhouse contract.[61]

Harnessing the Columbia River quickly proved to be a more formidable challenge than anyone had imagined. Although Kaiser's older son, Edgar, was only twenty-five and Clay Bedford slightly more seasoned at thirty-one, Henry Kaiser was confident that they could jointly supervise the job. The young men moved up from Hoover Dam to the Bonneville site, where their biggest challenge was controlling far more water than at Hoover. Twice during initial phases of construction, floods roared down the river, wiping out cofferdams and thousands of man-hours of work. Years later, Edgar Kaiser recalled his baptism under fire: "[It] was, without question, the most difficult construction job we have ever built."[62]

With the Bonneville job in hand and work nearly finished on Hoover Dam, in June 1934 Henry Kaiser confidently sought the contract for Grand Coulee Dam. The proposed location was 350 miles east of the Bonneville Dam, on the Columbia River. Cheap water would benefit chiefly eastern Washington, but inexpensive power would help the entire Pacific Northwest.

Even to experienced construction men, Grand Coulee represented one of the most challenging building tasks yet undertaken. It was larger than Hoover Dam or any single structure ever built. Several early-twentieth-century studies of feasibility and potential benefits were conducted. The most influential was provided in 1922 by Major General George W. Goethals, chief engineer on the Panama Canal job. Like Hoover Dam, the Grand Coulee would create an enormous reservoir, to be called Lake Roosevelt, 151 miles long, with an average width of 4,000 feet and depth of 375 feet. Unlike Hoover Dam, the Grand Coulee would be long and low. It would be anchored by a concrete base 500 feet thick, reaching a height of 550 feet; at the top would be a 30-foot-wide roadway across the 4,173-foot-long dam. Engineers estimated that three times the concrete used on the Hoover Dam project was needed. The overall job dwarfed the Hoover Dam contract; from a budget of $404 million, $209 million was for irrigation canals, $181 million for the dam and power plant.[63]

To their shock, Kaiser and several Six Companies partners lost the bid on preliminary work to the Mason-Walsh-Atkinson-Kier (MWAK) combine. However, when bidding opened for the superstructure early in 1938, they were ready. Kaiser sponsored the bid and was joined by MacDonald and Kahn, Pacific Bridge, Morrison-Knudsen, and Utah Construction. They also brought in former rival MWAK and the General Construction Company of Seattle. The combine was named Consolidated Builders, Inc. Harvey Slocum, who had helped MWAK figure the bid that whipped Kaiser in 1934, organized a rival group called Pacific Builders. When the envelopes were opened, the tables were reversed; Consolidated Builders bid $34,442,240, beating the competition by $7 million.[64]

The Grand Coulee job, begun in 1938 and finished in 1942, marked a significant transition in Kaiser's career. It was his last major construction contract before becoming heavily involved in manufacturing and the production of building materials. There were key developments within the Kaiser organization at Grand Coulee. Perhaps the most significant was experimentation with what became the Kaiser Health Plan, under Dr. Sidney Garfield. Henry and Edgar Kaiser also gained valuable experience with labor unions, which benefited them in later years. Another important development at Grand Coulee was that Kaiser and his top men established a highly successful strategy of "cutting the dam in half," with two crews competing for the lion's share of the work—and glory. This tactic was to yield spectacular results in shipbuilding and other corporate endeavors.[65]

At the end of the 1930s, another major dam-building opportunity arrived. Shasta Dam, located twelve miles east of Redding, California, was to provide cheap water and power for the five-hundred-mile-long Central Valley region and control spring flooding along the Sacramento River. Once again, Kaiser and some partners formed a consortium of nine operators. A competing group, Pacific Constructors, counted a dozen members. Bids were opened on June 1, 1938. The presiding official read the Kaiser combine figure of $36,202,357; Kaiser confidently anticipated yet another major contract. Then he read the rival bid, and Kaiser thought his ears had malfunctioned: the competitors had bid $35,939,450, and he had lost the Shasta contract by a mere $262,907.[66] Convinced that his competition had misrepresented certain costs, Kaiser quickly regained his composure. Still fighting for the contract, he ordered his engineers to build a model of the dam, so that he could prove to Bureau of Reclamation officials that his bid was actually lower. Despite his powers of persuasion, Kaiser failed to change their minds.[67]

There might appear to be a cyclical pattern in the outcomes of job bids, each success followed by a failure and vice versa, but this would be a highly misleading perception. Smaller jobs were extremely competitive; in some cases, a dozen or more bids might be submitted. Kaiser and his men by no means ignored small projects, and they lost more bids than they won. Still, by the late 1930s big jobs were their primary targets. They were involved in far more than dam building. Several key jobs were visible from corporate headquarters in Oakland. They erected the pilings for the eastern half of the San Francisco–Oakland bridge and also won the Broadway Tunnel contract in Oakland. In addition, Kaiser and assorted partners built many piers and jetties along the Pacific Coast.

Failure to win the Shasta Dam contract indirectly led Kaiser into manufacturing durable goods. By 1939 Kaiser had spent a quarter of a century in construction; his men had used millions of barrels of cement. Never at east when subject to the whims of others, particularly delivery of a critical commodity, Kaiser had considered entering the cement business in 1933.

Angered at prices charged by West Coast producers, he urged his engineers to scour the Bay Area for deposits of limestone and clay, main ingredients of cement. Kaiser was considering challenging five large producers.[68]

Kaiser was unconvinced by industry representatives' claims that, with plants operating at 28 percent of capacity in the throes of the Depression, price fixing was inconceivable.[69] However, he was so busy with dams and other jobs in 1933 that he postponed building his own cement plant. Losing the Shasta job provided him the incentive he needed. The "Big Five" cement producers confidently expected a lucrative contract at Shasta; who could challenge them? Kaiser entered the list. Time was one ally; he knew it would be more than a year before Pacific Constructors required cement deliveries at Shasta.

Still, Bureau of Reclamation officials were incredulous when Kaiser informed them he intended to bid on the cement contract. From his office in Denver, Chief Engineer R. F. Walter opposed Kaiser's plan on several counts. His most significant objection was based on disbelief that a single plant could maintain steady deliveries of cement over three years, in the face of possible labor problems, machinery breakdowns, and faulty batches of cement. Kaiser noted that the bureau planned to obtain sand, gravel, and other materials from single suppliers; if the chief's logic applied to him, it should also affect other potential vendors. Bureau engineers also stressed that Kaiser had neither experience nor a cement plant.[70]

Kaiser informed Walters that he had already taken steps to enter the industry. Engineers located plentiful limestone deposits along Permanente Creek in Santa Clara County, and Kaiser leased the land with an option to purchase. Kaiser's assistants also arranged financing from the Bank of America for plant construction, and arranged with railroads for delivery to Redding, which was close to Shasta.[71]

Kaiser faced a tough battle persuading government officials to take him seriously, but he had one significant advantage. West Coast cement suppliers had established a pattern of submitting nearly identical bids on contracts. Kaiser learned that this practice had alienated Ickes, who abhorred even the hint of price-fixing. A month before bids were opened, Kaiser presented a list of the "monopoly's" trangressions to Ickes' office. In addition to its usual activities, the cement trust had allegedly interfered with construction of his cement plant, organizing neighborhood protests against his planned facility, pressuring railroads to hike rates for shipment of Kaiser's cement, and engaging in other restraints of trade.[72]

Despite Kaiser's bold initiative, industry officials were still surprised at the outcome of the bidding for cement at Shasta in the summer of 1939. The West Coast combine came in at $1.41 per barrel, close to negotiated prices on many other jobs. They were shocked when Kaiser bid $1.19 per barrel and tried to convince bureau officials that accepting Kaiser's bid was far too risky.

Bureau officials wavered. Combine leadership included some of the West Coast's most powerful men: A. E. Wishon of Pacific Gas and Electric; George Cameron, publisher of the _San Francisco Chronicle;_ and others. Yet government officials signed papers in June 1939 for $6.9 million worth of cement from Kaiser. A few years later, a California railroad man observed: "If Kaiser's life can be said to have a turning point, it was then. He licked a tough bunch. From then on, he wasn't afraid to tackle anything." [73]

Six months later Kaiser was launched as an industrialist. On Christmas Day, 1939, the men at the new Permanente Cement plant presented him with the first bag from what eventually became the largest plant in the world. Yet delivering cement was only one of his challenges. Kaiser also won the bid to supply aggregates for the dam. Other West Coast materials suppliers, angered at losing to Kaiser at Shasta, tried to complicate the job of fulfilling his contracts. Kaiser had access to sand and gravel pits located just ten miles from Shasta. Unfortunately, local railroad men demanded what Kaiser considered a prohibitive rate of $.27 per ton for the short haul. Kaiser believed that the cement combine encouraged the railroad's intransigence; he wanted to beat the "monopolists" again. He confronted them indirectly; his engineers rigged up an ingenious ten-mile-long conveyor belt from the sand and gravel pits directly to the dam site. Billed as the world's longest continuous conveyor belt, the "rubber railroad" moved a thousand tons of aggregates per hour, day and night, for four years, for $.18 per ton. [74]

These successes should not suggest that Kaiser easily met his commitments. Before the contracts were completed, at times he was sorry he had won them. The reason was that demand for cement increased sharply in 1940 and 1941 because of the escalation of war preparations on the West Coast. Suppliers who had inveighed against the Bureau of Reclamation encouraging another cement producer when their plants were operating far below capacity suddenly found themselves with more orders than they could handle. Prices reflected the increased demand. Kaiser soon found himself at a disadvantage. He had to deliver 200,000 barrels each month to Shasta; at $1.19 per barrel he supplied cement for about $.30 less than the old combine received on new contracts. [75]

By 1942 the Permanente plant had four kilns, with a total capacity of 16,000 barrels a day. If the plant operated continuously, without work stoppages, equipment breakdowns, or interruptions in supply, it could yield roughly 500,000 barrels per month. However, even before Pearl Harbor the government was gearing up for war in the Pacific. Demand ran into millions of barrels, and military agencies pressured producers to expand capacity as quickly as possible. Thus, in the midst of the confusion caused by rapid expansion of plant capacity and lucrative contracts to supply cement to military bases in the Pacific, Kaiser was obligated to send almost half of his output to Shasta Dam, at unattractive prices.[76]

Despite later Kaiser Company public relations claims that Kaiser provided all the cement for the Shasta job, the facts are slightly different. In June 1942, Bureau of Reclamation officials provided a small measure of relief for Permanente Cement. The dam builders requested total deliveries of up to 257,000 barrels per month until November 1942. Estimates of total cement needs for the last year of construction exceeded original projections by almost 20 percent, and bureau officials had little choice from either a legal or an ethical standpoint but to wheedle the remainder of the Shasta cement from other suppliers. Kaiser was clearly nettled that his rivals got $1.44 to $1.55 per barrel, while his cement brought only the contract price of $1.19. In fact, Permanent supplied nearly 95 percent of the cement for Shasta.[77]

By late 1942, however, Kaiser had more important things on his mind than one cement contract. Anticipating America's involvement in World War II, he was preparing to enter other industries: magnesium, steel, aircraft, and shipping. When Kaiser delivered his last bag of cement at Shasta, involvement in dams was largely behind him. By then, he was turning out more cargo vessels than any other ship builder in the nation. The men who built dams in the 1930s and stayed with Kaiser in 1942 emerged into a wholly different world.

5

Patriot in Pinstripes— Shipbuilding

Henry Kaiser had been interested in boats as long as he could remember. He spent much of his youth within eyesight of the Erie Canal and was fascinated when old-timers recalled its heyday. As a teenager, he enjoyed boating on lakes and streams near Utica. Later he worked as a photographer on tourist flatboats in Florida. At Lake Placid, he courted Bess Fosburgh in canoes and small powerboats. After the move to Oakland in 1921, boating was his only significant hobby. He enjoyed tinkering with outboard engines with his son Edgar. In the 1930s Kaiser built Fleur du Lac, a retreat at Lake Tahoe. He used the facility more for business than pleasure, but his chief recreational outlet there was skimming over the deep blue water in high-powered boats.

Despite this lifelong fascination with boats, becoming a shipbuilder was far from his mind when he was building dams in the early 1930s. The origin of Kaiser's first inkling that he might build ships is uncertain. In later years, his public relations staff claimed that the U.S. Maritime Commission had persuaded him to build ships. There was some supporting evidence for this view. Testifying before a congressional committee hearing after World War II, Vice-Admiral Emory S. Land, chairman of the commission, recalled: "He was certainly one of the key men in the Six Companies, and it took us two years to land him. He came down to my office at least three times, and I do not know how many times to Admiral Vickery's office before we could get them mixed up in the shipbuilding business."[1] Testifying before a Senate subcommittee in the summer of 1942, Kaiser was asked by Senator Harry S. Truman if he had been involved in shipbuilding before 1940. Kaiser replied, "No, I had never even seen a ship launched."[2]

Neither Land nor Kaiser deliberately lied; the magnitude of Kaiser's feats in shipbuilding after 1940 simply dwarfed what transpired earlier. But

Kaiser's entry into the field was neither capricious nor sudden. Some evidence suggests that it wasn't Kaiser's idea. According to one account, Six Companies associates John A. McCone and Stephen D. Bechtel first considered shipbuilding in 1937 and decided it was "about ripe to become big volume business . . ."[3] At first, Bechtel and McCone aroused little enthusiasm among other partners, but Kaiser became a convert in 1938. The idea took off. By October 1938, Kaiser was working clcsely with Roscoe "Jim" Lamont, who was organizing the Seattle-Tacoma Shipbuilding Company. Kaiser's employees constructed shipways for Lamont's company, and he sensed enormous opportunities for himself and his partners.[4]

In the late 1930s, shipbuilding was still in the doldrums. After the World War I boom, many of the large shipyards had suspended all, or most, of their operations. In the Depression foreign trade had declined precipitously, and there was little demand for new vessels. The industry was dominated by several large companies, including Newport News, American, Bethlehem, and Sun shipbuilders. There was a stirring of activity when the Merchant Marine Act of 1936 authorized adding five hundred merchantmen over ten years. Most of the new ships were built in Atlantic Coast shipyards, and easterners still dominated the field. Jim Lamont initially introduced Kaiser to John D. Reilly, president of Todd Shipyards, an eastern company.[5] The two men explored possibilities for an alliance; they believed that in the event of a major buildup, the Maritime Commission would spread contracts between eastern and western shipbuilders.

Kaiser kept his partners informed about these talks. The western men were reluctant to form a partnership until they had an order in hand. In September 1939, shortly after the German invasion of Poland, the Maritime Commission asked for bids on five C-1 cargo ships. Kaiser's partners sensed an opportunity to test the waters in shipbuilding without a large financial commitment. Todd and Six Companies joined the Seattle-Tacoma Shipbuilding Corporation on a fifty-fifty basis and won the $9 million contract.[6] In fact, Todd was sponsor, and Six Companies had only a financial interest. In 1939 none of the westerners possessed sufficient expertise to sponsor the job; in the short run, they followed Reilly's lead. Todd personnel built the C-1 ships; Six Companies people constructed the shipways, watched the shipbuilding—and learned.

Under "normal" circumstances Kaiser and his partners would have had difficulty entering the business; in fact, they would have had no reason to do so. But the outbreak of war ended "normal" times. It took over a year for big eastern firms to gear up for large-scale production. Conditioned by two decades of hard times, industry forecasters did not fully anticipate future demand. But orders poured in; by the summer of 1940 huge backlogs had piled up. By the end of 1940, government officials were hard pressed to find shipbuilders capable of filling their orders.[7]

In fact, government officials cautiously expanded shipping through 1940. Isolationist sentiment remained entrenched in American thought, and the President—who was angling for a third term—feared political reprisal if he boosted the shipbuilding budget too much. Initially, most orders came from overseas. Reich Marshal Goering's Luftwaffe pounded British yards, severely wounding their shipbuilding capabilities. Even worse, Admiral Doenitz's U-boats were sinking British vessels three times faster than they could be replaced.[8] The British consequently scratched for ships anywhere they could be found; they were not choosy. Late in the year a special British commission came to the United States to let a contract for sixty cargo ships. Knowing that the Maritime Commission wanted to expand shipbuilding capacity on the West Coast, and realizing that the task was too large to be handled promptly in a single yard, Todd and Six Companies aggressively pursued the contract. The Americans proposed building thirty vessels on each coast. The British endorsed the idea. Two new companies were formed: Todd-Bath Iron Shipbuilding constructed vessels in the East, Todd-California in the West. Each group held a financial investment in the other's yards. In December 1940, the British agreed to underwrite construction of the West Coast yards and to pay $160,000 over cost for each ship.[9]

This marked the beginning of Kaiser's direct participation in shipbuilding. Once the British contract was signed, events quickly snowballed. Initially, the westerners' major responsibility was to build the shipyards; experienced Todd men would turn out the ships. As 1940 ended, Kaiser's interest was largely financial. This would soon change.

Kaiser approached this task with his customary enthusiasm. The Grand Coulee Dam job was winding down; there would soon be five thousand seasoned construction men looking for work. Within weeks it was clear that shipbuilding represented a mother lode. In January 1941, Admiral Howard L. Vickery of the Maritime Commission launched the Liberty Ship program. There would be plenty of business for everyone, but announcement of this program fed Kaiser's competitive juices. He hoped to become the biggest and the best. Just as he and his partners had confounded experts by building dams faster than was thought possible, he dreamed of producing ships at unprecedented rates.[10]

But Kaiser first had to build the shipyards. On the day the British contract was signed, he phoned Clay Bedford at Corpus Christi, Texas, where he was helping construct a naval air station: "Clay, you're going to build a shipyard." The young, but seasoned construction man knew his boss seldom joked. Although Bedford had barely seen a shipyard, he simply asked, "Where?" Kaiser replied, "Richmond." When Vickery's program commenced the following month, Kaiser sent Edgar to the Portland/Vancouver area to build additional shipyards there. At first, the situation in Portland was uncomfortable for Edgar. Six Companies founded the Oregon Shipbuilding Corporation (Oregonship) and Charlie Shea was nominally in charge. Shea was dying of cancer, although his partners did not realize it. They only knew that he lacked his customary vigor. Thus, Edgar had the delicate task of accommodating Shea and cooperating with personnel from Todd; all had firm ideas about how shipyards should be built. Shea died within a year; relations with Todd soured quickly. In a bit more than a year, the Todd partnership was dissolved.[11]

On a rainy morning in late December 1940, O. H. McCoon, one of Bedford's foremen, stood on the eastern shore of San Francisco Bay, gazing at the planned site of the first Richmond yards. It was a dismal setting, and rain was unrelenting. When McCoon ordered a tractor into the marshy terrain to clear a service road, it sank from view. Bedford's first task, obviously, was to create solid ground so that shipways could be built. Experienced engineers predicted it would take six months, but Bedford and his foremen ignored such talk. In three weeks, working round the clock, the Kaiser men built the land. Trucks dumped 300,000 cubic yards of rock on the eighty-acre plot. Decades later, one engineer recalled that the men built shipways before plans were drawn. On April 14, 1941, they laid the keel for the *Ocean Vanguard,* the first of 747 vessels to slide down ramps at Richmond.[12]

Few imagined the transformation Kaiser's shipyards would bring to Richmond. In 1940 it was a small industrial city of twenty-three thousand people, about four thousand of whom worked at the Standard Oil refinery, a Ford assembly plant, and other small plants scattered along the shoreline. A blue-collar area, Richmond possessed a small-town flavor; most residents lived in modest wood frame bungalows. They shopped in stores on the "main drag," MacDonald Avenue. Local citizens were generally law-abiding and self-supporting. There were few demands on city officials.[13]

Nobody was prepared for the events about to engulf the city, but for a few months, they seemed under control. When the British awarded the contract to Todd-California on December 20, 1940, local residents viewed the decision as an early holiday present. The first trickle of engineers and construction men was barely noticeable. Bedford and his foremen initially recruited Bay Area workers. By the summer of 1941 there were still only 4,500 workers on the Todd-California payroll. Local merchants enjoyed increased business, and most workers returned to homes elsewhere when shifts ended. However, the Kaiser yards operated around the clock, and longtime residents soon noticed that streets and stores were crowded at all hours.

The shock of Pearl Harbor brought a huge upsurge in local activity. As in hundreds of other cities, the sudden declaration of war created both the excitement and the traumas of a frontier boomtown. With approval of the U.S. Employment Service, Kaiser sent recruiters across the country to bring thousands of workers to the new yards, which mushroomed along the bay. Trainloads of "Okies," "Arkies," and "Texies" arrived and were given crash courses and assigned to dozens of shipbuilding tasks. First arrivals were fortunate; they rented rooms or tiny apartments nearby.[14] Later arrivals endured far worse facilities.

Richmond was soon overwhelmed by the newcomers. By the end of 1942 the Kaiser yards employed about 80,000; a year later almost 100,000 men and women drew paychecks. Recruiters urged workers to venture west alone, leaving families behind until they found housing, but many ignored the advice. Each week hundreds of bewildered workers stumbled into the swarming city. All told, almost 38,000 came on the "special" trains; another 60,000 arrived in automobiles. At least they faced better prospects than the Dust Bowl victims a few years earlier. They found high-paid, steady work immediately.[15]

By the end of 1942 Richmond was in a state of siege. Living conditions were in chaos, and local government was on the verge of collapse. Old-time residents feared the hordes of newcomers, in part because they disrupted services. Their children overwhelmed local schools; in a three-year period enrollment tripled. School officials first tried double, then triple, and, briefly, even quadruple shifts. Qualified teachers were unavailable; the school board resorted to hiring shipyard workers' wives, who in some cases were only semiliterate. Other facilities were overcrowded. Crime exploded, and the city jail, with a capacity of nine, was jammed with fifty offenders on an average night.

If established residents were inconvenienced, their living conditions were luxurious compared to those which newcomers found. Once quarters within commuting distance were taken, later arrivals had little choice but trailer camps. The sewer systems quickly clogged, and public officials permitted offal to flow directly into the bay. Garbage went uncollected for weeks. Vermin multiplied to the point that public health officials feared serious epidemics.[16]

Newcomers reacted in various ways, but families experienced the worst conditions. A machinest and his wife and children lived in their jalopy for weeks. A social worker photographed their living arrangement in an open field and interviewed the wife. According to the woman,

> The car windows aren't broke. We had to put up something to keep the sun out of Daddy's eyes. He works nights and sleeps in the car days. The children and I sleep in it nights. I just wish we were home. War or no war, if I'd known there'd be no place in Richmond we could live, I just wouldn't have come. You can live like this just so long, then you can't stand it any more.

Single men fared better, being responsible only for themselves. During warm months, many slept on the ground; when it was rainy or cold, many slept under bridges or in factory lofts. One man described his daily routine:

> We deliberately choose to work the graveyard shift. We get off at eight in the morning, have breakfast. By then it's warm enough to sleep almost anywhere there's grass. Along about evening we get up, shave at a filling station, and bum around town—in the bars, mostly; where else is there? . . . until time to go to work at midnight again.[17]

Most endured such conditions stoically; they earned decent money and were not being shot at.

Workers discovered that even though paychecks were larger, high prices ate up most of what they earned. Southerners in particular were dazzled by wages ranging from a dollar an hour up to three dollars for skilled laborers. Some agents conscientiously warned recruits about higher prices; but most were shocked by wartime inflation. A worker from Idaho paid forty dollars a month for a two-room apartment which he shared with his wife and two children. He longed to return to Idaho, where houses rented for ten dollars. A 1944 survey in the yards showed that the average worker grossed sixty-one dollars per week. After taxes, food, rent, clothing, war bonds, transportation, and other essentials, he had six dollars left for savings and miscellaneous expenses. Since many succumbed to the temptation of San Francisco's Barbary Coast and assorted fleshpots, many workers spent four years in the Richmond yards without saving a dime.[18]

Living conditions in Richmond reached a nadir early in 1943. Neither Kaiser management nor the government was indifferent to the workers' comfort; but in the Allies' dark days of 1942, they faced more urgent priorities. Their initial efforts to ameliorate local living conditions were pitifully inadequate, but by the end of 1943 the Maritime Commission and Kaiser management joined hands to throw up twenty-four thousand units of housing. These accommodations were utterly lacking in charm: rectangular, multi-family wooden two-story apartment buildings, in undesirable, low-lying areas. Streets went unpaved for months; neither grass nor trees graced open areas. With units added in 1944, these apartments ultimately housed about half the workers; many felt fortunate to obtain space even in such drab quarters. The rest still fended for themselves. By early 1944 the housing shortage in Richmond was history.[19]

Despite the chaos of the early 1940s, both local and federal officials praised Kaiser management for its concern for workers. In 1938 Edgar Kaiser had persuaded Dr. Sidney R. Garfield to venture to Grand Coulee to set up an innovative prepaid health plan. In Richmond, Kaiser management deepened its commitment to health care. With thousands of workers pouring into the yards, many of them sickly, or bringing unhealthy dependents, the concept received an acid test. It was a rousing success; 95 percent of eligible workers joined. For eighty cents each per week workers could provide excellent medical care for themselves and their entire families. Under the direction of Dr. Garfield, emergency stations were set up in the Richmond shipyards, along with the 175-bed Permanente field hospital, staffed by sixty doctors.[20]

Due to the efforts of Kaiser management, public officials, and other entrepreneurs, by 1944 a semblance of order had returned to Richmond. Federal agencies funded new sewers, a beefed-up police force, more schools, and new recreational facilities. Schools went on double shift, and sewage was partially treated before being released into the bay. Although many workers preferred the saloons and gambling dens, there were several new movie theaters. Those who liked exercise could join softball, baseball, basketball, volleyball, bowling, and other teams. City officials were relieved that no epidemics struck; but they still worried about crime. In 1944 police averaged four thousand arrests a month, 95 percent of them newcomers. On the bright side, local officials found an easy source of revenue. With money in their pockets, workers could afford stiff fines. Ordinary drunks were fined $25, and drunken drivers could be docked as much as $250. In October 1944 officials raked in $34,000 in fines, compared to $800 for the same month in 1937.[21] Local officials worked valiantly to serve a population which grew 400 percent between 1940 and 1944.

Five hundred miles north, the Portland region experienced similar wartime stresses, but to a lesser degree. The boom accompanying rapid expansion of the Kaiser yards did not create quite the impact there that it did in Richmond. Portland had a pre-war population of 305,000 and expanded to 359,000 by 1944; across the Columbia River, Vancouver, Washington, doubled in size, from 50,000 to 99,000. Thus, the region did not grow as rapidly as Richmond. Portland also had a legacy of shipbuilding booms, the most recent during World War I. Portland officials believed they could control any influx in population accompanying new shipbuilding contracts. In December 1940, nobody anticipated the social dislocations resulting from community efforts to meet the enormous demand for shipping.[22]

Three weeks after Todd-California won half of the British order, Portland had a share of the work. With guidance from his father, Edgar searched for a suitable location for the Oregon Shipbuilding Corporation. On January 12, 1941, the *Portland Oregonian* announced that young Kaiser had acquired an eighty-seven-acre site on the Columbia River, and that work would begin immediately.

According to one thoughtful student of Portland's power structure, conservative business interests had long controlled decisionmaking in general and city government in particular.[23] Thoroughly familiar with the achievements of Henry Kaiser, who had done construction work in the area for twenty-five years, they were also impressed with Edgar's work at Bonneville and Grand Coulee. Although aware of the Kaisers' determination, local business groups believed that they could at least bend Six Companies' activities in directions compatible with their own interests.

Portland leaders thoroughly misread the Kaisers. Following the death of Charlie Shea and termination of the Todd alliance, Henry gave his son full control of operations in the region, just as Bedford ran the show at Richmond. For the next four years the two men competed fiercely to turn out vessels faster than each other. When Oregon Shipbuilding acquired the eighty-seven-acre plot in January 1941, Edgar knew that his rival in Richmond had a month's head start.

Thus, when Edgar arrived in Portland to manage shipbuilding, he "hit the ground running." Between October 1940 and January 1941, he made several visits to the Todd facilities on the East Coast, where he and several top engineers absorbed instruction about shipbuilding techniques.[24] He was understandably anxious to apply his recently gained knowledge. However, it was some time before Oregon Shipbuilding became a presence in Portland. Like Bedford, Edgar first brought in a small contingent of engineers and workers with special skills. During the first months after the start-up, Oregon Shipbuilding recruited workers in the Pacific Northwest: from construction jobs, orchards, fish hatcheries, lumber camps, and paper mills. Most were white and spoke in familiar accents.

The first visible signs of Kaiser's presence were the enormous shipways and ancillary buildings sprouting up along the river in 1941. Like Bedford, Edgar built yards before blueprints were completed. The Kaiser men knew the ships were critical to England's survival. However much they needed the vessels, the British, masters of the sea for two centuries, must have shuddered at depending on neophytes in shipbuilding, but His Majesty's naval officers soon developed enormous respect for the Kaiser organization, which delivered the last of their ships five months ahead of schedule.[25]

Even as the Kaiser yard turned out British vessels, the Maritime Commission began sending work their way. Kaiser managers quickly realized that the faster they added shipways, the more work they would get. Pearl Harbor provided added stimulus. Following the declaration of war, the Portland area hummed with activity. Before the attack, the Kaisers operated only the Oregonship yard; in early 1942 two more yards were quickly built in Vancouver and at Swan Island. The Kaisers sent labor recruiters across the country, into the Midwest, East, and South. Soon, trainloads of men with Brooklyn and Dixie accents arrived in Portland, along with separate carloads of black recruits, chiefly from the South.[26]

With a combined population of 355,000 in 1940, Portland and Vancouver were better prepared to meet the influx than Richmond. Early arrivals found better quarters than those hired later. Two such men were the Haughey brothers from Michigan. Clifton Haughey, a well-placed engineer, rented a spacious two-bedroom bungalow in a pleasant neighborhood. His younger brother, Phil, was not quite so lucky. Phil also had an engineering degree, but he arrived a few months after his brother. He and his wife camped in Clifton's living room for two weeks while searching for quarters. By June 1942, they leased a one-bedroom apartment overlooking a parking lot. Phil Haughey described its shortcomings in a letter home: "We have an electric range which Frances swears at three times a day because it is so slow after our gas in Detroit, and there is no regulator on the oven." He concluded: "Of course, the whole thing makes us sick when we compare it to our own, but it is adequate and we get along."[27]

The Haughey brothers were more fortunate than workers arriving later without college diplomas or family resources. By the spring of 1942 the vacancy rate in Portland was a miniscule 0.5 percent. Edgar prodded the Portland Housing Authority (PHA) to build more units. He was distressed that by the summer of 1942 the PHA had only 4,900 units under construction and that valuable workers were leaving the yards due to inadequate housing. Projections estimated that 32,000 additional units were needed. Ultimately, Edgar and the Maritime Commission took matters into their own hands. On August 18, 1942, the commission authorized Kaiser to build 6,000 units at government expense on a floodplain on the Columbia River. Three days later, Kaiser's tractors broke ground, and workers began slapping together seven hundred buildings. Less than four months later the first tenants moved into the new community, called Vanport. Later, many more units were built; the worst of the housing crisis in Portland was over by mid-1943.[28]

Out-of-state workers venturing to Portland had a better chance to find housing than those in Richmond. By May 1943, Vanport housed nineteen thousand people, and projections were that it would soon contain forty thousand. Oregonship's company newspaper, *Bos'n's' Whistle*, touted Vanport as a totally planned community, with many amenities, including a 750-seat movie theater, gymnasiums, libraries, and lounge rooms for parties and club meetings. Five new schools, a 250-bed hospital, a combined fire and police station, post office, and shopping centers on both sides of the town were either built or in the planning stage by spring 1943.[29]

Over four thousand single men (and some families) resided in single or double rooms at Hudson House, a huge dormitory complex located a quarter of a mile from the Kaiser yard in Vancouver. Besides proximity to work, Hudson House offered bargan rates. Doubles cost $3.50 per week, private rooms $5.00. Company publicists claimed that a "world-famous" chef provided excellent food cafeteria style for $1.45 per day. Estimated average room and board of $53 each month permitted prudent single men to accumulate sizable nest eggs by war's end.[30]

In promoting Vanport and Hudson House, company publicists grossly exaggerated their virtues. But two Kaiser Company efforts attracted praise at the national level. As in Richmond, the company offered the Kaiser Permanente Health Plan to workers and their families. Another Kaiser initiative won the admiration of Eleanor Roosevelt, who visited the yards for a ship dedication by the President in 1943. The First Lady singled out the company's day-care center for children. For $.75 per day for the first child, and $.50 for each additional child, workers could drop off pre-school-age youngsters for the duration of their shifts. The children were cared for by qualified professionals, who arranged playground activities, indoor games, hot meals, and a daily nap. Parents could also take hot meals home. Company officials were obviously motivated partly by self-interest; women now comprised over a quarter of the employees in the yards. Surprisingly, workers were slow to take advantage of the day-care service; a year after the centers in Richmond and Portland/Vancouver opened, company officials were still devising strategies to increase their use.[31]

Despite the efforts of Kaiser managers and government officials to provide a humane environment, World War II was a difficult period for social experimentation. Showcase day-care centers accommodated a tiny fraction of shipyard workers' offspring, and mixing married and single persons in housing units created problems. Morally upright residents soon became disgusted with life in Hudson House. Much of the fault lay with the other residents, not the facilities. Former workers recalled that even the most innocent young men heard every conceivable combination of four-letter Anglo-Saxon oaths within hours of moving in. Buildings were desegregated by law, but race relations were tense. The races ate at separate tables and held very different cultural values. When a black worker kept his radio on despite complaints, three hundred whites gathered at Hudson House, bent on violence. It took a vanguard of police to prevent bloodshed, or even a race riot. But race relations alone provide an inadequate explanation for the constant tension. A local observer noted that the men comprised a cross-section of America, and disputes were constant, despite the vigilance of house police. "The daily and nightly brawls earned the hotel the sardonic nickname of 'Hoodlum House.'"[32]

According to one former resident, "Vanport was never more than a huge collection of crackerbox houses strung together fast and cheap." But those unable to gain access to Vanport may have been even less comfortable. A former worker who endured several months' residence at the Maritime Commission's facilities at nearby Ogden Meadows wryly recalled his experiences. He reported to three separate agencies before finally being assigned space. Leaving the swing shift at midnight, he hoped for a good night's sleep in his "permanent" quarters. But the walls were paper thin; he swore he heard conversations in normal tones two apartments away. His first night coincided with a party given by next-door neighbors:

> The party was still in the building-up stage when we arrived. It was a modest effort of clinking glasses, a blaring radio, and an occasional squeal of protest. By 3 A.M., however, other couples had arrived and the party had better sound effects. A rousing fist fight broke up the orgy about 4 o'clock. Then a drunken argument raged between a man and a woman. There was a crash of glass and a man's bitter cursing. . . . The argument droned on, and sleep came to us.

But the worker's slumber was all too brief. At 6:30 A.M. a baby in another unit started crying and did not stop until the parents woke up around 9:00 A.M. The worker understood their seeming indifference; exhausted themselves, they had learned to sleep through virtually anything.[33]

During the war years it was noisy everywhere. The racket was loudest in the yards, where rumbling cranes, clanking metal plates, and shouted warnings and directions all contributed to the constant din. To the worker coming off a shift and heading for some entertainment downtown, street sounds probably resembled a murmur, but the uproar amazed old-time residents. On Main Street in Vancouver, the taverns were busy at all hours. Workers lined up to enter legal gambling joints, where some lost a week's wages in a couple of hours. Others found amusement in bowling alleys, where inflation was not so evident. Workers who enjoyed the thunder of crashing pins after an eight-hour shift found cheap entertainment at ten cents per game. When movie theaters were not jammed, tired workers might enjoy a show and a box of popcorn for about thirty cents. Current magazines sold out quickly. One Kaiser employee recalled workers leaving news stalls with stacks of magazines. Reading was about the only sure way of avoiding trouble in rollicking Portland and Vancouver.[34]

Those who ventured west to the Kaiser yards ran the gamut from illiterate sharecroppers to Ph.D.s from elite colleges, but almost all shared a deep commitment to hard work. One is repeatedly struck by the seriousness of purpose in the words of most who recounted their wartime experiences.

But before Americans went to work, West Coast unions demanded that they be organized. In the words of one Kaiser manager, the boss "got religion" and realized the advantage of cordial working relations with unions during his years on the Grand Coulee job. It was difficult to recruit and retain excellent workers, particularly at remote job sites. Kaiser believed that a few extra dollars in wages and benefits were returned severalfold in more efficient work by experienced, satisfied workers. But he and his managers soon learned that good relations with unions on one job did not assure similar success elsewhere. Conditions differed between regions.

They also discovered that even dealing with different locals of the same union often required different strategies.

Labor unions experienced enormous internal stresses during the war years. The war brought both opportunites and problems to union leaders. Instant prosperity created unprecedented demand for labor and prospects for huge membership gains. These in turn brought welcome revenues— initiation fees and monthly dues. All this meant increased power for the unions signing up the bulk of the new workers. In the early 1940s, internecine warfare between rival unions was the rule rather than the exception. The radical Industrial Workers of the World (IWW) had declined after the Red Scare of 1919, but loyalists still hoped to rebuild its strength, at least in the West. In many areas, the American Federation of Labor (AFL) and the Congress of Industrial Organizations (CIO) were bitter rivals; locals often quarreled more among themselves than with management. Yet union leaders faced other sticky problems. Wartime brought federal sanctions against strikes and, after 1942, strict limits on wage hikes. Unions had little room for maneuvering management. Too often, labor relations consisted of petty squabbles over work rules. Finally, local unions risked alienating old-time members by absorbing too many newcomers at once. Skilled workers often resisted expansion of an elite labor pool. When minorities comprised large percentages of newcomers in local economies, labor relations occasionally became explosive.

Even conscientious managers had trouble avoiding labor problems in Portland, and Henry and Edgar Kaiser found themselves in hot water. By 1940, they had accepted the closed shop. They signed contracts with AFL locals when there were only 66 workers at the Oregonship facility and, later, with 191 employees at the Vancouver yard. Nobody gave the contracts much thought at the time. But by 1942 thousands of workers had arrived, and CIO officers realized what was at stake. Philip Murray, president of the CIO, claimed that it was patently unfair for a few workers to decide the union affiliation of thousands entering the yards later. Murray challenged the validity of the AFL agreement on the ground that there had been no union elections. Local CIO officials criticized high AFL initiation fees and dues; initiation charges ranged from $12.50 to $53.00 and monthly dues were scaled from $1.25 to $4.50.[35]

Edgar and Henry Kaiser felt like innocent bystanders. They had initially signed with the Boilermakers, whose local leader, Tom Ray, turned out to be an unsavory character and a promoter of racial and sexual discrimination. Blacks and women were not allowed full voting membership in the union, although they paid full dues. Following complaints from blacks, women, and officers of the CIO, the National Labor Relations Board (NLRB) ordered an investigation late in 1942. Among other indiscretions, the board discovered that Ray had spent $250,000 on a private social club for himself and his friends. To image-conscious labor leaders, he had become a liability, so national AFL officials dumped him. The NLRB also invoked a rule that closed shop contracts were illegal unless they had been approved by 50 percent of workers in the yards. The Board overturned the AFL contracts and ordered new elections.[36]

But national AFL leaders were powerful and clever. Purging Ray and appearing to give blacks and women full representation helped the local clean up its image. More to the point, AFL leaders effectively manipulated public opinion. Americans had little tolerance for management-labor conflicts during the national emergency; squabbles between rival unions aroused even more disgust. Hence, the AFL claimed that the CIO "interruption" of smooth-running operations was highly unpatriotic. The local yards were setting records producing ships. President Roosevelt urged a speedy settlement of union representation in West Coast yards, and Emory S. Land of the Maritme Commission strongly opposed reopening the issue. Under severe wartime pressures, the NLRB let the AFL contracts stand.[37]

When company officials recruited workers from across the country, they aroused the hostility of some employers and union officials. Public officials in some regions complained that Kaiser agents disrupted wartime production; in other cases, Kaiser felt compelled to disprove association with a few unscrupulous recruiters.[38] By the time Allied fortunes turned in mid-1942, Kaiser had experienced the hazards of reconciling union demands, military needs, and bureaucratic policy.

According to conservative critics, Kaiser was a "soft touch" for labor. A few disaffected workers wrote to columnist Westbrook Pegler, who publicized their revelations in his nationally syndicated column. One complaint was that Kaiser's yards were overstaffed, and that workers wasted time waiting for critical supplies or simply "goldbricking." Other letters described continuous crap games in the holds of ships. Another claimed that sleeping on the job was so prevalent that some workers held full-time jobs elsewhere. Kaiser's critics in Congress chided his solicitousness toward workers. At one appearance before the Senate Special Committee to Investigate the National Defense Program, headed by Harry S. Truman, Kaiser was lectured by Senator Ralph Owen Brewster (R-Maine). "To what extent is it possible," asked Brewster, "to communicate to the workmen the idea that if they do have to sacrifice a little of their comforts during the period of crisis that they are still better off than the boys at Guadalcanal?"[39]

There were also charges from the left of unfair treatment of workers in the Kaiser yards. The Fair Employment Practices Commission (FEPC) investigated several complaints from the National Association for the Advancement of Colored People (NAACP) that blacks were relegated to low-paying jobs with few promotion opportunities. There was considerable truth to the charge. An FEPC study of the three yards in Portland and Vancouver in September 1944 revealed that 7,892 blacks comprised 8.8 percent of the work force, but only one earned more than $1.80 per hour. Even Edgar Kaiser, remarkably liberal concerning race issues, resisted FEPC demands for black supervisors over non-segregated crews. He feared, with good reason, that whites might riot. Rita Cowan, a clerk in Portland, charged that she lost her job simply because she was Jewish. Few women complained, since they received equal pay for equal work, but a postwar analysis revealed that they were clustered in lower-level jobs and were first to be laid off after the war.[40]

Kaiser's yards employed almost 200,000 people for four years, and the number of documented problems appears low. Except for Kaiser's unrelenting critics, most observers praised the esprit de corps in his yards. In fairness to Kaiser and his managers, most complaints were directed against prejudiced local union officials, proprietors, and white co-workers. Edgar Kaiser resisted a black supervisor's suggestion that he create an "all-Negro" shipyard. To his credit, he met frequently with leaders in Portland trying to get them to persuade intransigent proprietors to give black patrons fair treatment.

The men in the yards admired Edgar Kaiser; although workers seldom, if ever, saw Henry Kaiser, many revered him. When Eleanor Roosevelt came to Vancouver on April 5, 1953, to christen the first of fifty "baby flat-top" aircraft carriers, she received a tumultuous welcome. But one newspaper account claimed that the "biggest ovation" was reserved for the boss. Years later, a former shipyard worker recalled another christening where Edgar introduced his father. Henry Kaiser started to speak, but was drowned out by a murmur of discontent from thousands of gathered workers, which grew to a roar of disappointment. Only a few hundred workers could see Kaiser, and those who could not yelled until he came forward into full view. In the words of the worker, "No finer tribute could have been paid—or paid more spontaneously—than Henry Kaiser's men and women paid him that day." Perhaps nobody captured the predominant attitude toward the boss better than a writer for *Nation* in December 1942: "The men are quite possessive about the yards and just as paternalistic toward Kaiser as he is toward them, regarding him with a fond and fatherly incredulity." They sensed his commitment, and they wanted to repay him in kind.[41]

Henry Kaiser clearly returned their affection. Close observers of Kaiser's managerial style stressed his ability to analyze issues from the viewpoint of the worker. After government statisticians revealed that absenteeism in his yards was above average, critics urged him to stand firmly against "treason." Kaiser endured their barbs for a time, but he finally blew up. In a passionate public statement he turned the tables:

> The talk about absenteeism has been grossly overdone. Much too much has been said and printed, and thought, about the small minority of people whose absenteeism is chronic. . . . Let's talk about PRESENTISM. My hat is off to the 93% *faithful* in the Kaiser-operated shipyards in the Portland and San Francisco areas. . . . With hands and hearts they are fashioning complete victory as surely as if they were on the fighting front.[42]

Cynics smirked that his rejoinders contained more bathos than Edgar Guest's poems, but ordinary workers sensed his sincerity.

Without question, good morale was a key element in permitting Kaiser's yards to smash previous records for output. Production figures present only part of the story, but they were spectacular. Between 1941 and 1945 his yards yielded 1,490 vessels; Clay Bedford and Edgar Kaiser wound up in a virtual dead heat in ships launched. Richmond turned out 747; Portland/Vancouver yielded 743. Kaiser and his men produced thirteen different types of ships; most were merchant vessels, including 821 ten thousand-ton "Liberty Ships" and 219 "Victory Ships." The latter were slightly improved versions of the former. Of 107 warships, fifty "baby flat-top" aircraft carriers were produced in Vancouver. The Kaiser yards turned out over 15 million dead weight tons of shipping at a cost of just over $4 billion.[43]

More than any other activity, shipbuilding made Henry Kaiser a national hero. Millions of Americans who followed public affairs heard the Kaiser shipbuilding saga repeatedly. Important as the Six Companies dams were, they were located in remote areas and their obvious benefits were regional. Shipbuilding was critical to the international war effort, and Kaiser was entering an even higher-stakes game. He started out in the shadow of John D. Reilly of Todd Shipyards. In some ways, Reilly's vision matched Kaiser's. He anticipated the huge increase in shipping needs as World War II loomed and sensed the absurdity of most yards being on the East Coast when control of the Pacific Ocean was so vital to the nation's security. But the men approached their tasks from different perspectives. Reilly was a salaried employee in an old, established firm. His company had achieved success with traditional shipbuilding techniques. Reilly valued his position and did not challenge convention. By contrast, Kaiser was almost contemptuous of traditional methods. His partners had long since despaired of getting him to follow customary procedures. While other partners were used to Kaiser's propensity for tackling several jobs at once, Reilly was not.

Within two months of signing the British contract, it was clear that Kaiser made Reilly very nervous. Reilly assumed Kaiser was devoting every waking hour early in 1941 to building shipyards in Richmond. He was dismayed that Kaiser delegated that job to Bedford and spent time dickering with federal officials over entry into steel, aluminum, and magnesium. Kaiser, generous almost to a fault, offered pieces of these proposed new enterprises to virtually any partner who might be interested, including Reilly. The easterner informed Chad Calhoun, a top Kaiser aide, that he opposed these projects. Reilly informed his partner that he wanted to send an observer to Kaiser Company board meetings to watch and report "every detailed movement" of his company.[44]

Kaiser endured such "meddling" until his men learned shipbuilding, but he and his men boiled inwardly. When Bedford's crew built Richmond yard no. 1, Todd men constantly checked their work. James F. McCloud, a young Stanford graduate in mechanical engineering, joined Bedford's team in June 1941 and immediately noticed that something was amiss: ". . . even one as inexperienced as I could feel the tension that existed between the old-time shipbuilders and the construction men who formed the nucleus of management and supervision of the Kaiser group."[45] Kaiser wanted "out" of the partnership at the first opportunity, and Reilly evidently reciprocated the feeling. The agreement ended when the last British ship was delivered in 1942.

By then, Kaiser's people were reaping accolades for speedy work. Although Kaiser took pride in workmanship and awards from naval inspectors for quality, his top priority was volume. Liberty Ships traveled at only ten knots when fully loaded; they made plump targets for submarines, and many were sunk. Hence, Kaiser's draftsmen and laborers stressed function, not perfection. They produced more ships faster than any other builder. The westerners ignored many traditional procedures and approached shipbuilding with fresh perspectives. They conquered bottlenecks which hampered other producers.

A traditional challenge to shipbuilders was crowded work space. The conventional method was to lay a ship's keel, then send hundreds of workers swarming into cramped quarters to perform many different functions. Workers handled heavy, dangerous tools, and some jobs were back-breaking. One of the most difficult tasks was riveting, particularly when the operator had to fight gravity. Avoiding accidents and maintaining high productivity was difficult. Kaiser's managers challenged convention from the start. As builders, they were experts at coordinating workers and materials. They decided to prefabricate large sections of a vessel, then bring them to the ship's hull only when they were to be attached to the keel or to other sections already in place. As dam builders, they had experience with heavy cranes; the only limitation was the maximum lifting capacity of their tools.[46]

Contrary to corporate myths, Kaiser and his engineers did not invent the subassembly technique. The British tried it prior to 1940, and a few eastern yards used it too. But it was difficult to implement in many older yards where space was at a premium, because it required ample room for spreading out subassemblies. In contrast, Kaiser's engineers built new shipways in uncluttered areas. Unburdened by obsolete yards and hidebound managers, they perfected the subassembly method.[47]

But Bedford and Edgar Kaiser could properly claim credit for other innovative shipbuilding techniques. When studying basic manufacturing skills late in 1940, Bedford visited a Ford plant assembly line. He noticed that auto workers learned many jobs in hours, whereas apprentices in eastern shipyards needed weeks to master several complex tasks. Riveting, the technique by which most ship parts were joined prior to World War II, required three weeks of training. Bedford and Edgar Kaiser never matched the simplicity in production achieved on the automotive assembly lines. Shipfitters in the Kaiser yards and elsewhere still required two or three months of intensive training to understand blueprints and how certain parts fit togther. However, many jobs were greatly simplified. A good example was welding. Supervisors learned that welding provided adequate strength for most part joints. It was faster and cheaper than riveting, and it required far less muscle. They also learned that women were excellent welders. Their key adjustment was positioning the subassemblies so that almost all welding was performed "downhand," assisted by gravity. This simple change made the welder's task far less physically tiring and enhanced worker productivity.[48]

A major factor contributing to the production records was intense competition between Kaiser yards. When one yard produced a vessel in record time, the new record became a target for supervisors in rival yards. By the end of the war, other yards typically yielded cargo ships in about two months, while the Kaiser yards averaged between thirty and thirty-five days. A few vessels were built much faster. When Edgar Kaiser's men turned out a cargo ship in ten days, Bedford wanted to halve that time. He carefully lined up men and materials, and they laid a keel at the stroke of midnight, November 7, 1942. Working eight-hour shifts around the clock, the men produced a ship in the incredible time of four days, fifteen hours, and twenty-six minutes.[49]

Critics charged that Bedford's feat was a cheap publicity stunt. One disgruntled Kaiser worker wrote to Westbrook Pegler a few months later:

> . . . I am prepared to testify that he took almost two months setting that ship up—that is, getting everything in readyness [*sic*], welding almost all of it into sections and segments . . . and then in these FOUR DAYS, all he did was slap it together. That ship, due to the special preparations, cost about four times as much as the ships he builds in 40 days.

Bedford admitted that he had employed unusual techniques in readying the sections for assembly. He compared the episode to a laboratory experiment, claiming that his men learned a great deal about moving far heavier parts than they had before and had gained other technical insights.[50]

Henry Kaiser was remote from day-to-day operations, but he consistently defended his managers. A few days after Bedford's feat, he testified before a Senate subcommittee: "There are many people in the country who believe that the ten-day ship . . . and the four-day-and-fifteen-hour ship are publicity stunts. If that is all they were we shouldn't do it. I think if they are truly valued they could be called incentive stunts." Kaiser claimed that after Edgar's men built the ten-day vessel, workers provided 250 suggestions for producing ships even faster. Kaiser stressed that he shared his yards' innovations with other shipbuilders. When Bedford surpassed Edgar's record, there were observers from "all the other yards to see what we have discovered."[51]

Government officials, and Navy officers in particular, strongly influenced shipyard production. A noted naval historian has observed that bureaucratic red tape frequently delayed output. Various procurement agencies claimed that their needs should be met first; squabbles over priorities consumed weeks and created confusion. Conflicts over allocations of skilled workers also wasted precious time. High-ranking naval personnel often demanded design changes, without informing procurement agencies. Such conflicts, inevitable during peacetime, were even more critical in the national emergency.[52]

Business leaders, including Kaiser, contributed to the confusion. By 1942 or 1943, Kaiser was an old hand at dealing with government officials. He was convinced that he should take any shortcuts necessary to produce ships fast. He firmly believed that he and his managers would be exonerated in follow-up investigations. But on one issue, Kaiser experienced continued frustration. From the start of shipbuilding, he almost never had enough steel plate and other important supplies. To keep vessels rolling down the ramps, Kaiser mastered evasion of bureaucratic regulations.[53] In the early fall of 1942, Office of Price Administration (OPA) officials charged him with paying black market prices for steel from a willing supplier in Cleveland. In the ensuing ruckus, columnist Raymond Clapper rose to Kaiser's defense: "If you have to be a scofflaw to get steel out of the arsenal of bureaucracy, then that's okay with me. If that's the way Old Man Kaiser has to get his steel to build ships to carry American forces to the fighting fronts, then I hope the old fellow breaks every law in the books."[54]

But federal officials generally winked at Kaiser's end runs. When local War Production Board (WPB) officials in Portland accused Kaiser of hoarding scarce materials, their superiors urged them to overlook it. Their reasons for excusing Kaiser were not wholly selfless. While agreeing that Kaiser played "fast and loose" with the rules, national-level bureaucrats sensed that nitpicking would complicate the WPB's image problem. Vice-

Admiral Land of the Maritime Commision took a similar stance. With his intimate knowledge of shipbuilders' special problems, he argued that they needed more lead time than other venders to line up critical supplies.[55]

In later years, Kaiser's public relations people claimed that his projects received more critical scrutiny from federal officials than those of other contractors. In fact, the boss spent a lot of time testifying before the Truman Committee and other "watchdog" agencies. Yet even Kaiser's representatives admitted thet the organization often received crucial assistance at the highest level. One oft-told tale concerned how the Navy fought Kaiser's proposal to convert cargo ships into miniature aircraft carriers. Top-level officers ridiculed the concept. But Kaiser, with help from prominent New Deal fixer Thomas G. ("Tommy the Cork") Corcoran, arranged a presentation to the President. Roosevelt had a well-known fascination for what others considered crackpot schemes, and Kaiser eventually received an order for fifty of the innovative vessels. The "baby flat-tops" did yeoman service in the Pacific Theater.[56]

In some cases, the government provided even quicker assistance. When the Maritime Commission authorized Kaiser to build more yards in Richmond shortly after Pearl Harbor, he learned that Richfield Oil, which owned most of the needed land, wanted an outrageous price. This incensed Kaiser, and he explained the situation to Paul D. Page, solicitor for the commission. Page was an unusual bureaucrat, who moved with Kaiser-like speed. Within four days, he flew from Washington to Oakland, drew up a new land appraisal, received a Department of Justice authorization for condemnation proceedings, and secured title from startled managers at Richfield.[57]

Kaiser's most extensive and personal contacts with government officials concerning shipyard operations were with Admiral Vickery, vice chairman, and Vice-Admiral Land, chairman, of the Maritime Commission. Vickery's needling was legendary, but he had enormous respect for Kaiser. Late in the war he stated flatly in a congressional hearing that the Portland yards were "the finest operation in the United States." More often, however, he used achievements at one yard to pressure other builders. When Bethlehem Shipbuilding laid its first keel for a 200-ship contract in April 1941, Vickery wired Kaiser: "I trust this start by Bethlehem will inspire you to at least try to deliver the first ship." His targets included Clay Bedford and Edgar Kaiser. When the latter produced several more ships one month than did Bedford, Vickery teased the Richmond chief: "With Oregon's delivery, you now understand what it means to be in first class competition. Don't you ever get out of the second divison?"[58]

But when Kaiser and his men needed help, they relied on Vickery. In mid-summer 1943 the first "baby flat-top" was launched, and it tested well.

But House Maritime Subcommittee officials inspected the Vancouver yards in response to rumors that the ships were unsatisfactory. Vickery was annoyed by such bureaucratic meddling and defended Kaiser. By the end of the war the two men had developed mutual affection. On August 8, 1945, Kaiser wired Vickery: "The only war weariness I have is the weariness of being forced by your telegram to state that our war record has permitted you to turn the needle on shipbulders all over the nation, including ourselves. You know I love the needle, no matter how much it hurts."[59]

Kaiser's working relationship with Land was usually smooth, but not quite so free-wheeling; tensions surfaced occasionally. In his memoirs, Land's appraisal of Kaiser was not wholly complimentary. He recalled returning an expensive watch that Kaiser allegedly gave his wife at a ship launching. According to Land, the incident was a "somewhat painful ordeal . . ." He also claimed that "thanks to good press relations, [Kaiser] received credit that was not due him." Yet Land concluded that he would be "the last one to sell Henry Kaiser short. He built more Liberties than any other constructor, and if his public relations department worked overtime, so did the Boss."[60]

With billions of dollars in defense contracts let during World War II, Congress monitored performances by suppliers. The key watchdog was the Truman Committee. This group investigated thousands of contracts, but it also had to consider many crackpot ideas passed along by congressmen humoring constituents. Some proposals made entertaining reading, at least after the war was over. One suggested that each American soldier be outfitted with a single-seat helicopter, loaded with a few cubic yards of fertilizer, which would be flown over Tokyo. Japan would literally be buried. Another urged development of huge metal spheres, armed with giant spikes, which would roll along "chewing up armies and cities like a meat grinder."[61]

All contractors doing much government business were investigated; that was one of the rules of the game. On a few occasions, the Truman Committee grilled Kaiser. On January 16, 1943, S.S. *Schenectady,* an oil tanker built at Portland, broke in two shortly after launching. Unfriendly reporters wrote accounts of hasty, slipshod work in the Kaiser yards. Despite thorough investigation, experts disagreed over whether the fault lay in the welding, the plates supplied by Carnegie-Illinois Steel, or the fact that the ship was launched in unusually cold water. On yet another occasion, Edgar Kaiser was questioned closely by committee members when studies revealed that his vessels had a ratio of structural defects slightly higher than averages in other yards.[62]

On such occasions, Kaiser and his son convinced most witnesses. Following several investigations, the Truman Committee assessed Henry

Kaiser's performance in highly complimentary terms. He fascinated committee members; convinced of his honesty, their questioning was usually polite, even admiring. One reason Kaiser generally received cordial treatment was that he was a national hero, lionized by most reporters. Members who hectored him without clear cause endured reprisals from newspapers friendly to Kaiser. And Kaiser masterfully posed as supplicant, modestly doing his best for the nation.

An American tradition is that after wars, defense industry profits receive close scrutiny. Such exercises have occurred repeatedly, from the American Revolution forward. In the 1946 elections, Republicans regained control of both houses of Congress; with bitter memories of sixteen years of political exile, conservatives attacked hated symbols of the New Deal. His services were no longer indispensable, and Henry Kaiser provided an irresistible target. Enemies nicknamed the rotund westerner the "New Deal's Darling." Critics dismissed his entrepreneurial credentials, pointing out that from the Hoover Dam contract forward, the federal government had bankrolled his major ventures. The need for national unity during the war had exempted Kaiser from direct attack, but now there was no need to pull punches. Even more galling to some of Kaiser's critics, he had the nerve to invade such pastures of privilege as automobiles, steel, and aluminum. Reactionaries thirsted for revenge, and their friends in Congress sharpened their knives.

The controversy over wartime profiteering reached a crescendo late in 1946. To conclude that the issue of Kaiser's profits produced sharp disagreements would be a classic understatement. Ralph E. Casey, chief counsel for the General Accounting Office (GAO), charged that Kaiser had invested only $2.5 million of his own, yet reaped the unconscionable sum of $129 million. Casey stated, "I dare say that at no time in the history of American business, whether in wartime or in peacetime, have so many men made so much money with so little risk—and all at the expense of the taxpayer."[63] Although journalists such as the *Chicago Tribune's* Colonel Robert McCormick leaped to join the attack, others defended Kaiser. A *New York Herald-Tribune* editorial argued that "For sheer irresponsibility and unfairness it would be difficult to match some of the statements made . . . by Casey."[64]

In response to the uproar, Kaiser's public relations department claimed that the yards had actually *lost* $18.6 million. Kaiser publicists practiced creative accounting in deducting interest paid on a $110 million loan from the Reconstruction Finance Corporation (RFC) to build steel facilities at Fontana. They also argued that with highly efficient operations, Kaiser had saved the government $203 million on $4 billion in work.[65]

The truth was not determined in congressional hearings in 1946, and forty years later it remains equally murky. Historian Frederick C. Lane's painstaking study of wartime shipbuilding shed no light on Kaiser's profits. As Lane observed, "The corporate connections between Kaiser's shipbuilding and his production of steel and magnesium made it difficult to determine his final profits."[66] If anything, Lane understated the situation. Kaiser's financial dealings were extremely complex, as he and his partners all operated numerous companies and subsidiaries, and they invested in each other's companies, and often in their partners' subsidiaries. No hint of personal dishonesty emerged from the hearings, even if Kaiser's holdings seem to rival those of utilities wizard Samuel Insull in complexity.

With victory in the Pacific assured, the military need for Kaiser's ships vanished overnight. Therefore, Kaiser entertained a variety of outside proposals to maintain his interest in water transportation, and he developed some initiatives of his own. Kaiser explored possibilities of entering passenger lines, and he negotiated with Nationalist China about a joint shipbuilding venture. These discussions yielded no fruit. Civic leaders in Portland/Vancouver and Richmond pressured him to maintain at least small ship repair facilities. For a few months after V-J Day he acceded to their requests, before government agencies closed down the yards.

After the shipyards suspended operations, Kaiser's interest in large ocean-going vessels faded. In later years, he again dreamed of conquering the seas, but with jets carrying passengers from the Mainland to Hawaii. Although Kaiser's unglamorous cargo ships vanished from the public eye, they served for many years after the war. They carried food and clothing to war-ravaged Europe and the Far East. During the Suez Canal crisis in 1956, the world faced a shortage of shipping, and the belching veterans were pressed into service again. In the 1960s most produce traveled on ships carrying many times more weight than did Kaiser's clunkers. But European investors rescued a few of them. Because they had long ago been written off as investments and required minimal upkeep, they carried small loads cheaper than thirty-thousand-ton-freighters.[67] A few remain as historic relics.

Shipbuilding had a large impact on Kaiser's career, not entirely beneficial. Although he had been a beneficiary of large government contracts on earlier jobs, most notably dam building, Kaiser's World War II work enhanced the image of an entrepreneur who thrived only with federal support. Big loans from the RFC to build a steel mill reinforced that view. But shipbuilding launched Kaiser into many other fields and strengthened his determination to compete against the self-proclaimed champions of free enterprise. Shipbuilding also turned Kaiser into a public personage; anonymity was a thing of the past.

6
Man of Steel

In later years, Kaiser often claimed that difficulties in obtaining steel plate for ships late in 1940 and throughout 1941 drove him into the steel industry. Certainly Kaiser used persistent steel shortages as a lever to persuade government officials to authorize his plant. However, three months before he signed contracts with the British to construct ships, Kaiser envisioned his own fully integrated steel empire in the West.

In early discussions with steel executives and federal officials, Kaiser camouflaged his ultimate objective. He stated publicly that if steel producers met burgeoning needs for steel plate, he would abandon interest in the field. But deliveries were slow, and Kaiser obtained few solid commitments for future steel plate orders. This clearly hampered long-range planning in the yards. There were two basic reasons for the bottleneck. First, very little steel was produced in the Far West; supplies were shipped in from the East. Second, Big Steel leaders resisted expansion through the first half of 1941. Kaiser believed that such reasoning was timid, narrow, and unconscionably selfish; and this stimulated his interest in alternatives.[1]

Kaiser sensed a ripe opportunity to establish an industrial base in the West. A consistent pattern of natural-resource exploitation had evolved: minerals were discovered, only to be processed and consumed elsewhere. Steel basically fit that pattern. Although the West possessed significant iron ore deposits, most steel used in regional manufacturing was shipped in; eastern producers controlled supplies and distribution. There had been periodic attempts to develop integrated steel operations in the Far West before 1940. Edward H. Harriman purchased land with rich iron ore deposits in California's Mojave Desert in 1908; but his death in 1909 ended hopes for large-scale regional production. By World War I, there were several rolling mills in the San Francisco Bay area. But in 1940, the Far West had only a smattering of mills, most of which reduced scrap steel to usable forms. Until World War II, demand for finished steel in the West was so limited that eastern steel producers easily met it. In their view, it made no sense to develop new production facilities in the region.[2]

In late 1940, Kaiser required steel plate rolled to an unusual thickness. The product was relatively crude, not difficult to turn out. But Big Steel had to convert rolling mills on a significant scale to meet Kaiser's needs. In the eyes of eastern steel producers, Kaiser belonged at the end of the line. They first met orders of eastern shipbuilders, many of whom were old customers and friends. Eastern shipbuilders were also closer to supplies. By the spring of 1941 the U.S. Maritime Commission was handing out big orders as fast as it could find shipbuilders capable of filling them.[3] To Kaiser, eager to expand operations, the steel supply problem loomed increasingly critical.

Kaiser was not alone in his assessment of the situation. Other sophisticated observers shared his perception of Big Steel's listless response to frighteningly obvious national needs. Treasury Secretary Henry Morgenthau, Jr., bluntly expressed his views to the President in mid-December 1940: "No expert knowledge is necessary to see that the steel industry will be unable to handle the volume of orders that lies ahead. . . . an immediate major expansion program for the steel industry is clearly called for." But leaders in Big Steel insisted that they had the situation well in hand. Many other industralists were equally reluctant to expand plant capacity.[4]

When confronted with complex problems, President Roosevelt often created new bureaucracies. True to form, he founded the Office of Production Management (OPM) in 1940. One of its first tasks was to estimate future steel needs. But bureau officials stacked the deck; the primary author of its report was Gano Dunn, on loan to OPM from U.S. Steel. The "Gano Dunn Report" was first issued in February 1941. Dunn assured federal officials that Big Steel could meet any anticipated emergency with current plant capacity, and that surpluses were likely in the months ahead. Despite rapidly mounting evidence to the contrary, this view dominated government planning in the early months of 1941, as Big Steel was well represented in Washington. Between August 1939 and the end of the war, former U.S. Steel board chairman Edward R. Stettinius held several key positions in agencies forming supply policies. Thus, precious time was squandered.[5]

After the war, policy analysts lambasted Big Steel's lack of foresight, even charging criminal negligence. But criticism was hardly muted even in 1941. Richard V. Gilbert, director of the Defense Economics Section of the Office of Price Administration and Civilian Supply (OPACS), stated in April 1941 that the Dunn Report "could be demolished from a technical viewpoint." Gilbert concluded that the report was "nothing short of irresponsible. . . . Playing it safe from the viewpoint of industry has always meant restricting capacity. . . . It is high time our requirements and capabilities were estimated by people who play it safe for the country." Writer I. F. Stone, whose book appeared before Pearl Harbor, included steel producers when inveighing against the "grip of monopoly." According to Stone, big capital engaged in a "sit-down strike" until guaranteed huge tax breaks from the federal government. By Stone's account, Roosevelt initially believed that reports of steel shortages early in 1941 were "deliberate lies." A second Dunn report, issued in May 1941, admitted that shortages existed, but still resisted expansion. This time, however, OPM officials ignored Dunn's advice, and he soon resigned.[6]

By April 1941, Kaiser had pleaded fruitlessly with Big Steel and government officials for months. He finally determined that if Big Steel would not fill his orders, he would do it himself. He wangled an audience with the President and showed him preliminary plans for a $150 million steel complex, designed primarily to produce steel plate. He argued that with recently completed dams providing cheap energy, and with sufficient mineral reserves in the region, he could double the West's steel output and lower production costs. According to one source, a West Coast steel industry, independent of eastern control, had been a "pet project" of the President since 1939. Roosevelt liked Kaiser's enthusiasm, a sharp contrast to the somber cautiousness of many of the conservative businessmen he called economic royalists in the 1936 election.[7]

No detailed account of their meeting survived, but one can imagine Roosevelt cheerfully urging Kaiser to pursue his plans while promising him absolutely nothing. Unbeknown to Kaiser, government engineers examining his proposals were unimpressed. Three weeks after Kaiser's conference with Roosevelt, S. R. Fuller criticized his plan, claiming that it was based on very shaky suppositions. The westerner casually tossed around cost figures for new plants ranging from $50 to $150 million; in addition, he had no financing plan. Fuller noted that Kaiser presented alternative proposals for five plants in three states; further, he did not explore their postwar use. Finally, Kaiser's sources of raw materials were widely scattered.[8]

But Kaiser kept planning and talking. Newspapers and magazines speculated about where Kaiser would build his plants. In the meantime, Kaiser pressured Big Steel for deliveries, gaining enemies in the process. Late in June he sent identical letters to presidents of several large companies, lecturing them in patronizing tones, suggesting that if they met the crisis, he would not enter the business. He informed Ben Fairless, President of U.S. Steel:

The Government in its broader vision has not yet elected to let me do this. [But it] has elected to have the steel industry expand existing facilities. Therefore, it now becomes a greater responsibility of yours. Selfishly, I am happier with decreased responsibility, but sadly I view the dire consequences of shortage of steel for shipbuilding if it continues. Therefore, I can only sit and wait, and hope that you will measure up to your responsibility.[9]

If Kaiser's letter was disingenuous and sarcastic, he was only responding in kind to the steel producers' patronizing assurances that they knew best.

The enmity between Kaiser and the eastern steel men would deepen. While he never overtly questioned their patriotism, Kaiser implied that they were, at best, overly cautious and somewhat dull-witted. In his view, he was simply trying to wake them up. For their part, eastern steel men, reeling from a decade of depression and external attacks, were deeply annoyed when an upstart westerner, who had made a fortune in lush government contracts, a man with no experience in the field, instructed them how to run America's most basic enterprise. Kaiser was one of the earliest and most vocal critics of the Dunn Report. That events proved Kaiser right while they were so spectacularly short-sighted hardly softened their attitudes toward him. Kaiser's patronizing "I told you so" letters to Fairless and to Gene Grace of Bethlehem Steel undoubtedly raised their hackles.[10]

Despite his disclaimers to the steel men in June 1941, Kaiser did not sit back and wait for supplies to meet demand. In fact, government officials finally decided to expand steel facilities in the West. But they rejected Kaiser's bid in favor of a government-owned facility at Geneva, Utah, to be operated by U.S. Steel. The decision barely slowed Kasier's drive to develop his own facilities. He based his reasoning on two points. He believed his people could deliver steel plate to the yards faster than anybody else, and he insisted that the West would benefit from expanded facilities after the war. OPM officials rejected both arguments; they weighted experience more heavily than enthusiasm. But two government analysts sympathetic to Kaiser's position stated in an early November 1941 memo to National Defense Advisory Commission (NDAC) member Leon Henderson:

> Mr. Kaiser has undoubtedly received a run-around in Washington. . . . The fundamental issue is whether the government will take a chance on an independent operator in the hope that construction will be speeded up by someone who is thoroughly convinced of the need for expansion and costs and prices will be reduced by a person who is anxious to adopt all modern processes.[11]

Melvin de Chazeau, one of the analysts, ripped the backward-looking perspectives on OPM bureaucrats: without compiling data independently, lazy staff members simply accepted Big Steel's assurances that there would be insufficient markets for expanded steel production after any future conflict. Their primary logical flaw was accepting Big Steel's demand projections from the mid-to-late 1930s, according to which steel expansion ". . . East as well as West, will be worthless after the war."[12] Despite support from de Chazeau and other prescient government officials, in early December 1941 Kaiser's chances for authorization to build a steel mill still appeared remote.

Pearl Harbor seemingly changed the situation overnight. With war declared, there was no time to be lost; but government bureaucrats still resisted Kaiser's initiative. In an angry letter to W. A. Hauck, an OPM engineer who persistently opposed him, Kaiser unleashed his frustration:

> . . . I made every possible effort to meet you to discuss our steel needs but was not accorded the courtesy of having you wait a few minutes for me at our Richmond shipyard, although I am told you devoted considerable time to this with officials from the steel companies. So far we have seen no result from these efforts and steel deliveries for shipbuilding are pitiful, at this hour of our greatest need. . . . I feel you are still in a position to help, to rectify past mistakes, and to relieve this desperate situation. . . . What will you do?[13]

Military projections based on catastrophic scenarios ultimately affected approval for a western mill. Some strategists feared destruction of the Panama Canal, which could seriously impair deliveries of eastern steel to western shipyards and other defense plants. Although most public officials assessed realistically the limitations of Hitler's strategic goals, a few imagined the impact of an Axis invasion of the East Coast upon the nation's industrial heartland. Cataclysmic visions did not seem far-fetched in the frightening early weeks of 1942.[14]

Even when the government finally authorized Kaiser's steel plant, it attached some unappealing conditions. Although government officials financed the U.S. Steel–operated mill at Geneva, Utah, Kaiser had to borrow the necessary funding—with interest—from the Reconstruction Finance Corporation (RFC). In addition, he was not permitted to select his own site. Kaiser hoped to build the facility on the coast, near Los Angeles. But military officials, fearing bombardment by the Japanese, wanted the facility at Fontana, California, fifty miles east of Los Angeles. Less accessible to attack, it was also less convenient to suppliers; the inland location cost Kaiser dollars and delays.[15]

High drama, punctuated by comic scenes, marked the end of Kaiser's tortuous quest for government approval. In mid-February 1942, officials at the War Production Board (WPB) approved the deal, provided Kaiser could locate a turbo-blower for the blast furnace. Kaiser had no idea what a turbo-blower was but nonchalantly assured them he could. At the first opportunity, he asked Chad Calhoun to enlighten him. Equally uninformed, Calhoun called the California outfit supplying engines for ships at the Richmond yards. Joshua Hendy engineers soon reported that they could build a "turbine-blower" in three or four months. Kaiser and Calhoun casually added this information to a preliminary written agreement. Fortunately, WPB officials failed to study the agreement carefully, or were equally ignorant of steel mill operations. They accepted Kaiser's assurances; later he got his blowers straight. With that hurdle cleared, final WPB approval was in order. One witness recalled how Kaiser personally followed final authorization forms from room to room, while they collected signatures from countless bureaucrats. With the precious papers in hand, Kaiser dashed over to Director Jesse Jones' offices at the RFC. Jones, a tough, no-nonsense Texan, knew that Kaiser was ignorant of steelmaking and briefly held up progress. Before releasing government loans, he demanded assurances that established producers would provide critical technical assistance. Despite their differences with Big Steel, Kaiser and Calhoun had worked hard lining up support from others in the field. The westerners' perseverance finally paid off. In a national emergency, even hard-boiled steel men offered help; within twenty-four hours Kaiser had commitments from two men at Republic Steel who would later become fierce antagonists, Tom Girdler and Charles White. Jones finally approved the RFC loans for the mill at Fontana in late February 1942.[16]

With typical exuberance, Kaiser did not wait for final approval to get started. Fourteen months earlier he had commandeered the services of Clay Bedford in setting up the Richmond shipyards. In mid-February 1942, he called chief engineer George Havas and rumbled, "George, you're going to build me a steel mill." Havas, as familiar as Bedford with his boss's style, asked, "What kind of a steel mill?" Kaiser replied, "Oh, just a steel mill, a small one." Yet from the beginning, Kaiser had no intention of being limited to a "small" mill. The initial RFC loan was a modest $22 million, but Kaiser was back in Jones' office within weeks, seeking another $100 million for plant expansion. Even with promises of technical assistance, many thought Kaiser would fail. Hauck strongly opposed Kaiser's follow-up request, arguing that U.S. Steel could produce more quickly and economically at the Geneva plant: "[Kaiser] . . . has not this organization and would have to create one from grass roots, which is not easy." Despite continued opposition from Hauck and others in the WPB, once Kaiser's foot was in the door at RFC, it was difficult to dislodge. Eventually, Kaiser borrowed over $100 million for his brainchild emerging next to vineyards and orange groves in southern California.[17]

Havas and his engineers wasted no time building the mill. Few had any experience with steel, but that only increased their sense of adventure. Engineer Lou Oppenheim recalled his experience at the plant: "We rushed drawings from Oakland to Fontana, but parts of the plant were built before there were any designs." It was the shipyard experience all over again. Critics who had scoffed when Kaiser promised steel in 1942 held their tongues when he presided proudly over the "blowing in" of the first blast furnace, named "Bess No. 1" for his wife, on December 30, 1942.[18]

It was a momentous occasion. During 1942, Henry Kaiser had risen from a virtual unknown to a renowned public figure. At the dedication, he outlined present and future objectives. He repeated his pledge to government officials: his first priority was steel plate for ships. After thanking Big Steel for technical assistance, he delivered his real message: the Fontana plant augured a new era in western development. With a real industrial base, the region might break its generations-old dependence upon eastern manufacturing. Kaiser outlined the long-term future, concluding:

> The new world of the postwar period will have to be supported by a volume and variety and a quantity of production heretofore unknown. That challenging prospect will be met in many regions of the earth, but nowhere will its fulfillment be more convincing than here on the Pacific coast where the outlines of the future are traced in bold relief for all who have the courage to read.[19]

For decades, Kaiser had helped develop the region's infrastructure and provide inexpensive water and power, all prerequisites of industrialization. Finally, he was poised to share the fruits of these earlier endeavors.

Kaiser's gesture toward Big Steel and other suppliers probably masked his true feelings. Just days before his speech, Utah Fuel, a potential supplier of coking coal for Fontana, refused to guarantee deliveries. Kaiser was concerned about alternative sources. Since the Utah coal fields, the nearest sizable source, were six hundred miles away, he had reason for worry. Any warm feelings he held for eastern steel men were fleeting. In a baccalaureate address at Washington State College in May 1943, Kaiser lambasted reactionary business leaders: "Unhappily the remnants of monopoly and vested interests are still with us. They are always selfish, short-sighted, anti-social. They are willing to pay any price to perpetuate their privilege and to prolong that which they think is to their advantage."[20]

Kaiser was a maverick in many ways; he challenged tradition in almost every business he entered. In the 1940s, nearly everything he did generated controversy. Kaiser proved repeatedly that he was a formidable rival, but his penchant for publicity and his ability to attract government support incensed some competitiors. In some industries he entered, the rivalry was relatively good-natured. For example, after the war, Big Three auto producers joked about the westerner and his "orange juice and sunshine boys" from California; privately many auto men respected, even liked him. Kaiser traded friendly insults with Henry Ford II, Charlie Wilson, and other auto men. In aluminum, officers at Alcoa knew that the Department of Justice intended to break up their virtual monopoly after the war. If they did not welcome Kaiser with enthusiasm, they cooperated when they had to.[21]

But Kaiser's relations with Big Steel ranged from mutual distrust to open hostility. These feelings were briefly submerged in the national crisis of 1942. Old-time steel men provided short-term technical assistance and were startled at how quickly their pupils learned the business; Fontana yielded steel plate three months ahead of Geneva. But cooperation soon ended. Big Steel executives assumed that Kaiser would quietly fold his tent after the war. Conventional wisdom, and their studies, showed that the West only needed one mill. To them, Kaiser was a flash-in-the-pan. Even if he succeeded at Fontana, Geneva was far more advantageously situated with respect to raw materials. During the war, Kaiser occasionally discounted his postwar ambitions. On occasion he implied that his loans were so burdensome that he would have to default and forfeit a chance to own the steel operation. In a June 1943 meeting with two business reporters, he claimed, "If Fontana ever becomes worth anything I can't own it, because it would set my family back so far they could never get started." [22]

Kaiser was ambitious and optimistic; this smoke screen was particularly disingenuous. Available evidence reveals that Kaiser planned to retain postwar control of Fontana, and that he intended all along to expand operations. Virtually alone among steel men, he sensed the enormous postwar potential for economic growth, particularly in the West. Some influential, tough-minded power brokers thought he was crazy. In a face-to-face meeting in November 1943, RFC head Jesse Jones told Kaiser that he was "spreading himself out too much and was riding for a fall." Ironically, in the same meeting, Jones fanned Kaiser's ambition for a postwar steel empire when he suggested that the RFC would write off half the loan on Fontana. Kaiser might save $55 million, plus interest. [23]

This assumption became central to Kaiser's planning for postwar operations. The government built $9.2 billion worth of defense plants; most business leaders and policy analysts held that the majority of these facilities would become white elephants after the war and assumed that they would be sold to private interests at low prices. Such expectations encouraged Kaiser to plan in expansive terms. [24]

In February 1944 several western states held a conference on postwar regional economic development at Carson City, Nevada. Kaiser sent Chad Calhoun as his personal representative. Calhoun heard several Utah speakers argue that if only one western steel mill remained open, Geneva was the clear choice. Kaiser interpreted this as a thinly veiled power grab by Ben Fairless of U.S. Steel. In a lengthy telegram to conference delegates, Kaiser portrayed Fairless as an outsider, trying to divide westerners. In the wire, read by Calhoun, Kaiser implied interest in taking over Geneva and expanding operations at Fontana: "I am a western operator, and Geneva could be a western industry. Anybody who knows anything at all about Henry J. Kaiser knows that I am for the development of the West by any industrialist who is passionately and primarily devoted to its best interests." Kaiser reminded delegates that Big Steel had bypassed earlier chances to develop western steel facilities, and that U.S. Steel was only a tenant. He deftly raised the specter of easterners pulling out after the war and "leav-[ing] Provo a ghost town."[25]

In the waning months of the war and during reconversion, Kaiser and Big Steel threatened raids on each other's turf. The easterners grabbed headlines in February 1945 by stating interest in buying Kaiser's mill. Kaiser, angered, retorted that "Fontana is not and will not be for sale." Most dismissed his rejoinder that he might go after Geneva. In fact, he and his advisors set up preliminary negotiations with surplus board officials in December 1944 to consider combining Fontana and Geneva. In July 1945 Kaiser officials submitted a preliminary offer to the Defense Plant Corporation (DPC) to lease and operate the Geneva plant for five years, with terms renewable every five years thereafter. Kaiser and his managers explored other strategies for enhancing their presence in western steel. They discussed an independent western steel combine, including Colorado Fuel and Iron (CF&I) and Wickwire-Spencer Steel. Perhaps fearing domination by Kaiser, officials from other companies suspended the negotiations.[26]

Before pursuing such grandiose dreams, Kaiser wanted to renegotiate the RFC loan. This became a top priority in steel from the summer of 1944 until 1950, when he finally paid the loan in full, plus interest. At first, Kaiser and his advisors were optimistic about chances for concessions from the RFC. Kaiser's publicists realized that they first needed to do some fence-mending. Cautious public servants were confounded by announcements of Kaiser's interest in entering many new enterprises. In a July 1944 memo to his boss, Calhoun analyzed the company's image in the eyes of RFC officials. He observed that, according to the bureaucrats, "We have been operating on the hit or miss system. We operate on the 'brain throb' method and hastily decide on changes without thorough study or analysis." Kaiser and his men received high marks for prompt, decisive action; but their managerial style unnerved bureaucrats. Far more worrisome, in Calhoun's view, was talk around Washington about "favoritism" for Kaiser in RFC lending. Despite such obstacles, Calhoun was "confident that the solution and correction of this is relatively simple."[27]

To Kaiser and Calhoun, the case for reduction of the RFC debt was overwhelming. In a lengthy analysis of Kaiser Steel's position, Calhoun reminded federal officials that as early as 1940 Kaiser had expressed a desire to set up a "wholly integrated plant to serve the wide range of Western steel requirements," but that RFC loan terms limited production to steel plate. While that commodity was required for ships, it served little use in peacetime. Calhoun documented steps taken by the company to assess postwar uses for the plant. Extensive market surveys, beginning in 1940, projected rising consumption patterns in the region. Since plant authorization in 1942, the company had "taken steps to induce steel consuming industries to move to Southern California." Calhoun argued that government involvement in steel was a hindrance and that the WPB red tape would complicate Kaiser's efforts to retool for peacetime production. The RFC had refused loans for plant modernization and expansion. Finally, Calhoun reminded RFC officials that they had chosen the Fontana site. Surely, in the interest of fair play, federal officials would give the company a fair opportunity to compete with other steel producers.[28]

By late 1944 the political situation in Washington had changed significantly; Kaiser and his advisors sensed that renegotiating the RFC loan would be a struggle. One of their top lawyers in Washington, Hugh Fulton, observed that, however justified their claim that they had built the Fontana plant for patriotic reasons and at highly inflated costs, "the RFC might answer that Kaiser Company took that risk with its eyes open and gambled on big profits that might have been obtained if the need for steel had lasted long enough." Fulton prophetically cautioned that "equity alone is not a good enough argument."[29]

The new political reality was that despite Roosevelt's reelection in November 1944, New Deal liberalism had seemingly run its course. The president's precarious health was a well-kept secret, but there was no denying his shortened coattails. The 79th Congress elected with him had a distinctly conservative cast. Politicians were anxious to cut government costs; Republicans and conservative southern Democrats sharpened their knives, anticipating an all-out attack on bloated bureaucracies.[30] New Deal friends had praised Kaiser as a consummate patriot, and he had not shied away from favorable publicity. Kaiser and his publicists learned that glory had its price, and that powerful antagonists were eager to puncture his bubble.

In November 1943, Jesse Jones had warned Calhoun that it would be much easier for the RFC and other government agencies to work with Kaiser "if he would keep his name out of the papers and not go around making so many speeches, etc."[31] Kaiser tried to follow this advice, and he gradually developed a public relations organization to enhance his public image. Yet even had he wanted to, Kaiser could not have disappeared from public view entirely. He was seriously considered for the 1944 vice presidential nomination; the Truman Committee kept probing his wartime activities; and public curiosity about his postwar plans also kept Kaiser in the limelight.

Even before the 1944 election, Calhoun sensed a stiffening of attitudes toward Kaiser among the bureaucrats. According to Kaiser's vigilant troubleshooter, middle-level RFC staff members conceded the company's case for generous loan terms. In July 1944, Calhoun traced the trouble to the top of the hierarchy, where "the prevailing climate is definitely chilly, banker type, on spending any more money on Fontana."[32]

After the 79th Congress was seated in January 1945, RFC officers were even more wary of Kaiser's requests. The reasons were transparent. Like many New Deal and World War II agencies, the RFC was on very thin ice. Whether motivated by genuine concern over taxpayers' dollars or naked opportunism, politicians probed the RFC and other agencies for signs of weakness—or a whiff of scandal. The RFC loan to Kaiser figured to become a prime target; enemies called Kaiser the "New Deal's Darling" and far less flattering names. Kaiser had been one of the New Dealers' heroes; he now became one of the Republicans' favorite whipping boys. Whatever the merits of Kaiser's case for debt reduction, RFC officials realized that they might sign the agency's death warrant by making concessions. Such fears among RFC officials were beginning to emerge in 1945; they intensified over the next several years.[33]

Such political realities were obvious only in hindsight. As the war drew to a close, Kaiser underestimated the RFC's growing resistance. When agency officials perceived the compelling logic of his case for debt renegotiation, they would presumably come around. Almost before the ink was dry on the 1942 loan agreements, Kaiser's managers began marshaling arguments for eventual debt reduction. In the weeks after V-J Day, they believed that relief was simply a matter of time, that the only issue was the percentage to be trimmed. Some conservative business leaders conceded that Kaiser had a good case: nobody would bid anything close to the cost of construction of Fontana if it was sold. In fact, before they fully realized their own precarious position, high-level RFC officials introduced specific numbers for debt reduction in the fall of 1945. Director Sam H. Husbands considered reducing Kaiser's first mortgage debt from $103 million to $58 million, a compromise he called "liberal and extremely fair." Husbands was surprised when Kaiser officials found the terms too stiff.[34]

In early 1946, Kaiser's future in steel was unsettled. He wanted to expand, but uncertainty over the RFC debt hampered his flexibility. In addition, eastern steel producers camouflaged their western strategy effectively. The government put the Geneva plant on the auction block and set a bid deadline of May 1, 1946. Kaiser considered leasing the facilities, but government officials preferred outright sale. Between V-J Day and the following spring, Kaiser's corporate picture changed markedly. By early 1946 the westerner was rapidly entering other fields, and rival steel men discounted prospects of a Kaiser bid for Geneva.[35]

No other producer challenged the Geneva tenants. U.S. Steel submitted the only purchase offer, and government officials accepted its $47.5 million bid. Since the plant had been built at government expense for nearly $200 million, U.S. Steel acquired a modern plant for one-fourth the cost of construction. Further, since the government financed Geneva, U.S. Steel owed no accumulated interest. Publicly, Kaiser expressed satisfaction: the West needed steel output from both Geneva and Fontana.[36]

Kaiser's reasons for endorsing the sale were no mystery. With this precedent established, simple justice suggested that Kaiser receive similar consideration on Fontana. This principle dominated his negotiations with the RFC. For a time Kaiser remained patient. Calhoun, in almost daily contact with the RFC officials and politicians at the Capitol, urged his boss to maintain a low profile. In the summer of 1946 he advised Kaiser that, although the RFC still favored eventual concessions, "present sniping in Washington" suggested that no deal was likely for two or three years. To the sixty-four-year-old industrialist the delay seemed an eternity, and debt interest mounted daily. Impatient by nature and eager to keep moving in many other ventures, he nevertheless contained his frustration as long as possible. But in early 1947, Kaiser wrote two letters to President Truman alleging discriminatory treatment from RFC and rehashing his case for relief.[37]

Much had changed in the White House between 1945 and 1947, and Kaiser no longer enjoyed easy access to the executive branch. As head of the Senate committee investigating performance of defense contracts during the war, Truman respected the industrialist's ability and integrity. But Truman was also aware of Kaiser's emerging skills as a publicist and political operator, and his top advisors were wary of the westerner. In a note attached to a January 1947 letter from Kaiser to the President pleading his case, White House aide John A. Caskie observed, "Kaiser makes a case for himself. . . . What the other side of the picture is we do not know."[38]

Caskie's memo, which was directed to Dr. John A. Steelman, one of Truman's most sophisticated troubleshooters, seems disingenuous, in that U.S. Steel had successfully presented a one-sided case in buying Geneva. But Caskie reflected a growing impression among critics, both within and outside of government, that Kaiser did not always play with a straight deck. The industrialist charged discrimination on the Fontana refinancing while quietly accepting as his due government favors in other industrial endeavors. For example, in Truman's first year, Kaiser received bargain rates in leasing the Willow Run plant for automobile production; he eventually purchased the facility for a fraction of the cost of construction. Kaiser also benefited from the Justice Department's effort to encourage competition against Alcoa. In February 1946, Kaiser leased two plants near Spokane, formerly run by Alcoa, at bargain rates.[39] As Kaiser's critics saw it, Willow Run was an indirect subsidy, and his break at Spokane paralleled U.S. Steel's windfall at Geneva. They were tired of Kaiser's continual wailing about unfair treatment in one industry. It was high time, in their view, that Kaiser faced real competition in at least one business, and they turned increasingly deaf ears toward his entreaties.[40]

In retrospect, Kaiser's chances for debt reduction at Fontana probably vanished with the Republican resurgence in the congressional election in November 1946. For the first time in eighteen years, the GOP controlled both houses. Kaiser had no intention of giving up, but he sensed the need for a new strategy.

By spring 1947 it was clear to Kaiser that the postwar boom, particularly in the West, exceeded even his most optimistic dreams. His vision of rapid postwar migration to the Southwest and unparalleled demand for products supplied by new basic industries was fast becoming reality. But he had hoped that shipbuilding orders would bring sufficient profits to repay much of the RFC loan; the abrupt end of the war dashed that expectation.[41]

Kaiser clearly needed to establish more political pressure against the RFC. To Kaiser, Fontana symbolized the West's industrial potential; if the region hoped to share the fruits of solid economic growth, other western leaders should help him secure relief. Chad Calhoun proposed such cooperation at the 1944 Carson City conference, but generated little interest. In May 1947 he stressed the same idea: "The Western group must realize that and be prepared to convince the leaders of the Republican Congress that an adjustment of the Fontana financing is necessry for the best interests of the West." Conceding that congressional support for Kaiser had diminished, he added, "It is not something we can take too active a part in. Our task will be to get the Western businessmen to act; to follow through. We can only aid and advise. It must remain a 'Western' problem."[42]

Kaiser and his managers were not alone in perceiving the symbolic importance of Fontana to the West. When in August 1947 the RFC again blocked Kaiser's application for debt reduction, the *New Republic* commented, "Neither will the West forget the RFC decision was a ruling against the West in its attempts to build its own steel mills and free itself from control by the East." But Kaiser was again disappointed at lack of support from western businessmen and politicians. They also failed to rally to his cause when several western railroads lowered rates for carrying U.S. Steel's products from Utah to Pacific Coast cities but refused to grant similar reductions for Utah coal shipped to Fontana. As Kaiser saw it, western fabricators perceived immediate benefits of lower-priced steel controlled by eastern interests, but failed to understand that Fontana's disadvantage augured higher average steel prices in the long run.[43]

Hence, Kaiser management failed to convince other western decision-makers that the RFC fight was their battle too. Between 1945 and 1947 Kaiser Steel earned modest profits, but they barely covered interest on the loan. Even worse, RFC officials still resisted Kaiser's efforts to expand and diversify, thus tapping markets which would have enhanced profit potential significantly. In Kaiser's mind, it was time to play hardball. After the RFC turned down yet another debt reduction proposal in August 1948, he shocked western consumers by raising the price of steel thirty dollars per ton. In a period of severe shortages, Kaiser knew he could demand higher prices, but he also conveyed strong messages to the RFC and his customers. He claimed that RFC policy forced him to "gouge" western steel consumers:

> RFC and others in the government seem to think they will be extracting this money from me. They are making a toll collector out of me, though, by forcing me to charge high prices, collect the money and pass it on to RFC. I just don't think it is fair, and I don't relish gouging the public just to satisfy the RFC's stringent demands.[44]

Being deferential had never been easy for the senior industrialist; in 1948, he returned to his natural style, confronting critics head on in a widely circulated booklet, *Outrage in Steel*. His arguments were not new; what was different was the accusing tone of his rhetoric. On the Fontana issue, he no longer believed the government was dealing in good faith. According to Kaiser, the RFC was deliberately "crushing Fontana by favoritism to Geneva," a policy he called "an outrage against the people."[45]

Responding to Kaiser's charges, new chairman John Goodloe claimed that the RFC was justified in demanding full repayment for Fontana. Between the end of the war and January 1948, "the present day replacement value of the plant has grown to a point where it is now substantially equal to the amount of the RFC's indebtedness." This was a subtle way of pointing out that Kaiser was a beneficiary of postwar inflation, a condition federal officials generally downplayed. In addition, argued Goodloe, Kaiser distorted the government's sale of Geneva to U.S. Steel. Rather than the $40 million price that Kaiser quoted so casually, the real figure was closer to $100 million. Just as Kaiser manipulated the figure downward, so did Goodloe maneuver it upward. Goodloe also argued that since the westerner admitted it would take two years to increase output significantly, "The matter . . . [of debt reduction] can hardly be regarded as an emergency measure to alleviate the current steel situation."[46]

Neither side budged over the next two years, but Kaiser finally accepted reality; given the direction of majority political thought, continuing the fight would waste time and money. But by 1950 repayment in full did not spell doom. His predictions had proven spectacularly right; Fontana's financial picture had brightened considerably. Contrary to some eastern competitors, Kaiser consistently urged rapid expansion of output, so that prices could drop. But unmet demand kept prices up, which benefited his mill's short-term economic fortunes. So did a $53 million order obtained by Eugene Trefethen and Clay Bedford from Transcontinental Gas Pipe Line. By the summer of 1950, Fontana obtained private financing to pay off the RFC loan and expand plant capacity. The Giannini family, which controlled the Bank of America, had underwritten many of Kaiser's projects. They believed in Fontana, but told Kaiser that he would not achieve real respect in the national business community until he raised money on Wall Street. They introduced him to George Woods of the First Boston Company in New York. Woods, a sophisticated and high-powered financier, put together the deal. Kaiser Steel raised $125 million: $60 million in bonds, $40 million in stock, and the rest in cash.[47]

Feeling enormous relief, Kaiser presented a check to RFC officials for just over $91 million in early November 1950, wiping out his largest debt to the government. He returned $1.23 for every dollar borrowed; he did not mention inflation in publicity releases. After paying off the RFC, $34 million was left for working capital and much-needed expansion.[48] In the fall of 1950 Kaiser produced only 1 percent of the nation's steel, but he felt well positioned to compete effectively with Big Steel. Kaiser relished the challenge. No longer could bureaucrats hamper his moves, repeatedly permitting opportunities to slip by.

One of Kaiser's strengths was his intuitive sense of future trends; as the war ended, he was nearly alone in perceiving glorious prospects for Fontana. In March 1945, economic journalist C. H. Grattan allowed that Fontana might play a "supplemental role," but predicted that Geneva could produce "most of the needed steel for the western industry." A month earlier an *Iron Age* reporter had been even less sanguine about Fontana's prospects. He could not find "a single substantial consumer of mill products [who] seems to have present confidence that Fontana can or will produce and sell its products postwar to compete with . . . eastern mills . . ."[49]

Despite such negative assessments of Fontana, U.S. Steel executives clearly recognized the importance of opening moves in the fight to control western steel markets. Most industry analysts assumed that the easterners would either gobble up Fontana or put it out of business. Big Steel pressured the RFC to collect in full the Fontana loan. But Kaiser had learned to play their game too. When several western railroads lowered rates for Geneva steel but refused Kaiser's requests for similar relief, his associates in Washington persuaded the Interstate Commerce Commission (ICC) to overturn the rate differentials.[50]

Kaiser's basic strategy in the national arena was to portray Big Steel as conspiring to limit supplies and maintain artificially high prices in the West. In a sense, Kaiser promoted himself as an industrial populist. In 1942 he had predicted that postwar supplies of many producer goods would fail to meet demand. Events proved him right. A period of postwar economic adjustment was inevitable; Kaiser conceded that it would take some months to convert steel plants from military to civilian production. However, when two years passed and steel remained in critically short supply, he lost patience. Despite continuing evidence of strong demand, nationwide production dropped from 95.5 million short tons in 1945 to 91.2 million in 1947. Kaiser charged that Big Steel's short-sighted policies threatened the national economy.[51]

During the early 1940s, Kaiser had become very friendly with New York Mayor Fiorello H. LaGuardia. The mayor arranged for Kaiser to address the nation over the Mutual Radio network on the need for more steel. On August 9, 1947, Kaiser ripped Big Steel, particularly Gene Grace of Bethlehem, claiming that Grace and other steel moguls had colluded to keep smaller producers from expanding production. He urged listeners to pressure Congress to investigate the persistent bottleneck in steel production. His words echoed William Jennings Bryan's attack against eastern financiers a half-century earlier.[52]

Kaiser and his men were genuinely bewildered that Big Steel, with hundreds of millions of dollars at stake, appeared so blind to mounting postwar demand. In fact, by the fall of 1947 Kaiser was just one of many influential Americans trying to prod Big Steel into increasing output. Big Labor, led by Walter Reuther of the United Auto Workers (UAW-CIO, key politicians from steel-using regions, and others shared his concern. By late September, critics persuaded the Senate's Small Business subcommittee to investigate persistent shortages. To the disgust of Big Steel, Kaiser was the star witness. While representatives from the big companies insisted that 95 million tons was sufficient for projected annual demand, Kaiser grabbed headlines by insisting that 1947 output should be 120 million tons. As one columnist put it, "It will be interesting to dig this subject up again—come 1949—to see who was right. Bull Henry Kaiser or the 13 Big Bears."[53] As it turned out, Kaiser was.

Other than personal antagonism toward Kaiser by old-guard steel men, there appeared to be little reason why they targeted him for special treatment. In 1949 Kaiser Steel was still a pygmy; Fontana produced 1.13 million long tons, just over 1 percent of the nation's total output. Kaiser ranked thirteenth on the list, behind Ford Motor Company. In contrast, U.S. Steel turned out 32 million tons, Bethlehem 15 million, and Republic 8.7 million.[54] Despite Kaiser's minor share of the national market, he did produce one-third of western steel. However, by mid-century, eastern steelmakers had tacitly conceded that Kaiser was right about western market potential; they wanted to keep it for themselves.

Beginning in 1950, Kaiser was finally ready to increase his share of western steel. Free of RFC restraints and with access to private capital, operations expanded rapidly. Kaiser's location in southern California revealed his foresight. Conventional wisdom held that mills should be located adjacent to mineral resources; while important, access to markets was a secondary consideration. Industry analysts had assumed the Geneva mill would be the linchpin of the western steel industry. The Utah facility was much closer to iron and coal deposits. From a production standpoint, Geneva had significant logistical advantages over Fontana. In 1945 raw material costs for pig iron averaged $15.83 per ton at Fontana, only $10.76 at Geneva. Yet Kaiser correctly anticipated the increasing importance of accessibility to markets. By the mid-1950s Kaiser Steel sold 65 percent of its output within sixty miles of Fontana; in contrast, Geneva shipped more than three-fourths of its steel to the West Coast. That was why U.S. Steel pressed railroads so hard for lower rates. In the early 1950s Geneva paid almost $15.00 per ton for shipment to both Los Angeles and San Francisco; Kaiser's rates were $1.82 and $7.00 respectively. Fontana eclipsed Geneva in both ingot capacity and blooming and sheet rolling output. From less than 60 percent of Geneva's ingot capacity in 1945, Fontana caught up in 1954, and in 1960 turned out 2.93 million tons to Geneva's 2.3 million. In blooming and sheet rolling, Fontana had three-fourths of Geneva's capacity in 1945; twenty years later it doubled the Utah mill's output. When Kaiser died in 1967, his company was the pacesetter in western steel.[55]

Big Steel producers could no longer pretend Kaiser was a minor irritant; by the early 1950s they confronted a maturing competitor. Where Kaiser was vulnerable, Big Steel had always been quick to challenge him. Kaiser remained convinced that Big Steel would try again to pressure western railroads into discriminating against Fontana on shipping rates for iron ore and coal from Utah. Early in 1950, with Fontana pushing out steel at 110 percent of rated capacity, Kaiser sensed an opportunity to protect his weak flank. Federal courts had ordered that his chief supplier, Utah Fuel Company, be auctioned off to satisfy bondholder claims against its parent company, the Denver and Rio Grande Railroad. Kaiser wanted Utah Fuel. According to *Newsweek*, which usually treated Kaiser roughly, U.S. Steel helped jack up the price. The company offered loans to Utah Fuel executives, who were trying to retain control. But Kaiser was even more determined. The opening bid was $2.75 million; he finally paid $6.8 million. The westerner got his coal, but the easterners made him pay top dollar.[56]

Steel supplies matched demand in 1949; but the Korean War created new shortages, and sniping between Kaiser and Big Steel continued. Kaiser, a comparative lightweight, could not slug it out with the powerful eastern firms. Nevertheless, he delighted in keeping them off balance. He bought a small blast furnace in Cleveland to supply steel for cars, then planted a rumor that it would be the core of a new eastern steel combine. He passed the tip to Washington columnist Drew Pearson, who publicized the story. Kaiser simply wanted to shake up Big Steel. By 1951, Kaiser-Frazer was producing many fewer cars than in earlier years of high demand. Kaiser no longer needed the Cleveland plant, which he sold to Bethlehem Steel.[57]

The sale of the Cleveland plant suggested that by the early 1950s the cold war between Kaiser and Big Steel showed slight signs of thawing. Kaiser's payoff of the RFC loan in 1950 forced rivals to accord him at least grudging respect. Even the most cynical steel man admired the tough competition Kaiser provided in the West.

But mutual suspicions could be rekindled in an instant, and nothing irritated Big Steel men more than Kaiser's labor policies. Steel moguls claimed that Kaiser demonstrated socialistic tendencies which had no place in private enterprise. With the exception of the widely publicized work stoppages by John L. Lewis' United Mine Workers (UMW) during World War II, labor-management relations had taken a back seat to the exigencies of winning the war. Despite the earnest efforts of the Office of Price Administration (OPA), prices crept up inexorably during the war; but wages failed to keep pace. By V-J Day, consumer goods were in short supply, prices were high, and black market selling was rampant. Labor was understandably restive. Union leaders read about record-breaking wartime profits in basic industries and realized that they had shared little of the new wealth. They scornfully rejected government reports that underestimated inflation; by ignoring black market prices, such documents failed to gauge the real cost of the goods their members went without. Industrialists claimed that they faced enormous reconversion costs, and that abrupt wage hikes would force more layoffs and bring back the Depression. In the months following V-J Day, labor-management relations deteriorated rapidly.[58]

Nowhere were labor relations more tense than in steel. Among the nation's basic industries, Big Steel had been one of the last holdouts against organized labor. Until the mid-1930s and the Steel Workers Organizing Committee's (SWOC) attacks against the industry's open shop practices, unions made little headway. In the infamous 1937 Memorial Day Massacre at Republic Steel in South Chicago, police had killed several workers and wounded many in a conflict reminiscent of labor violence half a century earlier. But by 1945 the United Steel Workers of America (USWA) were well organized and militant and were led by one of the nation's ablest union leaders, Philip Murray, Jr.

Late in 1945 the Steel Workers made their initial moves. Their contract was due to expire, and they threatened a strike if Big Steel did not grant a substantial increase. President Truman persuaded Murray to extend their deadline to January 21, 1946, and created a fact-finding board to determine an equitable wage adjustment. The board recommended a basic hourly increase of $.185. Murray accepted it, but Big Steel would not budge from a "final" offer of $.15. Industry leaders would grant the full amount, but only if the government abolished price controls. Truman would have none of it and considered seizing the companies.[59]

That was where matters stood on January 17, 1946, four days before expiration of the deadline. Truman invited Murray and Fairless to the White House, but the meeting stalled, and the steel man left in a huff. The next day, Kaiser, who "happened" to be in Washington, showed up at the White House and announced that he would accept the $.185 increase. He realized full well the impact his concession would have. Kaiser unctiously stated: "I have informed the President . . . that I have sufficient faith in this great nation to humbly take the lead in peace—as I did in war—in helping our people and our world establish the sincere and honest relationship which these critical times require." He chided his competitors: ". . . three-and-a-half cents is two percent of steel wages. Who can estimate costs down to two percent? Can anyone hesitate to save his country for three-and-a-half cents?" Murray chimed in, calling Kaiser's concession "a great contribution to the nation."[60]

Once again, Kaiser won a media contest with his rivals in steel. The reactions of men such as Bethlehem's Grace and Republic's Tom Girdler have not survived, but their thoughts toward Kaiser must have been unprintable. In their view, Kaiser had simultaneously committed two unpardonable sins. That he had broken the ranks of "solid steel" was hardly surprising, since he had always been an outsider; but his break weakened their bargaining position.[61] Far worse, he had openly consorted with the enemy and had the gall to condemn their penuriousness from the most visible forum imaginable. To Big Steel, this was unconscionable grandstanding.

Kaiser's dealings with the USWA set a pattern which prevailed for the rest of his life. He repeatedly settled with the union ahead of his competitors. In 1952, a nearly identical situation arose. By then, Kaiser Steel was emerging as the dominant company in the Far West. If Big Steel hoped to present a united front against union demands, Kaiser had to be included in their strategy sessions. Kaiser had learned hard lessons about controlling costs; he could not pay appreciably higher wages than competitors. So he joined his erstwhile enemies; warily, the antagonists touched hands. For more than two months, Kaiser and his advisors sought solutions with other steel producers. Ironically, the union demanded the same wage increase settled on six years earlier: $.185 per hour. Repeated strike deadlines came and passed. But early in April, the USWA was prepared to walk out; Kaiser again announced that his company would settle. This time his break from Big Steel was not so dramatic. Several small producers settled ahead of him, and he minimized differences with holdout companies. His statement was low-key, almost lost amid the excitement caused by Truman's announcement that he would not seek reelection that fall. Still, a few steel men sourly noted Kaiser's early departure from the fold.[62]

In 1959 Kaiser Steel had yet another run-in with eastern producers. By then, many of the actors had changed, but old feelings occasionally surfaced. The script followed a familiar pattern. When the USWA struck in the summer of 1959, industry leaders formed an alliance. Edgar Kaiser, who had taken over much of the day-to-day management of the company, joined the group. For more than three months, he helped plan strategy, telephoning his father on a daily basis. Neither father nor son could stand delay; Edgar negotiated privately with USWA head David J. MacDonald. In late October, Kaiser Steel dropped out of the combine and settled ahead of the others.

Big Steel's public response to Kaiser's decision was surprisingly moderate. Acknowledging that no company was bound to a group decision, other steel men observed that a generous wage settlement would be less damaging to Kaiser Steel, with its newer, more modern plants. They noted that the western firm was not saddled with as many outmoded work rules as Big Steel. But reporters picked up hostile comments behind the scene. According to *Newsweek*, some steel men viewed Edgar as a "shill" for MacDonald, and a "traitor to America." Edgar evidently reciprocated their feelings; he stated that, henceforth, the company would not join industry-wide bargaining.[63]

Henry and Edgar Kaiser had always been most comfortable marching alone, not in the ranks. The bitterness between producers and the USWA in the 1959 strike, which lasted 104 days, bothered them; they were determined to avoid similar experiences in the future. Rather than distancing themselves from union leaders until the contract neared expiration, the Kaisers sought to resolve their differences in a relaxed, unhurried atmosphere. MacDonald was agreeable, and the union and the company formed a semi-permanent group to deal with fundamental issues. A key member of the committee was Dr. George W. Taylor (Ph.D.), a labor expert from the University of Pennsylvania. Taylor represented the "public" and chaired the group.

By the end of the 1950s, experts acknowledged that labor-management relations had changed dramatically since the end of World War II. Earlier generations of workers were primarily concerned with "bread-and-butter" issues: the right to organize, hours, and wages. By the late 1950s, younger workers had not directly experienced the Depression; many were interested in participating in decisionmaking, job satisfaction, and other intangible issues. The beginnings of decline in domestic "smokestack" industries were not yet evident, even to top managers, let alone rank-and-file workers. Foreign competition was growing, but it was still a minor concern.

As the 1960s dawned, environmental hazards in the workplace were not as worrisome to most workers as seniority rules and the specter of technological unemployment. At Kaiser Steel, committee members wrestled with the division of benefits from technological and other "cost-saving" innovations. After months of discussion, they agreed that workers would receive one-third of the cost savings effected when wasteful practices were eliminated. Workers received monthly "bonuses," dependent upon rank, seniority, and minimum attendance requirements. They also agreed that any union member displaced by technology or reorganization of work was guaranteed a job; even if "demoted," a worker received the same pay. This did not include workers laid off due to declining business conditions.[64]

Edgar Kaiser carried much of the load for the company in these negotiations, with guidance from Eugene E. Trefethen, Jr., Jack L. Ashby, C. Fred Borden, and others. Yet Henry Kaiser was a constant presence, via conference calls and occasional visits. He patiently goaded committee members to keep working even when issues appeared hopelessly complicated. And he received most of the credit for the precedent-breaking agreements. In 1964 the AFL-CIO honored the octogenarian with the prestigious Murray-Green Award, a symbol of labor's regard for a leading industrialist.[65]

However cordial Kaiser's relationships with top union officials were, conflicts occasionally surfaced at Fontana. In the mid-1950s, problems emerged between old-line Kaiser supervisors and some newer union members. Tensions became so serious early in 1954 that Henry Kaiser met personally with MacDonald to seek a solution. Both pledged cooperation, but local union members remained angry with management. An unidentified worker writing to Henry Kaiser in March 1955 charged that the "old-guard Kaiser men" had spies in the plant. He continued: "There is so much jealousy and hurting each other in the plant. The impossible orders the foolish things they ask the men to do. I have never heard so many angry men." In early October 1955, David Walton, president of the local union, informed Vice President and General Manager Jack Ashby that "Human attitudes here have changed. The employees no longer have the respect for the company that they used to have. . . . Labor relations between your company and this union are today at an all time low." Upon that point, at least, local management and labor leaders could agree. A management report listed forty-seven work stoppages between January 1954 and October 1955, including three which shut down the plant for several days. The most recent had interrupted production for seventeen days.[66]

Tensions eventually eased. Some supervisors needed basic lessons in interpersonal communication, but most workers sensed the company's good intentions. Workers appreciated the health care program, and they initially reacted with enthusiasm to the bonuses awarded for cost savings in the early 1960s. No wonder; the payouts were considerable at first, averaging $810 per eligible worker in 1963.[67]

Local boosters had welcomed Kaiser Steel with open arms. By the late 1940s and early 1950s, it provided the industrial anchor of the eastern end of the San Gabriel Valley, including six to seven thousand jobs. But the mill exacerbated environmental problems. When smog became a serious hazard in the mid-1950s, rapidly expanding operations at Fontana came under rigorous scrutiny. Kaiser Steel installed the most sophisticated smokestack and furnace emission screening devices available. Such efforts were not totally effective, but company officials received high marks for cooperation from local boosters. When Los Angeles County Supervisor Warren Dorn charged early in 1959 that Kaiser Steel was a major contributor to the smog problem, Riverside County politicians and journalists leaped to the company's defense. A *Rialto Record* editorial observed that prevailing winds almost always blew from west to east, and that Riverside County suffered far more from automobile smog generated in Los Angeles.[68]

The quarter-century between the founding of Kaiser Steel in 1942 and Henry Kaiser's death in 1967 was marked by enormous changes in the operation's fortunes. From a crude, "single-function" mill in its early years, Kaiser Steel became the dominant integrated steel facility in the West. Kaiser did not live to see the gradual withering of his steel empire. Ironically, his own companies helped sow the seeds of Fontana's decay and eventual shutdown in the early 1980s. Kaiser Engineers helped develop energy and mineral resources in the Pacific basin. These new resources were vital to the overnight emergence of a potent Japanese steel empire. In the early 1960s Japanese imports made significant inroads into the increasingly lucrative West Coast steel markets.[69] By then, however, Kaiser and his organization had expanded into a dozen other enterprises and far beyond the western shores of the American continent.

7

Creating an Image

Without question, World War II made Kaiser a national, even an international celebrity. Although he was an important contractor before the war, he was known only by certain business leaders and politicians. Between 1939 and 1941, his initial endeavors in industry and rapid rise in shipbuilding expanded his visibility in these circles. But when the Japanese bombed Pearl Harbor, Kaiser was still unknown to the American public. Three years later his fame rivaled that of war heroes like MacArthur and Eisenhower. His triumphs in shipbuilding and widely publicized proposals for cargo plane production and postwar planning vaulted him into the limelight. He became such a renowned public hero that President Roosevelt seriously considered him as his running mate in 1944.

From the outset of his business career, Kaiser was a promoter. Ever aggressive in searching for new opportunities, he instinctively knew how to "package" his abilities. Even at the turn of the century in Lake Placid, the sign above his photography store encouraged passers-by to "meet the man with a smile." Over the years, Kaiser assiduously honed his skills in interpersonal communication. He was not a gifted public speaker, but few matched his dynamism in one-on-one situations. He was amazingly adept at selling himself to strangers; he specialized in convincing decisionmakers that he could, somehow, perform difficult jobs ahead of extremely short deadlines.

Although Kaiser was a prominent West Coast businessman by the end of the 1920s, his "marketing" techniques were very ordinary. As a rising businessman, he engaged in conventional public service activities. He joined a few fraternal orders, first at the local and later at the regional level. In 1916 he became a member of the Elks Lodge in Everett, Washington. He later became active in several social and service organizations in Oakland. Although he seldom exercised, in 1930 he joined the Athens Athletic Club and the Claremont Country Club. The same year, he joined the Commonwealth Club and Associated General Contractors (AGC), both in San Francisco. As noted earlier, in 1932 he served as national president of AGC.[1] He used such organizations to form useful friendships and promote business.

One reason for the slow emergence of Kaiser's natural publicity skills was that few contractors were flamboyant promoters. Most pursued contracts aggressively; beyond competitive pricing, they made personal integrity and dependable performances under contracts their primary watchwords. Neither Kaiser nor his Six Companies partners revolutionized their publicity efforts. When they received bad press in the summer of 1931 because of conditions at Hoover Dam, they simply presented the facts as they viewed them in letters to newspaper editors and in rare personal interviews. Their limited advertising was confined to professional journals with small circulation. Apparently this suited Kaiser. As a sand and gravel man and a road builder in largely rural and isolated regions, he perceived little need for advertising or publicity.

When Kaiser ventured to Washington in 1931 as Six Companies' designated "point man," he operated essentially as a lone wolf. Although his son Edgar occasionally accompanied him, he often went by himself. He soon learned his way around Washington's bureaucracies. Important men immediately noticed his enthusiasm and prodigious energy. Distracted as he was in the last year of his beleaguered presidency, Herbert Hoover acknowledged that Kaiser was a man on the move: "He would be very helpful on any committee or group which may be set up to consider expansion of government activities." By the fall of 1932 Kaiser was spending enough time in Washington to make him a regular customer at the Shoreham Hotel.[2]

After Franklin Roosevelt moved into the White House, Kaiser conducted enough business in the capital to need considerable local legal assistance. He retained the influential laywer Thomas G. Corcoran, primarily to facilitate access to New Dealers. Interior Secretary Harold L. Ickes claimed that when Kaiser sought authorization for a magnesium plant, Corcoran pulled the required strings: "Tom got the President on the telephone from my office just before the Cabinet meeting. Apparently he did a good job because the President started in to crowd Jesse Jones on the issue. Jones didn't like it too well either, but the President, in effect, ordered him to take care of Kaiser."[3] Kaiser worked informally; despite many large federal contracts, as late as 1940 he still had no public relations organization.

Kaiser attracted little attention from the national press until he won Liberty Ship contracts. The first nationally circulated stories about him claimed that he preferred to work in secrecy. In March 1941, *Time* claimed that "Although his engineering feats are among the greatest of all time, his name is unlisted in *Who's Who* and rarely seen in the news—partly because he dislikes publicity, but also because no one can make him sit still long enough for an interview." *Business Week* described Kaiser as "still a mystery man," who was "publicity shy." In the spring of 1941 the *Saturday Evening Post* assigned veteran reporter Frank J. Taylor to write the first in-depth story on Kaiser for a major periodical. According to Taylor, Kaiser still had a reputation for secrecy, "shunning publicity." Kaiser initially encouraged this perception. Early in 1942 *Life* sent reporter Gerard Piel west to research another in-depth story about Kaiser. Upon learning about the prospective story, Chad Calhoun wired another executive: "Mr. Kaiser is reluctant to have this story come out at all but has agreed with Peel [*sic*] to have you furnish him with any material with the understanding that we are to approve any material used and might even request that nothing appear at all."[4]

Calhoun's telegram suggested that by 1942 Kaiser sensed the benefits of "going public." Except for the steel situation, before 1942, he had bypassed many opportunites for political "grandstanding." But he became fully aware of his emerging potential for shaping public opinion when in 1942 he proposed building a fleet of five thousand cargo planes. Although he did not fully anticipate the enormous public response to his ideas, he carefully staged the unveiling of the proposal. He outlined his ideas at a ship launching in Portland on Sunday, July 19, a day when the maximum number of workers could hear his address. He passed out advance copies of his speech to reporters, so that they would give accurate accounts of it in Monday newspapers in the East.[5] Still, the rousing reception his cargo plane initiative received amazed him. From then on, he was a national celebrity.

Kaiser would have become a folk hero even without the cargo plane proposal. In the weeks before the Portland speech, several Hollywood movie moguls courted him. They had ideas of producing, at the very least, short film-clips documenting his meteoric rise. Harry Cohn of Columbia Pictures proposed a feature-length movie of his life, arguing that such a film would stimulate American patriotism. After the Portland speech, the motion picture industry made many offers to Kaiser, and fraternal lodges and service organizations inundated him with requests for personal appearances. Within ten days of the speech he presented his views to the President, and the nation's press and radio news networks acclaimed him. Senator Abe Murdock of Utah informed Kaiser that his name was "becoming a household word throughout the country," and that many of his constituents asked why President Roosevelt did not simply "put Henry Kaiser in charge of the war program."[6]

Much as he enjoyed the glory, Kaiser realized by the fall of 1942 that he needed a public relations organization, if only to shield himself from impossible demands on his time. Publicly, he denied personal interest in such matters. In October he told a *Christian Science Monitor* reporter: "I hired a public relations man once. He set out to try to publicize me. That wasn't what I wanted at all. I wanted to get away from being publicized, but I wanted the force and favor of publicity behind my projects."[7] This disclaimer was disingenuous; behind the scenes, several consultants were already providing direct help. Dr. Paul F. Cadman (Ph.D.), an economist with the American Bankers Association, cautioned Kaiser against excessive public speaking: "It will take more out of you than you think. Its effect can be ruined by too many appearances, and the acclaim which follows should be heavily discounted." Palmer Hoyt, the hard-driving editor of the *Portland Oregonian*, counseled Kaiser about responding to inaccurate or unfavorable printed accounts of his activities.[8]

Although Kaiser was portrayed as a "miracle man" by many reporters and radio commentators, he initially lacked confidence in his speaking ability. After he came into the national limelight, he frequently sent advance copies of his speeches to trusted associates. Before addressing a businessmen's banquet in Boston in early November 1942, he sent an advance copy to Charles Gow, president of Warren Brothers, who reassured him that his speech would go over well. Dr. Cadman was not always so kind. After Kaiser's address to the National Association of Manufacturers (NAM) in early December 1942, Cadman lectured him like a schoolboy: "The speech, and particularly the latter part of it, suffered severely from too rapid a reading. . . . Your short sentences are well handled and effective, but you did not do well with the long sentences." Kaiser eagerly sought Cadman's approval. Two weeks later, after an address in Los Angeles, he claimed that he "received a standing ovation at the end of the speech. . . . I have never addressed an audience where such superb attention was given. One could have heard a pin drop."[9]

Cadman, a few outside consultants, and several of Kaiser's top-level executives organized a small public relations staff late in 1942. Cadman offered his services as an unpaid volunteer, provided Kaiser would contribute "substantial sums . . . to certain activities in which I have a deep personal interest." He continued in an informal role with Kaiser for several months. Others made greater commitments, presumably with Kaiser's approval. In December 1942 Bill Netherby set up an advertising department; in early 1943 Kaiser's public relations staff added more outsiders. Milt Silverman, a reporter for the *San Francisco Chronicle*, wrote publicity material for the Kaiser companies.[10] Corporate offices printed several brochures and "in-house" magazines, including *Kaiser: The Permanente News* and monthly issues of *Kaiser Digest*.

Despite such documents, public relations initially evolved on an informal, ad hoc basis. In June 1943, however, Chad Calhoun strongly urged his boss to set up a full-time organization. According to Calhoun, "in the absence of our taking any definite action in this respect our many opponents, enemies, and those who act through sheer stupidity and ignorance, a terrific picture can be built up very adverse to you personally and to your best interests." Calhoun advised Kaiser to establish a group which would "have a definite plan and policy established by you and those you choose from your staff." He urged Kaiser to appoint someone else to "do the actual work" but offered his services for direction, guidance, and review. Kaiser followed Calhoun's advice. He set up a marketing committee and hired an outside advertising agency in August. He also established a Washington office consisting of a "Chief Expediter," five assistants and seventeen support personnel. Monthly office expenses amounted to just over $10,000. In November, Dr. Cadman finally accepted part-time employment with an annual retainer of $6,000.[11]

By 1943 Kaiser had become such a public figure that he needed a sizable staff simply to protect him from admirers. Even the *New York Times* enhanced Kaiser myths; a Sunday magazine issue in January 1943 characterized Kaiser as the West's Paul Bunyan, performing seemingly impossible tasks with three blue oxen. The lead ox was Imagination; hitched to it were "two stalwart beasts" called Organization and Perspiration. Ordinary citizens flooded his office with testimonials; their letters revealed how fully he had captured the nation's imagination. A South Carolina high school teacher tested her students on characters from Christopher Marlowe's *Doctor Faustus*. One student forgot that the "face that launched a thousand ships" belonged to Helen of Troy, substituting Kaiser's name instead. Another writer who had read a misinformed story dwelling upon Kaiser's personal unhappiness wondered, "Why are you so miserable when you have done so much good for others?" Hundreds of autograph-seekers simply sought his signature, to which his publicists responded that he wouldn't finish his work if he gave in to all requests. Others made pathetic appeals for contributions. Requests came from around the globe. Sister Marta Czapiewska of Vancouver, British Columbia, wrote to Kaiser in Polish, asking for "some hundred" dollars for dozens of children in an orphanage: "I am turning to you with tears for some help, because we die of hunger if not cold."[12] Records do not reveal whether Sister Czapiewska received a donation, but the staff at least had the letter translated. To respond more effectively to hundreds of other "worthwhile" organized charities' requests, Kaiser began planning a family trust in 1941.

Inevitably, many were disappointed or disgruntled. When Kaiser's office denied an autograph, one citizen took umbrage, claiming that other famous Americans such as Henry Ford had not been too busy "to grant such a small favor." Newspaper columnist Westbrook Pegler accumulated a file of letters lambasting Kaiser. "The great American hoax which Henry Kaiser has foisted on the population [was] by means of his 'Hollywood

Style' publicity agents," claimed a former worker at the Richmond yards. A writer from Stockton, California, denounced Kaiser directly: "Your publicity is making you look ridiculous by playing you up as a 'Superman' which, of course, you are not." When Kaiser's publicists solicited funds for the United Seaman's Service, one of the few charitable organizations to which Kaiser lent his name during the war, a Chicago businessman replied: "I don't need any prodding to do my job and I am trying to do it without publicity or grandstanding."[13]

Kaiser would have been in the news constantly even without a public relations department. Although feature article writers for national magazines tried to get their stories directly from Kaiser, many reporters and radio broadcasters simply padded oft-told stories with innovative hyperbole. In the spring of 1943 Frazier Hunt provided just such mush over his General Electric news broadcast; "Kaiser does things in ways and quantities and speed that have never been done before. He's a sort of a Henry Ford, and Boss Kettering and Charlie Wilson all rolled into one. He's terrific; he's colossal; he's completely unbelievable. . . . He's the master Doer of the world. . ."[14]

Kaiser fully realized that he was a highly influential personage. Eleanor Roosevelt invited him to lunch in Febraury 1943, but he was too busy to accept. Either that, or he knew about her dreadful White House cuisine. During the same month *Time* asked him, "as a prominent person," to offer his views on the future of postwar relations between the United States and the Soviet Union. A story appeared in the *Chicago Times* of an army officer who, on the strength of his military priority, unwittingly "bumped" Kaiser off a flight from San Francisco to Washington. Once the plane was airborne, the stewardess informed him that he had taken Kaiser's seat. "Kaiser?" exclaimed the officer, "I'm flying to Washington just to see him." The story was probably apocryphal; on at least one occasion even Henry Luce relied on Kaiser's "pull" with government authorities to secure pullman tickets.[15]

Kaiser and his advisors were acutely aware of his growing national reputation, and they monitored it closely. His publicists polled 381 Americans and discovered that all but 47 knew who Kaiser was. This was an astonishing level of name recognition, particularly in a pre–electronic-media age. According to their figures, 76.6 percent made only favorable comments, while only 2 percent held negative views.[16]

Presumably, such name recognition was a major reason why many groups and individuals promoted Kaiser as a presidential candidate for 1944. As early as 1942 he received scattered letters insisting that he would be a superb candidate on either party's ticket. By 1943 a trickle of letters turned into a steam, and some notable Americans endorsed him. Francis Townsend, father of the Social Security Act, stated: "Henry J. Kaiser is a remarkable man. Can't we persuade him to run for President? He would sweep the country. The Republicans would grab him in a minute if they were not all darn fools."[17]

Early in 1944 national newspapers reported that "Kaiser for President" clubs were sprouting up across the country. The Republican nomination was wide open. Although he had lost to Roosevelt in 1940, Wendell Willkie was still in the hunt, as were Ohio Senator John W. Bricker and New York Governor Thomas E. Dewey. Publicly, Kaiser disavowed all interest. He directed aide Llewellyn White to follow the activities of one Vandorf Gray of Chicago, self-anointed mastermind of the "Kaiser for President" clubs. Kaiser insisted that his monitoring of Gray's activities was simply to "nail" any unauthorized claims or statements, but his disclaimer is not entirely persuasive. Publicists sampled reaction toward him in scattered cities; they also inquired into advertising prices in many urban newspapers, including several printed in foreign languages.[18]

If running for President seemed far-fetched early in 1944, few realized how close Kaiser came to being chosen as Roosevelt's running mate. Few Democrats opposed a fourth term, although thoughtful party leaders were deeply concerned about the president's rapidly eroding health. But there was rampant speculation over who Roosevelt would choose as his running mate, since many privately feared that this individual would soon reach the Oval Office. Henry A. Wallace had replaced two-term Vice President John Nance Garner in 1940, but his liberalism generated a strong "dump Wallace" sentiment among party leaders. Roughly half a dozen serious contenders were considered: Alben Barkely, William O. Douglas, Sam Rayburn, James F. Byrnes, Harry S. Truman—and Kaiser.

According to distinguished biographer James M. Burns, "the President never—not even in 1940—pursued a more Byzantine course than in his handling of this question."[19] He kept even his most trusted confidants in the dark, while asking them for data on several potential running mates. Kaiser's role in the drama is equally mysterious; in later years conflicting versions surfaced. The President invited Henry and Bess to Hyde Park for a two-day visit in April 1944. According to one Kaiser associate, the industrialist left the meeting bewildered over its purpose.[20]

But Kaiser was indeed a serious prospect. Roosevelt ordered a full FBI report on him following the Hyde Park meeting. Ickes recalled his surprise when Roosevelt mentioned Kaiser's name at a meeting in late June. In Ickes' words, "this was a strange political fish to appear upon the platter." Roosevelt asked Ickes to make further inquires about Kaiser. Presidential advisor Samuel I. Rosenman recalled that Roosevelt like the notion of a liberal businessman on the ticket. Oscar Ewing, acting chairman of the Democratic National Committee, also remembered serious discussion of Kaiser, as did Robert G. Nixon, an *International News* correspondent with a nose for White House leaks. Some years later Jack Smith, a respected national columnist, claimed that after receiving the FBI report, "FDR decided then and there that he wanted Henry J. Kaiser for Vice President," but old-line party bosses talked him out of choosing a man who had never held public office.[21]

There is even more mystery over why Kaiser was not chosen. Rosenman claimed that Roosevelt lost interest in him only when he learned that in a 1942 speech Kaiser had endorsed a large sales tax to finance the war. Ickes offered a different account. By 1944 Kaiser and Corcoran had become antagonists, due partly to a disagreement about legal fees. At a meeting in the Oval Office just days before the convention, advisors promoted their preferred candidates. Corcoran pushed Supreme Court Justice William O. Douglas; Rosenman still promoted Kaiser. According to Ickes, Corocran claimed that columnist Eliot Janeway had circulated the rumor that Kaiser was a Jew. Corcoran professed disbelief in that claim, noting that *Who's Who* listed Kaiser as an Episcopalian. Ickes asked Rosenman "if he wanted to make antisemitism an issue." Rosenman affirmed that Kaiser was not a Jew. As Ickes recalled, "My answer was that a lot of people thought he was and many would believe it, with the effect that the thought would be the same." Ickes concluded, "Truman was brought into the conversation, but not seriously."[22]

Roosevelt used Kaiser's name as a trial balloon and tested party sentiment without risk. Last-ditch maneuverings in the final days before the convention deeply involved Edwin Pauley, a major party fund-raiser. Pauley pushed Truman, and he saw Barkley, Byrnes, Douglas, and Wallace as the chief rivals; he never mentioned Kaiser. John W. Partin, a careful student of the vice presidential nominating process, argued that Wallace and Byrnes were the front-runners, and that Douglas, John Winant, and Truman were originally in the second rank of competitors. Partin did not mention Kaiser either. If Ickes' recollection is accurate, Kaiser was a possibility until days before the convention, but then was dropped.[23]

Although not on the ticket, Kaiser was actively involved in politics in 1944. He was national chairman of the Non-Partisan Association for Franchise Education. Corporate advisors feared that he would become involved in controversial issues such as civil rights and loyalty oaths; such involvement could damage corporate concerns. But Kaiser ignored their admonitions. He appeared on radio and in newsreels, urging Americans to register and vote in the November elections. On the civil rights issue, he avoided controversy.

But he had some embarrassing moments. On one occasion, Kaiser had mimeographed copies of a speech passed out to guests at New York's University Club. After lunch was finished, he ascended to the podium and asked, "Any questions?" Someone called out, "If your outfit is non-partisan, how come this?" and held up a mimeographed paper titled "Businessmen for Roosevelt." According to a reporter, "There was silence. The guests gazed over their demitasse cups at Mr. Kaiser. Strong men at the speaker's table paled. . . . A bottle of Scotch at a WCTU convention couldn't have caused more embarrassment." Kaiser blurted out, "There must be some mistake." At that very moment, a representative from the printing company rushed into the room and explained that Kaiser was right. In the words of one reporter, the delivery boy had "run afoul of pixies," and had dropped off speeches for separate functions. Some in the audience had the right one. Kaiser was off the hook.[24]

Like others achieving instant fame, Kaiser learned that glory had drawbacks. He and his family had lived in relative obscurity before the war; they now were frequently surrounded by reporters and popping flashbulbs when they ventured outside homes and offices. Kaiser's comments were subjected to careful scrutiny, from new friends and enemies alike. Naturally gregarious and friendly, Kaiser realized that to function effectively, he had to shield himself and his family.

Celebrity status also threatened his relations with Six Companies associates. Several partners had invested in the shipyards, but Kaiser got most of the glory. This disturbed some of the westerners, Kaiser included. When Frank Taylor labeled Kaiser "Builder No. 1" in a 1941 article in the *Saturday Evening Post,* several partners complained that, in shipbuilding and other joint projects his contributions were overblown. A few weeks after Kaiser introduced the cargo plane proposal, Stephen D. Bechtel mentioned a need to "recement our mutual purposes." Bechtel continued: "I hope that very soon we can sit down together and spend sufficient time to clarify the atmosphere so that we may all have the benefit of each other's judgment and support, just as we used to have in the 'good old days.'"[25] Some partners were uneasy about Kaiser following his own course, even though they had declined his offer to participate in steel. Yet Kaiser placed great value upon business ties and personal friendships, and he and his publicists henceforth urged reporters to stress the contributions of others.

Kaiser believed at one point that certain reporters deliberately exaggerated his role in Six Companies. When *Fortune* published a feature article in 1943 emphasizing his rapid rise to prominence, he and his advisors were disturbed by inaccuracies. They requested a meeting with the editorial staff at *Fortune.* Kaiser scored their portrayal of his dealings with his partners. According to Kaiser, the article implied that he dominated his partners and insisted that they do things his way. During the meeting, Kaiser made one comment about interpersonal relations, which may have simply reflected the intense pressures under which he worked: "You can't work as hard as I am working to get production and pay any attention to personal relations."[26] Despite occasional misunderstandings, Kaiser remained personally close to his partners throughout their lives.

Kaiser company officials, including the boss, developed what occasionally resembled an "us versus them" attitude toward the press. At the meeting with the editors of *Fortune*, Kaiser sounded paranoid: "I don't expect you to write anything but what is bad." Just moments later, Henry, Jr., complained: "Your attitude is synical [*sic*] and sarcastic." Cadman, Calhoun, and other publicists read advance drafts of magazine articles submitted by editors for factual verification. In response to an article stressing negative implications of postwar demobilization upon the long-range economic and social prospects of Richmond, Henry, Sr., angrily wired the magazine's editor: "If I were a publisher I would not want to assume responsibility for the release of an article which is certain to critically injure the war effort in this area by misplaced emphasis." The editor tried to reassure Kaiser that the sole purpose of the article was to "study the stresses and strains imposed on a small community by the exigencies of war," but his honeyed rejoinder did not mollify the industrialist.[27]

Kaiser encountered opposition from many sources. One C. C. Crow, editor of *Crow's Pacific Coast Lumber Digest*, was obsessed by Kaiser's activities. Between 1942 and 1945 he chronicled Kaiser's purported misconduct with increasingly vitriolic prose, charging him with cynical coddling of labor union thugs, criminal misuse of public funds, egotistical pursuit of the presidential nomination in 1944, and other secret, nefarious objectives. A typical Crow broadside concluded that considering Kaiser's well-known capacity for gaining lucrative government contracts, "he is immediately exposed as one of the most brazen wastrels who ever fastened himself onto the pocket-books of the long-suffering public."[28] Kaiser finally lost patience and directed publicists to hire detectives to determine who was masterminding Crow's operation. They reported that U.S. Steel provided support. Kaiser's publicists claimed that there was "no doubt" concerning Crow's criminal liability, but they sensibly opposed a lawsuit, which "would merely give him the notoriety he seeks and would not help us any."[29]

Crow may have been Kaiser's most vitriolic critic, but he also attracted potshots from nationally syndicated columnists. Westbrook Pegler criticized Kaiser's dependence upon government contracts and his generosity in labor negotiations. Pegler observed in May 1945 that "this, of course, makes Kaiser a great liberal and a progressive industrial genius and accounts for his popularity with the unioneers."[30]

Months earlier Cadman had warned Kaiser to avoid links with too many liberal groups and causes. Cadman anticipated the postwar conservative reaction among business leaders and the general public in the aftermath of fifteen years of Depression and wartime federal regulation. He advised Kaiser to downplay his associations with New Dealers. The industrialist was invited by the Union for Democratic Action to speak at a testimonial banquet in December 1944 honoring outgoing Vice President Wallace. Kaiser accepted, but Cadman advised him to avoid further association: "As long as we refuse to affiliate with, sponsor, endorse, or donate to, or write articles and make statements for any and all of these organizations, we are on safe ground." When the American Council on Race Relations tried to enlist Kaiser's aid in "coping with [postwar] interracial frictions," Cadman strongly advised against "getting into these issues at this time."[31] Kaiser remained on cordial terms with many influential liberal Democrats, but after World War II he tried to remain apolitical.

But in 1945 and 1946, this was very difficult. As the war approached its climax, Kaiser neared his peak as a public figure; prominent Americans actively recruited him for countless national and international causes. Isador Lubin, a member of Roosevelt's White House staff, informed the President in late March 1945 that General Eisenhower wanted Kaiser to visit the troops on the European front: ". . . it would help the morale situation immensely to have a person like Kaiser pay a visit. . . . they would like to see the guy who built so many ships." Kaiser appeared on the fringes of international politics. When Soviet diplomat Vyacheslav Molotov attended an organizing session in San Francisco for the United Nations in the spring of 1945, Kaiser hosted him at the shipyards across the bay in Richmond. One of Kaiser's Russian-speaking engineers interpreted. The yards impressed the taciturn Soviet. One observer quoted Molotov: "This is the most remarkable day of my life." Gerard Piel, who had left *Life* to become a spokesman for Kaiser, informed his boss, "Mr. Molotov was profoundly impressed. You gave Mr. Molotov a splendid demonstration of the sources of our economic strength."[32]

Influential Americans sought Kaiser's advice on many issues. When Senator Robert F. Wagner drafted a new Social Security bill in May 1945, he sent a draft to Kaiser: "I hope that you will read the bill and let me have the benefit of your suggestions." Recently sworn-in President Harry S. Truman was equally intrigued by the famous industrialist; before an appointment with Kaiser, he jotted on his desk calendar that the industrialist "sees all, knows all, etc." When Walter White of the National Association for the Advancement of Colored People (NAACP) asked Truman to receive a small delegation of Americans concerned with racial equality, he proposed Kaiser as the sole representative of American industry. Although advisors tried to limit Kaiser's involvement in public affairs, he served in ceremonial positions for several national and international organizations. His public service offices between 1945 and 1946 included chairman of the Membership Committee of the Americans United for World Organization: director of United China Relief, Inc.; national chairman of the Victory Clothing Collection for the United Nations Relief and Recovery Administration (UNRRA); and symbolic posts in other UN-sponsored war-relief projects.[33]

Although his commitments to such efforts were brief and largely ceremonial, Kaiser remained in the public eye following the war. His daring venture into the automobile business aroused the enthusiasm of hundreds of thousands of Americans. His decision to remain in the steel business and to challenge Alcoa's near monopoly in aluminum earned him the respect of millions. Kaiser was in the news constantly; every month, it seemed, he opened another plant or entered some new enterprise. However, even Kaiser's publicists assumed that the fervor surrounding him during the war would wane, and that they would be able to settle into the routine types of promotional efforts conducted on behalf of most large-scale enterprises. Calhoun laid off several Washington staff members in October 1945 and moved back to Oakland. He soon discovered that it was difficult to cut back public relations activities; three months after his return to the West Coast, he discovered that he still spent most of his time in the capital. In February 1946 he told his boss that "events and changed conditions plus the enlarged scope of our activities now make it necessary . . . that your best interests require continued representation here—more so than ever before."[34]

With abrupt termination of wartime contracts, negotiations over possible entry into several enterprises, and aggressive expansion of existing operations, Kaiser faced most of the old public relations issues and a number of new ones. As a prominent, wealthy American businessman, he drew pitiful letters from hundreds of Eastern Europeans begging for money or jobs in the United States. But his publicists remained convinced that some organizations intended to exploit Kaiser's name. When Americans United for World Organization resisted his decision to resign, Cadman urged him to "stick to his guns."[35] As Kaiser moved into consumer products, his publicists perceived their paramount responsibility as shielding him from public controversy.

This was a major challenge. Magazines chronicled his plans; politicians probed wartime activities; and his publicists worked overtime to present company positions to the media. In Washington, Calhoun monitored federal legislation and its potential impact upon corporate interests. Whether or not Truman perceived Kaiser as a potential challenger, others did. Once again, admirers prodded Kaiser to throw his hat into what eventually became a very crowded ring in 1948. Homer Hardesty, self-proclaimed Global Secretary of the Global Citizenship Club of Daytona Beach, Florida, advanced Kaiser's name through the Democratic district-level primary. Hardesty grandly visualized convincing masses of southern delegates to switch to Kaiser after the first roll-call vote at the national convention. But Kaiser publicist Robert C. Elliott stated the obvious: most of those urging him to run were simply promoting their own interests.[36] Kaiser publicly dismissed all such blandishments; privately, one suspects, he may have felt at least a twinge of temptation.

With the emergence of his large, new private enterprises and expansion of the medical care program, the public relations staff faced new challenges. After he formed the automobile company in partnership with Joe Frazer in August 1945, Kaiser's dealings with labor unions were scrutinized even more closely than when he had worked primarily on government contracts. The postwar period was a difficult time for labor negotiations. With rampant inflation, unions demanded generous increases, but many managers sensed a rising tide of conservatism and fully intended to challenge labor.

Kaiser was entering new fields and had to attract skilled workers from competitors; thus, he frequently offered higher wages in basic industries. Early in 1946 Kaiser signed precedent-setting agreements with steelworkers and auto workers. Public opinion was mixed. A Baptist minister from Granville, Ohio, praised his Christian spirit: "Yours is a course which should lead the way for other men in industry and labor to find a basis of cooperation." But others were critical. A fixed-income pensioner from Temple City, California, complained, "How do you think it makes every retired person feel . . . to see the industrial employers gang up with their groups of workers to snipe away at the savings and value of the dollars all have saved up year after year?" Kaiser welcomed opposition from the rich and powerful. But committed as he was to prepaid group health care and higher living standards for working Americans, criticism from ordinary Americans disturbed him deeply.[37]

By the late 1940s the Kaiser organization had developed more effective responses to public criticism. A booklet, titled *Questions and Answers about Henry J. Kaiser,* which presented the organizational view of frequently asked questions about Kaiser and corporate operations was published in September 1946. In response to mounting congressional criticism concerning Kaiser's wartime profits and government loans, publicists provided simple explanations. They distributed several thousand copies of the booklet and planned periodic updating and reprinting.[38]

The Kaiser organization occasionally bungled efforts to sway public opinion and influence the decisionmaking process. Such lapses were particularly notable at Kaiser-Frazer. In 1948 Big Steel tried to induce federal officials to investigate the automobile company's takeover of the Cleveland plant providing steel sheet for auto bodies. Kaiser-Frazer officials "persuaded" dealers to ask President Truman for support. The President received hundreds of letters and telegrams, many of which referred to the automobile company as "Keyser-Frazier." When Congress in 1949 tightened credit regulation for new car purchases, the company mounted an effort to persuade members of Congress to reverse their decision. Dozens of the telegrams, purportedly from outraged Kaiser-Frazer dealers, were worded identically.[39]

By mid-century, some opinion-makers were impatient with what they perceived as Kaiser's oversensitivity to public criticism. In their view, if Kaiser planned to remain in the forefront among industrialists, he had to learn to handle criticism better. Pegler, a master at spouting invective, lectured Kaiser against complaining about "character assassination" with any critical newspaper story. According to Pegler, Kaiser's public gripes proved only that he had a "very thin skin." The columnist claimed that a majority of his own comments were "all for Kaiser." In response to another Kaiser letter complaining of unfair treatment, Henry Luce replied: ". . . it saddens me to think that the only time you write me . . . is when you're mad at me. We've had three or four stories on your affairs lately, and I'm quite sure that some of them must have been pleasant reading for you."[40]

At mid-century, experienced businessmen counseled Kaiser to reexamine the guiding purpose of his publicity. Banker George D. Woods believed that publicists overemphasized Kaiser's personal role. According to Woods, this approach had made sense at the beginning of his emergence as a public figure, but "that time has long since passed . . . at this stage it is better to talk about Companies . . ." Alex Troffey, a newcomer to Kaiser's staff, was particularly critical of *Questions and Answers*. According to Troffey, the booklet "had quite an ax to grind." In fact, concluded Troffey, "the book contains a lot of *propaganda* that cannot be erased simply by inserting a supplement."[41]

In a word, experts urged Kaiser not to take attacks on his companies as personal attacks, and not to respond in kind. At times he followed such sound advice, but occasionally he blew up. When *Business Week* published rumors of his plans to merge Kaiser-Frazer with several other Kaiser companies in 1949, Kaiser complained to editor Paul Montgomery. Brushing aside Montgomery's offer to print Kaiser's rebuttal, the industrialist charged that most readers assumed "letters to the editor" were written by cranks, and that they merely drew more attention to the original rumors: "Never in my history have I seen a reputable magazine publish baseless rumors that are so destructive and damaging to an industry or industries." Even Calhoun occasionally perceived attacks against Kaiser in conspiratorial terms. Late in 1953, following seemingly endless defenses against charges that Kaiser-Frazer had grossly mishandled a contract to built C-119 cargo planes for the Air Force, he vented his frustration in a memo to the boss. Calhoun was on reasonably firm ground in stating that Kaiser's interest had been under "severe, insidious, and effective attack" for years, but he overreacted in claiming, "We have never been organized to defend ourselves from such attacks."[42]

At mid-century, Kaiser and his public relations staff had largely curtailed their inclination to shoot from the hip. By the end of the Korean War, the organization had been tested by several investigations, by the sensationalism surrounding a messy stock-fraud lawsuit between Kaiser-Frazer and Cleveland financier Cyrus Eaton, and by other challenges. Above all, Kaiser's publicists learned the wisdom of short-term silence. Before responding publicly to criticism, they usually drafted position papers revealing deep thought about ramifications of alternative responses. Given the increasing stakes involved, this is hardly surprising; by the early 1950s Kaiser headed an empire comprised of dozens of companies with combined assets approaching a billion dollars. Hundreds of thousands of investors could be adversely affected by a serious public relations gaffe. But in his final years, Henry Kaiser believed that modern managers were too concerned with corporate responsibility and public service. In a highly revealing interview in 1963, Edgar Kaiser recalled that he and his father held differing views: "I'm willing to spend more time and more effort than he thinks I should. *His feeling is that our whole company is one big public service*" (emphasis added).[43]

This does not suggest that Kaiser was indifferent to such issues. In the early 1950s, he was deeply involved in what amounted to nearly an all-out war with the American Medical Association over prepaid medical care; charges and countercharges were ugly indeed. In most dealings with the media, however, Kaiser and his staff showed maturity and growing sophistication. In the late 1950s, after his semi-retirement to Hawaii, Kaiser entered radio and television. By 1962 the octogenarian industrialist had become a master of the media. Kaiser had come a long way in the three decades since he stepped off the train in Washington in 1931, a neophyte trying to learn the mysteries of dealing with the nation's decisionmakers.

Henry Kaiser's mother,
Mary, about 1884.

Henry Kaiser's father,
Frank, about 1885.

Henry Kaiser's birthplace, Sprout Brook, New York.

Henry Kaiser as an infant, about 1883.

Henry Kaiser as a teenager, about 1900.

Henry Kaiser cavorting with Flo Brownell,
daughter of his photography shop partner.
Such an intimate "candid" photo was very unusual
for its time. Unfortunately, no recollection
of Kaiser's relationship with the young woman
has survived.

Kaiser's first photography shop,
Lake Placid, New York, about 1900.

Bess Fosburgh, shortly before
her marriage to Henry, about 1907.

Kaiser the entrepreneur, about 1917.

Kaiser and unidentified business associates,
Vancouver, British Columbia, 1915.

Early road-building scene, Snohomish, Washington,
about 1916. Kaiser is at far right.

Road-building scene in Cuba, 1928.

Kaiser with Cuban officials, 1928.

Kaiser with yellow Marmon automobile, 1931.

Kaiser with Six Companies partners at Hoover Dam,
about 1935. Kaiser is third from left.

Barren Boulder City, Nevada, about 1932.

A weary, unshaven Kaiser at Hoover Dam, about 1932.

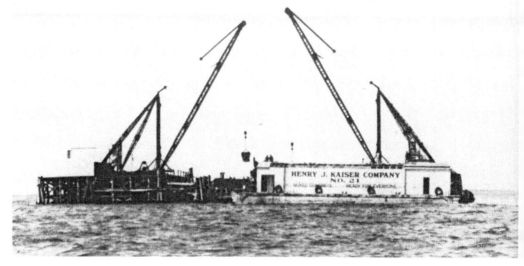

Kaiser equipment sinking Oakland–San Francisco Bridge pilings, 1934.

Looking down the world's longest conveyor belt,
Shasta Dam site, near Redding, California, about 1939.

Henry Kaiser, about 1946.

Kaiser–U.S. Maritime Commission housing in Richmond, 1943.
Dreary as these "barracks" were, they were
a huge improvement over the back seats of autos.

Living conditions in Richmond, California, about 1942.

Overhead view of Richmond shipyards, about 1943.

Female workers at Richmond Shipyard No. 3,
about 1944. At left, a shipfitter's helper;
at right, a steel checker.

Henry and Edgar Kaiser with President Roosevelt
at ship launching, 1942. Edgar is leaning over
the driver's seat.

Cartoon: The Important Thing to Washington.

Cartoon: "So far he's got Henry Kaiser licked by four hours."
Colliers, February 27, 1943, p. 62.
Used by permission of Michael Ponce de Leon.

Cartoon: Can't, Eh? By Reg Manning.
Copyright Phoenix Republic and Gazette Syndicate.
Reprinted with permission of *The Arizona Republic
and the Phoenix Gazette.* Permission does not
imply endorsement by the newspaper.

Bess No. 1 blast furnace at Fontana,
California, steel plant, 1942.

Henry and Bess Kaiser at a public appearance, about 1945.

Kaiser with Thomas W. McGowan, the hardware man
who gave him his first job in Spokane, Washington,
some forty years later in 1946.

Kaiser greets a press conference
at Oakland headquarters, about 1946.

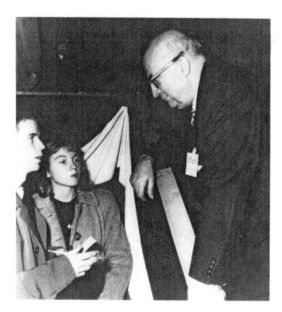

Kaiser talks to young reporters
aboard Friendship Train Tour, November 1947.

Kaiser as hard-working executive
in staged publicity photo, about 1946.

Kaiser Community Homes development,
Santa Clara, California, about 1949.

Kaiser Community Homes development,
Panorama City, California, about 1948.

Joe Frazer and Kaiser with plaster model
of one of their cars, 1947.

During happy days, Kaiser and partner Joe Frazer
ham it up at a "roast" in their honor, 1948.

Kaiser and UAW President Walter Reuther
sign labor settlement, 1949.

Willow Run auto assembly line, about 1948.

Henry and Edgar Kaiser pose proudly
with "Henry-J" automobile, 1950.

Industrias Kaiser Argentina (IKA) automobile plant, 1965.

C-119 cargo planes roll off the assembly line
at Willow Run, 1953.

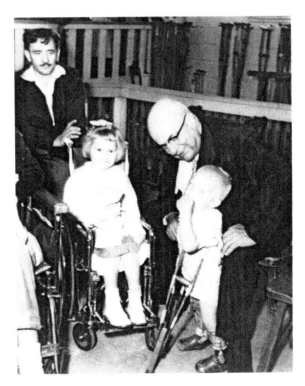

Kaiser with young patients
at Permanente Rehabilitation center, 1953.

Henry Kaiser, Jr., showing effects of advanced multiple sclerosis,
November 1959. He died in May 1961.

Dr. Sidney R. Garfield and Kaiser
examine a model of Walnut Creek hospital, 1953.

Edgar Kaiser with Israel Prime Minister David Ben-Gurion,
about 1958.

Kaiser and top managers pause long enough for a group photo, 1946.
From left to right, standing: Kaiser, Donald A. "Dusty" Rhoades,
Howard V. "Lindy" Lindbergh, Dr. Paul F. Cadman;
seated: Alonzo B. Ordway, Charles F. "Chad" Calhoun, George G. "Sherry" Sherwood,
Eugene E. Trefethen, Jr. (foreground), Tom M. Price.

Henry and Ale Kaiser, 1954.

Kaiser and band leader Guy Lombardo at Lake Tahoe, 1949.

Henry and Ale Kaiser clowning with comedian
Spike Jones and companion, 1955.

Henry and Edgar Kaiser pose with actor James Garner
on *Maverick* set, 1957.

Kaiser decked in lei at his eightieth birthday party, 1962.

Kaiser preparing to receive one of many honorary degrees
at June 1948 commencement, University of Nevada, Reno.

Kaiser overlooks Hawaii Kai construction, about 1961.

A slimmed-down Kaiser at Hawaii Kai
construction site, October 1966.

8

Planning for a Postwar World

During the late 1930s and World War II, American life was clearly in the midst of a profound transition, as recollections of the decades before the Wall Street crash receded deeper into memory. By 1943 or 1944 it was evident that the Allies would win the war, and thoughtful citizens wondered what peace would bring. Would the nation's economy slip back into a depression once the "artificial" stimulus of wartime spending was ended? Over ten million men and women served in uniform during the war; how would they be reintegrated into civilian life? Would the millions of women who had taken jobs in war industries be willing to make way for returning male veterans?

The concept of future planning touched many countervailing tendencies in American life. From the "Discovery," many European intellectuals saw the "New World" as the laboratory for development of the human future. The Puritans, the leaders of the American Revolution, the proponents of Manifest Destiny, and countless other Americans shared that vision. But Americans stoutly resisted centralized planning. In the 1930s, when several European nations had welfare capitalism firmly in place, the United States took its first timid steps toward a national agenda designed by federal planners. The National Resources Planning Board (NRPB) was founded in 1933; but its reports and recommendations aroused little interest or political support. Few mourned its passing in 1943.[1] Americans had a propensity to wait for crises before taking unified action. The nation had turned the tide of the war with little advance planning; certainly we could manage without it when peace returned.

But many thoughtful Americans sensed that the postwar world would present unparalleled social, economic, and political problems—and opportunities. While few anticipated the nuclear age, many thinkers realized that the end of the war would be an important watershed in world history.

Whether or not the United States took the lead in rebuilding the world, significant internal changes seemed inevitable. If government planners set no agenda, private groups and individuals had to grasp the initiative.

Henry Kaiser eagerly accepted the challenge. Fascination, even preoccupation with the future, which intensified as he aged, became a key component of his character. Tracing the roots of this interest is difficult; few clues can be found in Kaiser's upbringing. The rural region of his youth was a backwater; many of its economic functions were rendered obsolete by the tremendous technological and entrepreneurial changes sweeping the nation in the late nineteenth century. But older men such as George Warren and W. A. "Dad" Bechtel encouraged him to "think big" during his early years in construction. The nature of many jobs encouraged his future orientation. Between 1914 and 1942 Kaiser helped create much of the West's infrastructure. While building transportation, water, reclamation, and energy-oriented projects, Kaiser was keenly aware of their importance to the region's future.[2] The reluctance of others to take the initiative in satisfying what to Kaiser were obvious western needs encouraged him to seek more challenges. By 1942 his success in basic products like cement and steel provided Kaiser a solid foundation of confidence; he was eager to enter new fields.

In 1942 Kaiser turned sixty, an age when it would be natural to shorten risks and time lines for future projects. That was when Kaiser launched into a series of vast new projects with unlimited futures. However impressive his postwar achievement in several major industries, the list of additional options seriously considered but rejected is equally remarkable. It is not far-fetched to claim that no other American industrialist surpassed the depth and breadth of Kaiser's fundamental grasp of the nation's industrial prospects at mid-century.

Even before the United States entered World War II, Kaiser planned for peacetime. Although he emphasized that the steel plant was for defense, he clearly intended to supply postwar civilian needs. Several years before he entered the aluminum industry in 1946, he dreamed of its peacetime applications. He presented a general outline of his ideas for peacetime on December 4, 1942, in a major address to a black-tie dinner audience at the National Association of Manufacturers (NAM) meeting. Some highly influential business leaders, still gearing up for wartime production, were incredulous at his comment that "the problems of peace are already at hand."[3]

The ebullient westerner had become a media hero; some industrialists envied and resented his instant fame. They arched their eyebrows at his statements about the postwar era. Simply put, he was not a member of their club. Many corporate leaders considered him a government-financed bag of wind, whose meteoric industrial career would fizzle as soon as he encountered genuinely competitive postwar capitalism. Several critics directly challenged Kaiser's patriotism; in their view he was cynically manipulating government "favoritism" to advance his own selfish postwar interests.

In early December 1942, Kaiser perceived the situation very differently. What more could he do for the war effort? Production in the shipyards was shattering all known records; day-to-day management there was in the hands of two able and trusted subordinates. The mill at Fontana would yield its first steel plate within the month; he was already producing impressive amounts of magnesium; and he was trying to work with Howard Hughes on a cargo plane contract. Despite all these projects, Kaiser still had reserve energy; in his view, its best use included consideration of the industrial future of the nation, particularly the Pacific Coast region. To Kaiser, failure to plan for peace invited a crisis as serious as being unprepared for war. With his grade-school education he revealed a better grasp of historical parallels than many university-trained contemporaries.

There were other reasons for Kaiser's concern with postwar America. His companies employed over 200,000 workers, and demand for their products would almost disappear during peacetime. Experts predicted that less than 10 percent of four million workers in shipbuilding and aircraft would remain in those occupations after the war. Some advising Kaiser envisioned tens of thousands of frightened workers in the Richmond and Portland yards, plus millions more across the nation, once again facing long-term unemployment. Kaiser felt that such fears were largely unfounded; early in the war he correctly predicted a postwar age of abundance. In September 1942 he told listeners at a banquet in Oakland, "We have only time for a glimpse of what the future holds. At home our markets will be drained dry, and a pent-up consumer demand will be released, seeking satisfaction in every artifice and device we know how to make." One reason for his outspokenness was compassion for his workers. Kaiser hoped to spare them the anxieties they would experience by listening to the "doomsday" economists.[4]

It would be misleading to suggest that Kaiser was wholly out of step with mainstream business thought about the postwar economy. In fact, his ideas paralleled those of some widely respected corporate strategists. The chief difference was that Kaiser publicly stated his views many months ahead of other entrepreneurs. One highly influential postwar planning document was a report by financier and informal presidential advisor Bernard M. Baruch and his associate John M. Hancock. Historians of reconversion concluded that decisionmakers followed portions of their blueprint rather closely. Two key recommendations involved a master plan for public works in the event of widespread unemployment and quick resale of unneeded war materials and plant space to facilitate reconversion by private employers. Kaiser shared ideas with Baruch throughout the war. In

February 1944 Kaiser proposed that up to ten billion dollars' worth of self-liquidating public works projects be undertaken following the war. Ultimately, federal public works programs had many other sponsors and dwarfed even that figure. Although Kaiser clashed personally with future Committee on Economic Development (CED) chief Paul G. Hoffman, the two had joined other influential business leaders and public officials in preliminary planning for an interstate highway system in the late 1930s. Kaiser also proposed a network of six thousand airports as another major component of the nation's transportation infrastructure. Nothing came of the latter concept, but it suggested the magnitude of Kaiser's thinking.[5]

Kaiser never doubted the ability of private enterprise to create and distribute postwar material abundance, and he channeled his thought and energy in that direction. His ideas attracted favorable attention in high circles. In June 1943 Baruch wrote to President Roosevelt that Kaiser had "some wonderful practical ideas about postwar conditions." Kaiser disingenuously expressed the hope that he might stay "out of the limelight" in preparing for peace. In fact, he had already decided that others simply weren't taking the initiative, and that it was his duty to lead. Chad Calhoun and other advisors urged Kaiser to "go public" with his initiatives. In the fall of 1943, Kaiser expounded his ideas at length to reporters. His tentative master plan appeared in a September issue of *Modern Industry*. Kaiser reaffirmed his intention of staying in steel and emphasized the need for many items using lightweight metals and wood. He also called for West Coast automboile production. He proposed building ships for other countries "more economically than they [could] be produced anywhere else in the world." Idle shipyards might turn out freight and passenger cars for railroads all over the globe.[6]

At the end of 1943, Kaiser often felt he was fighting alone for public acceptance of any concrete postwar plans, let alone his specific proposals. He resented being treated as an outsider by "mainstream" business organizations, and he occasionally vented his frustration. In late 1943 the NAM followed his lead and drew up a postwar planning document outlining some general principles; but Kaiser complained that the organization treated him "more as a leper than they do as a welcome guest." Kaiser also voiced displeasure at receiving a cold shoulder from the CED, and Hoffman in particular: "He has never even taken the trouble to keep an appointment with me, much less discuss [postwar planning] with me." In December, the *New York Times* reported that Kaiser was urging military leaders to survey GIs to discover their visions of an ideal postwar nation. Kaiser suggested setting up volunteer groups in thousands of towns across America to collect and analyze responses from "their boys" overseas. These committees would serve as "draft boards in reverse," easing the transition of GIs back into civilian life.[7]

By 1944 growing numbers of Americans saw the end in sight, and Kaiser could more freely discuss his postwar plans. Several of his most influential advisors—Calhoun, Cadman, and Llewellyn White—suggested postwar projects. They encouraged Kaiser, as "America's leading business-man," to provide direction for economic reconversion. Early in 1944 White urged Kaiser to offer a future agenda which would exert the same type of impact upon the domestic economy as Wendell Willkie's book *One World* had upon the nation's commitment to internationalism. Kaiser and his advisors exchanged heavy doses of flattery, but their mutual encouragement to think the unthinkable and dream the impossible created a spirited, aggressive organization. By 1944 they were ready to present an ambitious, comprehensive, and specific agenda to the American public.[8]

It was Kaiser who personified this message—in speeches, interviews, and articles appearing under his name. Most of his public statements were prepared by others, but he often revised and polished preliminary drafts, and he spoke with obvious conviction. In a March 1944 address to the National Committee on Postwar Housing, he urged a unified commitment from federal and state governments, banks, businesses, and labor unions to attack the housing shortage. In April he busily promoted—unsuccessfully—a national system of airports. Undeterred by lack of interest in his airport network, he presented even more ambitious programs. In May, he submitted a remarkable document to President Roosevelt, promoting many of the liberal objectives which became reality from Truman's Fair Deal to Lyndon Johnson's Great Society. His suggestions included an interstate highway system even more ambitious than that already on the drawing board, a huge housing program, and a nation-wide system of prepaid health care. He differed from some liberals only in his faith that private enterprise could and would turn dreams into reality. The only possible stumbling block, according to Kaiser, was "selfish, short-sighted, and antisocial 'monopolists' willing to pay any price to perpetuate their privilege."[9]

Kaiser's remarks further irritated many corporate leaders, but he tried hard to restrain himself around those he would need in the postwar period. In particular, he directly courted large private lenders. To maintain and expand his corporate empire, he needed to borrow tens of millions of dollars of venture capital. In October 1944, before the New York Financial Writers Association, he defended his business credentials. He claimed that he fully understood the trials of competitive capitalism, noting that he had done well in construction and cement, two highly competitive enterprises. But Kaiser sought also approval from more disparate groups of Americans. He appreciated a *New York Times* editorial stating that he was on "solid ground" with many of his postwar reconversion ideas. And he undoubtedly pleased ambitious working women with his vision of their place in the work force; "Of course they will continue to work. Why shouldn't they?" From a late-twentieth-century perspective his next remark appears sexist: "Housework need no longer take up all of a woman's time." But for a wartime businessman, Kaiser was unusually aware of women's efforts. He believed they could be far more than temporaries, wartime workers in "men's jobs": "[Women] must find other things to do. [They] must work—no one is happy who is idle."[10]

Kaiser's postwar plans were temporarily postponed in mid-November 1944, after President Roosevelt summoned him to the White House. In the previous ninety days, employment in the Richmond yards had dropped from ninety-three thousand to about sixty-seven thousand. Many of Kaiser's workers had listened to his dazzling visions of postwar prosperity and—whether in response to the boss's ideas or for personal reasons—had left their jobs in the shipyards to get a head start seeking the best jobs in civilian industries. Roosevelt reminded Kaiser that the war was not over and worried that such serious attrition could hamper even the "miracle man's" output. After an hour-long chat on November 15, a sober, businesslike Henry Kaiser emerged from their meeting and urged workers across America to stay in their wartime jobs and buckle down to help finish the fight.[11]

Kaiser did not enter the private home construction field until the end of World War II, but he and his subordinates possessed experience in housing. At their dam sites in the 1930s, and in the shipyards, Kaiser and assorted partners had joined forces with federal officials to build thousands of dwelling units. In some cases they had also arranged for utilities, public safety, sanitation, medical care, and other vital services.

Long before the end of the war, Kaiser explored postwar prospects in home building. In December 1942 he discussed with designer Norman Bel Geddes the feasibility of producing prefabricated three-room steel-frame houses for as little as $1,500. On March 9, 1944, in an address to a conference of the National Committee on Housing in Chicago, he unveiled his ideas about postwar housing needs. Kaiser observed that the Depression had driven millions of families into cramped, antiquated facilities, and World War II had forced huge cutbacks in new housing starts. In addition, over a million GIs had married, leaving brides at home with relatives. Kaiser saw as "inevitable" that when peace returned, "there [would] be a spreading out, with extensive requirements for separate dwellings." If private builders failed to meet demands for several million new homes at the end of the war, the federal government would step in. Despite his government ties, Kaiser clearly preferred that private enterprise meet the nation's housing needs.[12]

Kaiser planned to assist the suburbanization of postwar America. He had mass-produced ships, and houses would be much easier to build. Two days after V-J Day he announced formation of a partnership with noted West Coast developer Fritz Burns. With a sharp eye for maximum publicity, the announcement coincided with a large United Nations gathering in San Francisco and visits by many delegates to the yards in nearby Richmond. Kaiser and Burns were equal partners, but their company was named Kaiser Community Homes. They would limit their activities to the West Coast and planned to offer two- and three-bedroom homes. They stressed that units would not be prefabricated, but mass production of kitchen and bathroom facilities would slash costs and hold prices down to about five thousand dollars.[13]

There is uncertainty concerning the number of units Kaiser and Burns planned to build. A *San Francisco Chronicle* reporter quoted Kaiser as hoping to expand to the point where he and Burns provided "millions of new homes and jobs." According to a *Chicago Sun* reporter listening to the same speech to U.N. delegates, "Kaiser admitted an ambition to do in housing what Ford did in automotive transportation after the last war." He probably got carried away by the euphoria of the moment. There is no evidence that Kaiser ever seriously considered supplying housing on such a scale. The largest figure mentioned by any officer at Kaiser Community Homes was 100,000 houses per year nationwide, and that ambitious goal could be reached only in collaboration with scores of local builders.[14]

Kaiser and Burns became high-volume homebuilders, but their innovations in design and construction methods attracted the most attention. Between 1945 and 1950, Kaiser Community Homes built only 0.2 percent of the country's new units. However, a few large builders, including Kaiser and Burns, were trend-setters in using new building techniques and materials. Certain methods employed in the shipyards were applied to homebuilding. Industry analysts were intrigued that a factory turned out panel assemblies, partly finished porches and roofs, and other sections requiring large, stationary machinery. Dishwashers, garbage disposals, and plumbing fixtures were produced in a converted aircraft plant in Bristol, Pennsylvania, and then preassembled in "standard" kitchen and bathroom units.[15]

The homes were centered in three West Coast metropolitan regions: Los Angeles, the Bay Area, and Portland, Oregon. How did the neighborhoods develop by Kaiser Community Homes between 1946 and 1950 compare to those by other developers? Kaiser and Burns did not offer five-thousand-dollar homes, due largely to rampant postwar inflation; but efficient building techniques enabled them to contain prices reasonably well. Kaiser's homes in North Hollywood and Panorama City went on the market late in 1946; prices ranged from seven to nine thousand dollars for two- and three-bedroom models. By 1949 and 1950 prices were between ten and twelve thousand dollars. By present-day standards the Kaiser models were cramped: the smallest two-bedroom houses were 730 square feet, whereas the largest three-bedrooms covered 1,086 square feet.[16]

Yet considering that Kaiser and Burns aimed at middle- and lower-middle-class markets, where primary wage earners were stable white-collar and blue-collar workers, their record appears impressive. The partners hired talented designers, who neatly camouflaged virtually identical kitchen and bathroom units and other rooms: buyers chose from four basic models: Cape Cod, Colonial, California, and Contemporary. Theoretically, the developers could provide 750 variations; in practice they offered 28.[17] The designers worked effectively with local planners and zoning boards, avoiding the monotony of the grid pattern of streets in favor of gently curved avenues. By varying garage locations and set-back lines, and by offering wide choices of colors, Kaiser Community Homes created reasonably distinctive neighborhoods.

Driving through the forty-year-old subdivisions in the late-1980s, one is struck by their ordinary character. Many houses show their age, with cracks, peeling plaster, and weathered window frames. Some are dwarfed by motor homes squeezed into narrow driveways. But in the late 1940s few were critical. Prospective buyers lined up for the first models offered. Real estate sections of local newspapers showed thrilled families receiving keys to new homes. Some Kaiser Community Homes neighborhoods seem drab now, but to families who had shared six-room flats with in-laws during the Depression and World War II, the houses looked like mansions.

For two or three years after World War II, Kaiser seemed deeply committed to the home-building program, which was interdependent with several other enterprises. Engineers developed new applications in home construction for many of Kaiser's new products. These innovations enhanced his impact upon suburban developments by creating a multiplier effect. By challenging western building suppliers who had enjoyed near monopoly conditions, Kaiser helped rein in inflationary construction costs. His cement, gypsum, sand and gravel, and aluminum were used in his housing projects, and by hundreds of other developers.[18]

By 1950, however, Kaiser's interest in and commitment to home building were dwindling. In 1946 he talked optimistically of finishing 10,000 homes that year; others in the organization spoke of eventually turning out ten times that many annually. Total output never reached 10,000. Kaiser and Burns planned to build 6,000 homes in 1947 but produced only 5,000. In 1948 they lowered sights to 3,000, but produced only 2,099 units. One reason Kaiser lost interest in the field was that by mid-century the nation's housing crisis was rapidly abating. Other builders with more single-minded commitments were filling the void. In 1950 alone, the nation's developers handed new house keys to nearly 1.4 million families.[19]

As World War II wound down, Kaiser was but one of thousands of Americans planning for peacetime. As one of the nation's best-known businessmen, he was approached by hundreds of would-be entrepreneurs with ill-conceived schemes, including a plea to invest in a string of chicken farms. Other offers were more sophisticated. In 1943 one "Champ" Pickens, a sponsor of the annual Blue-Gray college football all-star game, urged Kaiser to invest in Blue-Gray Motor Inns, a national motel chain. Pickens' concepts of tie-ins with local tourist attractions and national gasoline and restaurant chains revealed considerable thought, but the proposal did not capture Kaiser's fancy.[20]

Potential partners often approached Kaiser through influential mutual friends. A promoter of prefabricated movie theaters persuaded the president of Universal Studios to broach the idea during a private dinner with Kaiser. A few ideas were so enormous in scope that they may have startled even Kaiser. Tom Price, an early associate, proposed a series of tunnels through the mountains separating Los Angeles from the San Joaquin Valley. Price argued that they woud reduce rail and automobile trips between Los Angeles and San Francisco up to six hours. The project would take nine years and cost $500 million.[21] Unfortuantely, no record of Kaiser's response exists, but Price certainly took seriously his boss's encouragement to "think big."

In the early 1940s, Kaiser established a research and development laboratory in Emeryville, near Oakland; Howard V. Lindbergh supervised several engineers, who tested products with potential for postwar consumer markets. At "hobby-lobby," the first Kaiser automobile prototypes and many other experimental products were developed. Kaiser's engineers came up with dozens of their own ideas, and they tested many more. Inventors of gadgets attracting Kaiser's interest sent samples to Emeryville, where engineers examined them thoroughly. The handful meriting serious attention then were test marketed. After Kaiser started building houses, it seemed for a time that Lindbergh and his engineers specialized in home appliances. Between 1945 and 1948, the laboratory tested an endless stream of dishwashers, air-conditioners, washer and drier combinations, kitchen ranges and cabinets, lawn mowers, and vacuum cleaners.

Only a few products passed muster. In such cases, Kaiser usually bought the rights to manufacture the item, and production was turned over to Kaiser-Fleetwings, a small aircraft plant in Bristol, Pennsylvania, which he had acquired in 1943. In 1945 Kaiser's manager at Fleetwings, Sherlock D. Hackley, proposed turning out 100,000 dishwashers, featuring almost no moving parts. Those not used in Kaiser Community Homes kitchens would be marketed through two hundred retail stores within a four-hundred mile radius of Bristol. The eastern plant eventually offered four models. Kaiser's commitment to appliances paralleled his commitment to home construction: high initial enthusiasm followed by gradually diminishing interest. Yet as late as 1952, the organization was still cooperatively producing and marketing many kitchen and bathroom items through Sears, Roebuck, and Company.[22]

Two important industries considered seriously by Kaiser officials were fiberglass and paper. With his commitments to automobiles, houses, and light metals, fiberglass was a natural interest. Kaiser was less interested in turning out the product himself than in luring major producers to the West Coast. Harold Boeschenstein, president of Owens-Corning Fiberglass, loaned several engineers to Kaiser to help develop additional uses for the product. Boeschenstein visited "hobby-lobby" several times. He and Kaiser shared a vision of the product's enormous potential to create hundreds of new cottage industries generating, in turn, more uses for the material.[23] Kaiser's primary interest in fiberglass was its suitability for auto bodies and pleasure boats. The Kaiser-Darrin sportscar, produced in small quantities in the mid-1950s, was a masterpiece. In addition, his engineers designed some of the world's most sophisticated lightweight speedboats, which became highly competitive on the national and international racing circuit. Within a few years, major suppliers set up several fiberglass plants on the West Coast; as Kaiser and Boeschenstein had anticipated, they spawned hundreds of ancillary businesses.

Kaiser also considered entering the paper business after the war. Representatives for several mills in the Pacific Northwest, Texas, and the deep South entered serious negotiations with him. First approached late in 1944, Kaiser and his subordinates were sufficiently interested to negotiate possible acquisitions for several months. Some of the properties were very large; the Southland Paper Mills, centered in Texas, had total assets of $130 million. Kaiser drew in other potential investment partners, including Marshall Field's department store in Chicago, In May 1945, percentages of commitments were tentatively agreed upon. But the deal fell through.[24] Kaiser was simultaneously entering the automobile and housing industries and was examining prospects in many other areas; had circumstances been slightly different, he might have chosen paper over aluminum.

Another industry which intrigued Kaiser for years was railroads. He considered building and operating a line between Grants Pass, Oregon, and Crescent City, California, in the mid-1930s. A decade later, he no longer considered railroads, but dreamed of supplying rolling stock. The prospect of widespread unemployment in the shipyards stimulated this interest; he might simply convert some yards to production of freight cars. Such altruistic motives dovetailed nicely with developing new uses for lightweight metals. In 1943 he envisioned using magnesium in lightweight, high-speed railroad cars. Ralph E. Knight, Eugene E. Trefethen, Jr., and other Kaiser subordinates explored tie-ins between their organization and others. They also asked several large railroads to test the new cars on coast-to-coast runs.[25] Preliminary negotiations occurred in 1943, but wartime exigencies prevented immediate design and testing.

Prospects for railroad cars seemed bright during the war. Trefethen informed Kaiser that American railroads were operating overweight, obsolete stock and would soon need sixty thousand cars. But by 1945 postwar domestic growth prospects for the industry did not appear promising. The interstate highway system was on the drawing board, and commercial trucking already offered serious competition; commercial airlines would also make inroads into passenger service. But Kaiser still considered supplying railroad cars abroad. In May 1945, he casually informed Julius Krug, chairman of the War Production Board (WPB), that he would bid on thirty thousand railroad cars for the French government. The fact that he had little idea of how to meet such a contract bothered him not a whit. His people usually beat deadlines and made money; Kaiser believed they could turn out virtually anything.[26]

Despite Kaiser's imaginative, expansive proposals for alternative uses of the shipyards, for more than a year after the war he tried to remain in shipbuilding. He already knew shipbuilding; continuing in that field would require the fewest adjustments. In September 1943, when the yards were at peak production, he stressed the nation's postwar need to enhance the size and efficiency of its merchant marine fleet. Between 1944 and 1946, he actively promoted the use of ships and tried to convince government officials to keep the yards busy. His effort ultimately failed, and he was at least momentarily saddened when the yards closed down.[27]

Kaiser's concern for the disruption of his work force was genuine. In March 1944 he asked shipyard managers to survey workers concerning plans for the postwar period. The Portland poll indicated that 21.3 percent of the workers would definitely stay in the city; another 30.6 percent would remain if they had jobs, and 21.9 percent were undecided. The rest planned to return to their former homes. If the yards closed, upheaval in the lives of many seemed unavoidable. The futures of tens of thousands of people were at stake.

Kaiser first explored prospects of continuing to turn out cargo ships. By 1944 little remained of the decimated Russian fleet. Lend-Lease goods from America, so critical to the war-ravaged nation's survival, were carried in U.S. vessels. Dealing with the Russians was even more mysterious and complex then than today; one never knew which Soviets had authority to speak for whom. The U.S. State Department contributed to the confusion. Nevertheless, in the early spring of 1944, two Soviet representatives informed Calhoun that they hoped to obtain many cargo ships before the war ended, and that their leaders were interested in a long-term shipbuilding arrangement with one or more American firms. The Russians also requested technical assistance to rebuild their own yards. Kaiser's managers saw an opportunity to provide long-term work for many employees. Although W. Averell Harriman, U.S. Ambassador to Russia, warned Kaiser and Calhoun that the Soviets were difficult customers, for a time key men in the Kaiser organization believed that prospects for cooperation were promising. The closing months of the war brought rapidly escalating mutual suspicion between the two nations, and opportunities for cooperation evaporated as the atmosphere chilled. Still, Kaiser hoped to do business with the Soviets as late as June 1945, when he proudly toured the Richmond yards with U.N. Ambassador Vyacheslav Molotov.[28]

Kaiser and his organization made other efforts to continue in shipbuilding. It made little sense simply to dismantle the shipyards; as Calhoun observed in the late summer of 1944, they possessed significant competitive advantages: "[We] now enjoy strategic location, low-cost production, and an inter-national reputation through established records and world-wide publicity. There is an instant need to capitalize on these fully if favorable competitive position is to be assured."[29] For a time it appeared that participating in rebuilding the U.S. Merchant Marine was a strong possibility. Maritime Commission Chairman Emory S. Land recommended such a program to President Roosevelt in a "Personal and Confidential" memo in September 1944. He proposed building eight large passenger vessels, at a total cost of between $120 and $160 million. Kaiser offered to build half of the vessels at cost, plus a one-dollar profit. The President, an old "Navy hand," was favorably inclined and asked Land to find a yard on the East Coast capable of handling the other half of the order.[30]

But after he studied Kaiser's initiative closely, Land had serious reservations, which he conveyed to the President. He noted that none of the Kaiser yards had shipways of sufficient length to construct the vessels, and that the cost of refitting them would be prohibitive. Boiled down to essentials, one memo from Land to the President charged that Kaiser and other shipbuilders underestimated costs in initial proposals, and that they "had little or no incentive . . . to keep costs down . . ." Ironically, Budget Director Harold Smith accused Land of similar omissions in his original proposal, noting that the chairman had also ignored hidden costs, such as annual government subsidies for operation after the ships were built. Nor had Land submitted his proposal to other government agencies "established . . . to examine policy questions of exactly this kind."[31] Roosevelt's death in April 1945 cost the Merchant Marine a sympathetic ear in the White House, and postwar government belt-tightening ultimately cut maritime spending to the bone.

Kaiser remained flexible concerning postwar uses for the yards, and he explored remote possibilities. In July 1945 engineers at "hobby-lobby" proposed that the Navy mass-produce "V-Bomb Launching Boats." Six months later, Rear Admiral R. G. Bowen informed Kaiser that "the exact forms and techniques of use of so-called 'guided missiles' are highly con-jectural at this stage." By January 1946 the Navy felt little sense of urgency in producing new weapons systems.[32]

Kaiser consistently reassured city officials in both Richmond and Port-land/Vancouver that continuing operation of the yards in some capacity was a top priority. To Maritime Commission officials, Calhoun proposed that if ship-oriented activities at the Swan Island yard in Portland were not feasible, the organization might use the space for steel and aluminum fab-rication and general machine shop work, "and possibly the manufacture of housing equipment and . . . trailers, truck bodies, farm equipment, and buses." Between V-J Day and the end of 1946, Kaiser's managers submit-ted several proposals to the Maritime Commission and the War Assets Ad-ministration (WAA) for long-term leasing or purchase of the yards.[33]

Kaiser received no encouragement in any of these endeavors. In an early 1947 letter to the Maritime Commission, Calhoun reviewed months of frustrated efforts to use the Portland yards after the war. By March 1947, the Swan Island facility employed only one thousand men on small-scale repair operations. In April, the death-knell finally sounded. Edgar Kaiser informed the *Portland Oregonian* that the yard would close. The region's management-labor council praised the Kaisers' sincere efforts and simulta-neously blasted the "bungling" of the WAA, pointing out the hardships experienced by ten thousand "unemployed veterans in the area." But the decision stood.[34]

The yards in Richmond experienced a similar fate. The Maritime Com-mission chipped away at the operations; local management drafted one proposal after another to delay closure as long as possible. In August 1946 Richmond Yard No. 3 still employed 3,500 workers, and Kaiser manage-ment hoped to continue scrapping ships and salvaging parts. With steel in short supply everywhere, scrapping of ships was a valuable service, and managers in Richmond estimated that the facilities could meet scrap steel needs for the entire West Coast. But in October 1946 the Maritime Com-mission closed the great yards. Voicing "deep regret," Henry Kaiser in-formed local officials of the decision. Four decades later, Tim A. Bedford, who presided over the closing, blamed the decision on small-minded bu-reaucrats who had been "kicked around" by naval officers during the war.[35] A few yards were reopened, briefly, during the Korean War; but their glory years were history.

Henry Kaiser did not brood about dying industries or dwell upon events he could not control. Even as he tried to keep the yards open, he focused on exciting possibilities in related enterprises. Before the end of the war, Kaiser became interested in the global passenger ship business. Roosevelt, of course, shared his enthusiasm for such endeavors. In a May

1944 communication to Secretary of Commerce Jesse Jones, Roosevelt rhapsodized:

> There are a great many delightful places in the world which are not ordinarily visited by tourist steamers. We shall have plenty of ships after the war. Many of these places in the Pacific, the Indian Ocean, the Mediterranean and the South Atlantic have been scenes of combat in this war. I am convinced that there will be thousands of Americans who will have enough money at the end of the war to take a tourist cruise and would like to see places not hitherto visited by the American President Lines or any other.

For Kaiser, gaining a share of the Pacific passenger line business would dovetail nicely with existing interests in Hawaii and elsewhere.[36]

Kaiser's long-time associates in Six Companies avoided certain domestic industries not directly related to the construction business, but several with experience in overseas endeavors applauded the passenger line initiative. Stephen D. and Kenneth Bechtel, Felix Kahn, and John A. McCone encouraged acquisition of American President Lines. Kahn was directly involved in preliminary discussions with Vice-Admiral Land and other high-level government officials. Had negotiations borne fruit, any purchase would probably have been a joint venture.[37]

The passenger ship initiative fell through in mid-1944. The reasons remain shrouded. According to Cadman, Kaiser lost interest when it became clear that it would be very difficult to turn a profit. Cadman also noted that there was "too much regulation of services and type of vessles the line would operate." Most interesting was what Cadman's memo ignored. If the highly volatile international political situation bothered company officials, such concerns never intruded into internal corporate correspondence. During the war, Kaiser met high-level Nationalist Chinese officials. Chiang Kai-Shek's father-in-law, T. V. Soong, was one of the world's richest men and a sophisticated international operator. Like Kaiser, Soong maintained a suite at the Shoreham Hotel in Washington throughout the war, and their paths crossed. Kaiser and Soong probably discussed postwar possibilities for U.S. investments in China as early as 1942. Kaiser's associates negotiated with the Nationalist Chinese leaders through 1945. They investigated prospects in shipbuilding and repair, general manufacturing, and express cargo service. Unbounded faith in capitalism was orthodoxy in the Kaiser organization. Apparently, nobody doubted that Chiang represented enlightened leadership. Although he questioned the feasibility of passenger service, Cadman concluded in 1944 that "a Far East express cargo service offers an attractive investment possibility."[38] Kaiser, Cadman and other managers shared the fascination with Oriental trade felt by generations of American businessmen.

Huge commitments to other ventures and rapidly changing international economic and political conditions diverted Kaiser from large overseas investments in the immediate postwar period. But corporate investigations into long-term overseas potential underscored a stirring of foreign interest largely dormant since the Cuba years. Within months of V-J Day, Kaiser management invested in modest-sized overseas deposits of bauxite, to supply newly acquired aluminum facilities. This was but the beginning of significant expansion of foreign investments in diverse fields.

Although Kaiser decided against trans-Pacific shipping in 1944, he remained interested in the business. In 1960, when he was rapidly expanding cement and real estate development in Hawaii, he explored commercial shipping between the U.S. mainland and the Orient. Such a commitment to Far East shipping at that time would have been consistent with burgeoning investments in Oceania, Australia, and elsewhere in the Pacific.[39]

Analyzing the enormous range of major commitments Kaiser made between 1944 and 1946, one is struck by the fact that while many were outgrowths of months, even years of planning, others were almost whimsical. Insiders knew he meticulously planned a major effort to expand steel operations; and he hired automotive designers years before he plunged into the business in 1945. On the other hand, although he had explored postwar prospects in light metals, few in the organization foresaw the magnitude of his commitment to aluminum. The federal government opened a small window of opportunity in that field in 1946, and Kaiser and a few associates were brave enough to dive through. Had circumstances in half a dozen other fields been slightly altered, the organization might well have emphasized entirely different product lines in the postwar period. The years 1944 to 1946 thus marked a critical period, during which Kaiser made many of the commitments shaping the future of his burgeoning corporate empire.

9
Debacle in Detroit

The June 8, 1935, issue of the *Automotive Daily News* described an innovative concept in urban transportation unveiled recently at the International Automobile Show in Berlin: a tiny three-wheel covered vehicle, powered by a one-cylinder motor with 500 cc. piston displacement. In passing, the article mentioned, "The builder is Kaiser."[1] At that time, of course, Henry J. Kaiser was building dams, not automobiles. Close associates remember how Kaiser had enjoyed tinkering with engines with young Edgar, and that the boss enjoyed driving his own big cars at hair-raising speeds. The thought of making and marketing cars had probably not entered his mind by 1935; but the "Kaiser" story of a small car unveiled far away was a portent of the future.

A decade later, Henry Kaiser was deeply involved in automobiles. He delayed formally announcing his intention of joining the increasingly exclusive automobile fraternity until he and Joseph Washington Frazer formed a partnership on August 9, 1945. However, Kaiser had been "imagineering" automobiles for some time. In his widely publicized appeal for postwar planning before the National Association of Manufacturers (NAM) in December 1942 he urged Detroit to introduce 1945 models to future consumers. Some entrepreneurs rejected any distraction from the serious task of winning the war. Ironically, Joe Frazer led the charge, calling Kaiser's ideas "half-baked . . . stupid bushwah."[2] Although the westerner did not mention entering the automobile business, alert Kaiser watchers sensed that he was considering it.

In fact, Kaiser had already made his opening moves. Several weeks earlier, he had hired R. Buckminster Fuller to design a "1945 model Dymaxion." The two men shared a passion for unconventional thinking; Fuller proposed a three-wheeled vehicle seating four persons in the front seat. In addition to negotiating with Fuller, Kaiser encouraged Howard V. "Lindy"

Lindbergh and his engineers to pursue automobile ideas at "hobby-lobby."[3] Beginning in early 1943, they tinkered with automobiles and other products. Among dozens of enterprises, automobiles excited their boss the most.

Kaiser's automotive dream became the worst-kept "secret" in town. If any doubted his intentions, he ended the suspense at a New York press conference early in January 1943. Kaiser stated that if nobody else produced "lightweight, cheaper automobiles," he would. Publicly, Detroit "welcomed" his initiative. Alvan Macauley, president of the Automotive Council for War Production, praised Kaiser's "pioneering spirit," which could serve the country well in war or peace. Macauley admitted that "No automobile manufacturer believes he has built a perfect automobile," and there was "plenty of room for Mr. Kaiser's talent." According to the *Detroit Free Press*, established manufacturers lost little sleep over his challenge: ". . . the fact is that while the industry welcomes a new competitor, it is so well attuned to its job that the welcome is practically a dare."[4]

The badinage between Kaiser and Detroit auto executives in no way resembled his hostile exchanges with the steel moguls. By early 1943, Kaiser was used to trading jabs with government officers, and he deftly applied them to auto makers. In a mischievous letter to Fred Zeder of Chrysler, Kaiser commented on existing designs. Kaiser guessed that Chrysler executives seldom drove their own contraptions, leaving that chore to chauffeurs. His helpful advice to Zeder concluded:

> Oil pan should be lowered slightly so it will hit everything. The fact that it misses once in a while is very disconcerting to the driver. . . . Blind body corners don't restrict vision enough. Make 'em wider and watch the driving accidents increase. . . . Door handles of various assortments are wonderful. They'll do everything but pick pockets.

Auto men probably enjoyed these exchanges, since few took his threat seriously. By one account, they expected to "take Kaiser like Dewey took Manila."[5]

Even in his most optimistic moments, Kaiser never seriously considered creating a vertically integrated organization like Ford. He would have to obtain many parts from other suppliers. By early 1943 he was negotiating with manufacturers of engines and other key components. He bargained for engines with Continental Motors and Crosley. He also considered horizontal expansion into taxis, jeeps, trucks, and other service vehicles.[6]

While Kaiser sparred with auto makers and potential suppliers, his engineers applied themselves to immediate tasks. They disassembled existing automobiles to learn how the best were built and worked on body designs. In the summer of 1943, the Army considered using lightweight magnesium as a major structural component for jeeps and asked Lindbergh's engineers to build several prototypes. The Kaiser organization proposed manufacturing 100,000 jeeps: half on the East Coast, half on the West Coast. Engineers visualized reducing the jeep's weight by as much as a thousand pounds, between 40 to 50 percent. But tests revealed that light magnesium jeeps possessed insufficient tensile strength.[7]

Kaiser's engineers sought help in body design. Kaiser signed a contract with Detroit-based Harger and Probst, automobile designers. By mid-summer 1943, he envisioned filling the needs of hundreds of thousands of Americans who, in his view, weren't being served by Detroit. More than a year before Henry Ford II talked about producing a "low-priced, light-weight car," Kaiser announced hopes of mass-producing a $400 postwar automobile. He believed that ten million Americans would purchase such cars through service stations. Thus, he might avoid "middleman" charges of an expensive dealer organization. Experienced auto makers in Detroit chuckled at Kaiser's naïveté in sales, but they were less amused when he added disingenuously: "I'd hate for anyone to feel that I am out to hurt the existing industry. I'm aiming for a market that present cars reach only third or fourth hand."[8]

Why Kaiser spoke of turning out automobiles for $400 remains a mystery. He repeatedly brought up the subject in 1943 and 1944, but received no encouragement from experienced automobile makers. Harger and Probst urged Kaiser to concentrate on jeeps, even in the postwar period. In addition, they argued that Kaiser could produce inexpensive passenger cars only through an alliance with a major producer. Ralph E. Knight, a Kaiser engineer, agreed with Harger and Probst.[9] One plausible explanation of why Kaiser stuck with the $400 figure was that he was so busy with other projects that he never seriously figured costs. He was also an inveterate optimist, and he was stubborn. Perhaps he convinced himself that where demand existed, he and "his boys" could meet it. They had repeatedly achieved the "impossible." Why couldn't they produce a $400 car?

Kaiser was not a solitary visionary. In the summer of 1944 a few producers entertained similar thoughts. Such plans may have been prompted in part by Kaiser's challenge. Henry Ford II announced plans for "a modernized four-cylinder Model-A" priced at $500. Ford's rhetoric was a throwback to that of his grandfather thirty years earlier, stressing the need to serve the "thousands of persons who can't afford higher-priced automobiles." A few independents also considered models in this price range.[10]

By the spring of 1945, peace was clearly at hand. Postwar reconversion had long been at the forefront of Kaiser's thinking, and he was primed for action. In autos, he received enthusiastic encouragement from R. J. Thomas, president of the UAW-CIO. In a June visit to the West Coast, Thomas advised Kaiser on numerous technical aspects and urged him to go ahead with inexpensive, lightweight vehicles. As late as July 11, Kaiser considered joining forces with E. C. Mathis, who had already achieved modest success in the field. But several advisors opposed a partnership with Mathis, and Kaiser followed their advice.[11]

Had anyone told Kaiser in early July that within a month he would be in the automboile business, he would have beamed; had he been informed that his future partner was Joe Frazer, he might have registered stunned disbelief. Their relationship got off to a rocky start, considering Frazer's pungent reaction to Kaiser's NAM speech. In many respects, the men were direct opposites. Frazer, the son of well-to-do parents, had been educated at Hotchkiss, then Yale, and had spent most of his thirty years in the automobile business as an executive, most recently at Willys-Overland. One critic wrote that the only callouses on Frazer's hands came from swinging a golf club, but this was unfair. Frazer had a reputation as a hard-working manager, particularly effective in sales.[12]

Frazer possessed talents and experience Kaiser admired. Obviously the war created unusual opportunites, but jeep sales under Frazer's leadership at Willys-Overland jumped from $7 million in 1939 to $170 million in 1944. He quit Willys-Overland the latter year and bought controlling interest in Graham-Paige, a moribund operation that built a few cars and a good deal of farm equipment. In July 1945 Frazer had a small plant in Detroit and sophisticated designs for his own postwar automobile. His most attractive assets were two which Kaiser lacked: a proven record in consumer-goods sales and years of experience in the car business.[13]

For his part, although personally wealthy and the majority stockholder in Graham-Paige, Frazer needed huge amounts of fresh capital to succeed with his postwar models. Despite social connections and school ties, he was unable to raise sufficient funds from eastern investors. In early July 1945 he approached Amadeo P. Giannini, of the Bank of America. Although impressed by Frazer, Giannini wanted to develop California's postwar economy and was uninterested in automobiles in Detroit. He advised Frazer to look up Kaiser, since he knew that Kaiser wanted to enter the field and was seriously considering setting up production facilities in southern California. Together, the men might provide the backbone of a potent western automobile organization.[14]

Intermediaries arranged for them to confer in San Francisco. To the surprise of some, the July 17 meeting went well, as the former adversaries shared their visions of the future. Both Kaiser and Frazer were superb salesmen, and each was on his best behavior that day. For the moment, they buried basic differences which would plague their relationship in later years. Convinced that a partnership could succeed, they proceeded with breathtaking speed. Eight days later, they jointly announced creation of

Kaiser-Frazer Corporation. Initial capitalization was a mere $5 million, each partner putting up half. Two weeks later the company formally incorporated in Nevada.[15]

Although Kaiser was gaining a reputation as a friend of the worker, the primary reason UAW leaders encouraged his entry into the field was transparent. In early May 1945 Henry Ford, Sr., had announced that he had no postwar plans for Willow Run. If no other producer took over the enormous RFC-owned defense plant near Detroit, local union members might face hard times. New companies such as Kaiser-Frazer would need thousands of workers; this would obviously provide added leverage for UAW officials in bargaining with existing producers.

Kaiser-Frazer also received encouragement from another key source: the federal government. Ford's departure from Willow Run left RFC officials holding what might become a $100 million white elephant. Agency officials wanted to encourage new competitors, and they hoped to lease the plant to a company with a solid chance for long-term survival. But all parties realized that Kaiser-Frazer required a much larger capital base than it possessed. Following frenetic conferences with government officials, Kaiser and Frazer agreed to offer a substantial stock issue. Reassured, RFC agreed to a five-year lease on remarkably generous terms: $500,000 rent the first year, $850,000 the second, and $1.25 million thereafter.[16] Neither partner had well-established contacts on Wall Street, but Frazer called in Cyrus Eaton, a Cleveland financier. Late in September, the Securities and Exchange Commission (SEC) approved an issue of 1.7 million shares at ten dollars per share; eager investors oversubscribed the offering by a multiple of six.

With plenty of space and some start-up funding in hand, the partners now had to prove that there was action behind what some believed was boastful rhetoric. Jokes about the new combine were rampant in the lush offices and clubrooms of the Detroit establishment. One veteran said: "Kaiser hasn't found out yet that automobiles don't have bows, sterns, and rudders." Another doubter joked: "They got the wrong name for that outfit—they ought to call it Barnum and Bailey." A third offered a line which became an industry favorite: "What are they going to name their car, the Willit Run?"[17]

With peace at hand, automobile producers commenced a pell-mell rush to turn out vehicles. Consumers, frustrated by four years of empty showrooms, would buy almost anything on wheels. Detroit knew it, and manufacturers dusted off drawings for 1942 models, added a few strips of chrome, and rushed into production. Would-be buyers fawned over salesmen on showroom floors, seeking prominent spots on long waiting lists for new cars. Some impatient purchasers shortened waits with hefty bribes.

Industry analysts knew that the postwar period would bring major realignments. The cumulative demand created by sixteen years of depression and war presented opportunites for aggressive independent producers, or even newcomers. There might never again be such a good chance to crack the Big Three, which controlled 90 percent of the market in 1941. Experts respected independents such as Packard, Studebaker, Hudson, and Nash, but it was soon obvious that none of them would seriously challenge the giants. Tucker Motors made noises about becoming a major innovator, and a group of investors tried to create Playboy Motors. Neither thrived, and analysts eventually realized that Kaiser-Frazer had the best chance of challenging the Big Three. The other independents, it seemed, hoped basically to retain the specialized markets they had served before the war.[18]

Early in 1946, in an effort to impress both the industry and the public, Kaiser and Frazer hosted an auto show at New York's plush Waldorf-Astoria Hotel. The partners displayed models of two vehicles, the Kaiser and the Frazer. They flew in dozens of reporters from Detroit and a bevy of Hollywood starlets. Estimates of the cost of the extravaganza ran from $25,000 to $100,000. By one account, it manifested "a jubilant atmosphere combining a Billy Sunday evangelistic meeting, a world's series, a political convention, and a Tommy Manville wedding party."[19] But it was a bargain in terms of the favorable publicity generated. For four days, 156,000 prospective buyers formed blocks-long queues just to gain glimpses of the models. Although salesmen could not quote firm prices or delivery dates, New Yorkers ordered almost 9,000 of the prospective vehicles. At a banquet for company officials and guests, Kaiser and Frazer exchanged emotional tributes; Kaiser chirruped that they already had orders for over 660,000 cars and predicted they would produce 13 million. In the excitement of the moment, nobody challenged his figures, which he manufactured from thin air. But the public shared his optimism; that week, Kaiser-Frazer stock hit its all-time high of $24 per share.[20]

While gearing up for production, Kaiser-Frazer executives made a key decision profoundly affecting the company's ultimate direction and fate. Kaiser imagined producing inexpensive and innovative vehicles, featuring lightweight bodies and front-wheel drive. But when Kaiser-Frazer was formed, his visions were artists' creations, bold lines on drawing boards, and a few plaster models. Frazer urged going ahead with full-sized, conventional vehicles. Besides the fact that the easterner had thirty years of experience and workable plans, delivering cars to customers fast was a critical consideration, particularly for a new firm. If Kaiser-Frazer could turn out cars quickly, establish a record of dependability, and develop a solid core of loyal customers, the company might succeed.

Prompt, high-volume output was crucial, but Kaiser also had other reasons to accept Frazer's logic. Thousands of former auto workers needed employment; if managers could quickly gear up at Willow Run, they might attract experienced workers returning from the war who would otherwise rejoin the Big Three. In addition, now that they had sold stock, both partners' reputations among rival entrepreneurs were squarely on the line. They had to succeed, or they'd be the laughingstock of country-club locker rooms. Both men detested such images; they could tolerate animosity, but not ridicule. Perhaps the most compelling reason was their simple desire to get into production quickly and test the competition. Frazer's plan offered the quickest way.

Despite the hoopla surrounding the display at the Waldorf-Astoria, some experts still doubted that the company would turn out a single car. Before production began, formidable challenges had to be met. Dozens of expensive, complicated production machines had to be located and installed. Reliable sources of raw materials and parts had to be found. A network of sales and service centers was required. Union contracts had to be settled. A hundred more problems lay ahead, many of them unforeseen by the partners.

The difficulties were overlooked in the glow of enthusiasm during 1945 and 1946. Kaiser received dozens of letters from prospective dealers begging to market cars. Although most were from servicemen and other average Americans pursuing postwar dreams, he also heard from celebrities. From Boston came an inquiry by eighty-three-year-old retired mayor John F. "Honey Fitz" Fitzgerald, grandfather of a future President.[21] Frazer's contacts were even more critical in slapping together an organization of 3,500 dealers after eight months of operations. From the start, however, many were clearly marginal risks. A survey of forty-one dealers in northern California in April 1946 revealed average working capital of $29,183 and net worth of $78,949. As long as sales remained brisk and dealers held small inventories, undercapitalization did not hamper the dealer organization or operations at Willow Run. However, the situation portended major problems when competitive conditions returned. Historian Richard M. Langworth concludes that far too many Kaiser-Frazer dealers were simply "postwar profiteers whose only aim was fast sales and a speedy exit when the local market was saturated."[22]

Company managers hoped to recruit a skilled work force in short order. That the Big Three had most of the experienced assembly-line workers and seasoned managers at first seemed a minor competitive disadvantage. Of greater immediate concern was the plant location. Willow Run was thirty-six miles from downtown Detroit, much farther from homes of potential recruits than competitors' facilities. By the fall of 1946 Kaiser-Frazer was trying to overcome that disadvantage by constructing hundreds of single-family houses at West Willow, close to the facility. Fortunately, Kaiser-Frazer enjoyed an extended honeymoon with union officials. In January 1946, when on strike against other producers, the UAW shocked the Big

Three by announcing a one-year pact with Kaiser-Frazer. According to the UAW's R. J. Thomas, negotiations with Kaiser-Frazer had been "the most pleasant" in the union's history. He promised: "We are going to do all possible to see that Kaiser-Frazer becomes a successful company, and we will help them in every way." To cynical analysts, Thomas appeared barely able to hide his glee at concessions received from Kaiser-Frazer and the potential trouble that meant for the Big Three.[23]

During the first few months, Kaiser-Frazer experienced serious difficulties. Sophisticated observers did not expect the company to show immediate profits. The consensus was that the break-even point was 75,000 cars; in 1946 the company turned out only 11,754 vehicles, with $10 million in net sales, losing over $19 million. Some early investors who had expected quick profits doubted their wisdom. By August 1946, shares had dropped from a high of $24 to $15. When the cavernous plant yielded new cars only in driblets, cynics in Detroit hooted; "If you can't take a ride in a Kaiser car, take a ride on his stock."[24] The partners worked twenty-hour days, sorting out seemingly endless problems.

A year later it was their turn to celebrate. On September 25, 1947, Willow Run turned out its 100,000th car. Employees received a day off to celebrate the milestone; the plant produced 16,535 cars that month, and another 18,701 in October. Best of all, the cars sold well. Although underpowered compared to some competitors' medium-sized models, they were gracefully designed, with excellent front and side vision and several advanced safety features. All too soon, however, lines of buyers at Kaiser-Frazer dealerships disappeared. Company advertisements tried to turn this into a positive: "You can get a Kaiser or a Frazer." At Big Three dealerships customers still had to wait weeks, even months; in addition they accepted pittances for trade-in allowances. As late as May 1948, consumers regularly paid $500 over list price for Pontiacs and Dodges, $700 for Chevrolets. At Kaiser-Frazer dealerships, new cars were often discounted, and customers generally negotiated Blue Book prices for trade-ins.[25]

In hindsight, the market for Kaisers and Frazers clearly peaked just when corporate officials geared up for big-time competition. But there were few pessimists in 1947 and 1948. Kaiser-Frazer stock dipped to $7 in the summer of 1947, but by October it rebounded to $17. Those maintaining faith in the new company cheered when the 1947 annual report showed a pre-tax profit of $19 million. Equally encouraging, net sales skyrocketed from $10 million in 1946 to $260 million a year later.[26]

Knowledgeable insiders realized that producing 144,507 automobiles in 1947 was a remarkable achievement. Few companies faced more imposing obstacles to long-term success than Kaiser-Frazer early in 1946. The thorniest problem was developing and retaining dependable sources of steel, engines, and thousands of specialized parts. There were huge steel shortages, and everybody scrambled for supplies. Kaiser-Frazer competed with established producers who guaranteed suppliers huge orders into the foreseeable future. Even more important, whether or not they were influenced by the Big Three, many steel producers and auto-parts suppliers relegated the newcomers to the end of the line. As noted, steel producers had deeply resented Kaiser's entry into their field in 1942. They saw an opportunity to get even.[27]

Big Steel gave early indications that shipments to Kaiser-Frazer would be few and far between. In February 1946 Kaiser-Frazer obtained modest commitments from a few small independents, but shipments amounted to a trickle. During early months of production, the auto company received shipments from Fontana; but needs were far greater than the western plant could meet, and freight costs were prohibitive. On February 19, 1946, four days after settlement of a nation-wide steel strike, Edgar Kaiser and Joe Frazer called on Republic Steel in an attempt to open at least one door among the major producers. They were hopeful, since Tom Girdler had provided technical advice when Fontana was built. Their optimism was quickly dashed. They were prepared for Girdler's lamentations about being so oversold that he could not even take care of old customers. But his tone quickly became hostile. To Edgar's suggestion that if Republic refused to supply steel to new customers, the government might determine allocations, Girdler testily replied that he realized that "certain parties" might "get a stranglehold on this man Truman," as they had on Roosevelt. His allusion to Kaiser's previous government dealings was obvious. Girdler then launched into a tirade against Kaiser-Frazer. He charged that the company had deliberately embarrassed the Big Three by settling with the UAW just six weeks earlier when that union was striking against GM. He voiced outrage that Kaiser Steel had recently pulled a similar stunt against Big Steel. Joe Frazer recalled, "Throughout the entire conversation, Mr. Girdler was most profane and really abusive . . ."[28]

The two men were shaken when they left Republic's offices; and they anticipated a huge fight in obtaining crucial raw materials. But they recruited allies; among others, union leaders in Detroit provided help. R. J. Thomas wired President Truman, charging that Big Steel was colluding with GM over steel shipments. According to Thomas, GM hoarded huge quantities of steel to frustrate other producers. This was particularly curious, considering that the UAW strike against GM was three months old, with no signs of letting up. Thomas urged Truman to take "immediate drastic action to remedy a situation which may become a national scandal." Truman, having refused to intervene in the recently settled steel strike, rejected this demand also.[29]

Steel shortages plagued Kaiser-Frazer for two years. As late as September 1947 Henry Kaiser complained that U.S. Steel had reneged on an earlier pledge to supply steel. But shipments gradually loosened up. Early in 1946 Kaiser-Frazer received steel only from Fontana and four small, widely scattered eastern mills. Henry Kaiser eased supplies by gaining control of several small mills in the Midwest. Another source was Portsmouth Steel, recently organized by Kaiser's financial consultant, Cyrus Eaton. For a stiff price of $3 million, Eaton sold Kaiser one-fourth interest in that company. By late 1947, company officials were doing business with larger outfits such as Bethlehem, Weirton, Great Lakes, and Inland. But the established steel producers charged huge premiums, and Kaiser-Frazer had to pass extra costs along to consumers.[30]

Although Big Steel executives never revealed their reasons for gradual acceptance of the automotive newcomers, the reasons appear transparent. Undoubtedly, Kaiser-Frazer's early success impressed the steel companies. After the 100,000th car milestone in September 1947, it was clear that Kaiser-Frazer had staying power. By mid-1947 the company claimed 3 percent of the market. Steel producers realized that if they failed to make token gestures toward a potentially important automobile producer when supplies were tight, they would find closed doors at Kaiser-Frazer when competitive conditions returned to their industry. Perhaps even more important, several congressional subcommittees examined discrimination in allocations, both direct and indirect. From a public relations standpoint, Big Steel had little to gain from penalizing Kaiser-Frazer.

Regardless of Big Steel's policies, Kaiser-Frazer demonstrated ability to take care of itself. Managers became expert scavengers. In 1946 and 1947 scarcely a day went by at Willow Run without at least one supply crisis. Steel remained the most common deficiency. Late one afternoon body presses had almost exhausted the inventory of sheet steel. Within hours, alert "road expediters" (external troubleshooters) located forty-seven thousand pounds of the vital product at Bethlehem's works in Buffalo and rented six idle DC-3s in Philadelphia. At 4:00 the next morning the precious steel was unloaded at Willow Run. Similar anecdotes are told about procurement of dozens of other scarce components, such as axles, doors, and transmission assemblies. According to one analyst, Kaiser and his top executives continued scavenging just as they had during World War II. Kaiser-Frazer's jerry-built systems for obtaining supplies appeared designed by a deranged Rube Goldberg. Somehow, they worked.[31]

During a decade of automobile production, Kaiser-Frazer experienced only two profitable years, 1947 and 1948. Late in 1948, prospects still looked good. Sales were strong, and two new, improved models appeared. Although the Big Three lured away some large-volume Kaiser-Frazer dealers and weaker distributors showed signs of distress, the organization appeared stable, with roughly four thousand outlets. New car output rose from 144,507 in 1947 to 181,316 in 1948, and sales volume increased from

$260 million to $341 million.[32] That profits declined sharply from $19 million to $10 million worried top management, but to the rank and file and the public, corporate officials radiated optimism. Although Henry and Edgar Kaiser were keenly aware that competitive conditions were returning by the end of 1948, they believed that new models would bring continuing success and profits.

Unfortunately, 1947 and 1948 proved to be Kaiser-Frazer's high-water mark; from 1949 until suspension of conventional domestic vehicle production in 1955, corporate fortunes fell steadily. By the end of 1948 there was mounting evidence that the honeymoon between consumers and Kaiser-Frazer was over, that buyers were becoming choosy. Slower-moving cars were piling up in storage areas in Detroit. No longer would buyers gratefully accept anything that ran. They demanded something new: cars with engineering innovations and stylistic flair.

Kaiser-Frazer received high marks for pioneering in technology and style. For visibility, safety, and comfort, industry critics and consumers gave their models plaudits.[33] But this wasn't enough; in key respects their products came up short. Consumers had two major complaints: prices and quality. A few potential customers were disappointed that Kaiser never mass-produced a $400 car. One ex-GI, shocked at Kaiser-Frazer sticker prices of $2,400 to $2,700, informed Kaiser; "I managed to scrape together the $400 which you mentioned . . . But at that rate all I can afford to buy is 4 tires (with free air)." Industry analysts estimated that the cars were overpriced from $300 to $500, an obstacle not insurmountable when demand was high and competitors received large premiums over sticker prices. But it was only a matter of time until competitive conditions returned and overpricing became a severe handicap. Just as worrisome, Kaiser-Frazer customers complained about product quality and poor service at dealerships. One buyer listed fifteen defects in his four-month-old Kaiser, after only four thousand miles. He praised the local dealer's effort, but commented that retailers could not rebuild every car they sold. He concluded: "Gentlemen, when I put as much money into a car as the Kaiser cost I expect to receive something beside a lot of petty annoyances from it, and so far it was been nothing but an aggravation."[34]

Customer complaints, a trickle when supplies were scarce, became a steady stream as competitive conditions returned. One customer expressed disappointment at having bought a 1948 Kaiser Special for $2,465 in December 1947, claiming that a comparably equipped Buick 51 cost $300 less. Among other shortcomings, the buyer complained, "the motor is sluggish; the body, dust pans, bumpers and seemingly every joint and piece of the assembly rattle, creak, sings, and groans; rain leaks in through the windshield and windows. . . ." A schoolteacher from Chicago lamented that she had traded in her "good old Plymouth" for a Kaiser. "The paint was peeled off, and it had a drab, wan look, but it never caused me any trouble and took me many happy miles all over the United States. I now have 7,000 miles on my Kaiser and have had a perfect nightmare of a time."[35] Quality-control problems were easy to diagnose, but difficult to fix. Top management was dominated by Californians, with plenty of shipyard and construction experience. But they learned about cars on the job, as did assembly line workers. They gradually learned to build good cars; by then it was too late.

Other problems emerged. Although union relations were cordial by industry standards, Willow Run was not immune to labor tensions. Like the Big Three, Kaiser-Frazer experienced vexing work stoppages over what seemed to management to be petty issues. When fourteen workers walked off the job in April 1948 because of a dispute over rules for filing grievance charges, the entire 4,800-worker plant shut down. Some workers believed that the company followed the industry practice of hiring spies. Management held varying views concerning relations with the UAW. Henry Kaiser remained personally friendly with Walter Reuther and R. J. Thomas. And Clay P. Bedford recalled his union dealings in warm terms. But some lower-level managers believed the UAW deftly manipulated the inexperienced and vulnerable newcomers; they believed local union officers sensed that Edgar and Henry Kaiser were easy marks and often abused the Kaisers' sense of fair play. This assessment rings true. One former Kaiser executive claimed that Kaiser could place himself in the workers' shoes and he hated the idea of production delays and work stoppages. Hence Kaiser-Frazer settled contract talks quickly and generally paid slightly higher wages than did the Big Three. A former administrator of the Kaiser-Frazer UAW Pension Fund recalled a union meeting in which Walter Reuther advised local union members to eliminate some of their demands: "You will have to take them off the list because Edgar will give them to you and the company will go out of business." The official concluded, "The story illustrates . . . the desire of Mr. Kaiser to get along with the workers." Henry Kaiser and Walter Reuther treated each other as civilized statesmen. But local union officials, pressured by disgruntled workers, frequently confronted middle-level managers who had little experience with direct line responsibilities.[36]

By early 1949 it was increasingly clear that relations between Henry Kaiser and Joe Frazer were deteriorating. Basically, each believed he was more fit to run the business. No clear lines of authority were drawn at the start, although there was a vague understanding that Kaiser would handle production aand Frazer would manage sales. During the early months, both men expressed faith that problems would be worked out. But they interfered in each other's side of operations from the start. Rumors of a breakup surfaced even before they produced their first automobiles. In

June 1946 Kaiser heatedly denied the story: "I want to spike these rumors right now. They are totally unfounded and absolutely malicious." [37]

Despite Kaiser's disclaimer, tensions were palpable from the start. They centered about two basic differences: business philosophies and personal lifestyles. Frazer was aghast that Kaiser's managers pushed maximum production, while ignoring costs. In November 1946 Frazer returned from a fruitless trip east seeking additional funding; he warned Edgar: "We have gotten a reputation throughout the banking circles of being extravagant operators." Frazer believed Kaiser's managers were "living high, wide and handsome," and he listed numerous ways to reduce expenses. During 1947 and 1948 the company earned profits and Frazer hid his feelings, but his misgivings burst into the open when losses mounted in 1949. Frazer was also alienated by what he considered Kaiser men's pride in flouting established industry methods, a "we can do anything" arrogance. [38]

For their part, Kaiser and his subordinates cooled toward Frazer gradually. They believed that his concern over costs was short-sighted, and that economy could be achieved with high-volume production. The westerners increasingly considered Frazer an old-fashioned, "stick-in-the-mud" operator. Further, they held low opinions of some of Frazer's managers, whom some of them believed were Big Three rejects. Kaiser's managers also thought that the Yale man was hypocritical in criticizing their lifestyles. Frazer and his wife were socially ambitious; they spent time on the New York society circuit and yachting at Newport. The upshot was that Frazer resigned as president in 1949 and Edgar Kaiser took over. In a face-saving gesture, Frazer remained on the board with an annual salary of $75,000. But his influence waned, and most of his men soon left the company. [39]

Turning points in the history of Kaiser-Frazer are fairly easy to pinpoint. Prior to 1949 most signs were good; after that, almost all were bad. However, one episode in 1948 presaged the decline. As production peaked, the partners needed additional capital to finance continued expansion. Frazer had failed to locate underwriters on Wall Street. But their associates included Cyrus Eaton, who had handled two earlier public offerings. Early in 1948 the partners asked him to manage a third. They were somewhat disenchanted with Eaton, in part because as head of Portsmouth Steel he had ordered stiff price hikes, adding $5 million to Kaiser-Frazer's production costs. But the company needed more money, and the partners decided on a third stock offering. The consequences were disastrous; the primary result was a rancorous lawsuit which neither side won, but which damaged each severely.

Kaiser-Frazer needed $18 million and hoped to raise it by selling 1.5 million shares at $13.50 per share, less commissions. The sale was postponed in December 1947 and January 1948 because outstanding stock showed weakness. Finally, three underwriters, led by Eaton's firm, Otis and Company, and including Allen and Company and First California, tentatively agreed to sell the stock. They charged a stiff commission of $1.50 per share. The parties also agreed that to maintain a strong market Kaiser-Frazer would "stabilize" the issue before the offering by purchasing enough shares on the open market to keep the price at $13.50. The underwriters purportedly assured company officials that 15,000 to 20,000 shares would suffice.[40]

At this point things began going wrong. On February 3, the day before the scheduled offering, sell orders poured in and Kaiser-Frazer bought 186,000 shares at a cost of $2.5 million. Even worse, Bill Daley, president of Otis, informed Kaiser-Frazer that the underwriters wanted to cancel the deal. Henry Kaiser was incensed; although they had not yet signed final papers, they had reached a "gentleman's agreement." Under intense pressure from Kaiser, the underwriters finally signed a preliminary agreement to market 900,000 shares. Unfortunately, the underwriters' indecision had already done much damage. February 3 marked a general weakening of stocks, and widespread rumors of disagreements between Kaiser-Frazer and the underwriters eroded investor confidence even further.[41]

On February 4, the underwriters reluctantly tried to unload the stock. During the morning and early afternoon hours, they sold about half of their 900,000 shares. But sell orders came in nearly as fast, and they suspended sales. At 3 P.M. Eaton came into Kaiser's New York office and told him that it would be a grave mistake to keep pushing the issue on a sour market. When Kaiser insisted that Eaton was bound not only by honor but by a legal document, Eaton "flew into a rage" and threatened that "hell would be a-poppin'" if Kaiser held the underwriters to the contract.[42]

Although the underwriters had signed one document, Kaiser-Frazer did not actually deliver the stock to Otis and Company until February 9. As later court testimony revealed, Eaton spent the next several days looking frantically for escape clauses in the contract. Eventually his lawyers found two apparent loopholes. By law, if any Kaiser-Frazer stockholder filed suit against the new issue before it was finalized, Otis could cancel the contract. When lawyers for the two sides met in Cleveland on the morning of the ninth, Eaton's representatives consumed several hours meticulously examining each document. They were obviously stalling. After a long lunch, one of Eaton's lawyers pulled an early afternoon edition of a Cleveland paper from his briefcase. It revealed that one James F. Masterson had filed just such a suit earlier that morning in Detroit. Based on this new evidence, two underwriters canceled the deal (Allen and Company honored its commitment).

Six years of legal warfare ensued. Testimony revealed that David Martin, Masterson's lawyer, had earlier worked for Otis and Company. Eaton denied any recollection that Martin had ever worked for him, but he could not explain a flurry of phone calls involving himself and U.S. Senator Robert J. Bulkeley, Bulkeley and Masterson, and Masterson and Martin. Although evidence against Eaton was purely circumstantial, astute observers believed that, at the very least, the financier and his allies had "encouraged" the lawsuit.

Kaiser-Frazer absorbed legal blows too. Eaton's lawyers revealed that company accountants had substantially misrepresented fourth-quarter 1947 earnings. They charged that Kaiser-Frazer had entered fraudulent figures in a registration statement for the stock issue which the SEC had cleared. The dispute centered on a December 1947 inventory adjustment which hiked quarterly earnings from a projected $900,000 through November to about $4 million at the end of the year. For one of the few times in his career, Kaiser's honesty and integrity were challenged.[43]

The case dragged on through agonizing years of suits and counter-suits, awards of damages to one side or the other, and subsequent appeals. The case consumed thousands of work-hours, and created volumes of conflicting testimony. Predictably, only the lawyers profited. The trial damaged both principals' reputations. The SEC suspended Otis and Company for several months, but later evidence revealed that the commission had carelessly reviewed Kaiser-Frazer's registration statement. Kaiser-Frazer also had to counteract negative publicity. Following the opening maneuvers in the drawn-out fiasco, the price of Kaiser-Frazer stock plunged. A month after the new issue, it stood at $8.75.[44]

Eaton was a crafty, powerful enemy. Throughout the six-year fight, he deluged national politicians and opinion-makers with highly biased, unfavorable "facts" concerning Kaiser's automobile venture and other enterprises. The data supplied by Eaton provided grist for several government probes of Kaiser's activities.[45] Kaiser's publicists spent hundreds of hours countering Eaton's accusations in Washington. Ultimately, both sides tired of the fruitless struggle. With UMW President John L. Lewis uncharacteristically acting as a peacemaker, they eventually agreed to a truce.[46]

In retrospect, even if the stock-offering had succeeded, the company would still have been headed for trouble. Years later, Kaiser admitted that his biggest mistake was failure to raise $150 to $200 million when enthusiasm was at its peak. With a capital fund three or four times greater than the $53 million actually raised, the company could have spent tens of millions of dollars retooling with modern equipment and designing and testing new models. Instead, in 1946 Kaiser-Frazer introduced unexceptional products which, with a few cosmetic additions, changed little for three years. What customers had snapped up in 1946 drew ridicule in 1949. Meanwhile, Big Three firms invested heavily in research and development, resulting in more appealing vehicles in 1949 and later years.

The history of Kaiser-Frazer between 1949 and 1955 reveals isolated hope-inspiring incidents and a long list of numbing, depressing setbacks. Although the corporation set all-time sales records in vehicles produced and sold in 1948, monthly sales figures drooped at the end of the year. Rows of new cars remained in storage at Willow Run as dealer inventories grew. The new year brought disastrous results. Manufactuing output peaked in 1948 with 181,316 vehicles; in 1949 output plunged to a catastrophic 58,281. In 1948, Kaiser-Frazer's share of domestic car sales was 4.77 percent; a year later it dropped to 1.53 percent.[47]

As sales plummeted, so did dealer morale. The wife of a dealer in El-dorado, Illinois, recalled a pep rally for midwestern dealers at Willow Run early in 1949. In a "thank you" letter to Joe Frazer, she stated:

> We, my husband and I, thoroughly enjoyed every part of the splendid meal—the excellent entertainment and your gracious hospitality. When it was all over and the last speech had been said and the last new model had been shown, a sense of disappointment came over us. We somehow felt as though we had been built up for a big let down.

The bottom line, in her estimation, was that the "new" models were overpriced and out of date. Salesmen could no longer be motivated to ex-ceed quotas by tired old "incentives" such as pressure cookers and fur-niture sets. A former dealer from Tonawanda, New York, wired a bitter Christmas telegram to Henry Kaiser: "I lost all I had being one of your dealers. You made no effort to help. . . . I am a former Kaiser-Frazer dealer who is now broke." During 1949 hundreds of dealers quit. Corpo-rate officials publicly stressed that a trimmed-down organization was leaner and stronger. But Nina Kaiser, the second wife of company president Edgar, recalled, "The Big Three recruited many of the most successful dealers with the argument that they could do far better with an established company that was sure to survive. . . . Only a dealer of rock-solid integrity stayed with us during the retrenchment years." Clifford H. Keene, M.D., head of the Kaiser Permanente, Medical Care Program in Detroit, remem-bered the years after 1949 being filled with sadness. Many West Coast man-agers resented being in Detroit. As Keene recalled, "There were cases of severe personal traumas. Like Displaced Persons, we huddled together."[48]

The former dealer from Tonawanda reflected the feelings of many of his peers, but he was wrong on one issue: top management was trying desper-ately to reverse corporate fortunes. Henry Kaiser was acutely aware of the dealers' distress. At first, he hoped that traditional bromides would pro-vide a cure; in March 1949 he assured dealers that prosperity was just around the corner:

> Nationwide sales are picking up on our car. An intensive survey shows that sales are picking up more with dealers who are going out after the business. . . .
> Selling, as always, is a matter of believing in what you do and believing in

your product with all your faith and all your heart and then, most important, plying all your brain and brawn to getting it done.

But Kaiser's reassurances had a hollow ring; others in the organization considered more concrete steps to retrench and simultaneously promote sales. Frazer noted, "We know what we can sell our cars for—and it is not the price they are listed at now." In late March company officials bowed to mounting pressure from dealers and announced major price cuts on all models, averaging 10 percent.[49]

In addition to price cuts early in 1949, the company introduced several new models: station wagon sedans, called the Vagabond and the Traveler; four-door "convertibles" with steel tops covered by cloth; and the Kaiser Virginian, a six-passenger sport sedan. A few weeks later Henry Kaiser touted the new models with evangelical fervor. At a sales meeting, he challenged dealers who were in the doldrums: "You have a good product— competitively priced in the entire line. . . . Unless you are giving personally every ounce of your ability—giving every hour and minute of your time—living, breathing, and selling Kaiser-Frazer products—our partnership is not all it can be." Management offered direct incentives to consumers in September. Any prospective buyer could take delivery on a new car and, if not totally satisfied, could return it for a full refund within thirty days. All he would pay was one month's insurance, plus finance charges, if any. Even this unprecedented offer, inspired out of desperation, failed to reverse declining sales. Dispirited dealers sensed that the free-trial-period experiment advertised their weakness. To them, Henry Kaiser's magic had worn out. Investors shared their mood; by September, Kaiser-Frazer stock dipped to $3.50 per share.[50]

But company officials would not give up. In the spring of 1949 they considered returning to the basic idea which had inspired Kaiser's entry into the business: mass-producing a no-frills, inexpensive compact car. In May, Clay P. Bedford proposed a joint venture with other independents to produce such a vehicle named, perhaps, the "Roosevelt," priced under $1,200.[51] But if the company hoped to produce small cars, it needed new funding. With the collapse of the third stock offering and the plunge of Kaiser-Frazer shares, company officials knew they would find few willing lenders. The RFC offered $44 million, but only if they provided $10 million collateral in stock in Kaiser Aluminum and Permanente Cement. In other words, Kaiser and his top managers had to risk their investments in proven money-makers. Early in November 1949 top managers deliberated options at length. By then, company fortunes were so low that Henry and Edgar Kaiser considered quitting the business; total production that month was eighty-five cars. Accepting the RFC's terms looked like a huge gamble. But financial advisor George Woods reminded them that if Kaiser-Frazer collapsed in 1949, they might find recently opened doors closed when seeking public funding for other companies in the future. After weighing all factors, they accepted the RFC's terms and went ahead with the small car.[52]

At mid-century it was obvious that Kaiser-Frazer had to take drastic action. During 1949 the corporation had lost $30.3 million; it would have been even worse except for a $9 million federal tax rebate. Frazer, who had urged retrenchment, offered little advice; it was up to Henry and Edgar Kaiser to salvage the operation. Trying to camouflage thousands of car bodies produced for the 1949 models, they advertised "substantial innovations" in chrome and interiors of "more exciting" 1950 models of conventional cars. But they staked much of their future on a new, small car. Rumors soon circulated about its shape, size, and other features. Kaiser stimulated public curiosity about the mystery car by offering $200,000 in prizes for naming it.

In February 1950 the Kaisers proudly unveiled the unnamed new car at a pep rally for dealers at Willow Run. The car was a five-passenger, two-door sedan. Devoid of frills, it sported no chrome, no radio, not even a clock. The Kaisers hoped to deliver it to dealers by June, at a cost of about $1,175. If they succeeded, it would undercut the cheapest Fords and Chevrolets by about $250. Dealer enthusiasm appeared high; they finally had one competitive advantage in the struggle with the Big Three. But according to one source, sales manager W. A. MacDonald muttered to Hickman Price, another top executive; "Hickman, Jesus Christ! How am I going to sell this monstrosity? I just wonder if my salary is worth it." Evidently it wasn't; MacDonald quit shortly thereafter.[53]

After the car's public unveiling, hundreds of names were suggested. Frazer suggested naming it the "Mustang"; Edgar Kaiser demurred, preferring "Kaiser-Mustang."[54] One can only speculate whether choosing the name associated with Ford's dazzlingly successful entry a decade later would have made any difference in corporate fortunes. After weeks of poring over entries, Kaiser's managers finally decided on "Henry J." Mrs. Frances Atkinson of Denver, Colorado, won the grand prize of $10,000 for first submitting the name. Managers had hoped to offer the new car by the summer of 1950, but the Korean crisis, material shortages, and other problems delayed volume production until late in the year.[55]

For a shining moment, the inexpensive ($1,299 list price) little car looked like a winner. Attracted initially by novelty and economy (thirty-four miles per gallon), Americans ordered 30,000 in the first three months. Almost 82,000 Henry J's were produced in 1951, but in the words of one analyst, "Kaiser's baby was destined never to grow up." Interest fell off badly; in 1952 only 23,568 were manufactured. In desperation, Kaiser entered into an ill-fated deal with Sears to help market the car. Under the brand name Allstate, Sears sold a mere 2,600 vehicles. The tactic further demoralized many loyal Kaiser-Frazer dealers. Not only did they compete with the Big Three, but they also had to out-hustle other salesmen offering their own product. Although Kaiser-Frazer dealers generally expressed outrage at the "cheapening" of their product, the argument was largely academic. Only 124,871 of the vehicles were marketed under any brand name.[56]

One of the ironies in the declining fortunes of Kaiser-Frazer is that its worst years came just when management was learning how to produce excellent cars. *Consumer Reports* praised the new Kaiser-Frazer models in its September 1950 issue: 1951 models really *were* new. If the Kaiser had minor shortcomings, it was nevertheless "a very satisfactory car to drive and ride in, well-shorn of weight, and rating generally high as efficient transportation."[57]

But new and improved models in 1950 and 1951 did not reverse company fortunes. Initial enthusiasm for the Henry J increased production from 58,281 in 1949 to 146,911 in 1950, a 152 percent increase. Although sales rose from 73,822 to 112,055, the company faced the same old problem by year's end: mounting numbers of unsold vehicles. American car buyers of the 1950s were not satisified with cheap, dependable transportation. They wanted pizzazz. Henry and Edgar Kaiser were willing to compete at that game. In fact, in 1953 they introduced a new fiberglass-bodied sportscar named the Kaiser-Darrin, which earned rave reviews. But the Kaiser-Darrin was far too little, too late. The sportscar could not save the faltering company by itself; Kaiser-Frazer produced only 435 of these superb machines.[58]

By 1953 Kaiser-Frazer was awash in a sea of red ink. As the Big Three entered their glory years, Kaiser-Frazer and other independents desperately struggled for survival. During the early 1950s company officials staked their hopes on new models. Although the improved conventional car models held their own in 1951 and the Henry J temporarily boosted overall sales, they failed to enhance the company's competitive position in the industry. The Henry J was the sales leader in 1951, but it was discontinued in 1954. In 1952 and 1953 production of conventional vehicles slightly exceeded 30,000 each year. In 1954, although Kaiser offered some of the loveliest models ever produced, total output dropped to 7,039.[59]

Kaiser-Frazer's financial picture improved in the early 1950s, but only in the sense that the company was losing money less quickly. From 1949, when the company lost $30.3 million, fortunes improved significantly in 1950, when it lost $13.3 million; the 1951 loss was slightly smaller, $12.3 million. In 1952 losses shrank to $4.7 million, and company officials predicted that they were out of the woods. But fortunes nosed sharply downward again in 1953, when they lost a staggering $27 million. When Kaiser-Frazer lost a record $35.5 million in 1954, corporate officials talked bravely of continuing to fight. By then, however, they had directed most of their automobile activities overseas.[60]

In the early 1950s Henry and Edgar Kaiser blamed the Korean War for hampering new car production and interfering with potential profits. In retrospect, the conflict was both a blessing and a curse. The company received tens of millions of dollars worth of aircraft contracts, which kept the assembly line at Willow Run humming just when most signs indicated that Kaiser-Frazer was in deep trouble. This work probably prevented larger losses in 1951 and 1952. However, during the summer of 1953 the Air Force abruptly canceled Kaiser-Frazer's largest wartime contract for C-119 and C-123 cargo planes. Congressional critics charged that the company produced C-119s inefficiently at Willow Run. The Kaisers presented generally persuasive evidence explaining the cost differentials, to no avail.[61]

On the other hand, the airplane contracts distracted the fledgling auto producers from their primary objective. They might have been better served focusing all their energies learning to compete effectively in one of the world's most challenging enterprises. Even assuming the contracts helped lower corporate losses, they temporarily shielded the Kaisers from reality. Perhaps Henry and Edgar would have abandoned domestic car production more quickly had their losses been stiffer in 1951 and 1952. One could speculate that larger losses then might have led them to introduce their superb last-ditch entries, such as the Dragon sports sedan and the Kaiser-Darrin, earlier in the game. While unlikely, such timing might conceivably have led to a dramatic turnaround.

Corporate officials knew by the summer of 1953 that drastic steps were required for survival. They were being squeezed out of the conventional car market, but the company might survive by emphasizing specialized vehicles. Unveiling the Kaiser-Darrin in 1953 was one indication of such thinking. But the Kaisers had an even bigger surprise; they announced acquisition of Willys-Overland Motors of Toledo in April 1953. Rumors of the deal had circulated for some time, but many knowledgeable industry veterans had dismissed them; why should the venerable, profitable jeep manufacturer sell out to Kaiser-Frazer, a chronic money-loser?

There were at least three good reasons for the merger. First, the Kaisers offered Willys-Overland stockholders a handsome price for their company: $60.8 million. Second, executives in neither company had any warning that Kaiser-Frazer's defense contracts would soon be canceled. In the spring of 1953 the Kaisers had tens of millions in backlogged defense contracts and solid prospects of gaining additional work. But tax considerations were probably the key. With cumulative net losses stretching back four years, Kaiser-Frazer "owned" a tax credit estimated at $31 million. On the other hand, Willys-Overland had earned $6.1 million in 1952, but faced back taxes of $12.5 million. Accountants understood clearly that both companies would gain from the proposed merger.[62]

Although Kaiser-Frazer designed new models for 1954 and even beyond, in November 1953 the company capitulated to the Big Three in more than a symbolic sense. When a major fire ravaged General Motors' facility at Livonia, a suburb of Detroit, Henry Kaiser sensed a ripe opportunity to sell Willow Run. Old-timers in the organization differed over whether Kaiser sold the plant out of desperation or negotiated a good deal. Some argued that Kaiser made the best of a bad situation and astutely disposed of a corporate white elephant. Others believed that Charlie Wilson of GM knew Kaiser had little use for the plant and ruthlessly hammered down the price. Kaiser offered the facility to all of the big companies, and GM offered $26 million. Kaiser took the money, closed down Willow Run, and headed south fifty miles to Toledo.[63]

To most automotive historians, Kaiser's sale of Willow Run essentially signaled the end of his automobile venture. However, the company remained active in domestic specialized vehicle production and in conventional automobile production overseas. During 1947 and 1948, the Kaisers set up small assembly plants in the Middle East and Europe. When Kaiser died in 1967 the organization still had auto plants scattered around the world. In the mid-1960s Kaiser Jeep Corporation still produced fifty thousand or more specialized four-wheel-drive vehicles and heavy-duty military trucks annually. Kaiser Jeep had manufacturing plants in Toledo and South Bend, Indiana, and had 2,100 dealerships in the United States.

In later years, both Henry and Edgar Kaiser downplayed the fact that the auto company's total net losses over the first decade of operations amounted to a staggering $123 million. To their credit, they refused simply to cut their losses at the expense of investors in the company. Termination of domestic passenger vehicle production in 1955 was one of many factors leading them early in 1956 to reorganize the entire corporate structure. George Woods coordinated arrangements. Boiled down to its essentials, Kaiser Industries Corporation became a holding company for the Henry J. Kaiser Company and its operating divisions. Reorganization permitted Kaiser to borrow $95 million and pay off the auto venture's outstanding debts; stockholders in the auto company were permitted to trade in four shares for each share of Kaiser Industries. This arrangement was an honorable compromise, allowing investors who had hung onto Kaiser-Frazer stock to salvage something. Yet reorganization also served Kaiser's interests. With total shares in all companies carrying a quoted market value of $417 million at the end of 1956, Kaiser Industries gained sufficient clout in eastern money markets later in the 1950s to get financial leverage required for major expansions in profitable industries. More than a decade later,

Edgar called the hard lessons in automobiles "the best thing that ever happened to us."[64]

If the automobile venture was, in retrospect, a growing experience, the father and son camouflaged its benefits well at the time. Both men agonized over its failure. Henry Kaiser had been the inspiration in the preliminary stages, the one who possessed the burning desire to enter the auto business. He spent countless happy hours poring over prospective designs, and he was the final authority in crucial decisions, particularly after Frazer left the presidency. But Edgar bore the brunt of responsibility in running the business on a day-to-day basis. Edgar moved his family to Birmingham, Michigan, where he spent most of his time for almost a decade. Unlike his father, Edgar remained slender and retained much of his hair. However, the Detroit years quickly deepened his facial lines and grayed his hair. In the early years, Edgar faced the daily crises of short or nonexistent supplies. Later, he bolstered morale in a dispirited sales organization, negotiated with increasingly militant union leaders, and pleaded for time with impatient bankers and nervous government officials. Dealers complained that they only saw Henry Kaiser when news was good, at ceremonial unveilings of new models, or at "pep rallies"—in their view, when he wanted something from them. Some in the organization felt that the elder Kaiser was a rather remote figure, interested in the business when it was new and successful; when it turned sour, he dumped the problem into Edgar's lap.

Such a conclusion has elements of truth, but is an oversimplification. During the late 1940s and early 1950s, Kaiser's enterprises expanded on many fronts. Henry Kaiser did not have time to run the auto business himself; he had to remain at corporate headquarters. The fact that he placed not one, but two close associates in Detroit symbolized Kaiser's commitment to automobiles. That his son Edgar and Clay Bedford were there proved that Henry Kaiser considered the automobile venture of paramount importance.

Even more important, the elder Kaiser was deeply concerned by the company's future. Lambreth Hancock, a long-time personal aide, recalled driving Kaiser from Lake Tahoe to Oakland in 1954, when the company's future looked bleak. Kaiser, usually voluble and gregarious, was very subdued. Finally Hancock asked the boss what was on his mind. "I'm just trying to figure out some way to salvage Kaiser-Frazer." When Hancock said that many in the company were advising him to quit and were telling him that he was throwing good money after bad, Kaiser replied: "Handy, I can't give it up. I recently received a letter from . . . a retired railroad conductor . . . telling me that he had confidence in what I was doing and that he had withdrawn all his life savings and had invested it in Kaiser-Frazer stock . . . I can't let those kind of people down. I've got to find a way."[65]

Kaiser worried about his public image; but he also cared about people who depended upon him.

Although Kaiser put the best possible face on suspension of domestic automobile production, the American public viewed the auto venture as his single, spectacular failure. In later years, both privately and on rare public occasions, Henry did too. Nevertheless, just when Kaiser experienced what some considered a crushing, humiliating setback, almost all of his other ventures were experiencing their boom years. Kaiser had no time to ruminate over mistakes in automobiles. He was far too busy pursuing new opportunities.

10

Venturing Abroad

One of the hoariest myths about Kaiser, passed down through generations of his managers, was that the boss was so angered by demands from Cuban officials for kickbacks that he avoided foreign investments for the next quarter of a century. Publicist Robert C. Elliott claimed, "Henry Kaiser had been exposed to such a climate of bribery in his first big foreign venture—Cuba in 1927—that he said in effect, 'If that's the way it works, we'll never go overseas again.'" Other Kaiser men gave similar accounts of his indignant reactions to bribery attempts.[1]

Kaiser wrapped up the Cuban highway job in 1930; not until 1954, when he contracted with Argentina director Juan Perón to produce automobiles, did he make another major overseas commitment. The myth, then, possesses surface-level plausibility. The Argentina deal marked a significant change in the organization's posture toward international commerce. The commitment was sizable, highly publicized, the first major step in a rapidly escalating pattern of overseas investments. Upon closer inspection, however, Kaiser's Cuba experience by no means squelched his interest in foreign business. Far more important, until World War II, Kaiser had a small organization, and he was committed to many domestic ventures. Even so, from the moment he built his first industrial facility, Permanente Cement, he searched for overseas markets. Between 1940 and 1954, when he embarked on his renowned South American automobile venture, Kaiser investigated many opportunities.

After yielding its first bag of cement on Christmas Day, 1939, Permanente supplied most of the commodity for Shasta Dam. By the time the first carloads were en route to Shasta, Kaiser was thinking far beyond the dam. To challenge the "monopoly" of the West Coast cement producers effectively, he had to invade their territory, including the entire Pacific Basin. In the spring of 1940, a growing awareness of the Japanese threat led the armed services to reinforce gun placements, harbor facilities, airfields, and numerous other military installations. This required hundreds of thousands of barrels of cement, and West Coast cement producers would have to provide it.[2]

By early 1940 cement was coming into short supply; throughout 1940 and early 1941 prices increased markedly. But Kaiser found himself in a tough spot. He had agreed to deliver 5.8 million barrels of cement to Shasta Dam. By mid-1941 market prices had increased 25 percent, but he had committed over half of his cement to Shasta at low prices.[3]

The fact that Kaiser was "losing out" at Shasta made him determined to expand plant capacity and conduct more business elsewhere. Hence, when the military sought large volumes of cement for Pacific defenses, Kaiser and his managers presented a startling proposal. They would deliver orders in bulk in the holds of ships rather than in bags. Naval officers were highly skeptical. They feared that bulk shipment with no protection from the elements would produce lumpy, sticky, unusable cement and ruined ships. But they were intrigued by Kaiser's claim that bulk handling required one-fifth the time needed for bags. Kaiser convinced them by guaranteeing a quality product, arranging for shipment himself, and assuming all risks. At least for procurement of cement, military officials in the Pacific made a wise decision. Between October 1940 and the attack at Pearl Harbor, Kaiser shipped 484,000 barrels of cement which, with cooperation by the Dillingham family in Hawaii, were stored in silos in Honolulu. Rebuilding heavily damaged port facilities thus began within days of the attack. Kaiser's cement was used on numerous other outposts in the Pacific during the war.[4]

In the tense weeks prior to the Japanese attack, Kaiser also shipped cement to the Panama Canal Zone for construction of a third set of locks, fortifications, and other uses. These shipments were important to the nation's war preparations and portended Kaiser's growing interest in doing business beyond continental borders.[5]

For a time, Kaiser denied interest in such matters. At the bottom of a letter urging him to rehabilitate the water works in Havana, Cuba, Kaiser scrawled a reply, "You know I could not take an interest in foreign works now, and later I want to stay at home." Either his lack of interest was limited to Cuban projects or his views changed shortly thereafter. Kaiser's disclaimer was dated mid-November 1942; early in 1943, he sent a team of high-level executives on an exploratory mission to Latin America in search of opportunities. Specifically, the group pursued highway construction contracts after the war; Kaiser's engineers also sought work on Canada's Alcan Highway.[6]

One should interpret such conflicting directional signals cautiously. By the early 1940s Kaiser had developed a pattern of encouraging executives to develop bold proposals for future projects. Some of the stimulus to pursue foreign investments probably came from others. But early in 1944 Kaiser penned a revealing interoffice memo asking Eugene E. Trefethen, Jr., to identify "young and competent executives who might be willing to devote their time to foreign assignments." Less than two weeks later the *New York Times* reported that Kaiser had sent two engineers, George Havas and Tom Price, on a jaunt to Venezuela to discuss a development program with top officials. The men traded ideas with the Venezuelans on a comprehensive plan to help build hydroelectric plants, highways, and natural gas pipelines. They also discussed development of coal and diamond resources.[7]

The Venezuelan negotiations provided tempting glimpses of future possibilities and revealed consistency in Kaiser's thinking, since he also focused on helping industrialize the "underdeveloped" American West. He observed, "Everybody's standard of living has to be raised if we are going to raise our own." Unfortunately, wartime exigencies sidetracked further consideration of foreign investments. Kaiser probably had little inkling that Latin American negotiations would not resume for a decade.[8]

In the meantime, Kaiser maintained active interest in foreign investments elsewhere. Perhaps the most breathtaking opportunities presented themselves in war-torn China. As previously noted, Kaiser talked with international operator T. V. Soong, and their discussions went beyond shipbuilding. Both Kaiser and Soong were acutely aware of their roles in the courtship. Clearly Soong needed the capital and technical expertise the Kaiser organization possessed, but the Nationalists also sought the prestige accompanying any business alliance with the famous shipbuilder. Kaiser and his subordinates viewed the discussions partly as a gesture toward war allies; the thought of "helping" such enormous numbers of people may well have fed Kaiser's ego. An imaginative man, he invariably had large visions. At the very least, he reasoned that if domestic shipping orders dropped off drastically, as most predicted, he might gain customers for idle shipyard equipment. In early April 1945 the parties signed a memorandum of understanding to establish a small shipyard in Shanghai and to explore other possibilities.[9]

Complications arose almost immediately. Before the war, companies doing business with China had enjoyed extraterritoriality; they were exempt from Chinese law. In the spirit of the wartime alliance, that privilege was waived. After the war, American corporations would presumably be subject to local law. There was one major hitch; the Chinese had not yet drawn up new codes. Patrick Hurley, the U.S. ambassador to China, was initially optimistic that international legal snags could be worked out quickly, but he underestimated the difficulties. Donald M. Nelson, head of the War Production Board (WPB), asked that no announcement of the

Kaiser-Soong plans be made until "loose ends" were knotted. Since Nelson possessed considerable influence over disposition of surplus government property, Kaiser naturally honored his request.[10]

That was where matters stood at the end of the war. In the fall of 1945, a second consortium of Chinese business leaders approached Kaiser with a more grandiose, but vague proposal for a partnership. Percy Chen, like Soong, boasted important connections with high-level Nationalist Chinese officials. His proposal was very different from Soong's. He urged Kaiser to create an "engineering management institution" to provide technical training for "the many thousands of small industrialists who are so essential to an economy like China's." He proposed that it be established in the southern region, far from Mao Zedong's forces.[11]

Perhaps the magnitude of the proposal stunned Kaiser into uncharacteristic silence; more likely, its vagueness and impracticality disturbed him. By 1945 it did not take a China expert to divine that there were deep fissures within the Nationalist hierarchy, and that Soong and Chen were not mutual admirers.[12] Despite misgivings, Kaiser directed a trusted assistant to evaluate Chen's proposal; Gerard Piel substantiated his suspicions. Piel observed that the principals in Chen's grand scheme were unnamed and that the Nationalist government would probably control future expenditures on all major building projects tightly. He allowed that Chen's high-ranking contacts in the government might control much of the "liberal element" in future Chinese politics and that "they [could] be very helpful to us in any ventures that we contemplate." It might be wise to leave the door open just a crack. Summarizing, Piel advised Kaiser to provide an ever-so-polite brush-off.[13]

These negotiations with Chen still left hanging the matter of whether to proceed with the tentative commitment to Soong. Between the spring of 1945 and the end of the year, the international political situation had seemingly turned right-side-up again, following final defeat of the Axis powers. But Kaiser's situation had changed dramatically too. The organization had entered several major new enterprises, headed by automobiles and expansion in steel; it was also considering aluminum. Kaiser officials closely followed international events and became very aware of the irrepressible conflict between the Kuomintang and the Communists. Soong pressed for a stronger commitment, but the longer Kaiser held off, the less attractive the proposal looked. Calhoun finally proposed suspending talks "pending full clarification and stabilization of China's internal affairs."[14] The history of China's internal affairs between 1946 and 1949 is well known; with civil war raging, Kaiser's courtship with Chinese business interests ended early in 1946.

Following collapse of negotiations with the Chinese and similarly fruitless discussions with the Russians, Kaiser's interest in foreign trade appeared to dwindle. At mid-century, his domestic enterprises seemingly offered plenty of challenges. As far as the general public was concerned, Kaiser remained strictly a domestic manufacturer and contractor. But after he entered the aluminum industry early in 1946, he had to engage in international business, at least in staking out bauxite deposits.

Foreign investments appeared to be a minor concern in overall corporate strategy in the decade after 1945, but they were more important than many realize. Kaiser was one of the more innovative auto makers in exploring foreign market potential. In 1948, when his cars were at their peak in domestic sales, *Automotive News* announced an impending opening of a small Kaiser-sponsored assembly plant in Rotterdam, Holland. The plant began production in February 1949. Although output was modest, seldom exceeding one hundred vehicles per week, it provided a symbol of American commitment to a war-torn region, and a product which was temporarily competitive with scarce European models. Kaiser was sufficiently pleased with the Netherlands experiment to open similar facilities in Haifa, Israel, and Mexico City, in 1950 and 1951 respectively. He even ventured into the Japanese automobile market. During the immediate postwar years Japanese automotive engineers learned from U.S. production methods. In June 1951 East Japan Kaiser-Frazer, Ltd., rolled a Henry J off the line, the first American car assembled in Japan since Pearl Harbor. Company officials hoped that Japanese consumers would be more impressed with the compact than Americans were; initial production of Henry J's in Japan would be five hundred vehicles per week, with an increase if a market emerged. Kaiser-Frazer's commitment to foreign automobile production was more than symbolic. In February 1952 *American Automobile* reported that in ratio of exports of passenger cars to total production, "Kaiser-Frazer was the leader among American producers" in 1951. Admittedly, this was a hollow achievement in a year in which the company's share of the domestic market shrank to roughly 1 percent; it reveals, however, that Kaiser was interested in foreign auto markets several years before the Argentina venture. As late as 1964, when the organization's domestic vehicle production was a few thousand jeeps per year in Toledo, it assembled and manufactured a variety of vehicles in twenty-eight foreign countries.[15] From mid-century forward, Kaiser's overseas ventures mushroomed, as investments mounted into hundreds of millions of dollars. Several Kaiser companies became important multinational corporations.

In the minds of the public and many corporate executives, 1954 was a watershed in Kaiser's involvement in international business. That was when Kaiser contracted with Juan Perón to manufacture tens of thousands of automobiles in Argentina. Perón had originally asked Joe Frazer to consider a jointly owned automobile operation in 1947. Company officials then thought enough of the idea to propose a program remarkably similar to that adopted seven years later. Frazer proposed outright sale of a small assembly plant in Long Beach, California, established in 1945, when the partners planned a West Coast operation. By 1947, of course, all activities were centered in Willow Run, and they did not need the western facility. Frazer also proposed that initially almost all component parts would be produced in the United States; the Argentines could gradually develop integrated facilities to the point that eventually "practically all manufacturing operations would be performed at the projected Argentine factory." The plan fell through for at least two reason. In March 1947 the organization was energetically competing in a seemingly insatiable domestic market, and it was behind schedule in getting production up to 1,500 vehicles per day. Frazer pointed out the obvious: as long as the company easily sold everything it produced in the domestic market, management had little incentive to pursue Perón's initiative. But management at Kaiser-Frazer assigned engineer George Havas to perform preliminary investigations. In mid-summer 1947 Havas reported that the Argentines wanted Kaiser-Frazer initially to produce trucks. But the Americans preferred to concentrate on passenger vehicles. Nothing came of initial moves in 1947.[16]

Seven years later Kaiser's position in the automobile industry was desperate; Frazer was out of the picture, and the westerner was looking for some way to salvage his flagging operation. Perón, too, needed help, as Argentina's economy was stagnant. Despite Perón's vaunted industrialization program, no domestic plants produced cars. In a word, the two strong-willed men needed each other. Kaiser had become very friendly with New Orleans mayor De Lesseps "Chep" Morrison in 1951, when he built a huge aluminum plant in Chalmette, Louisiana. Morrison revived the idea of a South American automobile venture during a visit to Kaiser's Tahoe retreat in the summer of 1954. Morrison spelled out the possibilities in dramatic fashion. Once his enthusiasm was aroused at the vision of tens of millions of South Americans without a domestic automobile industry, Kaiser wanted prompt action, but Morrison persuaded him to delay a trip until it could be arranged by Mario Bermudez, a close associate of Morrison's. Bermudez headed the International House, a private New Orleans organization promoting Latin American trade, and had close ties to decisionmakers in South American and the Caribbean. The wait seemed interminable to Kaiser, but a few weeks later, he and his second wife, Ale, and a small entourage embarked on a tour of Latin America. Kaiser turned the trip into a full-fledged expedition: the party visited seventeen cities in nine countries during the twenty-seven day trip.[17]

The South American trip in August 1954 became legendary in corporate annals. During the mid-1950s the region appeared even less politically stable than usual. The first stop was Rio de Janeiro, where the party landed in the middle of a government crisis. Brazilian strongman Getúlio Vargas had survived many ouster attempts over a quarter of a century. A resilient, tough politician, he had always landed on his feet. Just days before Kaiser arrived, "unidentified" gunmen botched an effort to assassinate Carlos Lacerda, an influential newspaper publisher who had recently printed charges of government corruption and who was running for Congress against Vargas' son. Lacerda had been slightly wounded and a companion killed; opponents claimed that Vargas was behind it. When the Kaiser group arrived at Vargas' palace, they had to part an angry crowd brandishing signs reading "MURDERER," "GET OUT VARGAS," and less subtle suggestions.[18]

One may wonder why Vargas kept his appointment with Kaiser, but he had survived many ouster attempts and probably underestimated the seriousness of this latest contretemps. Why not go about business as usual? His recent public statements had emphasized revival of a faltering economy, and he felt pressure to deliver on his promise. Vargas needed Kaiser more than the American needed him.

Their meeting went well. Vargas welcomed Kaiser warmly, informing the American that he had read about him in John Gunther's *Inside U.S.A.* They discussed general economic opportunities in Brazil. Having established rapport, they agreed to explore specific proposals very soon. When Kaiser departed, he had no inkling that Vargas had less than a week to live. His end came swiftly. A military inquiry into the death of Lacerda's companion, a young, popular Air Force officer, moved rapidly. The ringleader of the plot was identified as the chief of Vargas' bodyguard. This turned the cabinet against Vargas. After an all-night session, cabinet officials realized that they had little choice but to rubber-stamp the military's demand for Vargas' resignation. Failure to do so might threaten their own safety, let alone political futures. The military chiefs went to the palace and presented their demands. Vargas agreed to a temporary leave of absence, then retired to his quarters. He avoided the disgrace of exile by committing suicide early the next morning.[19]

The Brazilian leader's problems were far from Kaiser's mind when he left Rio de Janeiro; he had more immediate concerns. He had learned a great deal about Perón in recent weeks. As their scheduled meeting approached, he uncharacteristically developed cold feet. According to Morrison, Kaiser tried to cancel the meeting before the plane left Rio de Janeiro: "Chep, I don't want to go into Argentina. Perón's a dictator; I'm told our rooms will be wired with microphones, they'll ransack our luggage when we're out, it's a gestapo state." Kaiser urged the others to go; he'd wait in Brazil and meet them on their way back. By Morrison's account, it took all of his powers of persuasion to coax Kaiser onto the plane to Buenos Aires. The mayor failed to budge the reluctant industrialist by protesting that for an

American of his stature to cancel the conference without warning would embarrass the United States; but when he talked of what it meant to him personally, and to his city, Kaiser gave in.[20]

But it was an unusually grumpy, suspicious manufacturing mogul who deplaned in Buenos Aires. Kaiser was stunned at the reception awaiting him. Huge banners reading "WELCOME KAISER" greeted the entourage. A red carpet stretched to the plane, and high-ranking government officials greeted the party. Perón had rounded up thousands of Argentines to line the motorcade route to the Plaza Hotel; they cheered and waved American flags. Kaiser's sumptuous hotel suite was showered with flowers, wreaths, and other gifts from Perón. Still, Kaiser resisted urgings by Morrison and others to loosen up and enjoy the festivities. That night he boycotted a city hall reception and an opera in his honor. The next day, Saturday, he grudgingly agreed to attend races at the exclusive Jockey Club; Perón was not present, and Kaiser refused an aide's suggestion to "drop in" on the dictator, who was watching a cycling competition.

If Perón was insulted by Kaiser's conduct, he hid his feelings well. Kaiser finally agreed to attend a Sunday luncheon at Perón's hacienda. As the party arrived, a corps of two thousand blue-shirted youths struck up a chorus of "The Star-Spangled Banner." Morrison introduced the two principals; although Perón was gracious, Kaiser initially appeared distant, distracted. By chance, a beautiful Mercedes-Benz was parked close by, and it attracted Kaiser's attention. Perón suggested a jaunt, and Ale Kaiser drove. Upon their return, Perón dropped the keys into Ale's hand and said, "It's yours, my lady." Understandably startled, she didn't know what to do. Morrison suavely explained that in Latin America, if a guest greatly admired a host's possession, the latter might offer it as a gift. He urged her to accept. Another member of the party, Bill Weintraub, suggested that they reciprocate by sending Perón an elegantly appointed Kaiser.[21]

Thus was the ice initially broken, and Kaiser slowly warmed up to the Argentine strongman. The gift, however splendid, did not sway Kaiser; he needed firm agreements. Typically, Kaiser wanted to discuss business immediately, but Perón preferred to show off his hacienda. They enjoyed a lavish feast, followed by a walking tour of the estate. The visitors departed late Sunday afternoon with assurances that serious discussions would begin early the next morning.

Still, formidable hurdles remained. Unfortunately, confusion over fiction and facts emerges. According to one version of the meeting, passed down for years by Kaiser company officials, the dictator took heavy-handed advice from one Jorge Antonio, a trusted confidant. Robert C. Elliott, a witness, claimed that Antonio balked at allowing Kaiser to set up operations unless he obtained a share of the profits. Antonio, who controlled the Mercedes-Benz distributorships, wanted to limit the number of automobiles, thus keeping prices high. By Elliott's account, when Kaiser realized that Antonio wanted sole distribution rights for all cars produced in the country, his face reddened and he stood up: "Gentlemen, I'm sorry, if you will excuse me. . . . I will not be a party to that type of dealing." With that, Kaiser and his group swept out. Arriving at their hotel, they purportedly received an urgent message from Perón, promising to continue discussions without Antonio.[22]

Elliott's account provides titillating reading and dovetails nicely with Kaiser's reputation for abhorring "foreign" bribery; but other evidence challenges it. Five days after the meeting, Elliot personally drafted a "confidential" memorandum to Edgar Kaiser and Eugene Trefethen, Jr. The document was remarkable for several reasons, including an almost verbatim account of the dialogue at the meeting. There was no hint of any under-the-table dealings; Antonio appeared wholly supportive and cooperative in welcoming Kaiser's automobile initiative. Elliott's memo also showed that the meeting broke up amicably. Further evidence of the "routine" nature of the meeting is a memo dictated by Kaiser just three days afterward. Kaiser mentioned a cordial luncheon with Antonio following the meeting and a tour of the Mercedes-Benz facilities in Buenos Aires that afternoon. Kaiser summarized the Argentina visit: "President Perón and [I] completely understand . . . each other's problems and objectives."[23]

These conflicting accounts raise more questions than they answer. Other evidence suggests that neither is wholly accurate but each contains some truth. James F. McCloud became president of the automobile company, Industrias Kaiser Argentina (IKA). Although not present at the original meeting between Kaiser, Perón, and Antonio, McCloud had ample opportunity to analyze their interpersonal dynamics. According to McCloud, Antonio remained in the background during the original business meeting between Perón and Kaiser, but made his move during a follow-up conference, when the American returned to Buenos Aires two months later. Antonio, as an automobile dealer and one of Perón's closest associates, assumed that the Americans would naturally "favor" him. Such arrangements were common in many countries. McCloud claimed that Kaiser calmly sent his son Edgar to inform Perón that he would not agree to any favoritism.[24] Kaiser was probably more offended by Antonio's desire to limit supplies of automobiles than by overtures for a "partnership." The American had developed a corporate strategy destined to deliver "necessities" at moderate prices, and Antonio clearly did not share these values. Perón promised to neutralize Antonio late in 1954, but according to McCloud, Antonio caused problems as long as Perón held power.[25]

Perón temporarily persuaded Kaiser that business dealing would be strictly "honorable"; on October 5, 1954, they signed an agreement. Workers in the Toledo plant had already begun to pack up about $10 million worth of idle automobile production equipment for shipment to Argentina; this represented most of Kaiser's initial investment in IKA.[26] A remarkable feature of the agreement was that the American did not want majority ownership; in fact, he insisted upon Argentine control. This was a critical decision. When Argentine underwriters offered IKA stock to local investors, the issue was snapped up in three hours. The Americans received token percentages of the stock, the government took 19 percent, and private investors got the majority. The agreement called for building the plant three hundred miles inland from Buenos Aires, in Córdoba, a city of 500,000. This would help decentralize the nation's industry, most of which centered around Buenos Aires.[27]

These terms convinced most Argentines that Kaiser cared about their interests. Unlike many American business leaders seeking easy access to raw materials, cheap and docile labor, and virtual freedom from taxation, Kaiser formed an equal partnership with the Argentines. But few international observers fully realized the importance of these terms at the time. Sophisticated columnists for leading U.S. newspapers argued that Perón and Kaiser were cynically protecting their own interests. Kaiser's move was interpreted largely as an effort to unload idle capital equipment. A four-part series in the *New York Times* in April 1955 emphasized the precariousness of Perón's position, arguing that the beleaguered general was desperately trying to meet long-standing promises to diversify the nation's industrial base and shore up the faltering economy.[28]

There was considerable truth in these views. Had domestic prospects for Kaiser's cars been promising in 1954, Morrison might not have revived suggestions for Argentine operations. But Kaiser's ego was also involved; he loved the idea of being a "provider" of greatly needed items for the "masses." That was one reason why he had entered the automobile business. If North American consumers rejected his product, South Americans might be more appreciative. Finally, of course, Kaiser received compensation for automobile production equipment he no longer needed.

Whatever the cause for Kaiser's involvement in Argentina, the wisdom of the shared partnership soon became evident. A military coup ousted Perón on September 20, 1955. By then, work was under way on the Córdoba plant, and the heavy machinery had been shipped from Toledo. Within weeks, the interim government froze the assets of nearly 100 companies, including IKA. In addition, 172 companies were investigated for possible illicit profits earned between 1943 and Perón's fall from grace. Henry Kaiser had semi-retired to Hawaii, and Edgar was the primary spokesman for corporate interests. Shortly before Christmas 1955, Edgar called on the country's new leaders and came away from the meeting "encouraged."[29]

Edgar's optimism was justified. In the following decade, Argentina suffered a seemingly interminable series of political upheavals. Although the first post-Perón government publicized certain questionable facets of the former dictator's "deal" with Kaiser and one newspaper labeled Henry Kaiser "El Gorila," IKA's assets were quickly unfrozen. Ground had been broken for the plant in April 1955.[30] Although interrupted on at least one occasion by picketing and fighting, work progressed rapidly. In June 1956 the first cars and jeeps rolled off the lines. Despite generally smooth sailing, IKA encountered problems. The agreement called for rapid conversion from American to Argentine parts suppliers. By 1958 IKA purchased half of its parts from local producers; unfortunately, almost one-third of them were faulty. This forced IKA to require inspections at every station for every vehicle; costs rose, and output fell behind schedule. Although the Kaiser product sold well, customers were often casual in meeting payments. Uncertain collections forced IKA to borrow, frequently at high interest. Edgar Kaiser announced losses for 1955 and 1956.[31] Ironically, Kaiser's automobile fortunes in Argentina reversed those in the United States, where early success was soon followed by irreversible, numbing losses. In Argentina, initial losses were quickly replaced by steadily increasing profits.

Kaiser's Argentine venture became a model for American businesses seeking viable foreign investments. The South American company steadily expanded vehicle output. In 1959 production exceeded 30,000 units. Imported Fords and Chevrolets cost about $15,000, while a locally produced Kaiser, called the Carabela, was available for just over $5,000. In the late 1950s the automobile market in Argentina appeared ripe. There were 600,000 automobiles on the road, but the average unit was twenty years old. With a population of twenty-two million, there was one automobile for every thirty-seven persons.[32] The venture clearly appealed to Argentine investors, some twenty thousand by 1964. In the mid-1960s, according to Elliott, IKA was the nation's largest manufacturing plant. The company employed nine thousand Argentines, many in skilled labor and managerial positions. Elliott counted only thirty-five North Americans on the IKA payroll; obviously, local citizens made important contributions. Argentine investors were gratified when IKA yielded profits of $6 million in 1960 and $9 million the next year. Early in 1961 the firm celebrated production of its 100,000th vehicle.[33]

IKA was a boon to Argentina, but it was also important to the parent organization. In 1956 Kaiser created Kaiser Industries, Inc., partly to facilitate access to important eastern-dominated sources of capital. Far more critical than the trickle of profits flowing north into Kaiser's coffers was IKA's enhancement of the corporate image. In the late 1950s and early 1960s the success of IKA induced financiers, who for years had dismissed Kaiser as the federal government's welfare child, to sit up and take notice.

Kaiser willingly took risks in a volatile region, and his corporate model in Argentina provided an alternative to the "old" colonial-capitalist system. It would be absurd to portray Kaiser standing alone as a symbol of enlightened capitalism; by the late 1950s and early 1960s Edgar Kaiser, Gene Trefethen, and presidents of various operating divisions sweated out most of the daily decisions. But Henry Kaiser remained active in creating overall policy. Early in 1964 Bernard L. Collier, Latin American correspondent for the *New York Herald-Tribune,* touted the organization's South American success: "Too many U.S. private enterprises fail, fear imminent failure, or never hazard a try in Latin America these days. Notable among the exceptions is the Kaiser Industries Corp." Collier concluded that IKA was "an example of what cooler economic heads agree is probably the only answer for flagging U.S. business in that troubling and trouble-ridden area."[34]

Kaiser's penetration of South American markets yielded other benefits. Foreign correspondents for prestigious national magazines praised Kaiser's enlightened dealings with citizens of foreign countries at all social and economic levels. The editor of *Harper's* stated: "Beyond its own self-interest, the Kaiser experiment has done a great deal to build respect for American methods and for Americans." A writer for the *Nation* observed that Kaiser had avoided the long-term government takeover that hampered other multinationals because he insisted that local investors hold control. Finally, *Business Week* pointed out that Kaiser's achievements in Argentina and elsewhere had prospered to the point that by 1966 multinationals around the world paid him the ultimate compliment; they invaded his new territory.[35]

IKA keyed the organization's initiatives in South America, but efforts in Brazil brought similar success. Following the initial visit to Perón, the Kaiser party was rudely shaken during a brief airport stop in Rio de Janeiro on the homeward swing when informed of the suicide of Vargas. But this did not deter them from negotiating with the new Brazilian government. Brazil's potential market was too tempting to ignore. Occupying half of the South American land mass and with a population approaching seventy-five million, Brazil promised good returns for daring investors. There seemed to be room for billions of dollars in foreign capital. Following Kaiser's initial visit, corporate strategists estimated that the country could support half a dozen car plants. They actually underestimated potential markets; by 1961 Brazil boasted seventeen automobile production facilities.[36]

Kaiser briefly considered an innovative and daring vision for automobile manufacturing in Brazil. Perhaps he and his organization could help that country become an exporter of cars and jeeps. Why not produce them in Brazil with comparatively low-cost labor and sell them in the United States? There were 2,800 Kaiser-Willys dealers; he had a sales organization in place. If he couldn't match the Big Three with a home-grown product, perhaps there was another way. Kaiser dazzled Brazilian officials with prospects of exporting fifty thousand units annually to the United States. Momentarily captivated, the Brazilian ambassador to the United States gushed, "It's a great idea. . . . That is what I have been dreaming of. . . . For years I have tried to tell the United States about the developments that should be done in Brazil, but Washington has not heeded. Now Henry Kaiser expresses what we have so long envisioned." Having established an auto plant in the United States without guaranteeing supplies of needed materials, Kaiser and his managers were wary of being caught unprepared again. They explored prospects for developing Brazil's iron ore deposits and and establishing dependable supplies of steel. Cheap power was also critical in establishing an efficient, competitive automobile industry.[37]

The government crisis of August 1954 delayed efforts in Brazil, and sober second thoughts convinced Kaiser to pursue a more limited agenda. Other industrialists contemplated supplying power and steel. When Kaiser returned to Brazil in October, he and new government officials proposed a more modest arrangement. The Kaiser-sponsored plant would concentrate on jeeps. Brazilian investors would control it, and parts would be supplied by local vendors, as conditions permitted. The new firm, Willys-Overland do Brazil (WOB), mirrored the success of IKA. By the end of 1963, WOB had more than 8,500 employees. Brazilians owned 52 percent of the stock, and ownership was even more "democratic" than in Argentina, as forty-eight thousand citizens held shares. In 1963 WOB sold almost 55,000 jeeps; total sales reached $182 million. During that year, total production of jeeps in Brazil passed the 250,000 mark. By then, company assets amounted to $83.2 million, and in May 1964 the directors announced a $32 million expansion program. In 1964 total units sales in the two South American countries passed the half-million mark.[38]

Kaiser's interest in Latin America in the mid-1950s reflected consistency in his thought. During the 1930s and 1940s, he had played a large role in the industrialization of the "underdeveloped" American West. Whether he would have participated in developing industry in South America without "Chep" Morrison's guidance is largely immaterial. By the mid-1950s, his North American industrial empire was firmly established, and he was in position to expand his horizons. Kaiser was an unabashed proponent of materialism. He was proud of making "more things—more services— more of the good things of life—for more and more Latin Americans."[39]

Measured solely against Kaiser's comprehensive vision for South American development, his achievements fell short of expectations. Because of international events beyond his control and his own changing agenda, many plans never progressed beyond the informal proposal stage. But in the fall of 1954, Kaiser's "imagineering" reached its zenith. His semi-retirement to Hawaii and departure from the corporate helm moved him to leave behind a general blueprint for long-range projects. Development of the Caribbean and South America was high on the list. In Mexico, Kaiser hoped to expand his modest automobile facilities into a plant turning out forty thousand units per year plus forty thousand engines for commercial uses. In Colombia, Kaiser envisioned producing automobiles, cement, sheet steel, gypsum, and coal. None of these ambitious projects were realized. In Latin America outside of Argentina and Brazil, the organization achieved little more than modest increases in jeep sales and an expanded network of dealers. Even in Argentina and Brazil, Kaiser gave way to more successful automobile manufacturers when they decided to develop major expansion programs. In 1967, the year of Kaiser's death, corporate holdings in WOB and IKA were sold for a total of $40 million to Ford and Renault respectively. If Kaiser did not fulfill all of his dreams south of the border, he nevertheless impressed business analysts. A *Cincinnati Enquirer* editorial in the summer of 1960 observed: "Through its formula for overseas investments, the Kaiser Industries Corp. has set a splendid example for all of American industry."[40]

11

Cargo Planes and Government Investigations

When Henry Kaiser's name is mentioned today, many are aware of his contributions to health care. When asked to list his enterprises, most cite aluminum and steel; those with a sense of history might add dams, ship-building, and automobiles. When informed that Kaiser was active in the aircraft industry for more than a decade, most are surprised. Although Kaiser explored numerous options in private aviation, most of his work was in defense contracts for the government. In 1942 he proposed a fleet of five thousand cargo planes. The plan gained considerable publicity, but little government support; aviation decisionmakers threw Kaiser a sop in the form of a contract to build three prototype giant cargo planes, including the famous "Spruce Goose." Until 1953, when the Air Force canceled his contract to build C-119 and C-123 cargo planes, Kaiser was active in the industry.

On November 2, 1947, the enigmatic Howard Hughes piloted the ele-phantine "Spruce Goose" a few feet out of the water in Long Beach, Cali-fornia. The first—and only—flight of the wooden airplane slightly ex-ceeded in length the first successful effort by the Wright brothers, and immediate acclaim for the pilot vastly surpassed that enjoyed by the mod-est inventors from Dayton, Ohio. Over twenty thousand curious observers witnessed Hughes' feat. The flight provided the aviator little more than grim satisfaction, however. From the inception of the project in 1942, ob-servers within and outside the aircraft industry had raised a crescendo of criticism, culminating in a highly publicized congressional investigation late in the summer of 1947. For Hughes, the whole experience was expen-sive, time-consuming, and exasperating. He probably wished he had never met the man who initiated the project, Henry J. Kaiser.[1]

Early in World War II, however, the project seemed urgent. The shock of Pearl Harbor had worn off, and the nation was grimly arming for war.

The spring and early summer of 1942 marked the nadir of the Allies' fortunes; their forces were retreating almost everywhere, and defeats piled up. The carnage wrought by German Admiral Erich Raeder's submarines against Allied shipping neared its peak. In the first eleven months after Pearl Harbor they sank over eight million tons of Allied vessels.[2]

By July 1942 shipbuilding had already made Kaiser a national hero. When he expressed opinions in public—about any issue—the press paid attention. Kaiser concluded that if submarines found cargo ships easy targets, it made sense to avoid them. On Sunday, July 19, 1942, he unveiled a provocative plan: he proposed that millions of tons of cargo be transported by air and claimed that he could produce a fleet of 5,000 seventy-ton cargo planes by the end of 1943.[3]

The concept was not original, having been offered as early as 1937 by Joseph P. Kennedy, who was then U.S. Maritime Commission chief. His idea was endorsed by aeronautical experts, including Major Alexander P. de Seversky, Grover Loening, and Francis H. Hoge, Jr. By July 1942 the Glenn L. Martin Company was producing the Mars, a seventy-ton cargo plane that performed well in tests, and the War Production Board (WPB) had recommended faster production of cargo planes.[4]

Yet prominent journalists and broadcasters, including Peter Edson, Boake Carter, and Raymond Clapper, portrayed Kaiser's proposal as a clarion call for immediate action. Within days of the Portland speech, nationally syndicated columnists made Kaiser's cause their own. The question why they ignored cargo planes until the westerner promoted them naturally arises. Joe Kennedy was not an expert, but the others, particularly de Seversky and Loening, clearly were. Glenn L. Martin and his competitors had built thousands of planes, while Kaiser had no experience in aircraft.

Two factors explain the enthusiasm for Kaiser's initiative. In the summer of 1942 the nation desperately needed heroes. Friendly journalists fawned upon Kaiser and nicknamed him the "Miracle Man." When he claimed he could do something, most people believed him.[5] Equally important, Kaiser developed keen instincts for exploiting his growing influence. Within days of the Portland speech, his cargo plane idea was toasted by the nation's press. Sensing opportunity, the ebullient entrepreneur packed his bag and headed to the capital to sell his plan. By 1942 he had a decade of experience in politics and close ties to prominent New Dealers. If newspaper pressure wasn't enough, powerful friends assured him a respectful hearing. Shortly after his arrival in Washington, he appeared in the Oval Office, where the President listened attentively to his ideas.[6] Kaiser departed with the belief that he had Roosevelt's support.

Despite media acclaim and his entree into high government circles, Kaiser faced two challenges. The first involved strategy. Military decisionmakers might order large quantities of the proven Mars seventy-ton cargo plane, but they were also intrigued by the potential of much larger planes in the two-hundred- to five-hundred-ton range. It might be smart to gauge the wind direction before irrevocably choosing a single approach. Kaiser also knew that aircraft manufacturers resented his entry onto their territory, just as steel producers had. Although the nation faced a grave emergency, it would have been surprising had they stood by idly while he entered their field.

Kaiser briefly bided his time, offering to assist whichever program military officials preferred. In an effort to ingratiate himself with established manufacturers, he requested their technical assistance in firming up his own proposals, while emphasizing that in wartime there was plenty of work for all. Industry veterans were naturally suspicious. Behind Kaiser's call for unified action they perceived a thinly veiled threat that their patriotism would be questioned if they withheld cooperation.

Initially, Kaiser seemed to make headway in his effort to get into aviation. President Roosevelt lent a sympathetic ear; so did Senator Truman's Special Committee Investigating the National Defense Program and Interior Secretary Harold L. Ickes. The latter believed Kaiser's proposed cargo planes "[could] be the turning point of the war in our favor."[7] Kaiser gave several speeches and hosted news conferences in Washington, all designed to drum up support for his initiative.

But behind the scenes established producers were lining up their legions, including senior military procurement officers. In hindsight, they had every reason to guard their turf carefully. Aircraft manufacturers performed splendidly during the war. When America began arming seriously in 1940, Roosevelt called for 50,000 planes per year. Many considered such a goal absurd. Yet production soared from 3,807 in 1940 to 85,898 in 1943. In 1944 production peaked at 96,318. Like Kaiser, the aircraft builders also performed miracles. In mid-1942 they were scrambling to meet huge demands; the last thing they needed was interference from outsiders.[8]

Opposition to Kaiser was often indirect, sometimes subtle. Admiral William D. Leahy of the Combined Chiefs of Staff reported that officers deemed the Kaiser initiative highly desirable *if* he could produce cargo planes "without taking material that is essential at the present time to our war effort." This caveat was critical. Military leaders knew full well that the worst bottlenecks in materiel were precisely the items Kaiser would need in quantity. Critics argued that Kaiser would waste time and materials retooling a shipyard to produce planes. In addition, he would have to "raid" other aircraft companies for competent personnel, thus impeding the efforts of experienced builders.[9]

For the record, aircraft manufacturers promised cooperation with Kaiser if and when he actually got government orders. In retrospect, evidence suggests that bureaucrats tried to placate Kaiser and keep him out of air-craft production. WPB head Donald M. Nelson gave Kaiser a tentative go-ahead to produce seventy-ton Mars cargo planes, but only if he could do so without interfering with present or prospective building programs. Nelson then appointed three established producers to a four-man commit-tee assessing Kaiser's qualifications. Not surprisingly, the committee con-cluded that permitting Kaiser to engage in experimentation was a luxury the nation could not afford.[10]

Kaiser had traveled a similar path with Big Steel; he had won that battle and did not quail before strong opposition. If the aircraft producers were too busy with conventional planes to help him, he'd find the right designer and build even bigger planes. At this point, Howard R. Hughes, Jr., entered the picture. According to historian Charles Barton, rivals such as Donald Douglas and Henry H. "Hap" Arnold acknowledged Hughes' brilliance, but many considered him a dilettante who could afford expensive toys. Hughes also alienated military decisionmakers by his bizarre social behavior and fared poorly in the contract sweepstakes. In later years, some accounts suggested that Kaiser pressured Hughes into a partnership to build giant cargo planes. While the shipbuilder did much of the courting after the ini-tial contact, Glen Odekirk, a close Hughes associate, approached Kaiser when his cargo plane proposal was attracting heavy publicity.[11]

While Kaiser and Hughes sized each other up, friendly newspaper col-umnists criticized Nelson and the military bureaucrats for giving Kaiser the runaround. The westerner's media friends were unimpressed with Nelson's provisional authorization for Kaiser to build planes. According to Eliot Janeway, this amounted to "telling Mr. Kaiser that, so to speak, he can have a ham sandwich if he can bake the bread, borrow the butter, and steal the ham." Raymond Clapper was even more incensed at the treat-ment of Kaiser:

> All he has to show is two mealy letters from Donald Nelson . . . Both are signed with the same rubber stamp. . . . Don't waste the time of such a valu-able man. Why kid a man who has his production record? Why kid the public into thinking Washington is behind him when nobody there has any intention of raising a small toe to help him?

The columnist concluded, "This is a piece of monumental fakery."[12]

Some bureaucrats believed Kaiser cynically distorted their positions to gain media support. Nelson and the WPB had defenders, but public offi-cials were bruised in preliminary encounters with Kaiser over cargo planes. Kaiser and Hughes formed a partnership and returned to Washington for further talks in early September. Government officials knew they had to handle the westerners carefully. Kaiser, too, realized that he and Hughes had to make concessions. Pursuit of a seventy-ton plane contract was useless; opposition from military leaders and manufacturers was too strong.[13]

Negotiations quickly focused on big experimental planes, and an accord was reached. The westerners agreed on September 10, 1942, to build three prototype cargo planes in the one-hundred-ton range. If performance tests warranted, production contracts might follow. Government officials committed $18 million for developmental costs but drove a hard bargain; no profit was allowed, and Kaiser and Hughes could not divert strategic materials from military production. Hughes had considerable experience with alternative materials in aircraft design and believed prototypes could be built with wood rather than metal. With little more than artists' drawings and optimism, the partners projected a plane with a gross weight of one hundred tons and a fifty-ton payload. Cruising speed would be 145 miles per hour, with a maximum range of 3,700 miles.[14]

Once the contracts were signed, controversy temporarily abated. From 1942 forward the aircraft industry performed miracles, and other producers attracted shares of glory. As Allied naval commanders learned how to fight U-boats and as the noose tightened about the Axis powers, the cargo ship crisis diminished. Military procurement officers experimented with hundreds of new weapons, most having far higher priorities than three prototype cargo planes. Whatever their reasons, bureaucrats left Kaiser and Hughes alone for a time.

But the Kaiser-Hughes project experienced troubles from the start. In retrospect, difficulties between the partners might have been anticipated. On a superficial level, they appeared well matched. Despite his later image as an eccentric recluse, during the 1930s and 1940s Hughes was a master manipulator of public opinion, who enjoyed the limelight as much as Kaiser did.[15] They also shared a fascination with technology. But they had little else in common. Henry Kaiser was a down-to-earth builder who worked with tangible goods and was fanatical about deadlines. But Hughes toyed almost compulsively with "final" designs and routinely ignored deadlines.

Their agreement called for Hughes to design and build the prototypes; Kaiser would produce the planes once the design received approval. Typically, Kaiser assumed that Hughes would work night and day until the design was finished. Hughes worked late at night in his secluded residence in Beverly Hills; Kaiser could almost never reach him. He often missed appointments; the shipbuilder wasted precious hours angrily waiting in Hughes' ramshackle Culver City office, while the latter's aides searched in vain for their boss. Hughes repeatedly ignored Kaiser's urgent appeals for information. When a business associate requested a letter of introduction to Hughes in February 1943, a Kaiser aide replied that Hughes was a "very independent operator" and discounted "any effect that a letter from us would have." By April 1943 Kaiser lost patience because, in the midst of many urgent tasks, he had to explain Hughes' delays to government officials.[16]

Some of their testy interchanges were simply caviling by two very proud, busy men, but they provided hints of more fundamental problems. Hughes hired a succession of project managers, but none could get along with the unconventional boss. On August 27, 1943, Ed Bern, general manager on the project for only two months, finally exposed mounting problems to responsible authorities. In an emotional phone call to Donald Nelson, Bern charged that Hughes' operations were a complete mess. According to Bern, who resigned later that day, Hughes had repeatedly frustrated efforts to establish responsible management. In addition, Hughes and his subordinates had distorted figures and lied to government inspectors. Bern warned Nelson, "We have a terribly chaotic situation out here. It is going to blow right up in your face."[17]

If Nelson felt satisfaction over difficulties on a project he had opposed, it was tempered by the knowledge that an investigation had to be handled with extreme caution. Above all, any probe must be free of the slightest hint of bias. Yet Nelson had no choice but to investigate Bern's charges. In the fall of 1943 the WPB studied the situation; it soon became clear that the first prototypes would be considerably overweight. This basic flaw obviously compromised their prospective payloads. Government investigators also determined that after more than a year, almost $10 million had been spent on a single aircraft which was nowhere near completion.[18]

Even with the best intentions, Kaiser and Hughes were unable to make rapid headway on a very complex task. In November 1943 WPB members and consultants held several meetings with the designers in an effort to solve engineering problems. Early in January 1944 a WPB inspection team visited Culver City to assess progress. Their highly critical report appeared to seal the project's doom. Inspectors concluded that project engineers had failed to remedy critical structural defects; it would take many months and large additional expenditures to overcome them.[19]

Nelson canceled the project in February 1944. In retrospect, his decision was sound; the military no longer needed large planes. But Hughes had friends in high places, who pressured the WPB to revive the project. With progress stalled and no relief in sight, Kaiser had dropped out of the picture months earlier, but it continued as a Hughes project. Government funding, however, was virtually eliminated; to keep the experiment alive, Hughes pledged to cover all expenses exceeding $20 million. The "success" of the "Spruce Goose's" test flight in 1947 is testimony to Hughes' grit and persistence, if not his financial acumen. Estimates vary, but he probably invested betwen $7 and $17 million of his own capital.[20]

By the time Hughes' "flying lumber yard" skipped out of the water late in 1947, the whole episode probably seemed a distant memory to Kaiser. The years from 1944 to 1947 were among his busiest, as he vastly expanded his industrial empire. But the partnership with Hughes was linked to his exploration of postwar possibilities in private aviation. In 1944 Kaiser actively promoted a national network of six thousand privately financed airports, scattered all about the country. Owners and operators of small private planes would have direct access to almost anywhere in the United States. Kaiser seriously considered producing airplanes for the consumer market. He purchased rights to produce the "Y-Model" airplane from inventor Dean Hammond, and he acquired similar rights from Stanley Hiller, Jr., to produce the "Hiller-copter." Both were extremely easy to fly. An average adult could master the controls after a few minutes of instruction. One of his engineers envisioned Kaiser as the "Henry Ford of aviation." However, other priorities, along with a realization that he had overestimated the market, sapped his interest; by the end of 1945 he had abandoned plans to produce private airplanes.[21]

Despite the breakup of their partnership, Kaiser and Hughes remained personal friends. When the government investigated the "Spruce Goose" contract in 1947, Kaiser made a brief appearance at the hearings, where he stoutly defended the flyer's integrity, if not his work habits. The episode seemed to mark a turning point in Hughes' life; he was in the midst of a personality change which made him a celebrated recluse. Unlike his former partner, Kaiser was not embittered by such experiences; he shrugged off criticism and temporary setbacks. Long before the investigation in 1947, Kaiser had moved in other directions.

In fact, earlier Kaiser initiatives in aviation had also received careful scrutiny. During 1943, before the full extent of the Hughes fiasco became apparent, Kaiser became involved in two other aircraft ventures. In early March, he purchased controlling interest in Fleetwings Aviation, a small manufacturer of specialized parts in Bristol, Pennsylvania. The Bristol plant would be converted to home-appliance manufacturing after the war. Of far more dramatic impact was his takeover of Brewster Aeronautical Corporation on Long Island. Brewster had a $275 million order from the Navy to turn out divebombers, and there were about twenty thousand workers on the payroll. But in March 1943 the operation was a shambles; production the previous month had been only eight planes. Labor-management relations were so bad that a parade of seven different managers had come and gone since 1942.[22]

As a favor to Navy Secretary James V. Forrestal, Kaiser agreed to try to turn Brewster around. In later years, public relations handouts implied that Kaiser worked instant miracles. This was not true. Seven months after Kaiser took over Brewster, operations were still so inefficient that Congress investigated the problems. Most of the committee's attention centered on union chief Thomas De Lorenzo, but Kaiser drew criticism for having spent only one day at the plant since he took over. The investigators believed that despite his prodigious energy, Kaiser was spreading himself too thin. Kaiser emphatically disagreed, claiming that he could get De Lorenzo to cooperate; the latter promised to do his part. Whether on account of Kaiser's increased attention, De Lorenzo's newfound commitment, or the workers' revived patriotism, plant output improved dramatically. In October 1943 output was 14 planes; in April 1944 Brewster turned out 123 aircraft. Kaiser and De Lorenzo became mutual admirers and cut the work force almost in half, to eleven thousand employees. Still, Kaiser was delighted to turn the plant back over to Navy officials in May 1944.[23]

When he testified for Hughes in 1947, Kaiser did not imagine that three years later he would be involved in aircraft on a far larger scale than before. Nobody, of course, anticipated the Korean War, and Kaiser had long since closed his World War II defense facilities. He was so heavily involved in production of civilian goods that gearing up again for war work was far from his mind.

Within days of the North Korean invasion, Kaiser offered to vastly expand production of durable goods, such as cement, steel, and aluminum. His purchase of Willow Run included a National Security clause permitting the government to convert it to defense production. In the Korean crisis, the federal government rationed automobile production. This action hampered the Big Three, but not Kaiser-Frazer, since Willow Run was operating well below capacity of three thousand vehicles per week. Both Kaiser and union officials realized that defense contracts could revive Kaiser-Frazer fortunes and stimulate local employment.

Kaiser expressed keen interest in military contracts, particularly B-47 bombers, C-119 transport planes, and jet fighters. In addition to his reputation in war production, bureaucrats had more immediate reasons to welcome his proposals. The Reconstruction Finance Corporation (RFC) had loaned tens of millions of dollars to Kaiser-Frazer. If the automobile venture failed, the government might not be able to collect on the loans.[24]

On December 5, 1950, Kaiser called on long-time business associate John A. McCone, then undersecretary of the Air Force. That afternoon, McCone's deputy asked Fairchild Aviation "in the interest of national security" to share production information on the C-119 cargo plane with Kaiser. The next day Henry and Edgar Kaiser and several engineers were the unwelcome "guests" of Fairchild officials in Hagerstown, Maryland. The situation was reminiscent of Kaiser's reception by established producers during World War II. As primary contractors of the C-119 cargo plane, Fairchild officials had little enthusiasm for cooperating with Kaiser.[25]

Only ten days later, Kaiser-Frazer received a contract to build 176 C-119 cargo planes for $467,000 each. Neither Kaiser-Frazer nor Fairchild was overjoyed with the $82 million contract. Henry and Edgar Kaiser had hoped for several times as much. Edgar later complained that heavy retooling costs had to be written off against a small number of planes; his company's performance evaluations would naturally suffer. But he and his father did not emphasize such concerns when they signed the contract. Air Force officials had their own reasons for doing business with Kaiser-Frazer. First, defense officials created second sources for most vital commodities, so as not to rely totally upon any single supplier. In addition, the Fairchild plant was approaching capacity; significant expansion of production would require major additions or another plant. Finally, UAW officials in Detroit lobbied hard for Kaiser-Frazer and convinced military officials that conversion of Willow Run would pose few problems. Certainly they could cite historical precedents, as unions and local manufacturers had achieved enviable production records in both world wars.[26]

Air Force officials tried to appease Fairchild by authorizing a small increase in its C-119 schedules, but battle lines were laid down quickly. A week after announcement of the Kaiser contract, *American Aviation Daily*, an industry organ, presented strong editorial criticism: "Industry observers are wrinkling their noses at the deal under which Kaiser-Frazer will build Fairchild C-119 Troop-Carrying transports . . ." Kaiser directly rebutted the editorial, charging that it circulated "an extremely misleading and distorted report on the announced contract."[27]

Early in 1951 over one million square feet at Willow Run were converted to aircraft production. The automobile assembly lines were redesigned; Fairchild reluctantly provided some technical assistance, blueprints, surplus tooling, and a few engineers. Suppliers of thousands of parts and subassemblies were located and delivery schedules established. Kaiser managers, of course, had plenty of experience with this type of challenge. Edgar Kaiser and Clay Bedford relied upon knowledge gained at the shipyards, and both spent much of their time at Willow Run in 1951.

Air Force officials assumed that they would recruit workers in Detroit who had assembled B-24 bombers during the previous war. This was an important factor behind their decision to award the C-119 contract to Kaiser. They did not take into account the impact of the booming prosperity in the region. Since the end of World War II, many skilled workers had achieved high-paying jobs and had built up seniority with the Big Three automakers or elsewhere. Many of these workers were in their thirties or forties; they had pension plans and little interest in jobs with no long-term stability. Neither Kaiser-Frazer nor military officials anticipated problems with the UAW contract then in force at Willow Run. When auto production slumped, laid-off workers had the right to "bump" aircraft workers from their jobs; if auto production increased, they could return to the other side of the plant. Inefficiency was built into the system; auto workers required several weeks of training before they were useful in air-craft production.[28]

It seemed that virtually nothing went right. Kaiser and his managers learned that assembling cargo planes with comparatively sophisticated equipment and delicate parts was tougher than putting together cargo ships. No top-level executives had aircraft experience. He recruited some middle-level managers and engineers from competitors, but established producers naturally kept high-level people if they could. Kaiser brought in several managers from the West Coast, each with a team of subordinates. By the end of 1951 there were ten vice presidents at Willow Run, none with aircraft experience; only three were in "line" jobs. The result was predict-able: administrative chaos.

Military liaison officers offered little help. In the crisis-laden atmo-sphere of late 1950, the Air Force initially took an "all-out, expenses-be-damned" attitude toward production. As performance evaluations on C-119s came in from the field, military officials demanded one modification after another. New specifications called for changes in data analysis, and voluminous new sets of figures, seemingly on a daily basis. Workers were constantly transferred between departments and from one pay scale to an-other; the payroll department had difficulty determining which costs should be charged off to each department. Little wonder: by the end of 1951 the plant employed fifteen thousand workers in the auto and aircraft facilities. According to several observers, workers took full advantage of the chaos. One worker might punch in time cards for half a dozen friends, who were paid.[29]

Despite the size of its operation, Kaizer-Frazer was a pygmy in the de-fense business in 1951, ranking forty-third in contract volume with $91.7 million. This amounted to 0.3 percent of all defense work. Nevertheless, by spring 1952, Kaiser's critics in Washington were prepared to strike. They were led by Congressman Alvin E. O'Konski (R-Wisconsin), who detailed a series of charges against Kaiser-Frazer. The most serious were that planes from Willow Run cost four times Fairchild's figure, and that Kaiser and his subordinates had used "connections" in Washington to secure the con-tracts. O'Konski charged that work went to Kaiser-Frazer because Clay P. Bedford was on leave to work for Mobilization Director Charles E. Wilson. O'Konski also perceived a conflict of interests in that McCone was on loan to the government from Bechtel-McCone, which owned 4,200 shares of Kaiser-Frazer stock.[30]

When O'Konski aired his charges, Henry Kaiser was livid. The one type of attack he could not abide was one against his integrity. Kaiser replied that not only was O'Konski "grossly misinformed on every single state-ment," but that he also had been "stimulated by persons wishing to dam-age the Kaiser-managed corporations [so] the congressman chose to make his malicious and unfounded statements under the cloak of congressional immunity . . ." Following the initial salvos between O'Konski and Kaiser, the two sides settled into a war of attrition. During the summer of 1952, McCarthyism was near its peak. Kaiser realized that during the Red Scare there were many victims of the "Big Lie," but he did not initially count himself among them. At first, he believed that once the congressman learned the facts, he would retract his statements. A retraction could not undo damage, but Kaiser hoped to contain it. He replied to O'Konski on May 26, 1952, and gave a copy to the press: "The malingerers who gave you the false information should immediately be called before the bar of public opinion and asked to substantiate their charges. We are prepared to meet these accusers in public before the press . . ."[31]

According to Chad Calhoun's notes, in a face-to-face meeting on May 31, O'Konski admitted that he had been "fed" material on Kaiser-Frazer. When pressed by Kaiser for his source, O'Konski admitted that it was "probably" Cyrus Eaton. Momentarily losing his composure, O'Konski blurted out, "They aren't going to make a sucker out of me. I owe it to the people of my district to straighten this thing out." According to a summary of a follow-up meeting between the same parties that afternoon, the congressman admitted that Eaton had dropped by his office personally to congratulate him for going after Kaiser-Frazer.[32]

If Kaiser and his men reached any truce with O'Konski on May 31, it was too late to prevent a second set of charges which appeared in *Aviation Weekly* on June 2. O'Konski's new broadside added minor details, but basically repeated earlier accusations. Kaiser consulted lawyers to determine whether he had sufficient grounds to sue O'Konski, Fairchild, or others involved. Attorney Walston S. Brown replied that grounds probably existed, but that his firm needed time to consider action against the congressman.[33]

Kaiser held his fire for several days, giving O'Konski some room and time to straighten things out. By mid-June, however, it was clear that the congressman was dragging his feet. Kaiser and his men invariably found him "unavailable" in his office, and he seldom returned calls. Kaiser and Calhoun demanded a public retraction printed in the *Congressional Record*. They prepared a long statement and wanted O'Konski's approval, but when they called on Friday, June 13, he was in Wisconsin, "visiting his constituents."[34]

After dozens of phone calls Kaiser's Washington office finally tracked O'Konski down. Following a lengthy telephone conference on Sunday, June 15, Kaiser and Calhoun thought that all had agreed on wording of a statement to be released from O'Konski's office early the following week. Here, Kaiser and Calhoun made a serious tactical error. O'Konski stayed away from Washington Monday; when there was no sign of him on Tuesday, June 17, they released the statement in O'Konski's name. O'Konski then charged that Kaiser and Calhoun had released "unauthorized state-ments," and that the so-called retraction was "erroneous." When he finally returned to his office on Thursday, June 19, he inserted a report in the *Con-gressional Record* claiming that Kaiser had presented him with an eighty-five-page rebuttal of certain charges, and that he had not "had sufficient opportunity to study the reply."[35]

It was obvious that clearing up "misunderstandings" was very low on O'Konski's agenda; he finally responded to Kaiser's document two weeks later. O'Konski was clearly a mouthpiece for others; his reply repeated al-most verbatim broad allegations made earlier by Cyrus Eaton. To Kaiser and Calhoun, O'Konski was copying the "Big Lie" tactics of Joseph McCarthy; it took far more time, energy, and thought to refute allegations than to make them. O'Konski continued his attacks until the November elections, in which he achieved reelection.[36]

Kaiser's troubles with Congress were just beginning. The election of 1952 marked a Republican resurgence. After two decades out of power, the GOP controlled the executive branch. Even though their edge in Congress was razor-thin, Republicans were eager to attack any remnants of "New Deal favoritism." Kaiser had repaid his biggest RFC loans, but his adver-saries had long memories. They revived unflattering nicknames, such as "the dimpled darling of the New Deal," and "Miss Democracy's best-kept boyfriend."[37]

O'Konski had a reputation as an unpredictable lightweight; Senator Styles Bridges (R-New Hampshire) was an opinionated but relentless ad-versary. Within days of Eisenhower's sweep, Kaiser heard rumors of Bridges' intention of getting to the bottom of the "C-119 mess." Seizing the ini-tiative, Edgar Kaiser wrote to Bridges urging a full and complete inves-tigation. Edgar claimed that he and his father were "proud of the effort we are making in the defense and civilian programs," and "ready and willing to submit any and all facts . . ."[38]

Bridges' suspicions mirrored O'Konski's, and the consensus in Kaiser's Washington office was that the two Republicans were working in concert. Editorial opinion was mixed. A *Time* story indirectly criticized Kaiser, stating that the "second source" policy of procurement by the Air Force encouraged inefficiency. The *Washington Post* lambasted Bridges for failing to "ferret out the facts before broadcasting his charges." Meanwhile, Calhoun and his staff tried to line up congressional support.[39]

In late November 1952 the Air Force inspected Willow Run operations. Considering the highly charged atmosphere, a dispassionate analysis may have been impossible; but Major General Mark E. Bradley, Jr., conveyed the team's concerns to Edgar Kaiser. The general cited numerous failures on the part of Kaiser's organization: imprecise and unrealistic delivery schedules, topheavy management, poor quality control, a loosely controlled labor force. While offering "advice and guidance on specific plant operations," military officials held that it was the contractor's ultimate responsibility to produce results. Bradley warned that if subsequent reviews did not reveal solutions that were "already long overdue," the government might cancel the contract.[40]

In his reply to Bradley's apparent ultimatum, Edgar Kaiser acknowledged "certain growing pains" that company management had experienced. But he defended Kaiser-Frazer's overall performance. The Air Force had cut the number of planes ordered; this obviously raised unit costs. So, too, did design changes demanded by the military. Kaiser claimed that the C-119s Willow Run produced had more modifications than Fairchild's. These factors explained most of the cost differentials. Kaiser denied that he and his father were dominated by labor, claiming that Kaiser-Frazer's UAW contract was typical for the industry. Finally, without naming Fairchild, he asserted that "there were errors in other technical data furnished, as well as long delays in furnishing some of the drawings, and complete failure in some cases to give the required information." He urged Air Force officers to compare his company not only with Fairchild, but also with "other contractors initiating new aircraft programs."[41]

Despite Edgar Kaiser's initiative, he and his father were clearly on the defensive late in 1952, trying to prevent cancellation of their cargo plane work. They actually had two contracts. While fighting in Korea continued in the summer of 1951, the Air Force announced plans for another cargo plane, the C-123. No unfavorable publicity concerning the C-119 contract had yet surfaced. Mike Stroukoff of Chase Aircraft was a brilliant designer and builder with big ideas but a small plant in West Trenton, New Jersey. He and Edgar Kaiser won a contract for 244 C-123s. The Kaiser interests initially acquired 49 percent of the Chase stock. However, misunderstandings between the partners surfaced quickly. Stroukoff assumed that Kaiser capital would be used to expand the Navy-owned West Trenton plant and that major subsections of the C-123 would be built there under his control. On at least one point the Kaisers and the Air Force agreed: with enormous capacity, Willow Run should turn out C-123s after the C-119 contract was completed. Even though they did not control the stock, Henry and Edgar Kaiser apparently assumed that their organization would dominate management at Chase, and that Stroukoff's basic role was to design the plane. With slow deliveries of C-119s at Willow Run, and the Navy's decision to take over the West Trenton plant, Stroukoff saw his dream in tatters. He blamed the Kaisers, and by early 1953 he was supplying information to their critics in Washington. For their part, Kaiser-Frazer officials were convinced that Stroukoff was in collusion with Richard S. Boutelle of Fairchild, trying to sabotage their C-119 contract. Boutelle's position appeared obvious to Kaiser executives; he had resisted their participation in

C-119s from the start. They couldn't fully understand Stroukoff's turn-about. Perhaps the designer hoped that cooperation with investigators might lead to a contract for C-123 subsections at the West Trenton plant.[42]

By early 1953, it was clear to even the most optimistic of Kaiser's managers that the organization's prospects in aircraft production were limited. In April Willow Run produced only forty-four C-119s. Air Force analysts believed that if all went well Kaiser might be able to complete his C-119 contract by March 1954. It was no surprise to Kaiser when the Senate Armed Services Subcommittee on Defense Procurement announced in mid-May 1953 its intention to hold open hearings to explore the issue of "second sources" for military contracts. Although politicians claimed that their primary purpose was to examine the general policy, Calhoun anticipated a quick shift in focus to specific cases, and he warned his associates to be prepared. Calhoun believed that Eaton was also feeding data to their critics behind the scenes. But even the acutely perceptive Calhoun was unaware of how hard Eaton and his allies were working.[43]

The hearings opened on June 2, 1953, with Bridges as star prosecutor. As Calhoun had predicted, Willow Run quickly became the primary focus. Bridges spent several days examining Air Force witnesses, but he called nobody from Kaiser-Frazer. He charged that Kaiser's C-119 contract was awarded much too quickly. Bridges "discovered" that Kaiser-Frazer had finalized an agreement with the RFC on a $25 million loan on the morning of December 5, 1950, and Henry and Edgar Kaiser had met with McCone around noon that same day. For the cameras and reporters, at least, Bridges acted incredulous that a major contract was awarded to Kaiser just ten days later. Bridges charged that the Air Force acted with undue haste, that there had been no investigation of the suitability of the Willow Run facility and no review of cost estimates for retooling and production.[44]

To some observers, Bridges' probing made him a conscientious public servant. Others thought that he oversimplified the situation and tried to manipulate it to his advantage—and that of his friends. Bridges conveniently ignored the conditions under which the C-119 contract had been awarded. In mid-November 1950, United Nations troops under General Douglas MacArthur appeared poised to drive North Korean forces into the Yalu River. One month later MacArthur's disorganized forces were in pell-mell retreat, hotly pursued by 500,000 Chinese. MacArthur called for drastic action against the Chinese, and worried strategists huddled around President Truman discussing possible Soviet responses to further escalation. In the tension-filled atmosphere of mid-December 1950, many feared that the nation might soon be immersed in a much larger conflict, possibly even nuclear war. Air Force planners believed that by 1954 they would require 1,800 C-119s, and that only a larger facility than the Fairchild plant could meet that schedule. Seen in that context, the Air Force policy of using Willow Run for C-119s appeared sensible; production could be expanded quickly in an emergency.[45]

All of this seemed ancient history, or eminently forgettable to Bridges in the early summer of 1953. By then, the crisis was past. Truce talks at Panmunjom, North Korea, were dragging into their third year, and the American public was restive at delays in "getting the boys home." Although a truce would be signed in July 1953, Americans did not rejoice. They were accustomed to total victory, not negotiated stalemates. Bridges sensed that the public sought scapegoats. In his view, Kaiser might have been a national hero during World War II, but only with a lot of help from spineless New Dealers. Kaiser had supporters in the Air Force, but Colonel Harry Smith reflected a commonly held view among Republicans when he telegramed Eisenhower: "Your administration will deserve and receive acclaim if it calls complete halt to further Kaiser raids on the treasury and recovers from him the multimillions he has already reaped at taxpayers' expense."[46]

The "findings" of the Senate Armed Services Committee were hardly revelations; basically, the Senators reconfirmed well-known facts and added a few details. As it had a year previously, when O'Konski leveled his original charges, the opposition press voiced surprise that Fairchild produced C-119s for $265,000 apiece, while the "same" plane cost five times as much at Willow Run. In the first few days of the hearings, several Air Force witnesses defended Kaiser, but the atmosphere in the hearing room was a cross between a witch-hunt and a circus. Top-level military leaders had careers and budgets to consider, and Kaiser was clearly expendable. Bridges skillfully maneuvered Lieutenant General Orval Cook, deputy chief of staff for materiel, into stating that the Air Force was "disappointed . . . in the performance of the Kaiser-Frazer operation."[47] Ten days after the hearings began, Bridges requested termination of the C-119 contract and announced that the hearings would soon end.

Deserted by former friends in the Air Force, Henry and Edgar Kaiser were still determined to defend themselves. They demanded to be heard and finally appeared before Bridges' committee on June 22 and 23. If either felt defensive, he did not show it. Henry Kaiser's testimony was impressive, and he commanded an amazing array of facts. He argued that comparing initial costs per airplane was absurd because retooling costs at Willow Run were so much greater. Air Force officials had been fully aware of this before making the commitment. Kaiser's most telling point was that by hiring him, the Air Force had purchased far more than cargo planes: it had bought capacity and flexibility.[48]

But neither the Air Force nor the senators were still listening; the former, under pressure from budget-minded Republicans, severed ties with Kaiser-Frazer. Henry Kaiser was in the midst of his second day of testimony, with Edgar at his side, when a Kaiser aide entered the room and handed a note to Edgar, who read it, then handed it to his father. They requested a private conference with Senator Bridges. The men retired to an anteroom and returned a few minutes later. Bridges announced that the hearings were recessed, without further ado.

Air Force Secretary Harold E. Talbott had cancelled the C-119 contracts. His decision made sense politically. Talbott, an Eisenhower appointee, had not been involved in awarding the C-119 contract. Certainly he felt no obligation toward the Kaisers. His primary concern was saving the Air Force from embarrassment. More important, with the imminent signing of a peace treaty in Korea, the Air Force no longer needed the planes. Obviously, decisionmakers sensed an opportunity to cut their losses with minimal political fallout.[49]

In a response seemingly out of character, Henry Kaiser refused to press the fight; if anything, he appeared resigned to the decision. As in the case of closing the shipyards, however, many workers would be laid off. Some twelve thousand employees would be dismissed within ninety days, and local UAW officials fought cancellation of the contract. Within days of Talbott's announcement, local UAW leader Emil Mazey collected signatures from over two thousand workers pledging to work for thirty days with no pay to help the company over the hump. Henry Kaiser always showed concern for workers, and it is curious that he withdrew on this occasion. He probably felt that in a boom economy in Detroit, fed by the rousing success of rival auto companies, laid-off workers would not suffer. Whatever the cause, he accepted the decision gracefully, at least in public. At a news conference shortly after recess of the hearings, Kaiser claimed:

> Throughout my career, whenever I have done government work, I have had a firm principle, and no action of today changes that in any respect. That is that I am proud of my government; I want to do the work and service that it wants me to do, and I want to relinquish anything which it does not want me to do.[50]

To supporters, Kaiser's graciousness in the face of unwarranted public humiliation confirmed their view of him as a great American. To cynics, his statement was a shabby imitation of MacArthur's "retirement" speech before Congress two years earlier.

Two weeks later Kaiser regained his characteristic fighting spirit. He delivered a few pungent remarks concerning the general lack of cooperation from Fairchild. He charged Fairchild with trying to "sabotage and undermine" production. He complained that corporate officials had dragged their feet in supplying technical information and had sold him obsolete, worn-out equipment when Willow Run retooled for the job. The Kaisers were angered when Talbott demanded unconditional surrender, asking Edgar to state publicly that his company would not bid on any future

C-123 contracts. Edgar Kaiser informed Talbott at a public meeting in July that his family resented being "threatened," and that "[We] were only conducting ourselves on one basis, and that was an honorable basis whereby we could sleep at night."[51]

Edgar refused to be Talbott's puppet, and his ally Emil Mazey gave the secretary some bad moments. Mazey presented figures showing that the first C-119s produced by Fairchild cost $6.5 million, a startling contrast to the $265,000 average cost figure frequently cited by Kaiser-Frazer's opponents. When Talbott stated that Kaiser-Frazer had been notoriously slow in "cleaning up" its labor problems, and that the Air Force had been amazingly tolerant in providing six months of grace to do so, Mazey observed that government officials had negotiated with the Communists for over two years in Korea without results.[52]

Henry and Edgar Kaiser realized that the cargo plane fiasco had consumed too much of their energy, time, and resources. Willow Run, and everything it represented, had become their most sensitive spot: however legitimate their government loans, they still owed heavy debts to the RFC. As Henry Kaiser observed shortly after the C-119 cancellation: "The quicker we get out of the RFC the better. Then they'll stop talking about Government financing."[53] Willow Run also symbolized mounting losses in automobiles; they sold it to GM a few months later.

In retrospect, it is clear that Kaiser underestimated the problems of successfully entering the cargo plane business. Certainly there were few reasons to anticipate insurmountable difficulties; it was basically an assembly-line job, and he and his managers had successfully overcome similar challenges. They were learning to build excellent automobiles, even if they could not sell them. With cargo planes, of course, "sales" were guaranteed. Although they struggled in automobiles, Kaiser's managers had enjoyed dazzling success almost everywhere else: aluminum, steel, cement, and many other fields. They were overconfident in approaching cargo planes. Whatever the causes, Kaiser failed to organize the project with his customary shrewdness.

Nevertheless, in the summer of 1953 Kaiser was as buoyant and full of new ideas as ever. He and his second wife, Ale, were planning to move to Hawaii, where he had important new projects. Aluminum promised exciting possibilities. Health care and hospitals were becoming an increasingly consuming passion in his life, and he was devoting enormous amounts of time and energy to that field. In the fall of 1953 he had far too many ongoing projects and future plans to worry much about mistakes in cargo planes.

12

Light Metals—Heavy Profits

Although the years after World War II were marked by monumental struggles in steel, automobiles, and cargo planes, Kaiser's industrial empire grew rapidly and prospered. Several enterprises made money from the start. Aluminum was his most spectacular long-term financial success. As with steel, the federal government initially opposed his effort in 1941 to enter the aluminum business. The similarity ended there; by 1946, the government actively encouraged him to compete against Alcoa. Reynolds Aluminum was active, but Kaiser was the only industrialist willing to provide new competition. Even with the government's blessing, Kaiser Aluminum faced major hurdles. Acquiring and transporting millions of tons of raw materials, meeting huge energy requirements, and creating markets for many new products, all had to be achieved before Kaiser Aluminum became a force in the industry. Kaiser's success in aluminum evoked another chorus of complaints of government favoritism. Kaiser and his organization overcame these obstacles; to the surprise of industry analysts, the company netted more than $5 million in its first year, 1946. Twenty years later, profits approached $59 million.[1]

According to seemingly authoritative accounts, Kaiser became fascinated with light metals during World War II, primarily for airplanes, jeeps, and automobiles, though he thought they could also be used as basic building materials. His initial effort to enter aluminum coincided with his first initiatives in steel. In February 1941 he proposed a fabrication plant for aluminum on the West Coast. It made no sense to produce aluminum ingots in the Pacific Northwest, ship them east for fabrication, then back west to be used. Kaiser had peacetime plans for aluminum even then. But in 1941, his offer to federal officials was simple and direct. The nation needed a western fabrication plant for national defense; he would provide it.[2]

Kaiser's proposal went to Secretary of the Interior Harold L. Ickes, who strongly supported it. The secretary shared Kaiser's strong belief that the nation would soon be a belligerent, and that existing producers, dominated by Alcoa, overestimated their capacity to meet wartime needs. Whether or not Kaiser's proposal prompted his outburst, Ickes charged Alcoa with "systematically scaring out of the field all private competitors except for their own kept satellites." He argued that aluminum fabrication was a major bottleneck in the defense program. Ickes backed a government-owned fabrication plant, run by Kaiser: "[He] is one of the biggest contractors in the country. I have had dealings with him and have found him to be a man of imagination and great driving energy . . . I would rather deal with him than with Reynolds because he is not afraid of the Aluminum Company of America and will stand up to that concern." [3]

Alcoa resisted expansion for the same reasons Big Steel did; its officers feared creating excess capacity and stockpiling too much aluminum. Such a response might deflate prices over the long run. Ickes got part of his wish; the government constructed western aluminum fabrication facilities, but Alcoa managed them. That settled the matter for a time. But Kaiser spent a good deal of his energy in 1942 and 1943 planning for the postwar years, and light metal uses remained prominent in his thinking.

Temporarily sidetracked in aluminum, Kaiser turned his attention to a closely allied product—magnesium. His first magnesium proposals had actually predated those for aluminum. After the fall of France in June 1940, military strategists understood the value of magnesium, both for lighter-weight aircraft parts and as an incendiary. By the fall of 1940 Goering's Luftwaffe had made that abundantly clear in France and England, or so Kaiser and his men believed. Germany produced eighty thousand tons of the product in 1940, while U.S. output, dominated by Dow-American Magnesium, was a paltry four thousand tons.

Dow management reassured public officials that they could handle any and all defense needs; as Kaiser saw it, Dow needed help. The magnesium situation mirrored those in steel and aluminum; the country would soon be caught short. In the summer of 1940 Kaiser ordered Harry Davis, manager of the Permanente Cement plant, to study ways to produce magnesium. The conventional means was the electrolytic process, used by Dow-American. Davis, however, had learned of Austrian expatriate Dr. Fritz Hansgirg, inventor of the "carbothermic reduction" process, which reportedly yielded a much purer end product. Following weeks of complicated negotiations in the winter of 1940–1941, Kaiser hired Hansgirg and borrowed $9.25 million from the Reconstruction Finance Corporation (RFC) to build a magnesium plant adjacent to Permanente Cement. Total borrowing for magnesium production eventually reached $22 million, and Kaiser repaid the entire amount, plus interest, in November 1945. [4]

Magnesium proved troublesome almost immediately. Hansgirg was a prima donna who despised the American concept of managerial team-work. Nine days after Pearl Harbor, the FBI arrested him as a security risk because Mrs. Hansgirg had contacted their son, the chief psychologist for the German army. As a result, Dr. Hansgirg was briefly confined in jail in San Jose, California. He was soon paroled to Black Mountain College in North Carolina, where he taught physics. Kaiser's association with a publicly identified security risk created misgivings among both public officials and critics. Advisors urged Kaiser to terminate his association with Hansgirg, but he refused. Although Mrs. Hansgirg charged Kaiser with blackmailing her husband into working at Permanente, Kaiser sponsored their immigration visa extension early in 1942.[5]

In addition to a public relations fiasco, Kaiser was also burdened with an operation which initially sputtered badly. Even before the plant was built, independent scientists and the War Production Board (WPB) warned that the Hansgirg process was untested and extremely dangerous.[6] The new plant launched production in August 1941, but mechanical "bugs" marred its performance in the early months. The Hansgirg process, brilliant in theory, proved devilishly difficult to apply in large-scale output. As government scientists feared, simultaneous experimentation and production proved risky. An accident in a retort furnace on August 28, 1941, killed three workers; weeks later, a second accident claimed two more lives. These events attracted more unfavorable publicity. So did the fact that the Hansgirg process initially yielded small amounts of the material at greatly inflated costs. In March 1942 Arthur H. Bunker, chief of the Magnesium and Aluminum Branch of the WPB, criticized these disappointing results; he claimed that even the normally ebullient Kaiser "had become very much discouraged." A WPB inspector visiting the Permanente plant in June 1942 concluded that the Hansgirg operation had created a "setback" in production of magnesium, partly due to "a too rapid push ahead attitude without much thought or study of all the factors that had to be considered and watched . . ." Over two years later, Maritime Commissioner John M. Carmody complained in a confidential memo to Admiral Land that "magnesium ghosts" and the memory of $7 million spent on failed experiments in magnesium were still causing him to sleep poorly.[7]

Despite repeated setbacks, the Permanente plant proceeded with magnesium production. By the summer of 1943 the most vexing shortcomings of the carbothermic process had been conquered. By then, Kaiser's managers were also operating three other magnesium facilities nearby. These included a dolomite quarry near Salinas, a seawater magnesium oxide plant at Moss Landing, and another magnesium reduction plant at Manteca. Most of Permanente's output was ingots, which were converted into lightweight frames, bomb-casings, and other military uses. A critical breakthrough came in late 1943. Kaiser engineers helped the Chemical Warfare

Service develop a frighteningly effective incendiary material, a combination of powdered magnesium, a distillate, and asphalt, nicknamed "goop." Military officers were so pleased with its destructive capabilities that early in 1944 the Chemical Warfare Service ordered Permanente Metals to produce nothing but "goop."[8]

From 1943 until the end of the war, Kaiser's work in magnesium was very productive. Permanente Metals turned out forty-one thousand tons of "goop" by V-J Day. If Kaiser or his men felt qualms over what happened on the receiving end of "goop," they hid their feelings well. Like most Americans, they perceived winning the war as a job to be done as quickly as possible. When the U.S. Army presented Permanente Metals the coveted "E" award for excellence in war production, the presiding officer emphasized that "goop" had been used on military and industrial installations, not civilian populations. If any present suspected that they had played a role in fire-bombings of Dresden or Tokyo, they did not talk about it.[9]

As noted earlier, Kaiser's feats during World War II made him a very controversial figure. But many public officials praised his work ethic. One admirer was Assistant Attorney General Thurmond Arnold, whom Roosevelt had appointed in 1937 to prosecute antitrust cases. Arnold's antitrust compaign was suspended during World War II, but he intended to press it when peace returned. When considering potential competitors for Alcoa, he thought immediately of Kaiser, to whom he wrote early in 1943, "I have long admired you more than any other business man . . ." With support in the Justice Department, Kaiser's men in Washington became privy to information about which companies might become postwar targets for prosecution. In early October 1944, Chad Calhoun predicted that the department would not let Alcoa purchase any government-owned facilities.[10]

By late 1944, Kaiser needed little encouragement to enter aluminum. He carefully considered potential uses for the light metal. In addition to its advantages in automobiles and aircraft, Kaiser realized that it could be used in ships, railroad cars, buses, trucks, home construction, and many other areas. Kaiser sought government-owned plants that might be shut down. As he told the Senate Small Business Committee in March 1945, "Idle plants are just so much scrap, and the junk value of scrap is only a fraction of their going concern value . . ." Kaiser claimed it was not "proper . . . to suggest what the government policy should be," then turned right around and criticized government officials for dragging out negotiations and hesitating to sell plants at discount. He urged them to sell plants promptly and keep them running.[11]

As demobilization began, many astute observers thought Kaiser took leave of his senses in entering aluminum. Most industry analysts thought that the market for light metals would virtually disappear after the war. Despite Alcoa's initial foot-dragging, capacity had increased sevenfold during the war years. Conventional wisdom held that finding uses for existing plants would be very problematical. Even George Havas, one of Kaiser's top engineers, underestimated long-term prospects in aluminum. Three partners in magnesium informed Kaiser they wanted no part of aluminum. The doubters were MacDonald and Kahn, Morrison-Knudsen, and Utah Construction. Finally, Kaiser needed major new lines of private financing, and the automobile venture promised to stretch his credit past the limit. Most of his advisors argued that it was pure folly to enter yet another capital-intensive industry simultaneously.[12]

Early in 1946, after months of dawdling, the War Assets Administration (WAA) finally put several government-owned aluminum facilities up for sale or lease. In Oakland, the midnight oil burned at Kaiser Company offices, where the boss and his key men discussed strategy. Initially, only Chad Calhoun and Eugene E. Trefethen, Jr., shared Kaiser's vision of the huge potential for aluminum in domestic consumer items, but Kaiser gradually swayed others to his point of view. His was the only vote that mattered, but he realized the need to convince the managers who would run the facilities on a daily basis. Although three partners declined to participate, three others stayed in: J. F. Shea Investment Company, General Construction, and Pacific Builders. At the end of the war, Permanente Metals had a surplus of $3 million, but that wasn't nearly enough to enter the business. A key factor in the decision to bid for aluminum facilities was that the Bank of America, after a good deal of arm-twisting by Henry Kaiser, provided $15.8 million in credit.[13]

The facilities Kaiser sought generated little enthusiasm elsewhere. The two plants, both in Washington, seemed to be large white elephants. A reduction plant at Mead had 101 structures spread over 234 acres; a rolling mill at nearby Trentwood was a huge building covering 52 acres. They had been built by the government for a total of $71 million in 1942 and had been idle since mid-1945; Kaiser's engineers discovered that they were in excellent shape. When the WAA officials decided to sell or lease the two plants, they invited bids from almost three hundred companies. There were nibbles, but Kaiser presented the only solid offer. Negotiations dragged on for several months. Doubters thought it appropriate that Kaiser formally entered the aluminum business on April 1, 1946: April Fool's Day. Kaiser leased both facilities for five years with an option to purchase; lease terms for the two plants totaled $9.87 million. In 1945 a U.S. circuit court had ruled that Alcoa, which controlled 90 percent of ingot production, had violated the Sherman Antitrust Act. Alcoa officials therefore cooperated in transferring the facilities to Kaiser.[14]

In addition to nine-tenths of ingot production, Alcoa controlled at least 70 percent of American capacity in all phases of aluminum processing, from raw bauxite deposits to extrusion of specialized forms. Like it or not, given the Justice Department's demand that the industry become competitive, Alcoa had to assist other producers. Clay Bedford recalled that Alcoa's chief executive officer, Frank McGee, was "really a very broad-minded, wise fellow," and that Kaiser's managers felt none of the hostility from the aluminum industry that they had attracted from Big Steel. The Justice Department "persuaded" Alcoa to supply all the bauxite Kaiser and Reynolds Metals could use. Kaiser also hired a number of Alcoa's managers and experienced technicians. The Pittsburgh-based company, anticipating sharp curtailment of demand, was retrenching, and Kaiser persuaded some key people that his outfit promised a more exciting future. Top management, however, remained in the hands of long-term Kaiser loyalists.[15]

Kaiser also acquired a plant in Baton Rouge, Louisiana, where raw bauxite was reduced to alumina. By May 1946 he had a partially integrated aluminum operation, but logistical problems seemed overwhelming. Initially, the bauxite purchased from Alcoa had to be transported 2,500 miles across the Atlantic from Surinam to Baton Rouge. The nearest available reserves of bauxite were located in Jamaica; even these resources were 1,200 miles from Baton Rouge, and it would take time to develop them. Conversion of raw materials into aluminum ingots was a complex, two-stage process. In Baton Rouge, raw bauxite was converted to alumina, which was sent to Mead to be reduced to ingots. Only then could the aluminum be converted into useful products. The Trentwood mill yielded only a few crude forms of rolled aluminum. For forms such as extrusions, Kaiser relied on specialized fabricators. Finally, although the Pacific Northwest had seemingly ample energy sources, so critical to alumina reduction, there were few regional markets for aluminum. The product had to be shipped long distances once again to major market areas. From raw material in Surinam to finished products in East Coast markets, some minerals traveled 8,000 miles.[16]

Despite obstacles, the Mead reduction plant yielded its first ingots in July 1946. Startled industry analysts soon learned that Kaiser, Calhoun, and Trefethen had been right about postwar markets for light metals. During the first year of operation, the Mead plant turned out almost 110 million pounds of aluminum, with sales of $45.4 million. Even more startling to industry analysts, the fledgling company, still under the name Permanente Metals, earned over $5 million. Donald A. "Dusty" Rhoades, who had nearly twenty years of experience in Kaiser's sand-and-gravel and magnesium operations, proved the right manager for aluminum. This was not simply the judgment of Kaiser's managers. A 1956 *Fortune* article called Rhoades "a fierce and shrewd competitor," who "wrung a much higher rate of production out of his plants than experienced wartime operators ever had."[17]

The late 1940s were a time of intense learning for Kaiser and his aluminum managers. The Pacific Northwest possessed plenty of cheap power; the dams Kaiser had helped build on the Columbia River a decade earlier supplied much of it. Still, it took little knowledge of the business to understand that the remoteness of his main plants was a decided handicap. In 1946 one analyst estimated that the cost of alumina was $0.32 per pound for Alcoa, while Kaiser spent $0.50. In addition, of course, Kaiser faced far higher costs in transporting rolled aluminum to markets. But as long as demand expanded, the company would probably make money.[18]

Kaiser's top priorities were obtaining more convenient sources of raw bauxite and acquiring more diversified fabrication. Although the Kaiser aluminum operation depended on Alcoa for most of its raw bauxite until 1953, the westerners also purchased and developed several thousand acres on Jamaica where they had discovered large bauxite reserves in 1947. In addition, they acquired a second reduction plant converting alumina to ingots at Tacoma, Washington, and several small fabricating plants in the East. A sharp, brief sales slump in the spring of 1947 forced Kaiser to cut back production in the Trentwood rolling mill to 40 percent of capacity. Inexperienced at the time, the managers feared that the softness in the market was a long-term trend, but this turned out not to be the case. In the late 1940s, Permanente Metals experienced a healthy growth rate. Sales grew from $45.4 million in 1946–1947 to just over $75 million in 1949–1950, and net income reached $10.5 million. In 1948 the company raised almost $9 million through issuing 600,000 shares of stock which it sold for $15 per share. With these funds, plus money from loans and retained earnings, Kaiser purchased the plants leased from the government. The Mead, Trentwood, and Baton Rouge plants cost a total of $36 million. In 1949 the company changed its name to Kaiser Aluminum & Chemical Corporation (KACC). The latter portion of the name referred to items produced at Moss Landing, California: dolomite for roofing, magnesia, and refractories for kilns and furnaces.[19]

By mid-century, Kaiser had created a new enterprise which promised to become an important supplier in a growing industry. Significantly, some decisionmakers did not think aluminum was growing fast enough. In the summer of 1949 Interior Secretary Julius A. Krug claimed that in the event of war, capacity in the industry would have to be doubled. Business leaders were ambivalent toward Kaiser's rise in the business. Some emphasized that he prospered only with his "old familiar crutch," federal subsidies. When he leased the government-built plants in Washington and Louisiana, critics charged that he got them "for a song." When Kaiser purchased them, they cried "fraud" and "favoritism." Kaiser officials claimed that they paid 36.1 percent of wartime costs of construction for the plants, while other corporate buyers of surplus plants paid an average of 33.3 percent.[20]

Other industry analysts thought such squabbles were irrelevant; they stressed the fundamental weakness of Kaiser's competitive position. In private communications, even the intrepid Calhoun was fully aware of Alcoa's ability to bury KACC if it had the chance. In a 1947 memo to his boss, Calhoun spoke of the "brutal history of Alcoa and its business practices" and warned that there was "no evidence to indicate that we are any exception, or that Alcoa's managers would follow any more lenient practices with us, once they are out from under the present Federal court order." Industry analysts believed that there had been little change in the overall picture in aluminum by late 1949. The Justice Department shared that view and closely monitored the activities of the eastern giant. Late in 1949 and early 1950, a congressional subcommittee probed recent suspicious moves by Alcoa. Kaiser tried to avoid testifying, informing the chairman of the House Subcommittee on the Study of Monopoly Power that the legal and technical issues being investigated were "too complicated." But the Justice Department insisted, and Kaiser appeared. He emphasized production ratios and profit margins, which compared favorably with those of Alcoa. But other witnesses believed that Kaiser Aluminum remained virtually a "satellite" to Alcoa.[21] The latter assessment is convincing, at least until 1950.

The Korean War gave Kaiser an opportunity to really challenge Alcoa. The conflict created conditions leading to the cargo plane fiasco, but it also marked the "breakout" stage for other Kaiser enterprises. The westerner exploited his opportunity in aluminum; KACC expanded rapidly and became more independent of Alcoa. Speed in recognizing new opportunities and presenting well-considered plans for expansion were the keys to Kaiser's success. Aluminum became a critical defense need, and Kaiser and his organization worked feverishly to help build up the nation's stockpile.

On July 8, 1950, two weeks after the outbreak of fighting, Kaiser volunteered to increase aluminum output 150 percent. For a few weeks, it appeared that his offer might be ignored. The United States had acted with unusual speed and efficiency in maneuvering the United Nations Security Council into placing a "peacekeeping" force on the embattled peninsula. However, the United States had geared up slowly for earlier wars, and no break in that tradition occurred in 1950. As in World War II, Kaiser again observed that bureaucrats held him back. Three months after he proposed expansion in aluminum, he still had no authorization. In October he complained to the Munitions Board that "Various national defense authorities have given up conflicting advices [sic], ranging all the way from statements that further long-range expansions will not be required to estimates of a stupendous Government expansion program." Patience was never Kaiser's long suit; he pleaded for prompt clarification of the government's position.[22]

Kaiser's entreaties were finally answered. Defense officials authorized doubling his current capacity in November 1950. The challenge shifted to where and how to do it. In 1950 power resources in the Pacific Northwest were strained to capacity. Aluminum processing devoured almost 60 percent of all hydroelectric power in eastern Washington; expanding the Mead and Trentwood plants would squeeze other consumers too hard. Kaiser's managers drew up detailed plans for new expansion and awaited word about where to build new plants. Naturally, facilities providing several thousand jobs were prized by politicians; state and local officials' lobbying had as much to do with the final location as Kaiser did. Two well-connected and persistent politicians were New Orleans Mayor De Lesseps S. Morrison and Congressman Hale Boggs of Louisiana. Kaiser considered a Texas Gulf Coast location, close to natural gas sources, but the Louisianans convinced both Kaiser and federal officials that some marshy land a few miles east of New Orleans on the Mississippi River would be a superior site. Morrison and Boggs simply "out-politicked" their rivals. In February 1951 Kaiser agreed to locate a huge new reduction plant at Chalmette. The location had historical significance, being where Andrew Jackson had routed British General Edward Packenham at the Battle of New Orleans.[23]

If federal officials expected gratitude from Kaiser, they were disappointed. Before the ink was dry on the authorization, he was back in Washington requesting increases in the original expansion objectives. In May 1951 Kaiser blasted Interior Secretary Oscar L. Chapman in a sarcastic telegram which he never would have dared send to Ickes. Kaiser charged that there were "reports" from Chapman's department that he wouldn't be allowed additional expansion "until and unless the government puts into the business some as yet unknown person or interests who might make aluminum maybe—sometime in the unknown future." When Kaiser visited Chapman's office a few days later, the secretary said that he had to give smaller independent companies a chance to expand. After informing Chapman that he wished federal officials would show the same attitude in the auto business, where he was a small independent, Kaiser stated, "I might as well tell the world that you don't want us to expand aluminum. You know you have given us the run around for dam [*sic*] near a year." Kaiser's forcefulness, plus the smooth political work by Morrison, brought additional expansion in November 1951. The Chalmette plant was authorized to double original capacity even before it produced its first ingots.[24]

Haggling with federal officials over expansion did not delay work at Chalmette. February 1951 brought a new invasion of the delta, this time by Kaiser's earth movers, overhead cranes, and hundreds of other big machines. Over thirty-five thousand wood pilings helped stabilize 280 acres of muddy, water-logged terrain. A mighty plant rose out of the swampland in just ten months. Natural gas piped in from Texas supplied power. Engineers estimated that at peak capacity, the plant would consume fifty billion cubic feet of gas a year. Gas-powered steam generating plants required almost twice the water consumed by residents of New Orleans. Fortunately, a bit of history was preserved. Engineers had originally designed the plant in a manner which would have eliminated a famous clump of trees known as Packenham's Oaks. Once the problem was discovered, plans were altered, and the grove became the centerpiece of a lovely park.[25]

In mid-December 1951 Chalmette began production. Defense officials were glad they had authorized the southern facility. The fall of 1951 brought a severe drought to the Pacific Northwest; had the plant been built there it would have been extremely difficult to meet military requirements for aluminum and regional power needs. On December 11, an array of federal officials, local politicians, and important guests watched Kaiser and Defense Mobilization chief Charles "Electric Charlie" Wilson tip a ladle pouring the first aluminum ingot. At a celebration banquet, Wilson recounted one visit by Kaiser and several aides a few months earlier. Wilson had named a production figure he hoped Kaiser could achieve, and the westerner had challenged Wilson to double it. An aide tugged at his sleeve and said, "Take it easy, H. J. Remember, Rome wasn't built in a day." Kaiser allegedly replied, "I don't know about that; I wasn't working on that job."[26]

Kaiser naturally stressed patriotic motives for expanding production. But he risked little; the government promised to purchase and stockpile all aluminum not sold in private markets for five years. This commitment enabled Kaiser to negotiate private loans he might otherwise have found very elusive. In fact, KACC borrowed $115 million early in 1951 from a combination of eighteen insurance companies and eight banks.[27]

The Korean War stimulated the aluminum industry in general, Kaiser's operations in particular. Between 1950 and 1953 KACC production capacity almost tripled from 143,000 tons to 428,000 tons annually. Industry analysts were not surprised that the war left KACC with almost twice the production capacity needed. In 1953 the company produced only 222,212 tons. What startled experts was that post–Korean War demand grew so rapidly. In 1954, Kaiser produced 357,000 tons and sold 388,000 tons. By the end of 1954, Kaiser was "big time" in aluminum. Alcoa was still the leader with about 40 percent of national sales, but KACC challenged Reynolds Metals for the number two position. By the mid-1950s, the company had also reduced dependence on Alcoa for bauxite. In 1953 KACC's Jamaica facility sent almost 666,000 tons to reduction plants; five years later shipments exceeded 4 million tons.[28]

Kaiser was enthusiastic about prospects for aluminum from the start; clearly the "metal of the future" had become the metal of the present by 1955. It was widely used in construction, and applications in the home were expanding almost exponentially. Recreational uses in boats, skis, camping and barbecue equipment, coolers, and many other ideas excited product managers. One industry study identified KACC as a leader in "the art of aluminum." The western firm did not match Alcoa in research and development, but it had several small pilot plants working on new applications.[29]

Kaiser's achievement in becoming a major supplier of aluminum was remarkable by itself. In 1954 and 1955 KACC broke free of dependency on Alcoa and prepared to challenge the easterners in their own back yard. Western markets were growing rapidly, but Kaiser wanted to compete nationally. Kaiser's move east reversed most previous industrial development, as western America had been dominated by eastern manufacturers.[30] To be sure, Kaiser had earlier "invaded" Detroit; but in the automobile business he had little choice.

In the early 1950s KACC acquired a few small fabricating facilities in Maryland, Ohio, and elsewhere in the East. Late in 1954 Kaiser announced plans to build a huge sheet and rolling mill at Ravenswood, West Virginia. The location made sense. With recently developed capacity to complete the two-stage process of reducing raw bauxite to alumina and then to ingots in Louisiana, KACC could ship the metal directly upriver to Ravenswood, located on the Ohio River. United Mine Workers (UMW) President John L. Lewis, who hoped to ease severe unemployment in the region, welcomed Kaiser's initiative. Lewis and Kaiser believed that the Ravenswood plant would attract specialized fabricators, which would further stimulate employment. Just as important as union cooperation, seemingly inexhaustible supplies of coal ensured cheap power. Finally, the Ravenswood mills provided easy access to eastern and midwestern customers. One industry magazine observed that before construction of the Ravenswood plant, eastern customers resisted buying KACC's products because deliveries from the West were much slower than those of competitors. With completion of Ravenswood, KACC finally competed in eastern markets on even terms with Alcoa and Reynolds.[31]

Kaiser had planned expansion into the East since at least 1951, when he purchased an option on a 2,650-acre site on the Ohio River, six miles below Ravenswood. When he exercised the option four years later, local papers were euphoric. In late May 1955, Kaiser flew to Ravenswood and was treated like visiting royalty. Marshall College in nearby Huntington, West Virginia, awarded him an honorary degree of Doctor of Humane Letters, undoubtedly because of the enormous economic stimulus KACC promised for the region. More than a thousand people attended the annual Five Dollar Banquet in Ravenswood and heard the rotund westerner praise regional potential and outline future plans. Kaiser charmed listeners by claiming that he had selected Ravenswood ahead of fifty other potential sites, not only because of its strategic location and vast coal resources, but "most of all because we like the people here; the spirit of cooperation and a substantial evidence that we would be welcome."[32]

Interest in future growth was very keen in Jackson County. Although the plant initially hired only five hundred full-time workers, Kaiser envisioned a fully integrated plant which would eventually employ several thousand. Within two weeks of his visit, more than nine thousand applicants visited the KACC personnel office. Officials in Ravenswood were dazzled at future economic prospects in the small town of 1,100 citizens; but they were wary of problems accompanying rapid growth. They believed that Ravenswood's population might multiply tenfold in the next five years.[33]

KACC managers received praise for helping make the transformation of the region as smooth as possible. A year and a half after Kaiser's visit, *Time* observed that the Ravenswood plant was "reviving the long-depressed Ohio River Valley." Growth came quickly, although not on the scale boosters originally estimated. Between 1955 and 1960, Ravenswood's population tripled to 3,410; in the mid-1960s it reached roughly 4,500 before leveling off. Nearby Ripley also grew from 1,813 to 2,750 during the 1950s. Company managers helped alleviate growth problems in Ravenswood. KACC built a twenty-room elementary school, which it leased to Jackson County for a dollar per year. In November 1963, Jackson County voters turned down a $420,000 bond issue for expansion of the school system. Kaiser offered to double every dollar raised on the next successful bond issue. He also helped underwrite a new hospital in Ripley. To be sure, it was enlightened self-interest; inadequate local schools and health care would make it hard for KACC to hire and retain able managers and workers in Ravenswood. But Kaiser had few critics in West Virginia after opening of the plant.[34]

Ravenswood was the most important addition to Kaiser's rapidly expanding aluminum empire in the mid-1950s, but there were other developments. At Chalmette, KACC added another potline, increasing plant capacity 13 percent and spent several million dollars modernizing equipment and smoke control. The company undertook similar expansion programs in the Pacific Northwest, at Mead, Trentwood, and Tacoma. Finally, KACC spent nearly $20 million expanding fabricating plants in the Midwest and the East. Kaiser matched competitors in producing a full line of industrial aluminum forms and developing new consumer goods. He was determined to create a fully integrated, competitive aluminum company. By the mid-1950s, he had achieved that goal.[35]

Completion of the Ravenswood plant convinced competitors that KACC meant business in all areas of aluminum production and sales. Thomas J. Ready, in charge of Ravenswood, estimated that it lowered transportation costs of sheet metal to eastern markets nearly 75 percent. With these savings, KACC lowered prices and grabbed a larger share of customers. By 1956 KACC had captured between 20 and 25 percent of the eastern foil market, and management confidently aimed for 35 percent. Although KACC experienced difficulties in consumer products, overall performance was excellent. Between 1957 and 1961, net annual profits ranged between $23.1 and $27.9 million, and KACC was firmly entrenched as the organization's top money-maker.[36] Although Kaiser bought a home in Hawaii in 1954, his move away from the mainland did not symbolize retirement from an active business life. The septuagenarian retained a driving energy and fascination with all corporate activities. Close associates recalled that he made few concessions to age, but he focused attention on the cutting edge of future business. In the late 1950s and early 1960s, finding new uses for aluminum provided some of his most significant challenges.

Kaiser was naturally interested in the bottom line, and profits in aluminum provided much satisfaction. KACC's position in producer goods was firmly established, but Kaiser dreamed of cracking Alcoa's and Reynolds' domination of consumer goods sales. Any bright designer with a new potential use for aluminum received an attentive hearing from the boss. Kaiser personally encouraged fabricators to conduct their own experiments. In offering aluminum at bargain rates to the research and development branch of Continental Can, Kaiser conveyed his enthusiasm to company president Hans Eggers: "I visualize the can industry as a vast new market of an entirely different nature than anything which the industry has ever experienced." Corporate offices were awash with drawings of all-aluminum automobiles, electrical equipment, railroad cars, even skyscrapers. The late 1950s marked construction of the first large aluminum office buildings: IBM in Rochester, Minnesota, the Texaco Building in Los Angeles, and others.[37]

Kaiser was intensely interested in aluminum boats. For years he had raced powerboats, both at Lake Tahoe and in national and international racing competition, and he worked constantly to improve his models. He closely monitored development of hundreds of different designs for both inboard and outboard boats, hydroplanes, catamarans, and other vessels. He explored possibilities in hydrofoil boats—large, fast vessels capable of carrying several hundred passengers on inter-island trips in Hawaii. However, most designs were for inexpensive outboards in the sixteen-to-eighteen-foot range. In the early-to-mid-1960s, the organization hired several small firms to build and market them. But Kaiser's designers never developed models with "sex appeal"; buyers perferred wood and fiberglass boats. Aluminum boats never caught on, but they gave Kaiser hundreds of hours of pleasure.[38]

One of Kaiser's widely publicized applications for aluminum was in some of the first geodesic domes in the late 1950s. Kaiser had disagreed with Buckminster Fuller on automobile designs in the early 1940s, but he hoped that geodesic domes would expand demand for aluminum. By early 1957 Kaiser was active in civic affairs in Honolulu. He urged Honolulu leaders to build a convention center and theater and contacted Fuller, who designed a comparatively modest 144-foot-diameter dome seating 1,800 persons. The structure required no supporting beams and offered un-restricted views from any angle. After building permits were secured, Kaiser's engineers erected the dome in two days.[39]

Fuller's dome was christened with a showing of Michael Todd's *Around the World in Eighty Days* in early November 1957. Todd appeared with his wife, Elizabeth Taylor, and many other celebrities. Kaiser believed that the geodesic dome was a harbinger of bigger things to come. Ever the opti-mist, he sensed the dome's potential for many commercial uses: amusement centers, armories, hangars, silo-type storage facilities, sports-complexes, and others. He talked of building a 14,000-seat basketball and indoor sports complex for New Orleans for under $1 million. But Kaiser and Fuller did little business building domes. In the late 1950s, they secured contracts for a few domes on the mainland, and in 1958 KACC established a dome sales office in Chicago. Company officials hoped to sell 250 per year. Again, however, Fuller and Kaiser had poor chemistry for a partner-ship; according to former associates, Kaiser found the designer's egotism irritating. More important, acoustical and structural problems diminished initial public fascination with Fuller's domes, and derisive nicknames soon cropped up. Kaiser's enthusiasm soon faded.[40]

Kaiser entered consumer products late in life, but with youthful enthu-siasm. According to aide Lambreth Hancock, it was his idea to slip cou-pons for free Hawaiian recipe books into every box of aluminum foil. Con-sumer interest appeared strong, and KACC sponsored Hawaiian cuisine contests in various regions on the mainland. Finalists in regional cook-offs won free trips to Hawaii, where they stayed in Kaiser's Hawaiian Village hotel. The promotion benefited his aluminum and resort interests, and it boosted jet travel and Hawaiian tourism in general. Kaiser presided over festivities at the "Kaiser Foil Annual Cookout Championships."[41]

Kaiser's penchant for promotion occasionally created conflict with top managers. Donald A. "Dusty" Rhoades was a superb production man, and under his direction KACC competed effectively with Alcoa and Reynolds in most areas. But Rhoades' marketing talents were geared primarily to-ward industrial sales; he initially had unsophisticated notions of consumer advertising. Milt Eisele, a former KACC executive, recalled a discussion in which Rhoades voiced suspicion of such an intangible "product" as adver-tising. Rhoades told Kaiser: "I can get newspaper boys to throw a [free] package of foil at each household [in Honolulu] for less cost than the advertising budget." Kaiser and Rhoades never achieved accord on advertising strategy. In an early 1955 memo, Kaiser informed Rhoades, "I am troubled, Dusty, with the fact that Alcoa and Reynolds spend so much money advertising foil . . . we, like ostriches, continue to bury our heads in the sand and ignore this." Kaiser concluded, "There must be some reason why they are spending all this extra money."[42]

KACC never achieved the success in consumer products enjoyed by competitors, but the company nevertheless thrived in Kaiser's last years. Between 1963 and 1966 net sales increased from $465.8 to $781.5 million. In 1966, net profits reached a record of $58.9 million. Aluminum was the organization's largest money-maker by a wide margin, dwarfing profits of other companies: Kaiser Steel, the next most profitable, earned $18 million, while cement and gypsum made $10.7 million. Other subsidiaries earned smaller amounts or sustained losses. The aging patriarch looked back on two decades in aluminum with satisfaction; entering the field after World War II had been one of his most brilliant decisions.[43]

13

Kaiser and the Doctors

Toward the end of his life, Kaiser claimed repeatedly that the Kaiser Permanente Medical Care Program (KPMCP), a prepaid health care system, would stand as his most significant achievement. He was right. Twenty years after his death, most of the companies in Kaiser's once dazzling industrial empire had either folded or been sold. However, the KPMCP continued to thrive. At Kaiser's death in 1967 the health plan covered 1.6 million participants; in the next twenty years membership more than tripled. Investment in hospitals and their appurtenances was $70 million in 1967; in 1985 it stood at $2.5 billion. By the late 1980s KPMCP was by far the nation's largest Health Maintenance Organization (HMO).[1]

On countless occasions, Kaiser told a poignant tale of how his mother had died in his arms when he was sixteen, because of lack of proper medical care. He recounted vowing at that moment that if he had the opportunity, providing the finest available medical care for the masses would be his primary mission in life. By his last years he had told the story so many times that he probably believed it. Kaiser had significant numbers of employees by 1914, but he paid little attention to health care until the late 1930s. Edgar Kaiser claimed that although such issues concerned his father deeply, the competitiveness of the construction industry and limited financial resources precluded earlier health care initiatives. The first Kaiser experiments in medicine in the 1930s copied features of long-standing programs. The Kaiser organization's real contributions were spreading availability of affordable health care to millions and providing advocates of more competition and pluralism in health care financing and delivery a successful model of those theories in action.

Kaiser first offered prepaid health care to workers at Grand Coulee Dam in 1938, but similar programs had existed much earlier. The nation's first private prepaid health plan was organized by La Société Française de

Bienfaisance Mutuelle in San Francisco in 1849. Most were developed in remote areas. In the 1860s, railroads, lumber, and mining companies offered company-funded health care, usually for employees only. In the 1880s the Homestead Mining Company in South Dakota claimed that it offered complete health care for families as well as employees, at company expense. There were many experiments with coverage. By 1888 several coal operators in the Lehigh Valley region in Pennsylvania offered prepaid group plans to workers and families for $.75 per month; single men paid $.50. By 1900 the concept was widespread, covering workers at New York City's Consolidated Edison Corporation, Northern Pacific Railroad employees in St. Paul, and thousands of others. Between 1914 and the mid-1920s, America's most famous industrialist, Henry Ford, claimed that he ran a "poor man's hospital" under a prepaid group plan. By the early 1930s, in California alone there were several hundred unregulated small health insurance plans.[2]

Although Kaiser gained a well-deserved reputation as a friend of workers, his initial involvement in health care was neither voluntary nor altruistic. When Kaiser was building roads during World War I, state laws in Washington, Oregon, and California required employers to share half the cost for injuries suffered on the job. Employers had an option of hiring physicians to care for injured workers or contributing to a state fund established for that purpose. In Washington and elsewhere, fraternal orders experimented with prepaid group plans, and some lodges even hired their own doctors. Portending future controversies, local American Medical Association (AMA) chapters in Washington objected to "lodge practice," claiming that lay groups "exploited" individual doctors.[3]

Kaiser complied with workers' compensation laws; he also joined the Elks Lodge in Everett, Washington, in 1916. Thus he was familiar with voluntary prepaid health care two decades before he offered it to his employees. It was years before the right opportunity arrived. For example, at Hoover Dam, Six Companies built a new town and provided modern hospital facilities. But Kaiser was busy in Washington, and other partners were responsible for hospitals in Boulder City.[4]

Yet the Hoover Dam years provided an important link in Kaiser's ultimate commitment to prepaid health care. Among other duties, Alonzo B. Ordway handled Kaiser's insurance. During the early months at Hoover Dam, Ordway learned of a young doctor who had set up a prepaid health care plan for workers on the Colorado River Aqueduct job in the Mojave Desert. Dr. Sidney R. Garfield was fresh out of residency at Los Angeles County Hospital and found few opportunities in the city during the depths of the Depression in 1933. Contract practice on government and corporate-sponsored reclamation projects promised economic and professional advancement . . . or at least a temporary livelihood. Starting with

$2,500 in savings, Garfield borrowed enough to build and equip a mobile twelve-bed facility in sun-baked Desert Center, which met the employer's legal obligations. He hoped to supplement his income by handling illness and injury beyond those covered by workers' compensation. Garfield attracted plenty of patients, but workers seldom saved money for unexpected, non-work-related illness and accidents. Nor was employer-covered service lucrative. The employers' insurance company generally paid the doctor's claims, but transferred serious cases to Los Angeles, denying Garfield more substantial fees. By late 1933 Garfield was deep in debt, his three-person staff hadn't been paid for seven months, and creditors threatened to close the hospital. In later years, corporate lore held that when a repossessor tried to reclaim his ambulance, Garfield pulled out a rifle and chased him away.[5]

Garfield had one bargaining chip; he provided excellent medical care, and the aqueduct contractors wanted to keep it. Ordway had close ties to Industrial Indemnity, which insured both Six Companies and the aqueduct contractors. He helped Industrial Indemnity and Garfield develop a new medical plan providing greater incentives for the doctor. The insurers agreed to pay a fixed portion of the workers' compensation premium for all on-site services Garfield provided. For an additional $.05 a day paid by workers, Garfield offered non-industrial coverage. This "fixed-fee" arrangement inspired Garfield to promote safety and preventive checkups, because he got paid whether or not workers suffered accidents and illness. Similar programs were used where employers guaranteed physicians extra income to keep them at remote or unattractive job sites. The contractors on the Colorado River Aqueduct endorsed the plan and agreed to collect the workers' monthly dues by payroll deductions. They also helped persuade 95 percent of all employees to sign up. The prepaid health plan was a financial and medical success. For five years Garfield tended patients in the desert. When the aqueduct project was finished in 1938, he sold the hospital for a profit and returned to Los Angeles to teach and practice medicine.[6]

In the meantime, Six Companies finished Hoover Dam and began work at Grand Coulee Dam. Edgar Kaiser made operating decisions, and he had to arrange decent medical care for several thousand workers at the remote construction site. Since Henry Kaiser had small investments in Industrial Indemnity and the aqueduct job, he probably knew about Garfield's medical program in the desert. But it was Ordway who brought Garfield's achievement to Edgar's attention; he located Garfield in Los Angeles and persuaded him to visit Portland to meet Edgar. As Garfield later recalled, their initial meeting was unpromising. Edgar was extremely busy, and the doctor cooled his heels for hours in his hotel room, with no word about when they would meet. Garfield recalled that he was about to return to Los Angeles when Edgar's secretary called. Fuming, Garfield went to

Edgar's suite in the Multnomah Hotel, intending to tell him bluntly that he wasn't interested in Grand Coulee. However, Edgar's wife, Sue, was there with a sick daughter, Becky. By the time Garfield had diagnosed her measles, he had forgotten his anger.[7]

For his part, Edgar Kaiser was not immediately impressed by Garfield. Dr. Paul de Kruif (Ph.D.), who later helped promote KPMCP, described Garfield as "a man whom you'd not pick out of the human mass as a leader. . . . His lean face was finely chiseled. . . . He was serious, yet smiled easily. . . . He was quiet and spoke in a hesitant drawl. He seemed bashful."[8] Garfield was flashy in appearance, with a full head of flaming red hair. A "natty" dresser in contrast to the somberly clad Kaisers, he wore dark-colored shirts and white ties. Later, Edgar told his father that nobody looked less like a doctor than Garfield. Despite unpromising initial impressions, the two men soon got on well, and Edgar persuaded Garfield to visit Grand Coulee.[9]

Except for an initial meeting or two at Grand Coulee, Garfield saw little of Henry Kaiser. Edgar persuaded him to set up a prepaid health plan at Grand Coulee. He had several selling points. Unlike the Desert Center operation, where "clients" were scattered over hundreds of miles, all of Garfield's prospective patients lived in the self-contained community of Mason City. Since corporate support was assured, Garfield had few financial concerns, and he sensed growth potential. Hundreds of workers remained from the initial phase of dam construction by another contractor, and Kaiser and his partners planned to hire thousands more.[10]

There was one drawback. The contractors on the first phase of construction work had provided poor medical care, and workers were suspicious of any management-controlled plan. Union officials had agreed to give prepaid health care a trial only after considerable persuasion. Garfield had to renovate an existing, abandoned hospital and dispense first-class medical care immediatley to win the workers' confidence. He established a sole-proprietorship medical organization, Sidney R. Garfield and Associates. Since the job site was remote, Garfield offered handsome salaries for the times: $500–600 per month, when many "fee-for-service" doctors earned half that. With that inducement, he eventually recruited Dr. Cecil C. Cutting, Dr. Wallace J. Neighbor, and several other young specialists. As Cutting later recalled, a team of seven doctors, most of them recent graduates from medical schools, supplied total health care for five thousand workers. The Grand Coulee medical operation thrived in a frontier town environment. Garfield and Associates eventually served workers, government bureaucrats sent to monitor work, and numerous prostitutes attracted to a town where large numbers of single men had settled. Accepting reality, Garfield and his colleagues performed health inspections and prescribed necessary remedies to the ladies of the night. The doctors' moral scruples were assuaged by the fact that in providing such services they supplemented their incomes nicely on a traditional "fee-for-service" basis. In return for the "live-and-let-live" attitude among the doctors, their wives found local madams generous donors to charity fund-raisers.[11]

Soon it became apparent to the workers that the commitment to medical care by Kaiser management went beyond providing minimum services required by state laws. Within a year union leaders were so impressed with Garfield's program that they negotiated coverage for workers' dependents. With few statistics to help establish equitable fees, Garfield decided to charge $.50 per week for each spouse and $.25 per week per child. Workers liked the program, and their health improved dramatically. Workers and family members learned to seek treatment before they were seriously ill; the preventive care principle was proven effective early.[12]

The successful experiment at Grand Coulee encouraged Henry Kaiser to make widespread affordable health care a major personal objective. By 1942, after completion of the dams, tens of thousands of workers migrated to the shipyards. Dr. Garfield had returned briefly to teaching and private practice in Los Angeles. Shortly after Pearl Harbor, he was preparing to enter the University of Southern California–Los Angeles County medical contingent going overseas. He had even purchased his second lieutenant's uniform. But Ordway asked him to manage health care facilities at the Richmond shipyards and persuaded the government to release Garfield from military service, because health care for shipbuilders was essential to the war effort. During the war, Garfield remained in the Bay Area expanding a health plan for shipyard workers, while other associates set up a similar program in Portland and Vancouver. Garfield persuaded Henry Kaiser to set up the Permanente Foundation as a philanthrophic enterprise to finance hospital construction and expansion. During the war, membership in the health plan mushroomed. At the peak of employment in late 1943 and early 1944, there were almost 200,000 workers and dependents at the Kaiser yards. The steel mill at Fontana also employed several thousand workers. Almost all eligible workers and families joined the program.[13]

The success enjoyed by Garfield and Associates during the war challenged organized medicine on the West Coast. In the shipyard regions, local AMA affiliates grudgingly accepted, yet subtly resisted the KPMCP during the war. Sheer numbers of newcomers would have overwhelmed local doctors and facilities. Thousands of workers arrived in poor health and worse financial condition. Many were racial minorities; white doctors in private practice resisted treating them, and there were few minority doctors in the East Bay, Fontana, or Portland/Vancouver. Established physicians realized that shipyard workers as a group were poor prospects for lucrative "fee-for-service" practice and that collections would be problematic. With the influx of "undesirable" potential patients and a severe doctor shortage, AMA leaders tolerated an uneasy coexistence with Garfield's organization.[14]

Garfield occasionally wished he had joined the army. Many of the shipyard workers were 4-Fs, rejected by the military as unfit for service. Thousands came from poor rural areas, with little knowledge of nutrition and basic hygiene. Dr. Cutting recalled that Richmond doctors treated five hundred cases of pneumonia during the first six months. Henry Kaiser provided crucial assistance by pledging shipyard earnings to guarantee a bank loan to his family fund, Permanente Foundation, which purchased and refurbished the Fabiola Hospital in Oakland. The foundation in turn leased it to Garfield and Associates.

Even with Kaiser's direct assistance and lack of intense opposition from local AMA affiliates, problems were nearly overwhelming. A field hospital in Richmond handled emergencies in the yards; it sometimes exceeded capacity. Garfield operated an ambulance service to distribute overflow cases to other area hospitals. This hardly guaranteed patients' safety. Cutting claimed that some drivers were quite unreliable. They occasionally visited taverns while delivering non-critical patients. One driver reportedly raped a patient. Another driver negotiating one of the region's celebrated hills lost a stretcher out the back of the vehicle. The patient received a free roller coaster ride, which he evidently survived. The war years were memorable for doctors and patients alike.[15]

Toward the end of the war, Garfield and Associates faced important decisions. Outsiders considered KPMCP a response to short-term demand, as it had been at Grand Coulee. As tens of thousands of workers left the yards, most assumed that Garfield and Kaiser would shut down the health plan and medical facilities.

But Garfield and Kaiser had other plans. Replying to an inquiry late in 1944 from Senator Robert F. Wagner (D-N.Y.), then seeking support for federal health insurance, Kaiser indicated his plan to continue the KPMCP. Declining Wagner's plea for support, Kaiser argued that health care was the responsibility of the private sector. He saw KPMCP as one model by which private enterprise could reform national health care: "I believe that if there could be a few more such examples, there would be a rapid development of this new type of medical service which would surpass anything thus far developed in the United States or any other country." In similar language, Garfield's doctors defended continuation of the program: ". . . we feel that a plan which provides so much care to the people at a cost they can so easily pay . . . has such merit that were it general [*sic*] adopted by the medical profession it would preserve private enterprise in medicine."[16]

Had Garfield and Kaiser anticipated the enormous future obstacles, they might have reconsidered their plan to continue KPMCP. Until 1945 they experienced no significant reversals; Garfield and the doctors shared a sense of adventure and professional satisfaction. In addition, they had never encountered much competition. But tens of thousands of workers left the yards, dramatically reducing workloads just when hundreds of "fee-for-service" doctors returned from duty overseas. The latter competed directly with Garfield and Associates for patients. The AMA had barely tolerated the Garfield group during the war; when Kaiser and Garfield announced plans to stay in business, both the national AMA and local affiliates were determined to undermine the program.

During the war, the AMA gave mixed signals to Garfield and Associates; in fact, organized medicine's response seemed guided by simple expediency. As workers poured into the shipyards and doctor shortages loomed, some local AMA leaders even extended a welcoming hand. Many doctors working for Garfield were admitted to local AMA chapters. The California Medical Association asked Garfield to help plan hospitals and clinics in the Bay Area. In March 1944 Garfield was invited to address the AMA-sponsored Annual Conference on Industrial Health; an old AMA antagonist, Dr. Morris Fishbein, even hosted him at dinner.[17]

But behind stiff handshakes, forced smiles, and occasional promises of cooperation from AMA leaders, Garfield and his colleagues sensed resistance from the moment they established facilities in the yards. On many occasions during the war, AMA hostility toward the group bubbled to the surface. Garfield's most energetic critic was Dr. Fishbein, editor of the *Journal of the American Medical Association* (*JAMA*). When medical experts testified before a Senate subcommitee in November 1942 concerning health care for civilian workers, Fishbein directly attacked Garfield and Kaiser, charging that they recruited doctors desperately needed by the military. But the two men were prepared for his broadside. They claimed that whereas the Army had one doctor for every hundred soldiers, the shipyards had one for every two thousand workers. Working in the yards was not as hazardous as battle, but it was certainly dangerous. More to the point, worker production was also vital to the war effort. Kaiser and Garfield recounted how doctors treated hundreds of 4-Fs, who needed extra attention before they could work effectively. Not content merely to neutralize Fishbein's charges, they went on the attack, claiming that local AMA affiliates did not have enough "fee-for-service" doctors to provide adequate health care. To Kaiser, AMA attacks against Garfield for using "unorthodox" methods to meet obvious needs was sheer hypocrisy.[18]

The Senate hearings elicited evidence very damaging to Fishbein and the AMA. Testimony from other witnesses revealed that Fishbein had an undistinguished medical background and had not practiced for over thirty years. Doctors with no ties to the westerners accused him of unethical practices, even criminal activities. Fishbein's critics cited specific transgressions, which fell short of indictable evidence. They claimed that he used his position as editor of *JAMA* to intimidate adversaries into silence. After 1942, whisperings against Fishbein increased, and the westerners received praise for challenging him. A captain in the Army Medical Services Corps wrote to Kaiser that Fishbein's influence in the AMA amounted to "a ruthless dictatorship in which he puts to shame the very dictatorships we are so actively fighting against. . . . he practices medical autocracy . . ." The authors of a scholarly study of AMA power shared this view, although they described him in less virulent terms: Fishbein "had become the symbol of old, reactionary leadership in the profession." By 1949 events had turned against the querulous editor. He was such a liability to AMA officials seeking an improved public image that they removed him as editor of *JAMA*. Kaiser and Garfield had outlasted their first implacable AMA opponent; but there were many others.[19]

Although the westerners decided in 1945 to retain the KPMCP and offer it to the public, the AMA had little immediate cause for concern. Kaiser's industrial empire quickly expanded after the war, but the health plan appeared to be in real trouble. At peak enrollment during the war, membership had reached 125,000; by late 1945, with the departure of most shipyard workers, it had plunged to 26,500.[20]

Several doctors recalled that the plan encountered severe hardships. With the return of real competition, local AMA chapters charged that Garfield and Associates was practicing "socialized" medicine. Of far greater concern to individual doctors was the threat, either covert or directly stated, that continued association with Garfield might cost them membership in local AMA chapters. Declining KPMCP membership obviously meant smaller revenues for Garfield's partnership and required severe belt-tightening. With varying degrees of horror and amusement, long-time associates recalled the hard times following the war. Some stories may be apocryphal, but doctors swore that they could not requisition new pencils without turning in stubs less than two inches long. Another claimed that Scotch tape was so rare that it was used "only as a dressing for patients sensitive to the usual adhesive tape."[21]

Despite their struggles, Garfield and the other doctors remained deeply committed to the program. They had witnessed directly the difference good medicine made in the lives of thousands of Americans previously unable to afford such a "luxury." They firmly believed in their basic operating principle: the plan provided strong incentives to keep members healthy. Although membership declined for a time even after Kaiser and Garfield opened it to the public, they hoped union leaders on the Pacific Coast would negotiate KPMCP coverage in future labor contracts. Although the federal government regulated prices and wages, fringe benefits were exempt from calculations; better yet, medical care was not taxed by the Internal Revenue Service (IRS). Thus, it became an attractive bargaining chip for both labor and management. As an employer, Kaiser had earned the respect of most union leaders, and it paid off after the war; within months of V-J Day, several labor leaders endorsed the program. In January 1946 the Alameda County Central Labor Council urged its AFL affiliates to push for KPMCP membership. Many locals joined in the following months. By the late 1940s labor support had reversed membership attrition. In 1948 membership equaled the wartime high. Far more spectacular growth lay ahead.[22]

By the late 1940s the relationship between Garfield and Associates and the AMA groups had changed; yet at the local level, the shift was very gradual. Garfield and his doctors had demonstrated resiliency; and after Fishbein's ouster, AMA leaders, sensing that direct attacks against the "Kaiser" plan might backfire, remained cautious. At the same time, Kaiser, Garfield, and the doctors appeared curiously ambivalent toward local AMA affiliates. On one hand, they worked hard to expand membership in the health plan, directly challenging the medical societies. On the other hand, they often adopted obsequious postures toward the local AMA leaders. Kaiser and the doctors deluded themselves with the hope that if they appeared ingratiating, AMA officials might react less negatively to competition. One reason for "kid glove" treatment of the AMA by the Garfield group was that although the medical organization could not control Kaiser, it could make life uncomfortable for the doctors. Indeed, as local AMA chapters watched the KPMCP grow, Garfield became the lightning rod for their anger. In October 1947 the AMA-controlled California Medical Board charged him with employing unlicensed physicians and interns. These cases involved minor technical violations of regulatory procedures. To warn Garfield, the state board placed him on probation for five years and suspended his license for one year. In a curious move, it then suspended the suspension, "provided he abided by state laws" in the future.[23]

For public consumption, Kaiser and the doctors at first shrugged off these aggressive acts by the local AMA groups. When an attorney for the Cooperative Health Federation of American sought documentation from Garfield concerning local AMA discrimination against his doctors, Garfield shaded the truth in his response. He claimed that no AMA action warranted legal action. Noting that the Kaiser hospitals often retained "outside" specialists on a part-time basis, Garfield concluded: "In fact, many of the physicians in the American Medical Association have assisted us a great deal in accomplishing our work." Kaiser also tried to placate local AMA groups. Although the Alameda County AMA filed new charges of unprofessional conduct against Garfield in June 1948, claiming that he was soliciting patients, and regularly denied membership to most young doctors entering KPMCP, Kaiser initially tried to smooth things over. Invited to meet with AMA leaders one day after the Alameda County chapter had suspended Garfield, Kaiser proffered an olive branch: "It is my deepest hope that you of the Medical Associations and ourselves will discover that we have certain common objectives that we both earnestly share. . . . Certainly we can explore and adjust whatever differences have arisen between us."[24]

Such conciliatory gestures did little good. Kaiser and Garfield tried repeatedly to resolve disagreements, but local AMA affiliates generally ignored their entreaties. In the early 1950s they persistently made life unpleasant for Garfield and his associates. The locals seldom questioned their competence, but denial of AMA membership limited the doctors in several ways besides threatening their prestige and status within the profession. Doctors not admitted to local AMA chapters were usually denied membership on specialty boards and access to non-Kaiser community hospitals which cost them "referrals" of potential patients by colleagues. Thus, they had fewer chances to develop lucrative practices if and when they resigned from Garfield and Associates. The AMA chapters also tried to hamper Garfield's recruiting efforts and weaken the cohesion and loyalty within his medical organization. In 1951 the Alameda County group spread rumors that Garfield was lining his pocket at the expense of patients; Kaiser retorted that by mutual agreement the doctor's salary was limited to $25,000 after taxes.[25]

According to key Kaiser advisors, AMA rejections also had strong political overtones that were a microcosm of national-level conflicts during the McCarthy era. The San Francisco AMA chapter rejected a membership application from one doctor on Garfield's staff because of alleged "communist or strong leftist" views. Kaiser did not challenge the propriety of such scrutiny of the doctor's loyalty; instead, he hired a private investigating service to disprove the AMA charge. He did not authorize "witch-hunts," but neither did he insist upon freedom of thought and expression. To Garfield's physicians, Kaiser appeared to yield to McCarthyism; he advised them that "loyalty to our government of all Permanente employees must be established beyond question." In fairness to Kaiser, he was far more worried about their vulnerable position than any "disloyalty" of doctors, but his unwillingness to defend constitutional freedoms drew criticism from a local ACLU chapter late in 1951.[26]

Although Kaiser and the doctors at first downplayed disagreements with the AMA, outside observers were not nearly so chary about confronting basic issues. Radio commentator Chet Huntley discussed the situation over the ABC network on September 10, 1952. Huntley allowed that under AMA control, the nation's doctors delivered "the best medical care in the world." Unfortunately, only the very wealthy could afford it; and the federal government underwrote care for some of the indigent. Middle-income Americans faced economic disaster in the wake of serious illness. Huntley did not blame the AMA alone, but he stressed that its leaders opposed most prepaid plans for allegedly "promoting socialized medicine." Huntley quoted Garfield on his chief philosophical difference from the AMA: "To the private physician, a sick person is an asset. To Permanente, a sick person is a liability. We'd go bankrupt if we didn't keep most of our members and their families well most of the time." [27] Huntley clearly sided with Garfield and Associates.

Despite all efforts to mollify the AMA leadership, opposition intensified, and Kaiser suffered a major defection by a key supporter. For years Dr. Paul de Kruif, a microbiologist and writer of popular articles on medicine, had been one of Kaiser's and Garfield's warmest admirers, and he was a superb publicist. In 1943 he had published a book, *Kaiser Wakes the Doctors,* a paean to the fledgling health plan. De Kruif remained close to Kaiser and Garfield in the first years after the war. Unfortunately, in the early 1950s he became involved in a contentious dispute with Kaiser and Garfield when the latter refused to hire several of his associates, who were researching controversial treatments for rare diseases. He joined their opponents, and both Kaiser and Garfield felt betrayed. Even more distressing, de Kruif published attacks in AMA-sponsored publications, and other critics took cues from him. A decade after his laudatory account of the plan, de Kruif argued that the KPMCP "closed-panel" plan required patients to accept blindly whichever doctor was assigned to their case. He claimed that this policy robbed patients of freedom to choose doctors, as well as control over treatment received. Finally, he criticized turnover among KPMCP doctors, claiming that many sought to "regain their dignity in private practice." Other AMA critics insisted that KPMCP constituted "lay practice" and control of medicine: ". . . we know that what Mr. Kaiser says will happen in Permanente usually happens," intoned one official. [28]

In the spring of 1953, occasional sniping again became open warfare between Kaiser and the AMA. Dr. Raymond M. Kay, Garfield's long-time friend and associate, was expanding KPMCP facilities in southern California. In early March, Dr. Paul Foster, President of the Los Angeles County Medical Association (LACMA), printed a vitriolic attack against KPMCP. Foster's diatribe raised Kaiser's blood pressure. He penned a highly personal manifesto, "AMA Declares War—The Challenge Is Accepted." His patience exhausted, Kaiser wrote:

> Fifty million Americans . . . can be the jury to decide for themselves whether the Government should enact laws to prevent the AMA monopoly from striking fear into the hearts of doctors, from intimidating them from associating

themselves together to be of greater service to their fellow man, and from cheating the people out of obtaining the kind of medical and hospital care for which there is such an overwhelming demand.

When Kaiser's top advisors digested his proposed counterattack, they quailed at the implications. Chad Calhoun wired his boss that he had "paced the banks of the Potomac, sat beneath the blossoming cherry trees on the Tidal Basin" trying to devise alternative strategies. Calhoun urged Kaiser not to release his reply. When Kaiser suggested legal action, Calhoun counseled him that a suit filed by a KPMCP doctor would be more effective.[29]

Kaiser temporarily restrained himself, but AMA attacks persisted unabated. In April, the LACMA declared that "closed panel systems are undesirable and injurious to the public." Furthermore, any doctor employed by such a system was "not acting in accord with the letter or the spirit of the principles of medical ethics of the American Medical Association." Some doctors were longtime members of the local AMA. Kay had recruited specialists with private practices who "moonlighted" occasionally. The LACMA threatened to expel members who associated with Kay.[30]

By the late spring of 1953, other parties were involved in the escalating confrontation. Several local unions supported the KPMCP. The *Long Beach Labor News* editorialized that the real, hidden reason the AMA objected to the Kaiser plan was that "it puts doctors on a payroll where they can't make huge profits at the expense of people's sickness." Kaiser and Kay received their own reports from AMA meetings. They learned that Foster attacked group plans in general rather than KPMCP alone only because he feared libel laws. But in the summer of 1953 Foster dropped all pretense; he was determined to smash KPMCP. In his most strident editorial yet he scored doctors who joined Kay. He lamented that certain physicians "fresh from medical school . . . are forced to succumb to the deceptively enticing lure of financial security" and join Kaiser. Others "failed to make a go of their own private practice and have found it simpler to pick up a monthly check from an employer." Foster vowed that the AMA would strike at all "lay-controlled, corporate-type, closed panel medical plans" by urging young doctors not to join them.[31]

Some AMA tactics amounted to little more than petty harassment, but others were serious threats. When the core of KPMCP doctors in a particular region was small, loss of a few key members seriously threatened the program. In 1945 hearings before a Senate subcommittee studying procurement of doctors for the armed services, Garfield had charged Fishbein with using political influence to subject key doctors to the draft.[32]

During the Korean War, Kaiser and Garfield were once again convinced that the AMA pressured local draft boards to call up Permanente physicians. Henry Kaiser became actively involved in protecting key doctors from the draft. Kaiser's eagerness to exempt Garfield, who was threatened with activation in the summer of 1952, was understandable. Garfield was "the very backbone of this program and could not be spared from seeing it to its completion, except at irreparable damage to the public welfare." But Kaiser also pleaded for doctors quite far down the ladder. In the case of Dr. Frederick A. Pellegrin, a lieutenant in the Naval Reserves, Kaiser claimed that compelling reasons of "personal hardship" should preclude his serving in Korea. Thwarted at local levels, Kaiser took Pellegrin's case all the way to the Under Secretary of the Navy and secured a deferment. More than three years later, one of Kaiser's top aides claimed that the AMA was still trying to get Pellegrin drafted. Early in 1957, his local draft board granted another deferment. Thus Kaiser delayed his military service for several years, but Pellegrin finally served a two-year stint in the Navy.[33]

The draft issue remained an irritant to the doctors. In the spring of 1954 Garfield was forty-eight years old, but the selective service board came calling again. Although he was even then relieving Garfield of major responsibilities in administering the KPMCP, Kaiser wrote a long letter to the draft board, explaining how indispensable his old associate was. When Kaiser appealed the case at the national level, Colonel R. L. Black, chief of the Army Medical Services Corps, jokingly told Garfield, "Wouldn't the AMA love to get Sid in the Army?" Kaiser won that battle, and Garfield never entered the military. In 1955 Kaiser was still sufficiently worried about AMA efforts to harass the doctors that he informed Selective Service chief Louis B. Hershey that more than 85 percent of KPMCP doctors had served in the military. Kaiser claimed that California boards scrutinized KPMCP doctors' records with extra care. Hershey reassured Kaiser that KPMCP would not lose key doctors, as the board passed up men older than thirty-eight and in another year the young doctors coming in large numbers out of medical schools "should fill the quotas."[34]

Kaiser's conflicts with the AMA appeared endless. As late as 1960, one scholarly account of national-level medical plans still characterized relations between KPMCP doctors and local AMA groups as "running from active hostility to an armed neutrality." Kaiser had seemingly tried every conceivable tactic to reach a modus vivendi. Occasionally he lost patience and vented his frustration. To a particularly offensive editor of *California Medicine*, he wrote ". . . I have come to the conclusion that to change your views from what they are to what they should be . . . would be like a lunatic racing through a forest attempting to bend old trees."[35]

Amidst conflicts with the AMA, however, Garfield and the doctors clearly gained public acceptance. In the decade after World War II, KPMCP membership grew almost twentyfold from its 1945 low. In December 1955 enrollment was 511,000. The Northern California Region accounted for more than half that number, with 293,000 members. The Washington and Oregon Region was small, with 22,000 enrollees. Much growth had occurred in the Southern California Region, where Kay and his staff had signed up 196,000 members. Over five hundred doctors were in the group, and KPMCP was big business. A $12 million construction program included five new hospitals and an equal number of new clinics in 1955. By the end of the year, patients had access to services in thirteen hospitals and thirty outpatient clinics.[36]

Union members formed the backbone of health plan growth; by late 1955 only one member in twenty worked for a Kaiser company. In the months following V-J Day, Kaiser put his emerging reputation as a friend of workers to good use; he and the medical administrators provided medical coverage to some large labor groups. In the Los Angeles area, following initiatives from union officials, KPMCP signed up the Retail Clerks Union and the International Longshoremen's and Warehousemen's Union (ILWU).[37]

Some spectacular conflicts with AMA locals over KPMCP contracts with unions occurred in the Northern California Region. In the spring of 1953, Kaiser and Garfield opened a "state-of-the-art" seventy-bed hospital in Walnut Creek, a rapidly growing suburb fifteen miles east of Oakland. They claimed that the location was natural, because of the rapid development of suburbs in the East Bay Area. Health plan members needed easier access to hospitals and clinics; those in Oakland were too inconvenient. But AMA physicians in nearby Pittsburgh, California, believed that the real reason was to challenge their dominance over services provided to four thousand workers at Columbia Steel, a subsidiary of U.S. Steel. The KPMCP had recently signed an agreement with U.S. Steel workers in South San Francisco; a new hospital and specialized clinics on that side of the Bay were key factors in winning the contract.[38]

In June 1953, zoning authorities in Pittsburgh received a request from the KPMCP for a variance on local property permitting construction of yet another hospital. A few days later, a local paper headlined a story titled "City Medics Ready Own Plan in Face of Kaiser Invasion." Subsequent newspaper accounts confirmed negotiations between KPMCP officials and United Steel Workers of America (USWA) Local 1440. "Fee-for-service" doctors were frightened and outraged. About thirty doctors practiced in Pittsburgh, a town of fifteen thousand people. Steelworkers and dependents comprised fully half of the doctors' patients; if KPMCP won the contract, their livelihoods would be jeopardized. They fought back, with help from AMA members from other East Bay towns. The local doctors and their allies cobbled together a "Doctor's Plan" to compete against KPMCP.[39]

Local union officials were unimpressed by the AMA doctors' sudden concern for their members' health. On July 7, 1953, they announced a contract with the KPMCP. The AMA doctors cried foul, charging that the union was run by "a small clique" giving orders to several thousand members. They demanded a referendum by secret union ballot; Kaiser and Garfield promptly accepted the challenge, and an election was set for Labor Day, September 3.[40]

The issue aroused intense feelings, reminiscent of battles waged a few years earlier in the automobile and steel industries over collective bargaining. The AMA doctors took out ads in local papers, charging misrepresentation of their initiative by "Kaiser doctors," and instructing union members how to choose "democratically" their "own" physicians. Doctors' wives and family members passed out leaflets at plant gates; sound trucks blared, "Don't be a captive patient" and "Retain your family doctor." KPMCP administrators responded in kind, claiming that their plan was by far the better option. More important, union leaders quietly, effectively promoted the Kaiser program. On election day USWA Local 1440 workers overwhelmingly endorsed the KPMCP by 2,182 to 440. Within weeks, KPMCP signed up over half the union members, adding nearly 10,000 workers and dependents to the rolls.[41]

A frequently voiced charge against the KPMCP in the postwar years was that members lost "freedom of choice" of doctors. Beginning in 1948, Kaiser and Garfield insisted that future union contracts include alternative health plans with unlimited choice of physicians. They were confident that once workers learned the full range of benefits offered, KPMCP would fare well in the competitive selection process. In fact, it took some years for the advantages of KPMCP to become evident. In northern California, and elsewhere, some well-known carriers provided stiff competition. In the early years of "dual choice," where workers chose between two or more plans, the Kaiser program progressed slowly. But in the mid-1950s it surged ahead of West Coast competitors. An independent study in 1956 of twenty-three large free-choice programs covering over forty-three thousand members showed that 65 percent chose KPMCP. In Southern California, medical administrators enrolled many workers in the plan. The Retail Clerks Union and the Longshoremen each provided several thousand members. Powerful union leaders, so contentious on many issues, offered sincere endorsements of KPMCP benefits. Widespread favorable publicity helped set the stage for even more explosive future growth.[42]

To outside observers, the Kaiser plan and hospitals appeared to be doing well in the mid-1950s. Certainly Henry Kaiser appeared satisfied with both the volume and the quality of service rendered, and the rapidly mushrooming modern facilities provided visible evidence of success. At many public gatherings, he cited KPMCP as his proudest achievement. But behind the scenes, Kaiser and the doctors were engaged in a bitter conflict. Garfield was in an extremely uncomfortable position. He felt great personal loyalty to Kaiser, who had provided indispensable support and financial assistance and believed he should call the shots. Yet Garfield also felt strong professional loyalty to his medical colleagues, who increasingly resented Kaiser's "interference." The struggle for control of the program threatened its very existence.

External controversy over Kaiser's involvement in health care was obvious from the beginning, or at least from establishment of the KPMCP in the shipyards. What most outside observers failed to perceive was the internal struggle for control over direction of the program. The doctors viewed Kaiser in very ambivalent terms. His high national profile and excellent reputation among workers attracted many new members, and that brought security and financial rewards to KPMCP doctors. When the medical group needed to expand facilities, Kaiser occasionally provided direct financial assistance; more often he helped arrange loans from other sources, usually the Bank of America. But many doctors were offended by what they considered unwarranted interference in professional activities. Local AMA chapters treated them as second-class doctors, in part because of what they called "lay control" of the KPMCP. Garfield's associates often cringed when the well-meaning industrialist exceeded the bounds of professional decorum in trying to protect their interests. Some male doctors never forgot snubs by AMA colleagues; their wives were frequently excluded by AMA doctors' wives from social functions which seemed important at the time. Many believed Kaiser's "meddling" in professional affairs caused their collegial difficulties. Fairly or otherwise, they took out frustrations against Kaiser, and some lost faith in Garfield for allowing him to interfere with their plan.[43]

At first, the doctors' reservations concerning Kaiser's involvement were muted. Undoubtedly, many doctors were embarrassed when Kaiser invoked biblical rhetoric in defending them from AMA attacks. In October 1947 he chastised Garfield's critics: "Of those who would do him harm, I can only say 'God, forgive them, for they know not what they do.'"[44] Most doctors stoically endured Kaiser's occasional outbursts with outward calm. But for a variety of reasons, including a desire to convince AMA critics of their independence from Henry Kaiser, the doctors formed a legally distinct partnership under eight physicians in 1949.

Many long-time KPMCP associates dated Kaiser's active involvement from early 1951, following Bess Kaiser's extended illness and slow death. He promptly remarried, and his new wife, Ale, actively encouraged her husband's deepening commitment to health care. She was a former nurse and hospital administrator with KPMCP. By the early 1950s, also, Henry Kaiser, Jr., had been diagnosed as suffering from multiple sclerosis, and his worsening condition further stimulated his father's deepening commitment to health care. It was at this time that internal conflict surfaced between the doctors and Kaiser's corporate administrators. Garfield sensed the growing tension and his own untenable position as mediator. He hired a very able assistant, Dr. Edward R. Weinerman, whose main assignment was to search for the roots of conflict. Within months, Weinerman thought he had isolated the most pressing issues. In his view, morale among KPMCP doctors was declining, along with quality of patient care. According to many doctors Weinerman interviewed, Kaiser expanded the program too rapidly and spent too much money on new medical facilities. They considered him a construction man who valued brick and mortar above professional opportunities and development. Many doctors believed Kaiser's pet projects took priority over research efforts, and one study revealed that KPMCP doctors earned about 15 percent less than their peers in "fee-for-service" practice.[45] The doctors' most immediate target was "lay management's" expenditure for the luxurious new hospital at Walnut Creek.

In his dedication remarks at the opening of the hospital in May 1953, Kaiser tried to "clear the air" between himself and KPMCP critics. But he insisted that with the Kaiser Family Foundation providing several million dollars for expansion, he and the hospital organization's trustees, including several corporate managers, should maintain ultimate control over building projects. In the early 1950s, Kaiser's personal memos to the doctors frequently revealed a patronizing, imperious tone. To one high-level doctor involved in new hospital construction, Kaiser directed specific orders and criticized previous actions taken. He concluded, "This is a constructive letter, but very firm and kindly. Please do not take this as criticism . . . but as a serious step which will eliminate costly delays." Kaiser even gave notice of his intention of taking charge of the KPMCP. To another administrator, he complained about approval of a health plan rate increase without adequate financial forecasting, "I was shocked yesterday to find that [you] have practically concluded, without any approval of either the Executive Committee of the Truestees [sic] a rate increase of $1.00 per family unit . . ."[46]

With Kaiser's growing involvement in daily activities of the KPMCP his relationship with Garfield became almost unbearably strained. In the fall of 1953, corporate advisors, including Eugene E. Trefethen, Jr., concluded that the KPMCP had grown to the point that Garfield could not manage it alone, and that its ability to secure long-term financing hinged on providing prospective lenders with detailed and accurate financial projections of the type expected of any well-managed business. Kaiser agreed, but remained convinced that his own helpful guidance could resolve the problems. On several occasions the two men sat down to map future plans, but Kaiser became impatient over Garfield's failure to follow suggestions. Kaiser once confided to Trefethen that he and Garfield had sat up "until the wee hours of this morning" trying to iron out their problems. Long-time colleagues recalled that Garfield was a casual administrator. Even when KPMCP membership exceeded 250,000, the doctor might jot down the agenda for a meeting on an envelope. As one associate put it, "Garfield ran the plan like a ma and pa grocery store." Although Kaiser was largely indifferent to "modernizing" his corporate structure, he realized that greater efficiency in running the medical program was needed.[47]

Despite their stress-filled professional relationship, Kaiser and Garfield retained a warm personal friendship. The debonair doctor married Ale Kaiser's sister Helen, and so the men were brothers-in-law. When both couples were in town, they regularly shared evening cocktails. But Kaiser fueled professional discord by deciding to revamp the KPMCP administrative structure. Late in 1953 a series of confrontations over administration culminated in Kaiser virtually ordering Garfield to appoint Clifford H. Keene, M.D., to help him run the program. Bringing in Keene generated enormous turmoil; it became one of Kaiser's most controversial mandates.[48]

Although he was to enjoy a distinguished career with the KPMCP, Keene's first months on the job were filled with trouble. According to Garfield, Keene was a fine surgeon, and Garfield had recommended him to Edgar as an ideal man to set up health care facilities at the auto plant at Willow Run. Keene established a good record in Michigan, and Edgar was very impressed with his management. But his personality was not ideally suited for the highly sensitive task of smoothing over relations between the doctors and Kaiser's corporate managers. According to one critic, Keene had been a lieutenant colonel in the Army, and he acted like one. Another claimed that Keene was "a disaster" with the western doctors. Yet another associate recalled that Keene could be abrasive in interpersonal relations.[49]

In fairness to Keene, he stepped into a hornet's nest. Keene claimed that he intended to refuse the assignment, but reconsidered when Garfield pleaded with him to step in and help out. Garfield never again mentioned the episode; years later Keene learned that Kaiser had pressured Garfield to make the overture. Even a person with highly polished communication skills might have found the situation impossible to remedy. The evidence strongly suggests that Henry and Edgar Kaiser exacerbated misunderstandings between Keene and the other medical men. According to several sources, they assured Keene that he would have a good deal of authority, and that he would ultimately administer the entire health program. But they misled Garfield, reportedly assuring him that Keene would remain his subordinate. Publicly, they introduced Keene as Garfield's "assistant," with no formal title. With their customary optimism, Henry and Edgar Kaiser assumed that misunderstandings would work themselves out in time.[50]

Garfield, Cutting, and other doctors perceived Keene as the industrialist's watchdog. Henry Kaiser anticipated their resistance. A week before announcing the appointment, Kaiser bluntly warned Garfield, "There could be harm only if you are unwilling to indoctrinate another individual into the day to day detail work that you have been doing in the area." Keene symbolized Kaiser's firm intention to involve himself in the minutiae of KPMCP administration. Garfield informed Kaiser that the doctors perceived management's overweening presence in medical matters as oppressive. For his part, Kaiser maintained that once the doctors understood the need for greater administrative efficiency, "a solution should be more readily forthcoming than at present."[51]

Misunderstandings between corporate management and the doctors intensified in 1954; by early 1955 the doctors reached the point of open revolt. On May 12, top KPMCP physicians, with the exception of Garfield and Keene, drafted a statement to Edgar Kaiser articulating their complaints. According to the doctors, Henry Kaiser and his corporate managers had engaged in "a series of unilateral actions [effecting] . . . lay domination" of the plan. They strongly urged a return to "the basic principles of integrated operation under physician management." Henry Kaiser waited a few days, then sent letters to all doctors who had signed the document. His message was both plaintive and acerbic. He lamented that the doctors had "made it clear to me that the medical groups believe that the help we are able to render is no longer needed." In response to their demand for greater independence, Kaiser lectured them like recalcitrant children: "It is unfortunate that some of you appear to have failed to realize the full measure that others have given to make your present success possible." Three weeks later Kaiser informed the doctors that "If we are no longer needed as trustees . . . we stand ready to step aside entirely . . ." The only catch was that the doctors had to assume all liabilities and pay Kaiser interests "fair value" on all assets owned by the nonprofit Kaiser Foundation Hospitals and other corporate entities. "These arrangements must be such as to assure our Trustees and me personally that we shall have no further legal or moral responsibility on account of such indebtedness."[52]

By the summer of 1955, a break appeared imminent. However, at Kaiser's request, Eugene E. Trefethen, Jr., intervened and both sides cooled off enough to arrange a peace conference at Kaiser's retreat at Lake Tahoe in mid-July. About a dozen top men from each group attended. According to several present, the three-day meeting was marked by passionate debate and raised voices. But both sides gave a little, and a truce emerged. Garfield was eased out as director of the KPMCP. The doctors accepted this under the condition that Keene would not replace him. Several other compromises were reached; an advisory council comprised of equal numbers of doctors and corporate managers was created. Regional management teams were formalized; future disagreements would presumably be settled by negotiations, not confrontations.[53]

The Tahoe conference did not end bad feelings between the doctors and the Kaiser organization, but tensions gradually eased. Rumors of maneuvering by one group or the other to grasp control of the KPMCP became less frequent. The regional management teams became cumbersome; according to Dr. Kay, they "proved very effective in bogging down any effort to get anything done."[54] The Tahoe meeting began to defuse suspicions on both sides, but the healing was slow. From the Tahoe conference and Trefethen's search for a compromise emerged a key principle in KPMCP's stability and success: the principle of a joint endeavor in which the doctors are represented by the nonprofit hospitals and Kaiser Foundation Health Plan, Inc. This principle guides KPMCP's organizational structure to this day.

Some physicians, including Kay's group in southern California, remained wary of Keene. Others resented the fact that Garfield had been summarily "put out to pasture." They considered his new position as executive vice president in charge of facilities planning and construction a transparent demotion. On occasion, Kaiser still treated Garfield like a schoolboy. Displeased with one set of Garfield's designs for a new hospital, Kaiser wired: "I am utterly disheartened, depressed and sad that we should receive from you nearly half thousand changes. . . . It is unbelievable at this late date you would create such costly troubles and put me in this embarrassing position." Garfield's reply was a detailed justification of the numerous changes; his wording clearly reflected his subordinate position.[55]

Yet by the late 1950s and early 1960s, relations between Kaiser and the doctors were clearly on the mend. Perhaps most important, the industrialist spent increasing amounts of time on Oahu, and he was involved intimately only with the doctors in the newly established Hawaii Region. Relations with the AMA also improved, and Kaiser's "interference" embarrassed the doctors less often. Most important, the KPMCP was an obvious success. The plan attracted large groups of new patients; between 1955 and 1965 membership ballooned from 523,510 to 1,328,761. Not only did the KPMCP carry more professional prestige, but the doctors enjoyed more competitive salaries. Most involved in the program experienced more rewards than frustrations. Strong differences surfaced on occasion even in the 1960s, but confrontations between the doctors and Kaiser's managers were far less frequent.[56]

By the early 1960s, Kaiser and the doctors were also thinking very much alike on a major public policy issue; government-"subsidized" medicine.

Although opinions varied, most managers and doctors associated with the KPMCP agreed that private enterprise should provide the nation's health care. Kaiser was thoroughly knowledgeable about the issues involved. He endorsed government assistance for group health programs. At least as early as 1943, he discussed prospects for a Federal Medical Loan Agency with Vice President Henry A. Wallace and others. The proposed agency would encourage group practice and help finance cooperative health facilities. In June 1945 Kaiser sent to Senator Claude Pepper (D-Fla.) his own draft of a bill providing federal guarantees of loans for medical facilities. But that was as far as he went; Kaiser opposed liberal Democratic government-funded programs. When President Truman's health care program became a warm political issue in the fall of 1945, Kaiser disappointed liberal Democratic friends by refusing to endorse the concept. To Mrs. Albert D. Lasker, he wrote, "Although there are many commendable features, the overall program is too comprehensive to warrant hasty action." Instead, he urged proliferation of innovative private plans.[57]

During the late 1940s and early 1950s, there was prolonged conflict in Congress over federal health insurance. After World War II, Kaiser's operatives in the capital monitored proposals involving health insurance or other medical matters. Historian Monte Poen determined that, apart from organized labor, there was little support for federal health insurance during the Truman years. Lobbyists for the AMA mounted a well-financed, powerful campaign against it. Of the significant initiatives suggested by advocates of federal health care during the 1950s, only a proposal to provide loans for constructing hospitals became law.[58]

During Truman's last months in office and the early months of Eisenhower's first term, Kaiser consistently supported expanded federal grants for medical facilities. In October 1952 he urged Congress to appropriate a billion dollars for a thousand separate facilities across the nation. According to Kaiser, each new hospital could serve thirty thousand Americans; this measure would "avert socialized medicine." During the Eisenhower years, Kaiser tried to persuade AMA lobbyists and legislators that prepaid group programs were a legitimate "free enterprise" solution to public health needs. He argued that if opponents thwarted them, public pressure would force Congress to consider drastic initiatives in "socialized medicine."[59]

Kaiser further argued that all Americans had a right to affordable health care and that prepaid group practice was "a constructive and positive non-government voluntary method" of providing it. He tried, unsuccessfully, to convert Eisenhower's newly appointed Secretary of Health, Education, and Welfare, Oveta Culp Hobby. He quickly sensed that the AMA had approached her first and that she had a narrow view of medicine. Just days after she was sworn in, she warned Kaiser to pursue "less strident tactics" if he hoped to make any headway. In a face-to-face meeting she imperiously lectured him: ". . . Mr. Kaiser, you are your own worst enemy because you have been talking so much about AMA opposition."[60]

By that time, Kaiser and his managers realized that their overt support for medical bills could actually damage prospects for passage. Late in 1953 Congressman Charles A. Wolverton (D-N.J.) asked Kaiser's Washington office to draft a bill for insured federal loans for hospitals. Chad Calhoun directed preparation of several drafts, checking constantly with the congressman and Kaiser about the wording and other particulars. Calhoun privately discussed facets of the bill with political allies, who cautioned against publicizing any notion that it was a "Kaiser bill." Calhoun in turn warned his employer: ". . . the inference was that . . . opponents would direct their attacks on Kaiser and therefore obscure the main issue."[61]

Kaiser and his Washington staff worked for over a year on the "Wolverton Bill," but it got nowhere. Eisenhower endorsed government aid to new hospitals and new diagnostic centers in his 1954 State of the Union Address, but verbal support did not bring action. The AMA remained hostile, and its lobbyists claimed that the Wolverton Bill was "an aid to bail out Henry Kaiser." In the mid-1950s, AMA voices strongly influenced Congress. Kaiser was frustrated that the hard work bore no fruit, and he vented his frustration in a lengthy memo to Calhoun.[62]

During Eisenhower's second term the AMA still dominated debate on federal aid to health. According to KPMCP executive Scott Fleming, most doctors in the program hoped to mend fences with the AMA in the late 1950s and early 1960s, and many of them opposed Medicare. But a few KPMCP doctors favored the idea, and Ernest Saward, M.D., KPMCP Medical Director in Portland and Vancouver, testified in favor of Medicare. By the early 1960s, Henry Kaiser was quite remote from the battle. Aide Robert C. Elliott wrote a memo to Kaiser in the midst of President Kennedy's losing fight with the AMA in the spring of 1962 analyzing testimony by others. Henry Kaiser issued no statements.[63]

Edgar Kaiser, then in his early fifties, was more active in the Medicare conflict than his father. He favored certain facets of the program and said so publicly. Still, by Kaiser standards, their roles were minimal. Nearing his eightieth birthday, Henry Kaiser remained vigorous, but confined himself to pressuring politicians through his Washington office for amendments encouraging his own type of private programs. After Lyndon B. Johnson's landslide victory over Barry Goldwater in the fall of 1964, Democrats had huge majorities in both houses of Congress, and passage of Medicare was assured. Edgar complained to President Johnson that the administration's bill discouraged participation by cost-effective, private health care systems such as KPMCP. Edgar accurately predicted runaway medical costs under a system of government-funded fee-for-service payments.[64]

The development of prepaid group medicine brought Kaiser many headaches, but the services the KPMCP developed also gave him deep personal satisfaction. He was prescient in his belief that he would best be remembered for contributions in medicine. At his death in 1967, the KPMCP boasted eighteen hospitals, and administrators were actively planning expansion east. Kaiser did not live to witness the truly explosive growth of the health plan bearing his name. Yet he had anticipated the future more accurately than most contemporaries. The KPMCP is recognized by most students of medical care as the nation's most successful HMO. Certainly it dwarfs its rivals in size today. But the 1970s and 1980s marked the emergence of numerous rapidly growing competitors.[65]

Were Kaiser alive today, he would almost certainly be distressed that even in the late 1980s only 13 percent of all Americans are covered by plans similar to KCMCP. He would be outraged at skyrocketing health care costs. But given his inveterate enthusiasm and optimism, he would probably argue that affordable health care for all Americans is just a matter of time. To Kaiser, the present day crisis in medicine would represent another "opportunity in work clothes."

14
Boss

From the day he hired his first employee in 1914 until his death in 1967, Kaiser's managerial style changed very little. Many growing enterprises created large, multi-layered managerial hierarchies in "rational" responses to the complexities of the modern business environment. Kaiser resisted "modernization"; he followed his instincts in organizing and promoting his employees. But year after year, Kaiser and his organization outmaneuvered most rivals, perceived opportunities where others did not, and consistently set new standards for speed and efficiency.

In their influential, widely read study, *In Search of Excellence,* Thomas J. Peters and Robert H. Waterman, Jr., traced managerial development in several dozen of the "best-run" American corporations. In many examples drawn from the 1960s and 1970s, they observed that the most effective corporate leaders were highly visible and practiced "hands-on," personal guidance of their operations.[1] Similar examples could have been drawn from Kaiser's managerial activities decades earlier. Kaiser's approach to management was hardly original or unique. His respect for his "associates" could have been borrowed from James Cash Penney, founder of the chain stores bearing his name, or from many other astute entrepreneurs. His skill in challenging bright young men to compete with each other might similarly have been patterned after that of Alfred P. Sloan, who created General Motors' famed "decentralized" system of separate automotive divisions. In refusing to permit important decisions to become trapped by "study" committees, in abhorring bureaucratic red tape, in sensing instinctively who in his organization could provide immediate assistance in a crisis, Kaiser resembled many successful industrial leaders.

Working for Kaiser was exhilarating and exhausting. Two decades after his death, senior executives still conveyed excitement when recounting the challenges he presented them daily. They remembered constant pressure, a sense of urgency; several fondly savored memories of brief moments of respite, when "the boys" sat around the office with Kaiser late in the evening after a strenuous day and basked in mutual camaraderie. The men who climbed the corporate ladder were tough survivors, a very select group. Kaiser thrived on twenty-hour days, weeks at a stretch, and few could stand his killing pace. Senior managers, to a man, recalled the utter exhaustion they experienced in their thirties and forties trying to keep up with Kaiser even when he was in his seventies. According to his son Edgar, "He got men to do things they never thought they could do." The survivors patterned themselves after the boss: they lived for their work. There is little mystery behind many victories; Kaiser and his men simply outworked their rivals.

When Kaiser entered the highly competitive construction business in 1914, he had to sharpen his leadership skills immediately. Just an important as shrewd bidding was the ability to manage workers. Seventy-five years ago road building was far more labor-intensive than it is today. Profit margins were often narrow. Inability to hire, motivate, and retain good workers hampered many contractors. One way of gaining loyalty and respect was showing commitment to employees as individuals. Unlike many contractors in this highly cyclical business who disbanded work forces in slack times, Kaiser found things for key men to do between jobs.

Other than figuring bids, Kaiser considered most desk work a waste of time, at best a necessary evil. Alonzo B. Ordway recalled the old days in road construction, when the boss spent most of his time out of doors, troubleshooting or traveling from one job to another. He loved being in the field with the workers. As Ordway remembered, treasurer George "Sherry" Sherwood had to badger Kaiser to examine accounts. When he found time, he called in his top men and reviewed figures quickly. At such times, he was often in a testy mood, grumbling over costs. Occasionally, he forgot paydays, until his men reminded him. Alice Price recalled that her husband, Tom, was inadvertently left off the payroll; it took him weeks to summon up the courage to inform the boss.[2] However friendly Kaiser was by nature, even in the early years everyone knew who was in charge.

Motivated in part by concern for workers, Kaiser insisted that they have the most modern tools available. He drove men to their limits with long hours, but he was very interested in lightening physically demanding tasks. As noted, he rigged up wheelbarrows with wide rubber tires, which were easier to push through gravel and mud than old-fashioned, iron-wheel models. He preferred to wear out machinery rather than workers. When he purchased new trucks, he had them outfitted with sideboards so they could carry larger loads. Ordway warned that trucks would break down more quickly under excessive weights. Kaiser replied, "Ord, our profit is in the overload."[3]

Kaiser realized that fresh workers performed more efficiently, with fewer accidents. He also knew that the maxim "Time is money" was a fact of life in construction. Beating deadlines meant interest saved on loans, quicker payments, and occasional performance bonuses. By meeting short and seemingly "impossible" deadlines, Kaiser also enhanced his image as a man on the move. His "office" was often the front seat of his car. When crews encountered problems, he was not above stripping off his jacket and grabbing a shovel or running one of Bob Le Tourneau's earth movers.

Although Kaiser could not have imagined the spectacular future of his corporate empire, he nevertheless recruited the core of his top-level managerial team very early. Although he added key men later, several "first-team" members were on board before he joined Six Companies: Tom M. Price, Alonzo B. Ordway, Joaquin F. "Joe" Reis, Donald A. "Dusty" Rhoades, Jack Ashby, George G. "Sherry" Sherwood, and several others. Young Edgar worked on road crews in the 1920s; later he brought along his college friend, Eugene E. Trefethen, Jr. Clay P. Bedford started in 1925 as a draftsman on California construction projects. Kaiser hired engineer George Havas off a plantation in Cuba. He recruited men with care; they, in turn, attracted bright young subordinates. The most able formed a nucleus around the boss. But Kaiser was accessible to men who had not yet reached the inner circle. He was devoted to those who shared his drive and were fascinated with new ideas. Edgar Kaiser once remarked, "He doesn't have just two sons, he has a thousand sons."[4]

Kaiser wasn't interested in personnel matters per se. He delegated "housekeeping" details to "Sherry" Sherwood and others. He focused intently upon the job at hand, and he assumed that all shared his passion for work. Kaiser ignored organizational structures until he joined Six Companies in 1931. The dam building jobs were so huge, and so many companies were involved, that some type of formal organizational structure was necessary. But Kaiser left detail work to those more interested in administration. He found no poetry in tidy, symmetrical flow charts.

In the mid-1950s Kaiser finally established a "modern" corporate structure with a conventional managerial hierarchy. Significantly, most of its development occurred after he moved from Oakland into semi-retirement in Hawaii. Other than appointing operating division presidents, Kaiser paid little attention to the management ladder. On the other hand, he remained deeply involved in major corporate decisions, and he continued to run his companies in the 1960s much as he had forty years earlier. He looked upon his top twenty or so executives as a "team," and he used "group management" or "modified committee" to reach important decisions.

This by no means suggests that by "group" deliberation executives could avoid individual accountability on tough, risky decisions. One who quailed at such a challenge might rise to middle management, but would never reach the inner circle. Typically, half a dozen top-level men would meet in someone's office and hash over an issue. Kaiser might order in lunch, after which the informal conference often moved to another office. Kaiser demanded that every man present his views; then a vote would be taken. On occasion he overruled such "ad-hoc" decisions. Kaiser listened carefully to his managers, whether or not he followed their advice.[5]

Kaiser enjoyed many of the benefits of a committee type of managerial system, but few of the disadvantages. His protégés gained valuable exposure to many fields at youthful ages. Kaiser benefited tremendously from the dynamics of the process. In selling ideas to his top managers, he consistently refined and sharpened his thought process. Bedford recalled that he sometimes argued both sides of an issue, testing his subordinates' mental skills. Nevertheless, when he was determined to do something, his decisions sometimes defied logic. Bedford claimed that many top executives, himself included, opposed the automobile venture. But Kaiser was determined to make cars, and they had to make the best of it.[6]

A Kaiser trademark was his ability to perceive hidden opportunities and make quick, sound decisions. He occasionally referred complex issues to "committees," but he did not tolerate time-consuming "studies." He typically selected a few men, challenged them to analyze an issue which might occupy a score of people for weeks in another company, and demanded an answer in "three or four days." Within forty-eight hours he started ringing up key members: "Do you have anything yet? How soon will you have it?" In such a fluid, unstructured environment, bureaucracies could not form, much less survive.

Kaiser developed much of his aversion to hierarchical bureaucracies from extensive dealings with federal agencies from 1931 forward. In his first weeks in Washington as spokesman for Six Companies he saw enough organizational dysfunction to last a lifetime. But he also learned valuable lessons in dodging bureaucratic tangles. Kaiser saved time in dealing with government agencies by quickly identifying key power brokers. The "Washington years" intensified his determination to avoid a top-heavy organization when his companies grew rapidly after World War II.

Kaiser's casual attitude toward organization sometimes bewildered business associates. When a Six Companies partner requested an organization chart, so that his people could deal directly with counterparts in Kaiser's companies, treasurer George Sherwood replied: "We have . . . not attempted to keep [flow charts] up-to-date as carrying as many operations as we do it is difficult to keep personnel always concentrated for any length of time."[7] The message was clear: those on top of developments in the Kaiser organization knew instinctively whom to contact concerning specific tasks.

So did influential outsiders, at least those involved in key decisions. Why should anyone waste valuable time creating detailed organization charts which soon became obsolete?[8]

Another key to Kaiser's managerial success was that he was a master communicator. A gregarious man who detested solitude, he constantly dealt with employees face to face. And he insisted that his managers talk with each other. In verbal communication, he tolerated extravagant expense; his telephone bill amounted to $250,000 a year as early as 1942. He hated paper work, but encouraged "instant communications" via telegram. Detailed exchanges between top-level executives on a daily, sometimes an hourly basis produced stacks of telegrams the size of Sears-Roebuck catalogs. One key difference between Kaiser and less efficient managers was that in his organization, paper usually represented instant communication, not aging committee reports which reached decisionmakers only after time-consuming journeys through managerial layers. When detailed staff reports were prepared, they were important; they usually reached top levels immediately. When Kaiser wanted truly quick answers, he often worked with the executive most involved with the project, regardless of rank.[9]

Kaiser encouraged his people to check constantly with each other and to remain aware of all important developments within their operating divisions. Engineer Louis H. Oppenheim recalled how Kaiser would ask one manager a question; then a few days (or hours) later he might ask another for the answer. Executives failing to maintain contact with peers quickly found themselves outside the decisionmaking process.[10] Kaiser never articulated this strategy; he practiced it subconsciously. Ambitious men thus developed versatility, and they faced the challenge of frequent changes in assignments. When a key man was needed on a new job, Kaiser could tap several subordinates capable of taking charge. Above all, Kaiser kept men on their toes.

Kaiser budgeted his time well. On rare occasions, when personally fascinated with a project such as automobile design, he immersed himself in details for extended periods. But after his organization expanded into a dozen industries, he resisted prolonged involvement in most projects until important commitments had to be made. He effectively delegated authority. When setting up Permanente Metals late in 1941, Kaiser approved several personnel assignments and then concluded in a memo to Gene Trefethen, "The purpose of this memorandum is to establish clearly the responsibilities of everyone, due to the fact that the allocation of my time is such that I do not believe it will be possible for me to follow the work outlined in any other way but through you."[11] His meaning was clear: run it yourself; consult me only when absolutely necessary.

What was it like to work for Kaiser? He was a workaholic. Over many decades his habits changed little; he maintained a killing work schedule.

He invested in expensive equipment to lighten tasks for blue-collar employees, but there were few labor-saving devices for managers. Kaiser baldly proclaimed his managerial philosophy: "You find your key men by piling work on them. They say, 'I can't do any more,' and you say, 'Sure you can.' So you pile it on and they're doing more and more. Pretty soon you have men you can rely on absolutely. You have an organization that can really get things done." Ambitious executives adopted the boss's work habits. William Soule, who joined Kaiser in 1941, recalled that it was "a challenge I could not refuse. I was drawn to it as a moth to a lighted candle." After an exciting but exhausting three-decade career, Soule reflected on those years: "Fortunately, when I was lucky enough to come into that cone of light I was not consumed by the flame. Singed, perhaps, but not consumed."[12]

Several former executives recalled their excitement when first invited to present their ideas in one of the inner-circle meetings. Tudor Wall remembered one such gathering. During the meeting, Kaiser was repeatedly interrupted by phone calls, which he took at his desk while keeping one ear tuned to the meeting in front of him. "I couldn't believe how he could keep eight balls in the air at once. There were calls about big union negotiations, $35 million deals, all sorts of things." Peter Hass, then with Permanente Cement, remembered a brief presentation he made just before Kaiser's move to Hawaii in 1954. According to Hass, Kaiser occasionally dozed off in meetings, only to snap to attention and ask a crucial question. "He liked to get people to make quick estimates. He's reach in the air and say 'Pick a figure.'" Hass learned that the best strategy was to stall for time: "I'd say 'I don't know,' then work like hell to get a solid estimate. . . . One sure way to get into trouble was to fake knowledge you didn't have." As Wall recalled, "Once we got an assignment, nobody ever checked on us. Top level executives would just say to get it done. It was up to us [to figure out] how to do it. It was an exhilarating feeling."[13]

In December 1951, several months after Henry and Ale Kaiser's marriage, they visited Louisiana to dedicate the aluminum plant in Chalmette. Mrs. Kaiser spoke to reporters. Some of her more intriguing comments concerned her husband's central values: "Mr. Kaiser believes a man should be just as interested in his home and his wife as he is in his business." Kaiser associates noted that, among top managers, there were few divorces.[14]

Family solidarity among Kaiser's top executives seems ironic, since the boss allowed them so little time at home. Even census takers noticed it. When visiting the home of Tom and Alice Price in 1950, the recorder mentioned that he had interviewed wives of about a dozen Kaiser employees, and ". . . none of the wives seem to know just what kind of work their husband do. However, they all seem to think they do work of some kind, for they don't seem to stay home much of the time." K. Tim Yee, the first person of Asian descent to rise to top ranks at Kaiser, recalled that he and his wife realized at the outset that they had to make enormous personal sacrifices. Another Kaiser executive, who retired in the upper-middle ranks, rejected the ultimate commitment. When asked to move from Oakland to a remote location, he declined: "From that point on, I knew my star was on the wane." With Kaiser, the job came first, family second.[15]

As exhilarating as working for Kaiser was for ambitious managers rising in the organization, it was hard on wives. Nearly half a century of dedicated service and memories may have induced him to exaggerate, but Clay Bedford claimed that he and his wife had moved forty times during his career. Corporate wives in decades past put up with intrusions few would tolerate now. Kaiser indulged in brief catnaps during meetings; he appeared never to sleep at any other time. His managers learned to expect urgent calls at all hours of the night. It might be 3 A.M. in Oakland, but it was 6 A.M. in New York, and groggy West Coast executives often picked up the telephone to hear Kaiser's cheery voice: "I didn't wake you, did I? Listen, you've got a ticket on the 7:15 flight to Detroit. I want you to spend a couple of weeks at Willow Run." Back then, few dared mention that they would miss a son's homecoming football game, or a daughter's christening, and that wives and children would be upset. In public at least, most corporate wives endured in silence.[16]

Kaiser considered vacations an irritant. Old-timers swore that when working on roads in Canada, Kaiser ignored U.S. holidays "because we were in Canada" and dismissed Canadian celebrations "because we were Americans." Thus they worked most holidays at standard rates of pay. Hass recalled planning a family vacation for months; it would be his first two weeks off in years. He and his wife devised an elaborate itinerary, purchased the tickets, and coordinated all reservations. The night before their departure, the boss called with a small problem. Years later Hass could laugh: "We never did get that vacation." One can well imagine Mrs. Hass's disappointment. Lambreth Hancock, Kaiser's personal assistant in later years, arranged a vacation, with the collusion of Ale Kaiser. The only hitch was that she persuaded Hancock and his wife to spend it at the Kaisers' retreat at Lake Tahoe, and the boss was there too. As Hancock recalled, Mrs. Kaiser laid down the law, demanding that their guest not be asked to do anything: "In fact, it occasionally became embarrassing when I would stop to chat with Mr. Kaiser, and Ale would come rushing out saying, 'Now boss, don't you dare give Handy anything to do.'" Kaiser met his wife's conditions for the full two weeks, but not an hour more. At 5 A.M. the day the vacation ended, there was a knock on the cabin door. "Handy, are you awake?" Hancock probably expected it. In as civil a tone as he could muster, he replied, "I am now, Mr. Kaiser." Kaiser entered the living room, sat down, and listed chores he had saved up.[17]

Taxing as their jobs were when executives could return home after sixteen-hour days, traveling with Kaiser was even more wearying. It was bad enough when he journeyed by train; exhausted aides must escape to Pullman berths for a few hours of fitful rest. When Kaiser was in his late sixties, he often traveled by airplane, and his companions had no place to hide. Tim Yee recalled rising early and putting in a solid day's work in Honolulu, then catching a "red-eye special" flight to the mainland with the boss, who hated "wasting" normal business hours. Yee was summoned to Kaiser's seat, and he spent the entire flight standing, talking business. In the small hours next morning, they landed in San Francisco. The "day" was not yet over. Kaiser whisked his aide over to the Oakland office and called a few of the "boys" into headquarters to talk shop. Yee finally escaped to a hotel in San Francisco about 3:00 A.M. He "slept in" until 8:00 the next morning, then hastily dressed and dashed back to the Oakland office. Kaiser was already there, bright-eyed and jovial. He teased Yee about his leisurely arrival. According to Yee, "He was loaded for bear."[18]

Tim Bedford recounted an even longer work marathon with Kaiser. During the South American automobile negotiations in 1954, Bedford remembered taking off for Brazil with Kaiser and several associates on a late afternoon flight from San Francisco. He assumed they would sleep in flight; instead, the men sat up all night talking business. They deplaned late the next morning into a hot, muggy climate. A scheduled luncheon presentation to key Brazilian business leaders left no time to stop by their hotel even to freshen up. The meeting dragged on for hours, amidst lots of food, drinks, and cigars. The Brazilians challenged some of their figures, so Kaiser asked Bedford to work up new numbers for a follow-up meeting the next day. That job was formidable, and Kaiser made it even harder by urging Bedford to join him and their hosts for a tour of the night clubs. Finally Bedford slipped away. He worked in his hotel room until 5 A.M., then collapsed into bed. At 7 A.M. the phone rang. Kaiser and Bedford reviewed the figures while breakfast was brought in. Bedford learned that Kaiser had been up all night, partying with the Brazilians. They went to the second luncheon, where Kaiser handled the entire presentation. As Bedford put it, "It was dynamite; he was just incredible."[19]

Even on "pleasure" trips with Kaiser, the pressure was on. Hancock remembered one weekend jaunt to Tahoe, with several carloads of people. The boss, of course, was in the lead car, and he insisted that everyone stay together. Following cars maintained breakneck speeds to keep up. They stopped at a little roadside cafe near Sacramento, because Kaiser loved its flapjacks. Kaiser bolted down his food, but Hancock was a slow eater: "I had barely started my breakfast [but] . . . after much urging from the Boss, I gulped [it] down. I will never forget as we walked out the door, he looked up at the sky and then down at his watch and lamented 'thirty minutes gone forever.'" When executives had to get away to maintain equilibrium, they stated their needs in apologetic tones. After informing Kaiser that he had not enjoyed a break for three years, Chad Calhoun, himself a workaholic, gave six weeks' notice of a planned two-week pack trip into a remote mountain area: "This is a vacation and trip that I very badly need. I am quite stale and desperately need the pick-up." Calhoun's destination revealed good sense; it was miles from the nearest telephone. Kaiser pressed him for a precise location of his campsite; he wanted to be able to send a helicoptor in after Calhoun if he needed him.[20]

Working for Kaiser could be exasperating, and some men simply resigned. Lambreth Hancock quit, only to discover that life away from Kaiser was too boring. He asked for and got his old job back. But he never forgot the two weeks following his formal notice: "Kaiser would look right through me, as if I were not there—I was completely invisible as far as he was concerned." Kaiser was absorbed by work and found total relaxation in his primary passion; he seemed unaware that his constant pressure wore people down. According to Tudor Wall, Kaiser badgered a top man in aluminum to the point of tears in the executive dining room in Oakland. Hancock experienced a similar incident. Kaiser had instructed him to be sure a fancy new engine for one of his powerboats was delivered to Lake Tahoe by a certain date. The deadline was nearly impossible, but Hancock contrived to meet it, at least on paper. Unfortunately, a fire in a railroad tunnel delayed the train carrying the precious cargo. Kaiser berated Hancock for not anticipating every conceivable contingency. Somehow, he should have known better than to route the engine through a tunnel! Hancock initially shrugged off such absurd criticism as due to momentary frustration, but Kaiser mentioned it repeatedly. For a time, Hancock bit his tongue. Finally, one day, he started blubbering in front of Kaiser. He hastily retreated to the executive bathroom, and cried uncontrollably. Kaiser, nonplussed, first sent a secretary to try to coax Hancock back out. That move was unavailing, so Kaiser came into the bathroom. Hancock blew off steam, telling the boss that he was through, that he never wanted to see him again. Finally composing himself, Hancock came out of the bathroom. Kaiser was at the door. Without a word, he embraced Hancock, took him into his office, apologized, and sent him home. According to Hancock, "I was a whole new man, he could still give pressure but he would give consideration too."[21]

Kaiser usually treated his employees with dignity and respect, but his concentration was so intense that he occasionally treated people like servants. He seldom carried money; he expected associates to "lend" him money for incidentals. Even top executives treated him like royalty. Hass recalled a visit to the Permanente Cement plant. It was windy, and Kaiser's suit attracted its share of dust. A top executive dusted him off by hand. On extremely rare occasions he appeared to demean people deliberately. During World War II, he asked a visitor if he'd heard a song called "Send for Kaiser," then making the rounds. According to a reporter present, he told the visitor, "Well, you'll hear it now." Whereupon he turned to advisor Paul Cadman and said, "Paul, sing it for him." Red-faced, Cadman dutifully sang the song about his boss.[22]

Hass's recollection of top executives solicitously dusting him is ironic, because Kaiser often ignored his clothing and appearance. Ale Kaiser recalled that before they were married, Kaiser often wore rumpled suits, mostly browns and greys. Hancock remembered one of the first times he ever saw Kaiser, at the main office at the Fontana steel mill: "It was a hot day; there was no air conditioning. Mr. Kaiser shuffled down the corridor in his socks, his shirt off, suspenders down over his hips." Another executive recalled how, when traveling, he was often called into the boss's suite. On at least one occasion Kaiser was clad in nothing but a pair of undershorts. He sat on the edge of a bed, with his enormous stomach hanging over his shorts. On other occasions he called aides into the bathroom while he showered. Doris Kearns, Lyndon Johnson's biographer, claimed that the President summoned aides into the bathroom when attending to his most private needs, simply to make them uncomfortable and test their squeamishness. There is no hint that Kaiser humiliated subordinates in this way. He was so fascinated with business that he simply hated to "waste" precious moments.[23]

Some employees were petrified at the thought of crossing the boss or refusing an assignment. On one occasion, this had dangerous consequences. One of Kaiser's powerful hydroplane boats was sabotaged just before a big race. Some bolts were placed in an air vent, and a propeller shaft was sawed part way through. According to Hancock, investigation by a private detective revealed that the culprit was an employee who had raced Kaiser's boats for years and who was fearful of the ever-increasing speeds the boats could reach, "yet he didn't have the heart after all those years of serving Mr. Kaiser to tell him that he was afraid to [race them]." When told of the employee's involvement, Kaiser recognized his real motive, forgave him, and kept him on the payroll.[24]

If Kaiser intimidated employees on occasion, he generally earned their admiration and affection. His visits to job sites usually boosted morale among the rank and file, even if such "state occasions" gave responsible managers indigestion. Yet top managers, those closest to him on a daily basis, also developed attachments to Kaiser. Sentimental expressions of affection marked interchanges between Kaiser and many key advisors, particularly on ceremonial occasions. They often exceeded ordinary testimonials exchanged between professional colleagues. As Henry Kaiser, Jr., aptly put it, "Dad likes a little hearts and flowers . . ." He probably loved the tribute paid him by one associate at a birthday banquet in his honor: "Great builder that [Kaiser] is, I think he has not ever crushed a flower half-hidden in the grass that he did not wish he might have walked some other way."[25]

Like many modern executives intent upon maintaining high worker morale, Kaiser sponsored frequent, elaborate awards ceremonies. He enjoyed overseeing many of the arrangements himself. For the "25 Year Service Awards Banquet" in December 1952, he rented the Colonial Ballroom in the St. Francis Hotel in San Francisco. Detailed arrangements prescribed not only the words, but the mood of the awards presentations:

> At the conclusion of the dinner the coffee is served . . . All service is removed from the tables. . . . Lights in house slowly dim while lights on the individual tables come on (This is the last function of the waitress at each table just before the change of lights). After a pause and on cue spotlight brightly on male octet in balcony behind the head table. Octet: "I am the builder. Come walk with me."

The singing continued softly in the background, while Henry Kaiser, Jr., speaking over a microphone but hidden from view, narrated a tribute to silver anniversary employees. The tribute was part poem, part song. At the end of a lengthy narration, the octet belted out "Give me some men who are stout-hearted men." Henry Jr., still concealed, intoned, "My father will now make the awards."[26]

Cynics hooted at such theatrical antics. However, as Peters and Waterman observed, the "best" companies create awards ceremonies and similar nonmonetary compensation on the flimsiest pretexts.[27] Few cynics worked for Kaiser, and most attending such banquets came away with good feelings. It was evident to them that the boss cared about employees.

Kaiser enjoyed being mentor to young protégés. Hancock recalled that he and Marty Wortman, another newcomer, were asked to supervise construction of a free-standing stairway in Kaiser's new home. An "old-country" Italian artisan was hired to do the work. Kaiser inquired several times how the work was coming. Hancock, pressured by other tasks, promised to visit the job site soon. He was so busy that he hoped Wortman would check the staircase. When the deadline neared, Hancock finally visited the job site. The artisan admitted that some materials had never arrived, that he had faked his reports, and that he would miss the deadline. Hancock and Wortman placed a conference call to Kaiser. To their surprise, the boss was not angry: "I suspected that all the time because the reports didn't follow the timing [they] should have been following." Kaiser asked, "Have you boys learned anything from this? As long as you've learned a lesson, the staircase isn't that important." To the harried young executives, the real lesson may have appeared that no matter how hard one worked, it was never hard enough.[28]

Kaiser's aides were acutely aware of the boss's ability in maneuvering people. His manipulation was often subtle, even gentle. In rare instances, he revealed a temper. But Clay Bedford, who knew him well for over forty years, claimed that he usually "play-acted" anger. Another subordinate recalled Kaiser loudly berating a business rival over the telephone, slamming down the receiver, then turning to a roomful of men, winking and chortling, "Well, let's see what the old bastard says when he calls back!"[29]

A key attribute Kaiser demanded in any executive was rock solid integrity. Ale Kaiser recalled that he loathed cheaters. Kaiser occasionally taught lessons in personal integrity even to "outsiders." When vacation cottages were being added at the Hawaiian Village complex in Honolulu, a city building inspector observed that two cottages were closer together than zoning regulations permitted by six inches. The inspector intimated to Kaiser that he might "overlook" the violation in return for other considerations. The discussion occurred on a Friday. Kaiser asked the inspector to come back the following Monday. Over the weekend, he had a construction crew cut off six inches, then plaster it over and repaint the wall. When the inspector returned, Kaiser casually asked him to check his measurements. He did, several times; soon he was muttering to himself. Finally he returned to Kaiser's office and said, "I must have been mistaken. I'm sorry." Weeks later the inspector asked him for the story. Kaiser told him and also said that he'd do the same thing "a thousand times" before he would pay anyone at City Hall a nickel.[30]

On other occasions, Kaiser used the integrity issue to teach lessons in management. A bright, aggressive young man had worked his way up from the mail room to salesman in one company. Unfortunately, greed overcame him and he offered a prospect an "under-the-table" deal. Kaiser called a conference to discuss the violation of company ethics. All present agreed that the culprit should be fired. Kaiser leaned back, lit a cigar, and started talking. He reminded them that the man had a superb record, except for one serious slip. He then turned to the salesman's superior and said, ". . . you have had this boy for all these years, you have trained him. You should have instilled in him all of the rights and wrongs and . . . that you never do anything under the table even if you loose [sic] the contract. If anybody gets fired, you're the one that should get fired." While the men sat, stunned, Kaiser said, "Now, let's go around the table again." Once more the vote was unanimous. The salesman kept his job and later headed his division. Everyone learned a valuable lesson.[31]

Another corporate policy involved internal competition. The Kaiser organization achieved partial vertical integration in several industries after

World War II. Kaiser subsidiaries were in position to earn sizable returns through sales to other "family members." The possibilities multiplied as the empire grew. But managers hoping to fatten up monthly sales figures through easy deals with other Kaiser companies learned caution. The boss did not tolerate "sweetheart" deals; in fact, he encouraged direct competition between the companies. In one case, when the state of California asked for bids on automobile license plates, Kaiser urged the steel and aluminum companies to submit rival proposals.[32]

Kaiser had never been much interested in office work; to the extent he could, he delegated paper work to others. He valued men like Eugene E. Trefethen, Jr., who deftly managed mountains of documents, government regulations, and internal memos. But by the mid-1950s, he had to confront the fact that his organizational structure was inadequate. In maintaining direct family control of his industrial empire, Kaiser had followed a fairly typical pattern. Two business historians observed recently that organizations expanding "without increasing the number or complexity of their products or markets found that centralized management systems could handle their needs . . ."[33] Until the mid-1950s, Kaiser's companies partly matched that profile. Corporate strategists, including Trefethen, studied closely the advantages of reorganization. Alfred P. Sloan had pioneered a dazzlingly successful decentralized corporate structure at General Motors in the 1920s. Ford and Chrysler did not follow suit until World War II, but some industry analysts believed that modern corporate structures helped them solidify positions as the Big Three.[34]

If a single event persuaded Kaiser and top managers to consider seriously "modernizing" the organization, it was hard times in the automobile business. As noted, Kaiser Motors suspended production of conventional passenger vehicles in 1955 and sold assembly-line equipment to Argentina. As cumulative losses since 1949 exceeded $120 million, Kaiser Motors' stock plunged. Bankruptcy was a distinct possibility. Henry Kaiser resisted acknowledging failure, and he wanted to provide stockholders at least partial recovery of their investments. Financial advisors, including George Woods, urged Kaiser to combine assets of his enterprises under one large holding company. Automobile company shareholders could exchange their stock for smaller numbers of shares in the new organization.[35]

Kaiser's corporate reorganization was not purely altruistic. By the mid-1950s, his highly personalized means of raising money would no longer suffice. Kaiser, his son Edgar, Trefethen, and other managers realized that recent fund-raising had been far too modest and often badly handled. When they needed tens or even hundreds of millions of dollars for future ventures, they never again wanted to rely on men like Cyrus Eaton.

An important intangible consideration probably entered the minds of decisionmakers in the Kaiser organization. Kaiser executives still overheard disparaging comments about government favoritism for Kaiser. They wanted to be taken seriously by other business leaders, to be accepted as members of the club. That was a major reason why Kaiser had paid off the RFC loan to Kaiser Steel ahead of schedule. Unfortunately, the government investigation of the C-119 cargo plane "mess" had concluded in the fall of 1953, and critics had long memories. By creating a modern, publicly owned holding company, Kaiser and his executives would formally join the elite among America's large corporations. In the future, when requiring bank loans or considering new stock issues, they wanted bankers and potential underwriters to court them rather than having to go begging to Wall Street. A "modern" corporate structure would ease the flow of venture capital from investors who might resist "old-fashioned" family-owned organizations.[36]

The financial experts presented other compelling arguments. A new umbrella organization would facilitate approval from the Securities and Exchange Commission (SEC) for future stock issues. Finally, under U.S. tax laws, Kaiser Motors had a huge, unused tax loss of $76 million that could be carried forward and written off by a successor company. All of these considerations led to the formation of Kaiser Industries.[37]

With reorganization approved overwhelmingly by the various Kaiser companies early in 1956, the organization took a giant step toward modernization. The new corporate entity absorbed all holdings of the Henry J. Kaiser Company, plus the Kaiser-controlled stock in steel, cement, aluminum and chemicals, gypsum, engineering and construction, fabricated metal products, real estate development, and sand and gravel.[38]

Kaiser remained somewhat removed from the day-to-day operations in his many enterprises. He approved creation of Kaiser Industries; when commitments involved tens of millions of dollars, he made the ultimate decision. However, he included promising subordinates in his deliberations. In addition, rising executives and established senior managers made many important operating decisions. The tougher the choices, the more men grew; he tolerated mistakes as long as men learned from them.[39]

Two decades after his death, several former Kaiser executives assessed his managerial skills. Although admitting their favorable bias, they nevertheless made some shrewd observations. Several noted that Kaiser's managerial performance varied considerably between different types of enterprises. Kaiser and his executives were superb at production, less skilled in other fields. The companies achieved their greatest triumphs in extracting and processing minerals; witness the success in sand and gravel, cement, aluminum, steel, and similar products. They also succeeded in government work, which was production-oriented. In both dam and ship building, they basically lined up and assembled aggregates. They quickly learned the ropes in producing automobiles, steel, and aluminum. However, they did not match that performance in consumer products and service industries. Although Kaiser was a genius at selling himself, he and his organization did not effectively market automobiles, household appliances, and aluminum foil. Exceptions included television and tourism in Hawaii, but Kaiser did not remain in the marketing end of these enterprises very long.[40]

Kaiser remained a workaholic all his life. In the spring of 1965 he suffered a heart attack during a visit to the mainland. While being flown back to Hawaii in an oxygen tent, he still talked shop. Whether he was in good or bad health, people found it exciting to be around him. There were some malcontents; this was unavoidable, given his strong personality. In Hawaii, a group of former Kaiser men organized an "alumni club." They occasionally met at a local bar and traded yarns of his high-handed treatment. Kaiser learned of a planned gathering of the "alumni." He swept into the club, joined them, and bought a round of drinks. He was soon swapping stories; when he left a couple of hours later, they cheered him.[41]

The "alumni-club" incident, and countless others, symbolized Kaiser: even to men who knew him for decades, he remained an enigma. He constantly surprised even old associates by doing the unexpected. Yet much as he loved unconventional thinking and men who shared his flights of fancy, he also valued sober-minded realists, who supplied a needed element of caution. One such individual was engineer George Havas. When riding a train, Kaiser saw a herd of sheep and told Havas that they had just been shorn. Havas followed Kaiser's gaze out the window. "Yes, Mr. Kaiser," he conceded, "it looks that way from this side."[42] People like Havas intrigued Kaiser, and he in turn fascinated his employees. Working for Kaiser was hectic, at times gut-wrenching, but never boring. Those who joined Kaiser knew the excitement of adventure, and many felt an acute sense of loss when they retired.

15

Global Development and a Pacific Paradise

Shortly after mid-century, Kaiser presided over an increasingly influential multinational organization. Overseas automobile assembly plants nearly circled the globe by the mid-1950s, and Kaiser Aluminum and Chemical (KACC) took delivery from widely scattered bauxite deposits. But the manifold activities of Kaiser Engineers were more significant contributors to Kaiser's international prestige. As his domestic industrial empire grew and prospered following World War II, many Americans assumed that the organization had retired from heavy construction, but the reality was far different.

Kaiser Engineers was organized in 1941, and kept busy during the war expanding the shipyards and helping build a third set of locks at the Panama Canal. Kaiser proposed massive engineering projects following the war, including a national airport network and other large public works. These initiatives failed, but Kaiser Engineers won many important domestic construction contracts, including nuclear power contracts that totaled $165 million by the late 1950s. The engineers sponsored a six-year expansion and modernization program for Armco Steel at scattered locations and a similar development program for Kennecott Copper's huge smelter in Utah. They built part of the Bay Area Rapid Transit (BART). In the 1950s and 1960s they dug tunnels and built bridges, hospitals and clinics, and port and harbor facilities. Symbolizing the diversity of their activities, even as they constructed nuclear reactors, they devised a master plan for pollution control and rehabilitation in San Francisco Bay and the delta areas of the Sacramento and San Joaquin rivers.[1]

However, after mid-century, many of Kaiser Engineers' most exciting projects were abroad. The postwar years marked a major increase in the nation's commitment to internationalism, and more American corporations became multinationals. Far-sighted men at Kaiser headquarters perceived opportunities to earn good returns, help spread capitalism abroad, and greatly enhance the organization's image. The Marshall Plan and other initiatives committed Americans to helping war-damaged nations rebuild. In addition, European colonial empires were quickly unraveling, and former colonies and protectorates needed practical guidance, not just new constitutions. In the late 1940s the United States was the world's unchallenged economic colossus, and ambitious nationalists around the world sought its technical expertise.[2]

Although Kaiser did not make large-scale commitments until the Argentine and Brazilian projects in the mid-1950s, other important preliminary moves occurred several years earlier, and the initiative did not always come from the Kaiser organization. In September 1947 a top Indian diplomat urged Kaiser to help the soon-to-be-independent nation develop modern industry. The Indian discussed long-range prospects in aluminum with Chad Calhoun, but his most immediate concern was expanding India's steel industry. Kaiser postponed pursuing this opportunity; political upheaval accompanying the transition from colony to independence may explain it.[3]

As in Latin America, Kaiser delayed follow-up on Indian initiatives for nearly a decade. However, in the fall of 1955, Kaiser Engineers signed a $130 million contract to expand the Tata Iron Works in Jamshedpur, a city of 250,000 located west of Calcutta. The commitment propelled the American firm into the Cold War, as the Soviet Union almost simultaneously agreed to build a government-owned plant. Since the Tata Iron Works were privately owned, capitalism and communism symbolically competed head to head in a pivotal Third World nation. According to western accounts, "communists" tried to foment unrest among thousands of local workers. *Newsweek* claimed that in the early months, Kaiser Engineers encountered delays because of "traditional Indian featherbedding," but that the Americans impressed local observers by working beside native laborers in 125-degree heat. If an operator had trouble with a big shovel, a Kaiser engineer would leap aboard and give an impromptu lesson. In this respect, little had changed since Cuba; but the equipment was far more sophisticated and expensive.[4]

Kaiser Engineers' experience in India differed from the automobile investment in South America in that the Americans were strictly hired hands in India. In other respects, the similarities were marked. As in Argentina and Brazil, the Americans were teachers who passed along engineering skills to Indian technicians. It would have been an insult to Indian pride to bring in large numbers of skilled workers. Instead, the Americans trained thousands of new draftsmen, engineers, electricians, equipment operators, welders, and other craftsmen. But the Americans also learned from their hosts. They hired experts to provide extensive orientation in Indian customs and traditions for Americans sent there. Despite, or perhaps because of, such orientation, relations between the Americans and Indians were friendly, but somewhat formal. As one analyst observed, although a few socialized with Indians, "as a rule they found it best not to hobnob with direct subordinates from the project . . . since Indian employees are very sensitive about signs of favoritism." But the reporter found considerably freer fraternization at the Tata works than between Russian engineers and their hosts. The western writer claimed that Soviet bosses tightly controlled their workers.[5]

Another important overseas Kaiser venture was helping build the infrastructure for industrialization of Ghana. Under British rule until 1957, this new African nation experimented with freedom under strongman Prime Minister (later President) Kwame Nkrumah. Cautious negotiations began in 1959. Edgar Kaiser led the American group, and discussions were fraught with tensions for many months. Nkrumah was an enigma. In the late 1950s the western press touted him as a foremost African statesman, an articulate opponent of neo-colonialism and advocate of pan-African unity. By the early 1960s he was accused of perceiving cabals behind every bush and turning megalomaniac in exercising power. Nkrumah proved very difficult; he alternately charmed visitors and imprisoned and tortured political enemies. Experience with African and other Third World leaders provided Edgar Kaiser advanced training in realpolitik; he later became an advisor on foreign affairs to Presidents Kennedy and Johnson.

Nkrumah masterfully exploited Cold War tensions to enhance his own power base. He was keenly aware that as one of the first powerful black nationalists, he would set the tone for future relations between African leaders and outsiders seeking business. In addition, Ghana possessed abundant natural resources: large bauxite deposits and the potential for hydroelectric power development along the Volta River. Aware of his position, Nkrumah pitted Russians and Americans against each other.

Henry and Edgar Kaiser were aware of the risks of major commitments in Ghana. So were other business leaders. When Americans first seriously considered development of Ghana's bauxite resources, Edgar Kaiser met with officials at Alcoa and Reynolds to discuss forming a consortium. Each of the three companies possessed the resources to do the job alone, but they explored spreading risks. They postponed the project; in 1957 and 1958 there was excess aluminum capacity in the United States. Nkrumah's gradual leftward drift also helped push the bauxite project into the background.[6]

Despite these considerations, in 1959 the Kaiser organization offered to help build an aluminum plant and develop hydroelectric power. The projects were inextricably joined: vast amounts of power were required for aluminum processing. But without heavy industry in Ghana there would be little demand for power. Nkrumah needed outside economic and technical assistance. Kaiser Engineers provided the design and supervision for the Akosombo Dam and its power transmission network on the Volta River; the project eventually cost over $200 million, underwritten chiefly by loans from the World Bank. Despite Nkrumah's "mailed-fist" approach to domestic dissent, Henry Kaiser warily endorsed plans to build the aluminum plant. Ground-breaking ceremonies took place late in 1964. The elder Kaiser lived to see completion of the dam and the aluminum plant, and also Nkrumah's ouster in 1966.[7]

In the 1950s and 1960s, Kaiser Engineers embarked on a series of overseas projects which required less deft diplomacy, but were more spectacular engineering feats. One example was the Snowy Mountain Range project in Australia. The lush eastern coastal regions of Australia receive ample rain, but the rest of the continent is tinder-box dry. Much of the rain falls in the Snowy Mountain region, midway between Melbourne and Sydney, from where it flows into the Tasman Sea. The Australians wanted to harness it but had no companies qualified to do the job in the mid-1950s.

The national development minister for Australia contacted state department officials in Washington in 1954; after bureaucratic channels were cleared, the Bureau of Reclamation drew up plans. Finally, the job was opened for bidding. Veterans of dam jobs in the 1950s recalled those big projects, and bidders were organized in a familiar pattern. Kaiser Engineers sponsored the winning consortium; six more companies joined the group.[8]

The job was huge. They had to store the water, harness its power, and divert it to arid western regions for irrgation. Seven dams were designed, and eighty-five miles of tunnels had to be bored through mountains. In addition, seventeen power stations were planned, plus four hundred miles of aqueducts to carry water to the interior. One of the world's largest water development projects, when completed the system would yield two million acre-feet of water and three million kilowatts of power annually. But bare statistics do not convey the magnitude of the challenge. Kaiser's share was two dams and much of the tunnel work. The dams were easy; they were comparatively small, and Kaiser's engineers had vast experience. Their biggest challenge was a single fourteen-mile-long cut, twenty-six feet wide, which diverted water through intervening mountain ranges. It was a dangerous job, and there were accidents, but safety precautions had been greatly improved since the 1930s. Still, the engineers confronted formidable challenges from nature. Blizzards buried several work camps for days before relief reached them; and electrical storms occasionally ignited explosive TNT charges prematurely. But Kaiser's engineering moles burrowed through rock at record-setting pace; as usual, the job was finished ahead of schedule in 1958.[9]

Henry Kaiser's personal involvement in the engineers' international jobs was very limited, particularly in his later years. Nevertheless, he was often the catalyst in negotiations with foreign leaders, some of whom were awed by the powerful patriarch. Kaiser executives recalled that although Nkrumah respected Edgar, his attitude toward Henry Kaiser approached reverence. In part, this feeling reflected Third World cultural values honoring age and experience, but after Nkrumah met Henry Kaiser in the early 1960s, he looked to the senior Kaiser for final decisions.

Until his death in 1967, Kaiser reviewed all but the least consequential engineering projects. According to corporate publicists, he approved some projects not because they promised large profits, but because they represented learning opportunities for younger men. All large corporations produce considerable puffery, but there is some truth in this claim. Kaiser was an organization-builder who believed that young men thrust into challenging situations eventually became capable managers. In the early 1960s Kaiser Engineers' publicity stressed large numbers of international contracts and the dollar volume of backlogged orders. But publicists seldom mentioned profits, because Kaiser Engineers generally lost money. In 1964 the company won $795 million in new contracts, but lost $16.6 million. Much of Kaiser Engineers' importance within the corporate structure was as a symbol of international prestige and as a training ground for promising managers.[10]

At the end of World War II, Henry Kaiser perceived one of the benefits of overseas expansion as creating abundance for more people. A cornucopia of material goods produced in partnership between American firms and local workers could be a powerful tool in selling the concept of free enterprise to neutral nations. Like most Americans, Kaiser failed to understand that neutrality made sense for many Third World countries. Until the mid-1960s the organization always conducted business outside the Soviet bloc. In 1966, Kaiser was in the final year of his life, and Edgar Kaiser was assuming command of the corporate empire. In May of that year, Edgar arranged for Kaiser Jeep's international division to send a convoy of products on a two-thousand-mile-long caravan through Poland, Hungary, Czechoslovakia, Rumania, and Bulgaria. Entente as a formal diplomatic strategy awaited the inauguration of Richard M. Nixon, but President Johnson advocated increased trade with Eastern European nations. Commerce Secretary John Connor called the Kaiser Jeep initiative "an imaginative technique to promote U.S. exports."[11] Edgar Kaiser coordinated the organization's thrust behind the Iron Curtain; under his guidance the engineering operations became truly global in scope. Nevertheless, under Henry Kaiser's stewardship, the organization had already set up enterprises in fifty countries.

After mid-century, Henry Kaiser was more personally involved in developing Hawaii than any other overseas venture. Late-twentieth-century

Hawaii is one of the world's great tourist attractions, but vast changes have occurred over the past three decades. Prior to statehood in 1959, most Americans thought Hawaii meant Pearl Harbor and pineapples; local hotels served less than 250,000 overnight guests in 1959 (as compared to over 4 million in the mid-1980s).[12] Henry Kaiser was the *malihini*, or new-comer, who exerted the greatest force in changing all that. Moving to Oahu in semi-retirement in 1954, aged seventy-two, Kaiser launched a daz-zling program of promotion and development. In addition to building hotels, he created beaches, a new city east of Honolulu, a hospital, and a cement plant. In his spare time, he built up radio and television on the islands. His "retirement" achievements alone constituted a career.

In contrast to local aristocrats such as the Dillinghams and the trustees of the Bishop Estate who pulled wires from off stage, Kaiser assumed a very high profile. Without question, he irritated some individuals. Hawaiians weren't used to his pace, and some believed he rode roughshod over local decisionmakers. But when they got used to him, most admired Kaiser. Workers were grateful to him for creating jobs. Few business moguls ever enjoyed more productive retirement years. For Kaiser they were joyful; he remained useful to the end.

Until Kaiser began his renovation projects along Waikiki Beach late in 1954, he was unknown to many Hawaiians, but he had economic ties to the islands even before World War II. As noted, in one of their few sound pre-war moves, military planners purchased and stored shiploads of Kaiser's cement at Oahu. Within days of Pearl Harbor, engineers were rebuilding with Permanente cement.

The decade following V-J Day was the busiest of Kaiser's long life, as he founded or expanded most of his largest enterprises. Yet the islands were never far from his thinking. In 1944 and early 1945, he considered freight and passenger ship service in the Pacific; Hawaiian tourism would have enhanced revenues. When Kaiser and Fritz Burns formed a housing part-nership in 1945, Kaiser stated that Honolulu would be a "likely spot" for several of their communities. He was a fairly frequent visitor in the late 1940s, and Bess loved Oahu. Henry planned a Lafayette, California, estate in a Hawaiian motif. Bess died before it was finished, but Ale Kaiser loved the islands too. In early 1950, a local development group tried to persuade Kaiser to spearhead an ambitious program for economic growth.[13]

Kaiser associates offered varying theories as to why Henry and Ale pulled up stakes in Oakland and moved semi-permanently to Oahu in 1954. Ale theorized that corporate operations had grown so complex by the early 1950s that Henry sought new projects that he could control from the ground up. Others suggested that Kaiser realized that as long as he resided on the mainland, even top-level managers would look to him for direction. His physical separation from the home office by 2,500 miles of ocean symbolically removed such close ties. This theory implies that Kaiser consciously forced second-generation managers to mature by themselves. Others in the organization held a radically different view: younger men took the initiative and encouraged him to move to Hawaii. Finally, a few individuals believed that Henry and Ale were affected by gossip about their hasty marriage and sought a fresh start.[14]

Both Henry and his young wife were strong-willed; it is hard to imagine them bowing to pressure to move. The couple certainly enjoyed the islands and made several visits in the early 1950s. Henry Kaiser was surprised that hotel space on Oahu was so limited. He and Ale solved their housing needs by purchasing a sumptuous Kahala Beach home, but Kaiser had far larger plans. One of his first pronouncements after visiting Oahu was, "It's nonsense to say that there's no room left to build more hotels on Waikiki Beach. Why not extend the world-famous beach and build a great vacation industry?"[15]

When interviewed years later about why he helped develop Hawaii, Kaiser claimed that he had "missed out" on the tourism and land booms in Florida during the 1920s and Palm Springs, California, after World War II, and he did not want to miss another chance. When he walked along Waikiki Beach in 1954, opportunity stared him in the face. The beachfront was developed, after a fashion. The Matson shipping interests controlled sixteen acres of prime Waikiki land and the Moana, Surfrider, and the fashionable Royal Hawaiian hotels. Old-guard locals owned most other hotels and eateries. Kaiser saw one major chance to break into Waikiki Beach: the Niumalu Hotel, owned by Jerry Zukor, a New Yorker, who had purchased it in the fire-sale atmosphere following the attack on Pearl Harbor. Frequented by a generation of servicemen, it had been immensely profitable. A collection of one- and two-story cottages "held together by termites within holding hands," the Niumalu was definitely at the low end of the scale. In April 1955 Kaiser brought it for $1,262,500.[16]

Kaiser wanted the land, not the structures. He and Fritz Burns conceived an elaborate plan creating an artificial lagoon and several hundred additional feet of beach space. After complicated legal negotiations with territorial authorities and other nearby landowners over dredging arrangements and littoral rights, the real work began. Kaiser and Burns originally acquired about eight acres; extensive engineering would double the space available for development.[17]

In the words of publicist Robert C. Elliott, "In a style unmatched since . . . the shipyards [Kaiser] began altering the map of Oahu. He scooped out a salt water lagoon (complete with island), trucked in 3,000 loads of sand to form a beach, and built a 100 room hotel in eighty-nine days . . ." By July 1955 his construction crews had turned the old structures of the Niumalu into beachfront "huts," with genuine thatched roofs woven by Samoan workers. In addition, they built a high-rise facility, set back from the beach. Even before this structure was finished, Kaiser and Burns were ready for serious entertaining at the Hawaiian Village.[18]

The two West Coast enterpreneurs met self-imposed deadlines, to the amazement and frequent discomfiture of their first paying customers. At 7:00 A.M. sharp, guests would be rudely awakened by clanking pile drivers, overhead cranes, cement mixers, and dozens of other pieces of heavy machinery. The first hotel manager, Lambreth Hancock, pleaded to no avail with Kaiser to let guests sleep in until 8:00 A.M. Just as he had driven managers on the mainland for forty years, so did he press Hawaiian contractors. One ingenious device he used to "hurry up" subcontractors was forcing them to work in close quarters. He did so by ordering landscaping to be planted very near main structures, thus forcing the subcontractors to squeeze cumbersome equipment into ever-dwindling amounts of space. Kaiser knew that subcontractors hated cramped work space. They worked quickly and indirectly pressured other subcontractors to pick up the pace. When Hancock complained that they trampled the landscaping, Kaiser replied that money saved from days cut off the schedule, plus additional room rentals, would more than pay for replanting.[19]

In his haste, Kaiser regularly violated building codes. There was no intentional malice; he simply hated paper work and delays. After architect Ed Bauer sketched a rough design for a complex of shops at the Hawaiian Village, Kaiser told him to start right away. Foundations were poured before Kaiser applied for a building permit. When city officials protested these high-handed tactics, Kaiser cheerfully admitted that his enthusiasm had run away with him and promised to be more careful in the future. But such incidents happened repeatedly.[20]

The hotel business initially fascinated Kaiser. But enthusiasm alone did not guarantee success, and he and Burns suffered some bruises. Kaiser hoped to win over the locals and hosted a huge bash to celebrate the grand opening. Cynics noted that some freeloading guests not only stuffed themselves with expensive food, but filled their purses as well. After the party was over, Kaiser and Burns congratulated themselves on their huge success. When they threw open the doors the next day, they assumed they would be trampled by paying guests. But few diners patronized their restaurants, and for the first few weeks, most overnight visitors were corporate managers from the home office on expense accounts. When the hotel issued credit cards to drum up local business, managers uncovered surprising numbers of "deadbeats" among Honolulu's elite.[21]

Other problems gradually surfaced. Hancock's background was in newspapers, and he had to learn the hotel business "on the job." He soon discovered that some bartenders and headwaiters were masters at cheating the house. Although Hancock eventually learned to ferret out dishonest employees, the constant battle of wits drained his energy. He eventually found solutions. The Hotel and Restaurant Union, one of the few strong unions in Hawaii, was headed by Art Rutledge, a tough, seasoned negotiator, who realized that Kaiser provided hundreds of jobs and saw him as a businessman to be nurtured, not opposed. Rutledge helped Hancock root out dishonest workers.[22]

Kaiser and Burns paid top dollar to lure the best musicians and entertainers. Many of them were from the mainland, including big names like the Martin Denny combo and Lawrence Welk, but "locals" benefited too. Henry and Ale "discovered" a talented native singer named Alfred Apaka, whose music they so enjoyed that they hired him away from Donn the Beachcomber and helped further his career. When Apaka wasn't doing mainland stints at Las Vegas or Lake Tahoe, he was often the featured entertainer at the Hawaiian Village. In bringing in top performers from the mainland, Kaiser helped raise pay scales on the islands. Just as his enlightened labor policies had distressed Big Steel, Kaiser's generosity with local entertainers and workers irritated Hawaiian competitors. As K. Tim Yee, former vice chairman of the Kaiser Development Company, observed, "The old Anglo families were frightened by Kaiser. They misunderstood him; he moved too fast. But working-class people, non-whites generally loved him; he was creating jobs, opening up the economy."[23]

In the mid-1950s there were too few tourists to go around. Kaiser predicted huge increases, but they weren't coming in as fast as expected. The hotel business was extremely competitive, and rivals developed predatory tricks. As newcomers to the game, Kaiser's managers were usually on the receiving end. Many guests with reservations failed to show up; rival operators paid taxi drivers "bounties" for each guest diverted from a competitor. Eventually, Kaiser's managers learned to reply in kind. Rival hotel managers and boat operators charged them with degrading the beachfront ambience by hawking catamaran rides on the beach and tried unsuccessfully to persuade public officials to ban Kaiser's boats. In the summer of 1957 Kaiser and Fred Daily, who ran the Waikikian Hotel on adjoining property, traded unneighborly charges.[24]

The hotel business was rough going, particularly in the beginning. Three months after the fall 1955 opening of the first sixty-nine units of the Hawaiian Village occupancy averaged under 20 percent. Managers estimated that the hotel needed three-quarters occupancy just to break even. Similarly, the bars and restaurants had too few patrons and too many employees. In March 1956 Hancock reported that occupancy was almost 50 percent, but that many patrons cut stays short and checked into rival hotels because of noisy construction. He concluded, "we have really got to sell and sell fast on the mainland!" In 1956 the Hawaiian Village lost money, but in 1957 it made a tiny profit of $15,000 with occupancy averaging 64.5 percent.[25]

Henry and Ale Kaiser enjoyed some facets of the hotel business. Henry was happiest when supervising general construction, and Ale provided good ideas for decorations, entertainment, and recreation. The couple frequently attended evening shows, and Ale enjoyed hobnobbing with Hollywood entertainers. But by the late 1950s Kaiser was tired of being an "innkeeper." He complained to Eugene Trefethen, Jr., of the "awfully burdensome load . . . of [trying] to find the time and spirit for seeing many of the persons that demands are made upon me to see," and he urged the home office to screen "important" visitors more carefully. Certain self-designated "big shots" created intolerable headaches. One congressman created an ugly lobby scene over allegedly poor service. Hotel manager James E. Durham complained, "Regardless of the stature of [the] Congressman . . . it is impossible for me to condone the treatment and abuse handed out to our employees." Kaiser no doubt heard about this and numerous other complaints.[26]

Kaiser learned that being an innkeeper required constant attention and supervision; there were hundreds of details to keep track of. The enterprise involved Kaiser's family and home office as well. When Edgar Kaiser visited the Hawaiian Village a year after it opened, he was amazed at the progress in construction, yet noticed many details demanding attention. He observed that with hasty building, some detail work was shabby; subcontractors should be called back to modify their original work. There were other irritants. Henry Kaiser was weary of requests for "freebies" by various corporate "friends" and minor celebrities. As he noted in 1957, "Honestly, I feel we could fill half of the hotel with this type of give-aways." Kaiser delighted in fully booked weeks, but these were rare. He constantly urged managers to fill the lobby with paying guests.[27]

Soon after opening the Hawaiian Village, Kaiser realized that his executives did not have the inclination or flair to manage the hotels successfully themselves. He therefore arranged with Edward E. Carlson of Western International Hotels to turn day-to-day operations over to professional managers. Western's first manager failed to understand Kaiser's work ethic, evidently believing that eight-to-ten-hour days were sufficient. Kaiser was annoyed that he took swimming breaks in the middle of the day; he didn't last long. Subsequent managers evidently proved satisfactory; no doubt they were carefully briefed about Kaiser's expectations before leaving the mainland. Western International ran operations until Kaiser sold the complex to Conrad Hilton early in 1961.[28]

Even before he purchased the Niumalu Hotel in 1955, Kaiser had promoted Hawiian economic growth. As the Hawaiian Village's multi-storied towers sprang up out of the sand, the vision of empty rooms bothered him, and he urged all involved in tourism to work together to bring hundreds of thousands of mainlanders to the islands. He promoted "Magic Island," a major expansion of usable beachfront land just off Ala Moana Park; his own construction company finished the first phase of the project in 1962. He was an enthusiastic supporter of statehood, and when Hawaii became a state in 1959, he urged his staff in Washington to help its representatives compete for federal appropriations for public works.[29]

During the 1950s promoting local tourism was one of Kaiser's top priorities. He personally visited large travel agencies on the mainland with a slide projector and promotional filmstrips. He had retained his touch as a salesman, and his visits often yielded large bookings. Kaiser also badgered the Honolulu Chamber of Commerce to drum up convention business more aggressively, claiming that every dollar invested in promoting conventions returned $100 to the Hawaiian economy. In 1957 he built the 1,800-seat Kaiser Dome, which could be used as a convention hall. He often promoted tourism in speeches. When asked to address the American Society of Newspaper Editors at their Honolulu convention in 1957, his topic was "Free World Travel as a Factor for Peace."[30]

Early in 1960 a local reporter urged Kaiser to estimate the growth of the tourist industry in the next decade. By 1959 the industry had barely started to grow; Kaiser predicted that a decade later there would be a million tourists a year. For once, he was too conservative; in 1969 over 1.5 million visitors arrived. One reason why Kaiser underestimated growth was that it was still costly and time-consuming to get to Hawaii. In his view, the major air carriers provided poor service to the islands. Even worse, they were unimaginative in promoting tourism themselves.[31]

By early 1960 Kaiser was seemingly engaged in a one-man war with the airlines. Before he moved to Oahu, most travel to Hawaii had been by steamship, but advances in air transportation were changing that. By the mid-1950s, DC-4s could reach Honolulu from the mainland; jet service was just over the horizon, or so Kaiser believed. With jet service, tourists with a two-week vacation could spend most of it on the islands. But the airlines resisted opening new routes and spending millions on jet aircraft until they were assured large loads. Kaiser considered such attitudes timid and short-sighted. In the late 1950s, he was rapidly expanding hotel space, as were other operators. The innkeepers were doing their part, but hundreds of rooms were vacant every night. At one point, Western International estimated that if all carriers fully booked every flight to Honolulu, hotel rooms would still be available. To Kaiser, the solution was simple: if airlines scheduled more flights, all would prosper.[32]

At first Kaiser believed that reason alone would convince airlines to promote tourism more aggressively. He tried to create good will with management, but United Airlines and Pan American were reluctant partners. According to Kaiser, in 1955 Pan American officials claimed that they were "throttled" in developing their Hawaiian traffic by lack of hotel space. That was valid in the mid-1950s, but the airlines reacted slowly to rapid changes. By 1958, available rooms had doubled, but air service was almost unchanged. Kaiser stated that he had given Pan American personnel first-class Hawaiian Village rooms at third-class prices but that Pan American had responded by using his rates to force better deals elsewhere, and that airline personnel also diverted passengers to other hotels. Despite these alleged provocations, in 1958 Kaiser was still in a cooperative mood. He wrote to Pan American President Juan Trippe: "[We] . . . do not want a current impasse between Pan American and ourselves to break up our past relationship and destroy our opportunities to accomplish a great deal by working together."[33]

Two years later Kaiser and his men felt less generous toward the major carriers. In late January 1960 the Hawaiian Village manager blamed Pan American for a poor Christmas season, largely because of duplicate airline bookings. The airlines claimed low occupancy ratios, but the manager recounted numerous cases of would-be patrons canceling reservations because of inability to secure passage, even during alleged "slack" periods in airline travel. Kaiser was so fed up with the airlines' lack of cooperation that he ordered the home office to work up costs and potential revenues for his own air service to the islands. He discussed a partnership with Robert F. Six of Continental Airlines. Whether this was an elaborate bluff or a sincere intention, Kaiser's attorneys initiated the cumbersome paper work required for a federal charter to operate planes. Edward E. Carlson warned Kaiser that if he started his own air service, other carriers would sabotage the Hawaiian Village. Kaiser dropped the idea. In retaliation against both Kaiser's and other hotel operators' complaints, a Pan American vice president supposedly threatened to lodge tourists in private homes. Kaiser drafted an open letter to mainland travel agents identifying major carriers, particularly Pan American, as the chief villains preventing millions from enjoying the "vacation of a lifetime."[34]

The brouhaha following the dismal Christmas season of 1959 evidently persuaded all involved to negotiate. Precisely who extended the first peace offer is unclear; very likely, second-level managers at Kaiser offices and the airlines initiated peace talks, and exchanged drafts of compromises. In May 1960 United Airlines President W. A. Patterson announced a 44 percent increase in the number of weekly flights to Oahu. Shortly thereafter, attorney Lloyd Cutler informed Kaiser that discussions with Pan American officials had reached the point where they were "willing to call a truce." In effect, if Kaiser stopped publicizing poor air service, Pan American would cease complaining about "inadequate" hotel space.[35]

By June 1960 hotel space in Honolulu had grown from 6,825 in 1959 to nearly 10,000. Kaiser, who was sponsoring the popular television series *Maverick,* proudly informed the major carriers that their airplanes would be prominently featured in a one-minute advertisement promoting Hawaii in the next episode. Later that summer Robert B. Murray, Jr., executive vice-president of Pan American, informed Kaiser that while disagreements remained, his company was "heartily in accord with your expressed wish that the hotels, airlines, and travel agents work together in harmony to bring about increased tourism to Hawaii." Murray suggested that airline and hotel operators regularly exchange data on advance reservations and cancellations so all parties could react quickly to anticipated lulls and times when either airlines or hotels were seriously overbooked. In September 1960 Kaiser announced that the Hawaiian Village and Pan American would jointly promote Hawaiian travel. With vacancy rates down and airline bookings up, hostilities eased.[36]

By the end of 1960 the Hawaiian Village was another success story for Kaiser. The original thirteen-story building was joined by two more high-rise structures nearing completion. The Diamond Head Towers, twin seventeen-story facilities, expanded capacity to over one thousand rooms. In a little over five years Kaiser had transformed the west end of Waikiki Beach. Profits were hard to figure, in part because Kaiser charged off so much corporate entertainment to other companies, and because Kaiser and Burns ran several sideline operations through one set of books. But close reading of yearly balance sheets suggests that over five years the hotel yielded a return of about 1 or 2 percent annually.[37]

Just when Hawaiians were growing used to Kaiser's methods, he surprised local business leaders by selling his share in the Hawaiian Village to Conrad Hilton for $21.5 million in 1961. Fritz Burns handled the negotiations, and Kaiser was absent from important meetings. Kaiser was actually surprised when the deal went through. On December 1, 1961, Burns and Hilton jointly announced a new partnership; each held half-interest in the renamed Hilton Hawaiian Village. Burns and his son would manage it. According to one insider, Kaiser believed that Burns had not been totally frank about all of his discussions with Hilton.[38]

Yet knowledgeable business people knew that Kaiser would not have sold out against his own interests. In fact, the sale fit neatly into Kaiser's normal pattern of operation. Basically, he was a builder, not a manager. The hotel complex was not quite finished in early 1961, but the key building decisions had been made. Those familiar with the relationship between Kaiser and Burns sensed that building with the speed and on the magnitude that Kaiser desired made Burns nervous. In the partnership with

Hilton, Burns worked with a finished product. In fact, the deal made sense for all concerned. For his part, Kaiser had found more exciting opportunities on Oahu, and he was ready for new challenges.[39]

Hotel construction and promotion of tourism were but two of the indefatigable *malihini*'s activities on Oahu. After the Hilton sale, much of his energy focused on a new residential city, Hawaii Kai, ten miles east of Honolulu in the shadow of Koko Head. He imagined a community of seventy-five thousand residents; in Kaiser's last decade, his vision and ambition grew exponentially.

When Kaiser first broached the concept of Hawaii Kai, financial advisors in Oakland shuddered at the capital which would be required before returns might be realized. Obviously, Kaiser could have simply ordered them to direct profits from mainland concerns into Hawaii Kai. But he seldom used naked force, particularly with his own managers. He would experience far less resistance if he obtained initial funding from another Hawaiian project. This helps explain the sale of his half of the Hawaiian Village.[40]

On April 27, 1961, Kaiser signed a formal agreement with the Bishop Estate to develop six thousand acres of property. But preliminary engineering work on Hawaii Kai had begun two years earlier, and Kaiser had envisioned such a project nearly a decade earlier. On a visit to Oahu with Ale in 1953, he had examined a large piece of property just east of the Waialae-Kahala district and had been sufficiently intrigued to consult with Burns, his partner in West Coast housing. For undisclosed reasons, they dropped the idea. Yet establishing a new city in Hawaii was never far from Kaiser's mind, particularly after he and Ale moved to Oahu in 1954. He anticipated that Hawaii Kai would accommodate chiefly the middle-class *haole,* or white "foreigners." But the project would employ native Hawaiians, and all would benefit. Kaiser's personal motto was "Find a need and fill it"; building Hawaii Kai would meet several needs at once.[41]

The community project receded into the background as Kaiser promoted tourism and built the Hawaiian Village. But in about 1958, publicist Robert C. Elliott built a home miles beyond the Kahala district, along the west slope of Koko Head, on Portlock Road. Construction of any sort interested Kaiser, and he visited Elliott's project frequently. He became enraptured with the spectacular view of the ocean and Diamond Head from this remote location and decided to obtain property nearby for his own home. The seven-acre site he wanted was owned by the Bishop Estate.[42]

The Bishop Estate represented a fabulous fortune, the legacy of Bernice Pauahi Bishop, the last of the Kamehameha ruling dynasty. The estate was established in 1884; in 1961 it owned 578 square miles of land, and conservative estimates set its assets in land alone at $250 million. However, most of it was undeveloped; annual revenue amounted to only $3 million, a miniscule return. Estate trustees sought investors interested in developing their properties; they were happy to lease the parcel on Portlock Road to Kaiser. During these negotiations, Trustee Atherton Richards started a selling job on Kaiser. He hoped to interest Kaiser in developing more Bishop property nearby.[43]

One with imagination could sense the development potential of the Kuapa Pond area. The property had a rich native history and contained several legendary sites; other tourist attractions were close by. The area offered wonderful views of Koko Head and Koko Crater, as well as Diamond Head and the entire Muanalua Bay. But the land near the pond would be hard to develop and had attracted little local interest. Kuapa Pond was swampy and infested with pests. The few inhabitants were largely pig farmers and flower growers; squatters living in almost hidden canyons regularly outwitted the trustees' rent collectors. There were a grocery store, a few dilapidated bars, and fishermen's cottages. Teenagers loved to "burn rubber" on the Kalanianaole Highway, which was lightly traveled at least at night.[44]

Leasing property for a proposed city of seventy-five thousand involved complex issues, and even after preliminary work began it took over two years to settle final legal terms. Kaiser received little support from his managers; most of his staff in Oakland opposed Hawaii Kai. Those who visited the proposed site left shaking their heads in disbelief. Kaiser invited Burns to join him on a fifty-fifty basis, but the size of the project and rawness of the land discouraged him. Burns estimated that $30 million would disappear into the project before profits would be earned. The terrain which was not marshy was rocky, much of it on severe slopes. One consulting engineer estimated that sewer costs alone would run $15 million.[45] On this project, Kaiser started out very much alone.

Despite negativism in the home office and discouraging reports from the planning consultants he hired, preliminary work began. Kaiser envisioned a community providing direct water access for the maximum number of homes, and one consultant advised him to visit Venice, Italy, to explore these ideas. Kaiser dutifully took Ale and a retinue to the famous city. His reaction to Venice was reminiscent of that of another famous American: when Ulysses Grant visited during his post-presidential world tour, he allegedly proclaimed that Venice would be a fine city if only it were drained. Kaiser made no comparable public utterance, but his lack of historical appreciation for Venice nearly matched Grant's. Ale Kaiser claimed that once he learned everything was old, he quickly lost interest.[46]

History did not interest Kaiser much; he focused on the future. He and the Bishop Estate trustees announced preliminary terms for developing the land in the spring of 1959. Kaiser leased parcels for varying periods. Kaiser assumed most development costs and was to receive most of the revenues. The unique nature and magnitude of the project created a lawyer's paradise. Impatient as always, Kaiser left it to subordinates to clean up legal loose ends. On October 27, 1959, he formed the Hawaii Kai Development Company and hired community developer David C. Slipher to supervise the project. Soon heavy construction equipment was dredging Kuapa Pond, building Hawaii Kai Marina, and reinforcing banks with semi-crushed boulders. The project brought back all of the challenges of the road and dam building years; in his late seventies, Kaiser was back in his element.[47]

Basic services had to be installed before houses were built, including a million-gallon reservoir. Kalanianaole Highway, a narrow two-lane road, provided direct access to Honolulu. It had to be widened, and legislators resisted funding an improvement which would primarily benefit a single builder. Another concern was creating a sewer system which would meet environmental standards. Unfortunately, the first crew to tackle the problem had little understanding of environmental factors and assumed they could pipe sewage directly into the ocean. When K. Tim Yee, who had worked for the City and County of Honolulu and for the Federal Housing Administration (FHA), joined Kaiser early in 1961, he inherited a mess. His predecessors had not obtained permits from government authorities. As a former public employee, Yee knew that such chores took time and patience. Yee's system required numerous pumping stations and was expensive, but after a year, his crews had met one of Hawaii Kai's major challenges.[48]

But Kaiser forced an even more formidable problem: once built, could homes in Hawaii Kai be sold? In the early 1960s, Hawaii Kai was far from the heart of Honolulu; with access to Honolulu's sewer lines, other developments closer in offered equally attractive homes at lower prices. Another obstacle to home sales in Hawaii Kai's early years was lack of charm in the immediate surroundings. Far-off vistas were breathtaking, but the adjacent landscape was covered with bare patches being worked by heavy machinery. The roar of trucks and cement mixers seemed constant, and choking dust was everywhere. Kaiser, ever the optimist, was eager to build more houses, apartments, and America's first condominiums. Kaiser's associates recalled that in assessing sales potential at Hawaii Kai, the boss had a blind spot. He believed so deeply in its eventual success that he assumed that buyers would materialize out of thin air. In the early 1960s, he was repeatedly frustrated by slow sales at Hawaii Kai.[49]

The first residents at Hawaii Kai felt like pioneers. Loose cattle from undeveloped areas of Kaalakei and Hahaione Valley often wandered the streets and trampled homeowners' shrubbery at night. Adventuresome children occasionally encountered packs of wild dogs and pigs when exploring nearby areas. Residents' descriptions of their first months often read like Dust Bowl diaries from the 1930s. Early in 1963, two years after the first residents moved in, Hawaii Kai still had a raw and unfinished look, but landscaping was improving. Residents sensed that management was making sincere efforts to alleviate problems.[50]

Sales remained worrisome. Early in 1963 A. A. "Bud" Smyser of the *Honolulu Star-Bulletin* asked Kaiser about "widespread rumors" that he was ready to unload Hawaii Kai. Kaiser claimed heatedly that such "vicious, damaging rumors" were patently false. But in memos to sales managers, he articulated his distress. In 1964 he informed the Bishop Estate that only 200 homes had been sold in 1963. At that, he fudged on the figure; an internal report revealed that only 135 homes changed hands that year. Yet nothing dampened Kaiser's irrepressible spirit. Trying to stimulate interest in the entire eastern section of Oahu, he urged the trustees to approve a plan for a major resort complex at the Queen's Beach area just east of Hawaii Kai. He predicted that if Queen's Beach went through, annual sales would reach 800 units, thus "finishing" the project in fifteen years.[51]

Despite such visions, by the end of 1963 Kaiser realized that his staff could not develop and market all of the projected homes at Hawaii Kai by themselves. Therefore he shifted strategy by inviting outside developers to participate in new home construction and sales at Hawaii Kai. By mid-1964 twenty-eight outside developers had invested $10 million in construction projects. Fortunately, Hawaii Kai did not become a hodgepodge of clashing architectural styles, as all builders had to secure approval not only from Hawaii Kai architectural experts, but the estate trustees as well. Bringing in outside builders helped Hawaii Kai turn the corner in the mid-1960s. The Koko Kai Shopping Center in the heart of the complex grew quickly. Local residents could find staple goods at competitive prices, and plans were on the drawing board for office space, banking facilities, restaurants, and specialty shops. New home construction tripled between 1964 and 1965. Sales finally picked up too. On December 30, 1965, total units sold reached 1,000; Kaiser presided at a ceremony welcoming the buyer and his family. Before his death in 1967, he knew that his final big project would reach maturity.[52]

Kaiser generally got along well with the trustees of the Bishop Estate. But most of the trustees were conservative men who moved slowly and postponed final commitments for excruciating periods. As an octogenarian, Kaiser was acutely aware of time; the older he grew, the more delays frustrated him. Inevitably, the situation created occasional conflicts. Hancock recalled one incident, very revealing of Kaiser's character. After repeated delays over one Kaiser proposal, the trustees finally sent a very stiff, formal letter stating that any further action could be taken only "at your own personal risk." Aides delayed showing him the letter, fearing a heated outburst. Hancock finally placed the letter on Kaiser's desk and watched with trepidation as he read it. Kaiser digested the contents with no expression until he reached the line about his "personal risk." Slowly a big grin wreathed his face: "They've done it. They've given me permission to do anything I want out here without their approval—so long as I do it at my own risk!" As Hancock observed, Kaiser had taken huge risks for decades: "All his life Kaiser was one who could turn a negative into a positive."[53]

In his last years, Kaiser needed his inveterate optimism in dealing with some persistent disappointments at Hawaii Kai. He had hoped that a proposed resort complex at Queen's Beach would make the area more attractive for buyers. In 1960, he envisioned a complex of golf courses, which were designed by renowned course architect Robert Trent Jones; two nine-hole courses were opened in 1962. But most of the facilities were still on the drawing board when Kaiser died in 1967, and Queen's Beach has developed slowly in the last two decades.[54]

Despite slow development of recreation facilities and other persistent problems, former associates were gratified that the founder lived to see Hawaii Kai show future promise. When Kaiser died, the infrastructure was in place; and most of the major residential sections of the development were started. In about 1963, Hancock asked Kaiser why he was beginning new sections when construction was far ahead of demand. Kaiser replied that he had only a few more years to live; he believed that projects begun during his lifetime would eventually be finished, but he feared that his successors might reject phases of the master plan which were but ideas and drawings. He planned shrewdly until the end.[55]

Hawaii Kai was Kaiser's last big building project, but he simultaneously pursued other interests in Hawaii. Some were projects designed specifically to improve life in the islands per se. Despite the opposition of Walter Dillingham, patriarch of an aristocratic family dynasty on Oahu, Kaiser built a cement plant on the west side of the island, at Waianae. Against the wishes of the local medical establishment, he successfully introduced the Kaiser Permanente Medical Care Plan to Hawaii. The octogenarian turned hobbies into minor projects. He tinkered with boat designs and considered introducing hydrofoil passenger ship service between the islands, and he explored several other challenges.

Kaiser even managed to convert passive pleasures into projects. As noted, when Henry and Ale came to Oahu they "discovered" Alfred Apaka, a handsome native singer who specialized in romantic ballads. The Kaisers were so taken with the sensuous Hawaiian singer that Henry formed a record company to promote his songs. Hawaiian Village Records was little more than a recording studio and distributing arm for Apaka's records. The record company lost money, but Kaiser cared little about financial results; he had fun picking up disc-jockey lingo and learning the record game. But their joy was broken when Apaka died suddenly of a heart attack at age forty. Kaiser abandoned the recording business almost immediately.[56]

By the time of Apaka's death in 1960, however, Kaiser was also involved in other forms of entertainment, including movies, radio, and television. He became involved in film-making in the mid-1950s, promoting the Hawaiian Village and consumer products. Hancock was put in charge of a half-hour sixteen-millimeter romantic drama titled *The Hawaiian Incident,* featuring several songs by Apaka and several Kaiser products. In the mid-1950s local television stations were shoestring operations, happy to use virtually anything free. The movie was shown in Hawaii and on some West Coast stations.[57]

The Hawaiian Incident achieved no critical acclaim, but it piqued Kaiser's interest in the media. Soon after he built the Hawaiian Village's first tower, Kaiser opened local radio and television stations, which operated out of the hotel. He imagined announcers constantly reminding tens of thousands of consumers that the shows were coming to them "live, from Kaiser's beautiful Hawaiian Village Hotel . . ." Kaiser used the stations to promote Apaka's music and provide all the local advertising he needed.[58]

Such "frivolous" enterprises distressed many of Kaiser's associates. The boss's usual powers of persuasion were compromised by the fact that his media mentor was Hal Lewis, a popular local disc jockey. Lewis was wacky, colorful, and controversial. He called himself J. Akuhead Pupule, which in Hawaiian stood for J. Crazy Fishhead; he lived up to the moniker through his stunts and practical jokes. Kaiser and Lewis worked up some numbers which convinced them that the radio station would be in the black in six months, television in a year and a half. No local stations had ever become profitable that fast, but Kaiser ignored warnings; most important, he wanted to do it. Even Kaiser was unable to restrain Lewis; observers were surprised that their stormy partnership lasted two years before breaking up in June 1958.[59]

Kaiser's venture into television coincided with radio and achieved more spectacular results. Production and distribution of *The Hawaiian Incident* aroused Kaiser's interest in television. In the mid-1950s Hawaii had only three stations, controlled by NBC, ABC, and CBS; the major networks may even have welcomed a newcomer. As in the automobile industry, Kaiser saw plenty of room for competition. He promptly received a charter to run Hawaii's fourth station from the Hawaiian Village. The station had the call letters KHVH-TV. For a while, it stumbled along in a distant fourth place; in December 1957 it captured less than 8 percent of the afternoon audience and only 5.5 percent of prime-time viewers. By 1960 it had emerged as the giant on the islands, burying its competitors by capturing a whopping 54.5 percent of viewers in that year. The primary reason was that it stressed local events, of primary interest to native Hawaiians. Another reason was that Kaiser's managers outworked rivals. Station managers Richard C. Block and John Serrao created a deceptively casual atmosphere; employees wore Bermuda shorts and mumus, but they worked hard.[60]

Kaiser's impact upon television extended beyond the islands. In the late 1950s and early 1960s, his name became familiar in virtually every American home with a television set, and not just because of a growing advertising budget. He entered the national television scene in the summer of 1956 by sponsoring the Kaiser Aluminum Hour. The drama series, which appeared on alternate Tuesday nights over NBC channels, alternated psychological thrillers and musicals, with an occasional high-level play; an example of the latter was an adaptation of Jean Anouilh's *Antigone*. The Kaiser Aluminum Hour appealed to consumer groups concerned over content; even rival producers praised the show's integrity. Unfortunately, such kudos could not overcome low ratings. The show faced tough competition from popular situation comedies and game shows.[61]

Kaiser's most spectacular success was his decision in 1957 to sponsor a pilot film for a proposed new series, called *Maverick*, on the ABC network. Robert C. Elliott claimed that when Kaiser polled his managers on underwriting a Sunday night western, there were thirty-one votes against and one in favor: Kaiser himself. This account may be exaggerated, but Kaiser was certainly enthusiastic from the start. He sensed that fast-rising young actor James Garner had star qualities. Warner Brothers produced the show; Kaiser and his strategists decided to air the program at 7:30 to get a half-hour jump on the Ed Sullivan and Steve Allen shows.[62]

Maverick was a major gamble. Kaiser invested $7 million, a big commitment at the time. Fortunately, *Maverick* was a sensation virtually overnight. It quickly became the number one rated show in America, as millions of viewers followed the escapades of Bret and Bart Maverick. There were a few critics. Arthur Hays Sulzberger, publisher of the *New York Times*, privately scolded Kaiser for the immorality of one episode he watched, "not sexual, just plain ordinary stealing in which the hero indulged." A publicist replied that the episode in question had reached twelve million homes and an estimated thirty million viewers, and that Sulzberger's was the *only* negative comment. Whether or not such a claim was true, the show was a rousing success.[63]

Maverick enjoyed several spectacular seasons, but Kaiser learned that success in television was fleeting. James Garner and several key script writers temporarily left the show, and Kaiser was displeased with the replacements. By the fall of 1960 he was receiving increasing complaints from viewers about deteriorating quality. Kaiser vented his frustration on Jack Warner and Bill Orr of Warner Brothers, complaining of excessive cost and the "awful shoddiness and worsening decline" of *Maverick*. He concluded, "You cannot sell us a Cadillac and deliver us a flivver."[64]

Kaiser sponsored other television shows, but he never recaptured the magic of the original *Maverick* series. In September 1960 he offered *Hong Kong*, an adventure series in exotic international settings, which received mixed reviews from critics, who liked the scenery and actor Rod Taylor, but generally deplored the plots. Perhaps no rival could have challenged NBC's reigning heavyweight, *Wagon Train*, a show that regularly attracted half of all viewers. After several weeks of trailing a distant third, Kaiser and ABC "reluctantly" dropped *Hong Kong*. Kaiser drew small solace from the Hollywood Foreign Press voting it "Best Show of the Year."[65]

Hong Kong was a minor critical success, but the fall of 1961 brought a Kaiser-sponsored fiasco called *Follow the Sun*, which lasted only a few weeks. Reaction was almost uniformly unfavorable; one group of critics awarded it top prize as "Worst Adventure Series." After it was dropped, some viewers urged Kaiser to revive *Hong Kong*. However, as his eightieth birthday approached, Kaiser became disenchanted with television. In the spring of 1962 he decided that his five-year association with ABC was no longer fruitful. He tried an abbreviated half-hour adventure series titled the *Lloyd Bridges Show*, aired by CBS on Tuesday nights. Unfortunately, this show did no better in the ratings than *Hong Kong* or *Follow the Sun*, and it, too, vanished. In the final two years of his life, Kaiser's subordinates established a small group of independent television stations in Boston, Detroit, Philadelphia, and Los Angeles, but the aging patriarch was inactive in these operations.[66]

Although Kaiser Broadcasting Company stayed in television and even expanded into new areas, the Hawaiian station was sold. Kaiser and his managers had demonstrated their ability to compete in yet another challenging field. Kaiser was in the winter of his life, but other projects aroused his interest. At the age of eighty-two, as he entered his second decade in Hawaii, he remained active in many corporate affairs. He devoted increasing amounts of his time to "useful" hobbies, but until his health finally gave out, he stoutly resisted devoting time to pure relaxation.

16

The Sunset Years

Henry Kaiser hated being alone; this helps explain his work habits and personality. He stayed up late, frequently talking to groups of people. By 4:30 A.M. he was often out of bed, talking long-distance to men scattered around the world. Whenever he had a new idea—and he commonly had a score or so daily—he reached for the telephone. His interactions with others were complex. He had thousands of acquaintances and hundreds of "associates," but few, if any, close personal friends. He appeared incapable of simply kicking off his shoes and ignoring business for a full evening, let alone for any longer period. Eugene E. Trefethen, Jr., was a protégé and a close associate for forty years; he recalled that Kaiser almost never mentioned personal matters. Others shared similar recollections.[1]

Yet Kaiser was very sociable. Edward R. "Ned" Ordway remembered that in the 1920s, Kaiser was likely to show up at his family's construction camp tent home at supper time with a few dozen eggs and boxes of strawberries and expect to stay for dinner. Years later, Ordway was an executive at Willow Run and planned a factory cocktail party. Kaiser heard about it and "dropped in." Kaiser could not fathom why his unexpected appearance might make others nervous.[2]

Kaiser may have shared his deepest secrets with nobody, but he appeared genuinely interested in others, especially young people. A young family friend recalled visiting the Kaisers' Waldorf-Astoria apartment. Admitted by a maid, she learned that Henry, Sr., was home alone. Having admired Kaiser from a distance, she was nervous about greeting him, afraid she might be intruding. She knocked timidly on the door of his study; he greeted her warmly and they talked for a couple of hours. During the early 1950s Kaiser developed affection for Mario Bermudez, who ran the International House, a New Orleans trade association. Bermudez had an adolescent son, Miguel, who was struggling with school in New

Orleans. Bermudez and Kaiser decided a change in scenery might be good for the boy, and Kaiser pulled the necessary strings to enter him in Honolulu's prestigious Punahou School. He lived at the Kaiser home for the year he was at Punahou. Kaiser was very concerned about Miguel and took time from his own schedule to work with the boy and write progress reports to his father. Mario Bermudez was very grateful for the interest Kaiser showed in his son.[3]

Newspapers and magazines often reported that Kaiser had no hobbies, that he relaxed only in work, but there were exceptions. Kaiser executive Todd Woodell recalled that on rare occasions the boss would interrupt business meetings in New York for half an hour to ice skate at Rockefeller Center: "A sight to behold in topcoat and Fedora among the more sportively attired skaters. He was a good and confident skater, which probably dated back to his early days in New York State."[4] Kaiser enjoyed few forms of recreation, but he pursued them with such energy that undoubtedly they resembled work to others.

He had always loved boats; in his youthful years at Lake Placid he owned a motorboat. He developed a taste for fast boats. Alice Price (wife of Tom M. Price) recalled that by the mid-1920s, he loved to race boats out in Oakland Bay. Bess didn't enjoy it, at least not the fast rides, but Alice Price occasionally joined him. He also enjoyed, on rare occasions, watching activities such as horse-racing, football, and boxing. He was rumored to be a cautious bettor at the race track, and he occasionally attended college football games in the Bay Area. According to one account, he was at Lake Tahoe in 1955 and wanted to see a fight between Archie Moore and Rocky Marciano. The writer claimed that he spent $5,000 to bring a closed-circuit telecast to his home.[5]

Kaiser's recreational retreats centered around boats and water. Not long after they moved to Oakland, Henry and Bess purchased twenty acres of undeveloped land on the west shore of Lake Tahoe. In typical manner, Kaiser decided to build an elaborate vacation facility in the shortest possible time. In the 1930s he "persuaded" A. B. Ordway and several other men to combine a "vacation" with fixing up a little place in the mountains. In less than a month they built a rustic but roomy and comfortable complex of structures, plus a pier and boat house. Those involved recalled that they had seldom worked so hard in their lives. Their boss managed to turn "relaxation" into another project.[6]

The "retreat" at Lake Tahoe was named Fleur du Lac. When the weather was good, Kaiser loved to spend weekends there. His passion was powerboats, and he enjoyed driving them in summer races at Lake Tahoe. In the 1930s he operated conventional boats with stock engines. The models were basically the same, so the best driver usually won. Kaiser was a skilled driver, and he won many trophies. Yet he was unable to curb his natural instinct to experiment with different boats and engines, in an effort to se-cure competitive advantage over rivals.[7]

By the late 1940s, Kaiser was a boat racing fanatic. He was in his late sixties, and as racing speeds increased, Bess and concerned associ-ates convinced him that it was silly to risk his neck in the biggest races. Kaiser reluctantly gave in and hired several famous drivers, including Guy Lombardo, a gifted sportsman and renowned musician. The band leader won several important races in Kaiser boats. In 1949 Kaiser entered both the national Gold Cup and the international Harmsworth Trophy races. He also planned an assault on the world speed record of 141 miles per hour in the unlimited hydroplane class.[8]

Boat racing and the use of Kaiser-made materials in boat building be-came fairly important company projects. Kaiser assigned several executives to racing; he treated the design of boats very much like that of autos, cargo planes, or other major projects. He spent hours poring over drawings, photos, and material-performance evaluations. In the spring of 1949, when things were going badly at Kaiser-Frazer, he found relief in plans to enter the Harmsworth Trophy races at Lake Placid, where he had been in busi-ness half a century earlier. He became deeply involved in elaborate prepa-rations; his crew arrived at Lake Placid a month early for tests and time trial runs. Unfortunately, bad luck dogged Kaiser's wake on Lake Placid, and his attempt at world speed records failed.[9]

Henry and Edgar both enjoyed the glamor of the racing circuit, and they got a kick out of matching wits and innovations against other wealthy sportsmen. They won many cups at prestigious local and national races. But the speed record eluded determined efforts for years. Finally, in the late 1950s, Kaiser's designers produced a hydroplane which captured the record. In 1957, *Hawaii-Kai II* set kilometer and mile speed records for propeller-driven boats and was the nation's Unlimited Hydroplane Cham-pion. During 1957 and 1958, *Hawaii-Kai III* set either lap, heat, or course records in every event entered. With success finally achieved, Kaiser retired from serious racing.[10]

Many of Henry and Ale Kaiser's social activities in Hawaii and at Fleur du Lac centered around the waterfront. Ale loved to water-ski, and Henry hired instructors to work with her and their guests. He spent hours at the dock, happily presiding over the activities. One day in about 1953 or 1954 at Tahoe, he decided that watching wasn't enough. He was over seventy and had never been up on skis, but he decided to try. Pleas by anguished asso-ciates could not dissuade him. After a couple of solo efforts to start up from the dock failed, observers feared he would drown. With typical te-nacity, Kaiser was reluctant to release the tow rope after he fell. Finally, with Ale on one side and an instructor on the other, he managed to get up, even though he lost one ski in the process. After a short, happy spin around a circle, Kaiser had proved he could do it. He was satisfied and never skied again.[11]

Bess Kaiser had died on March 14, 1951. For years she had suffered from high blood pressure, kidney failure, and complications caused by overeating and lack of exercise. When Bess was in her final illness, Henry and her nurse Alyce (Ale) Chester spent countless hours with her, talking about many things, including plans to expand the health plan and hospitals. Since Bess needed twenty-four-hour care, Ale lived at the family home; she and Henry drew very close. But family members and business associates were shocked when Henry announced less than a month after Bess died that he planned to marry the thirty-four-year-old nurse. Many strongly opposed the union: the mourning period seemed far too brief, and taking a bride half his age would surely stir up gossip. Many managers felt uncomfortable with Ale as the first lady of the Kaiser empire. But Kaiser was determined; he had seldom followed convention before, so why start as he approached seventy? He explained to his associates, "I haven't time to do what the average person does, to slide around corners. . . . This is a constructive move, and in sixty days I will be a sweeter, simpler, more useful person because of it."[12]

Kaiser announced his plans on April 7; three days later he and Ale exchanged vows before a few friends in Santa Barbara, California. Some blue-bloods in Oakland and San Francisco spread vicious rumors about the couple. Ale claimed that none of this bothered them much; Henry had always refused to look back, and even at sixty-eight his eyes were focused firmly on the future.[13] Kaiser often said he hoped to live to be a hundred; whether or not he achieved that goal, he was determined to enjoy the years left.

Ale Chester was raised in the Bay Area and entered nursing. In 1939, at twenty-two, she married artist Max Penovic. They had a son, Michael, born in 1945. Shortly after Michael's arrival, the couple divorced. She resumed her maiden name and returned to work as an administrative assistant in Kaiser's Oakland hospital. When Henry married Ale, he adopted her son. From all accounts, he became very attached to Michael.[14]

Those who saw Henry and Ale together claimed that they were well matched. Clearly Ale was fascinated by Henry's power and sense of command. She often called him "Boss" even around intimate friends long after they were married. Yet Ale influenced him as well. An able, intelligent woman, she was strongly committed to the health care program. Bess's death probably strengthened Kaiser's commitment, but Ale encouraged his growing personal involvement. They often claimed that their union was, in part, dedicated to carrying on work on the medical program.[15]

It is unlikely that altruistic considerations dominated their decision to marry. Without question, security and the dazzling lifestyle Kaiser offered attracted Ale. By prearranged wills, most of the family fortune went to the Kaiser Family Foundation, but she would become a wealthy woman. But Ale Kaiser was no gold digger; she was deeply attached to Kaiser, the man. She loved his energy, enthusiasm, and mind. Gossipmongers speculated that Ale had affairs with younger men, and much was made of the fact that they had separate bedrooms.[16]

If either was bothered by gossip, they did not show it; certainly Ale and Henry gave great enjoyment to each other. They moved to Hawaii, and Ale loved the tropical paradise. When Henry became involved in radio, movies, and television, she enjoyed the celebrities. Ale presided over a household seemingly populated by young people; Michael and his friends enjoyed the swimming pool and other sports. Her husband liked the commotion and took a deep interest in Michael and his friends. Ale recalled how he generously indulged her own or Michael's desires, then deducted twenty-five cents from Michael's allowance for lights left on. As she put it, "He'd swallow the elephant and choke on a gnat."[17]

Henry and Ale had disagreements. Lambreth Hancock recalled a Christmas when Kaiser racked his brain to think of the perfect gift for Ale. He finally decided on a Hammond organ and hired an organist to play it for her when she came down for Christmas dinner. Her face clouded over and she said, "I don't want it, take it away, I want a diamond." Dinner was a cold, nervous affair. Hancock later asked Ale why she had made a scene. She replied, "Handy . . . I've got to stay one step ahead of Mr. Kaiser and keep him guessing."[18] Ale certainly kept her husband's interest. Her presence enriched his final years in Hawaii.

During his last decade, Kaiser devoted more time to pleasures and "useful" hobbies than in the past, but work was never far from his mind. Even when confined to bed, he still spent hours "imagineering" new projects by telephone with associates and in conversations with family members. He never retired; well into his eighties, he worked twelve-hour days. He treasured his time left, which he used more effectively than ever. He might catnap during tedious meetings, but he snapped alert at critical moments. Kaiser loved life, and he occasionally grew depressed at the inevitability of his approaching death. But his final years brought exciting rewards both in his work and in public recognition. His home life was happy, lively, and serene. Until his final illness, he thoroughly enjoyed his "sunset" years.

When they moved to Hawaii in 1954, the Kaisers sold much of their property on the mainland, including a large estate in Lafayette, California. They maintained a suite at the Fairmont Hotel in San Francisco which they used during visits to the Bay Area, and Kaiser kept the retreat at Tahoe until 1960. In sheer opulence, the new estate on Portlock Road was more imposing than any previous residence. Kaiser enjoyed indulging his young wife and her son. By 1961, he had poured nearly $3 million into the estate, which included a dock and boathouse, dog kennels, guests houses, servant's quarters, and assorted recreational facilities.[19]

The aging patriarch and his family did not simply luxuriate in solitary splendor. Business associates, friends, teenagers, and servants passed through the gates, seemingly around the clock. Kaiser's longtime aide Hancock lived only a mile away in Hawaii Kai, and he spent several hours at the Portlock estate almost daily. Ale loved decorating and landscaping, and by the early 1960s the home was one of Oahu's showpieces. The Kaisers generally shunned Honolulu's "social whirl," but they regularly threw a New Year's Eve party with two hundred sit-down dinner guests. At the stroke of midnight, they put on a fireworks display that was enjoyed by residents all over Maunalua Bay. During Kaiser's years in media, Hollywood celebrities were frequent visitors. Life was seldom dull at the Kaiser home.[20]

Henry enjoyed most company, and he loved Ale. A major reason for their happiness was that they shared many of each other's interests. Ale was most concerned about health care, but she provided useful suggestions in other fields too. To a degree, Henry shared her leisure activities. She became fascinated with poodles and pursued her hobby in typical Kaiser fashion; her dogs won many prizes. Henry had had no interest in poodles before their marriage, but he accompanied her to some dog shows. He had always loved winning, and as her dogs garnered cups and ribbons, his interest apparently grew. Ale also loved fishing, and Henry sometimes joined her, even though he became impatient with waits between bites. She also enjoyed long boat rides, such as hundred-mile open-water trips from Oahu to Maui. Henry sometimes worried about her safety on the water. He once rescued her when her sailboat capsized far out in Lake Tahoe by jumping into a powerboat and rushing to the scene.[21]

In his last years, Kaiser developed a few interests not directly associated with work. He became friendly with construction magnate Del Webb, who owned the New York Yankees. When the Kaisers visited Manhattan, Webb frequently invited them to enjoy games from his private box. Soon both Kaisers were hooked on baseball. When Kaiser entered radio in Hawaii in 1956, he and Webb discussed broadcasting Yankee games over KHVH, but Webb could not break other local commitments. When the New York Giants moved to San Francisco in 1958, Kaiser carried live broadcasts. But thirty years ago the Giants played more day games than now, and even West Coast night games started too early to attract many listeners in Hawaii. The broadcasts were soon dropped.

Kaiser's interest in baseball was further aroused by Walter O'Malley, owner of the Los Angeles Dodgers, who hosted Kaiser at the 1959 World Series against the Chicago White Sox in Los Angeles. Home games were played in the Coliseum because the Dodgers' new stadium in Chavez Ravine was still under construction. In 1959 the sport was in a period of transition. Franchises were being moved, and baseball mogul Branch Rickey was planning a third major circuit, to be called the Continental League. Realizing that the westward movement of major league baseball franchises suggested the logic of parallel minor league franchise shifts, O'Malley and Kaiser discussed prospects for a Pacific Coast League franchise for Honolulu.[22]

Two Salt Lake City businessmen, Maurice Yates and Hal Tate, proposed moving the defunct Sacramento franchise to Honolulu and presented their ideas to Kaiser in the fall of 1960. Kaiser proposed a stadium seating fifty thousand fans in a "natural amphitheater" location in the Kaalakei Valley, above Hawaii Kai. But Yates and Tate told Kaiser that it had to be ready by April 1 if they hoped to persuade the league to award them the Sacramento franchise.[23] At that point, Kaiser realized the unrealistic time demands and the financial drain the project would entail. The setting was ten miles from downtown Honolulu, a formidable obstacle to attracting minor league fans. He abandoned the idea, and Chinn Ho, president of Capital Investments, spearheaded the successful drive to bring triple-A baseball into the renovated Honolulu Stadium. Although uninvolved in the final push for professional baseball on Oahu, Kaiser frequently attended Hawaii Islanders games. Friends and family members recall that even when doctors tried to confine him to his bed, he sometimes persuaded Ale to slip him out to the ballpark instead. When nurses were vigilant, Kaiser watched games on television. Evidently baseball mania was somewhat contagious within the family; Edgar was involved in early discussions leading to the move of the Kansas City Athletics to Oakland.[24]

In his final years, Kaiser reaped rewards for his contributions to American life. Honorary memberships and degrees were heaped on him, and he spoke frequently at commencements. Kaiser treasured such events, as he enjoyed sharing his personal philosophy with young people. He was never more positive or optimistic than in his last years, although his cheer was tinged occasionally with wistfulness and references to his advancing age. On public occasions, Kaiser repeatedly stated his profound faith in scientific progress and material abundance. The ideas he shared in the early 1940s were little different from those expressed twenty-five years later. Ever the optimist, Kaiser envisioned worldwide utopian abundance before A.D. 2000. Scientists could lick almost any problem, but they needed to be well versed in the humanities to avoid the pitfalls of assuming their own omniscience. He was not an unabashed material positivist. Kaiser had enormous faith in humanity, remaining convinced to the end that Americans would not succumb to "Godless materialism."[25]

By his eightieth birthday in May 1962, Kaiser's family members and business associates were becoming increasingly concerned over his health. Considering the way he abused his body, it was miraculous that his health lasted as long as it did. For decades doctors had urged him to lose weight. A medical report in 1944 accurately labeled him obese; at just under six feet and weighing 245 pounds, he was 80 pounds overweight. At times he ballooned up to nearly 300 pounds. Kaiser continued to be a gargantuan eater; Ale recalled that he loved rich, heavy foods. She realized he was headstrong and would satisfy his appetite somehow, so she slipped tasty health foods into his meals and snacks. Sidney Garfield recalled that when Kaiser contracted typhoid fever in Cuba, he was convinced that massive doses of pills cured him; ironically, the patron of sophisticated health care for others became a devotee of self-prescribed remedies for himself. He often carried a black bag full of pills and other mysterious remedies on business trips. When an associate with average stamina was worn out by Kaiser's punishing pace, the boss seldom prescribed rest. He might urge his subordinate to take a handful of pills instead.[26]

Kaiser was a rare individual who needed little sleep. Not surprisingly, considering his intensely creative mind, he suffered insomnia and regularly asked Garfield for quantities of sleeping pills. The doctor reluctantly complied, knowing Kaiser would get them elsewhere if he refused. But Garfield was horrified to learn in 1945 that Kaiser was taking large quantities of one self-prescribed drug that had dangerous toxic side-effects. The doctor urged him to cease taking the drug at once, "and no permanent damage will result." At times, Kaiser virtually chain-smoked cigars. Years later, Garfield shook his head in wonder when assessing Kaiser's longevity: "He really abused himself. He had incredible genes; if he took care of himself, he'd have lived even longer."[27]

Despite excesses in personal habits, Kaiser enjoyed remarkably good health into his seventies. He was slowed briefly by suspected heart and lung problems on widely scattered occasions in the early 1950s. In 1956 he was hospitalized by the first of a series of heart attacks. Still, medical reports concluded that other than normal aging and "considerable obesity," his vital signs were strong. Predictably, when hospitalized, Kaiser was a difficult patient. On one occasion, his examining doctor prescribed continued hospitalization but noted, "patient objects to this, refuses absolutely to follow the advice of bed rest and so forth. Insists he must go on to Honolulu." For years Kaiser acted as if rules of good health did not apply to him. He sounded a smug note when comforting construction partner Harry Morrison, who was laid up: ". . . I protest that they ought to put bars on the hospital windows because they are jails to me. Yet . . . I too have to obey doctor's orders now and then after resting and fuming at being confined. I have bounced back every time."[28]

Kaiser made light of others' concerns about his health; he also appeared reluctant to deal with the ultimate disposal of his fortune. Apparently he did not directly face the issue of dividing his assets until after World War II. He and Bess established the Kaiser Family Foundation in 1948, when he was sixty-six. Tax considerations clearly played an important role in inducing Kaiser to establish the fund before either of their deaths. When Bess died in 1951 the foundation gained its first important infusion of assets, nearly $15 million. Ultimately, the Kaiser estates and trusts yielded about $78.5 million to the foundation; by the mid-1980s the value had grown to approximately $250 million. Although Kaiser refused to take his own health seriously, he remained profoundly concerned over the health of others. Honoring the wishes of the founder, the foundation has awarded most grants to projects involving improvement of health care or allied research.[29]

In public addresses, magazine articles, and occasional church sermons, Kaiser predicted that "today's generation" of young people could achieve ages of one hundred years and even older, enjoying active lives until their deaths. He often expressed a similar personal ambition, but when he turned eighty he sensed that his own time left was short. Hancock recalled that Kaiser often became depressed around Christmas, marking the end of another precious year. This was why he initiated many projects toward the end of his life; he feared that after he was gone his empire would be managed by caretakers rather than innovators. He worked compulsively even in his mid-eighties. After a heart attack in the summer of 1965, he left the Kaiser Hospital in Oakland against doctors' orders. He insisted on flying back to Hawaii. Doctors persuaded him to recline on a stretcher, with an oxygen tent, but he spent the entire trip in strenuous discussion of unpleasant personnel decisions.[30]

In his last two years, Kaiser finally heeded his doctors' advice. With help from Ale, who fed him low-calorie foods, he finally lost weight. By his eighty-fourth birthday he had slimmed down to 225 pounds. He still had a large appetite. Tim Yee recalled that one of the few foods his doctors approved in almost unlimited quantities was sharkfin soup. Kaiser kept a pot of the delicacy and snacked on it frequently.[31]

In late 1966 Kaiser's enormous strength faded. Although he demanded to go outside and watch construction at Hawaii Kai, he spent increasing amounts of time confined to bed. Ale saw to it that he napped frequently. His mind remained sharp, and the telephone permitted him to keep in touch with dozens of managers. Occasionally, his strength revived and he managed a business trip to the mainland. James F. McCloud recalled seeing Kaiser for the last time in Oakland, about two months before he died. Kaiser was confined to a wheelchair, but he was "bright as a new dollar." He looked at McCloud and said, "My, aren't you lucky—you've got so many problems." For Kaiser the excitement of business never waned.[32]

By June 1967 Kaiser could no longer pretend he felt vigorous. His frail health took a turn for the worse, and once again he was put on a plane for Hawaii. This time it was evident that there would be no rally, that the end was near. For several weeks he lingered in bed at the Portlock estate. During his last weeks he spent many waking hours talking intimately to those close to him. His grandson Edgar F. Kaiser, Jr., then in his mid-twenties, recalled the hours spent with his grandfather as a key learning experience. The failing patriarch conveyed ideas about his philosophy of business and life; even then, Kaiser talked about the future, not the past.[33]

In late August 1967, Kaiser slipped into a coma, and close family members were summoned to Hawaii. He was conscious for brief periods, but the end was near. On the morning of August 24, the monitor recording his heartbeat gave its final "beep." Ale Kaiser and Hancock were in the room when he died in his sleep. Ale looked up and blurted, "Handy, he's gone." Then she broke into tears.[34]

An American institution had vanished from the scene. Edgar, the surviving son,[35] announced his father's death. Tributes poured into the home on Portlock Road and corporate offices in Oakland. President Lyndon B. Johnson sent condolences to family members: "Henry J. Kaiser embodied in his own career all that has been best in our country's tradition. His own energy, imagination and determination gave him greatness—and he used that greatness to give unflaggingly for the betterment of his country and his fellow man." An avalanche of letters descended upon Ale, from Kwame Nkrumah, Walter Reuther, David Rockefeller, W. Averell Harriman, Wright Patman, Jacqueline Kennedy, and hundreds of other notables. Newspaper editorials around the country stressed his great achievements. Edgar Kaiser, however, urged his associates to pause but briefly before returning to the tasks his father wanted them to complete. Edgar asked them to "rededicate [them]selves to the achievement of his goals . . . and carry on the work that he had begun."[36]

CONCLUSION

Twenty-two years after Kaiser's death, his industrial empire has largely dispersed. The original corporations bearing his name have been sold to outside interests. What happened? Addressing this question in depth would require another volume, but some reasons for the breakup of the Kaiser empire appear fairly obvious. They range from internal disagreement over corporate management to uncontrollable international developments. Henry Kaiser had such a forceful will and extraordinary vision that nearly any successor would pale by comparison.

Although Edgar Kaiser was a capable administrator, he was not the creator his father had been, and the gap between his and his father's ability to inspire others, or drive them when necessary, was significant. Henry Kaiser erred on the side of pushing even tough, seasoned men to the breaking point. By his death, he had largely worn out a generation of managers. Unconsciously, perhaps, Edgar overcompensated, and the organization never regained its momentum. Men liked Edgar, but they worked much harder for his father.

Edgar formally controlled the Kaiser empire from 1959 until his death in 1981, but Eugene E. Trefethen, Jr., made many important operating decisions too. Even while Henry Kaiser was still alive, Edgar and Trefethen added layers of new management. They were "modernizers." Most of the new managers were highly capable; some were brilliant. But managerial ranks grew faster than corporate business. Time lags between identifying problems and tough decisionmaking lengthened, and the corporate structure became more rigid.

When Henry Kaiser died in 1967, American enterprise still dominated world markets; foreign business leaders eagerly sought American guidance in modern management techniques. Few forecasters predicted that U.S.

business leadership would not effectively meet foreign competition. Despite investing billions in postwar modernization of plants, the nation's basic industries aged rapidly, particularly compared to those in Germany and Japan. Ironically, Kaiser Engineers played a key role in helping future competitors develop inexpensive natural resources and modernize industrial facilities.

Other factors were beyond the control of even the most astute managers. Although wage differentials have narrowed in recent years, American businesses still pay higher labor costs than most foreign competitors in most industries. American reliance on competitively priced imports created a rapidly mounting trade deficit in the 1970s and 1980s. Kaiser Industries produced such basic commodities as aluminum, cement, chemicals, and steel; they faced stiff competition in one or more of these industries from Germany, Japan, Korea, Taiwan, and elsewhere. Finally, the international energy crisis of the 1970s hampered all industrial powers, but American corporations, confronted with many problems simultaneously, appeared particularly vulnerable. Several of Kaiser's commodities were produced with energy-intensive techniques; the companies producing those items struggled. Yet it would be misleading to portray top management in the Kaiser organization as helpless bystanders. They sold several of the companies as they approached peak volume of production and sales, and some of the companies declined under new ownership.

Thoughtful Americans reading Henry Kaiser's obituary in late August 1967 realized that one of America's last business giants had passed from the scene. The founders of the nation's famous corporate dynasties, men who dominated entire industries by the sheer force of their personalities, were mostly gone: Carnegie, Rockefeller, Morgan, Ford, and others. By Kaiser's later years American companies still boasted many persons with superior leadership skills, but their individuality was often submerged by the demands of modern managerial systems. Today, with a handful of exceptions, such as Lee Iacocca, Donald Trump, and a few colorful corporate raiders, America's business leaders are generally portrayed as gray-suited team players.

Public attitudes toward big business and its leaders changed during the course of Kaiser's career. Once "captains of industry" were perceived as admirable, risk-taking visionary individualists, ambitious, even a bit ruthless. Their critics, from turn-of-the-century muckrakers through the Depression, often wrote highly personal exposés of antisocial behavior of individual business leaders. By the 1960s, social critics deemphasized individuals, focusing instead on less admirable aspects of big business: environmental damage, support for third world governments with dubious human rights records, sexist and racist personnel practices, and other shortcomings. Some of these issues were only beginning to emerge when Kaiser died; one may only speculate how he would have responded to them.

Kaiser emerged from the business culture of the late nineteenth century, when association with one or two key entrepreneurs could quickly present an up-and-coming young person to enormous opportunities, and when deals were often settled with handshakes. In the early twentieth century, Warren A. "Dad" Bechtel and George Warren became warm friends and informal mentors, who helped advance Kaiser's career. Throughout his long life, Kaiser enjoyed conducting business affairs on a highly personal, one-to-one basis. He was at his best hurrying along a huge deal in a ten-minute phone call, or providing wise guidance to a bright young protégé.

On the other hand, Kaiser owed a great deal of his entrepreneurial success to the emergence of big government and the military-industrial complex. A fundamental reason why Kaiser became such a controversial figure in the 1940s was that he worked his way into power circles in Washington and made the government his partner very quickly. Critics charged that Kaiser had not proved himself as an entrepreneur before he was blessed with government contracts. To some extent, their criticisms reflected envy; during the 1930s and World War II, Kaiser's government contracts and highly visibility generated not only large profits, but priceless publicity, as well. Opponents and critics repeatedly charged that Kaiser's government work was riddled with inefficiency, even fraud; and they made sure that his government work was frequently and closely investigated. On balance, Kaiser's record for speed, dependability, and economy in meeting government contracts was quite good, but his opponents were certainly on target in recognizing his expertise in understanding and working with federal bureaucrats.

But understanding these processes did not mean that Kaiser liked them. In the two decades after World War II, he frequently voiced frustration and impatience with the growing complexity of managerial decisionmaking. Even before his move to Hawaii in 1954, he delegated a great deal of authority over day-to-day operations to able subordinates. In his later years, almost all of Kaiser's creative energy concerned new enterprises, where he and a few associates could make important commitments immediately after intense consultation.

Kaiser's historical reputation will undoubtedly change over time, as others reassess his legacy. Two final questions remain. How did Kaiser compare to other entrepreneurial leaders in America? And what was his principal legacy?

Kaiser's overall contributions place him among the first rank of American business leaders. This is not simply the conclusion of a star-struck biographer; Kaiser was prominent among less than one hundred "laureates" in *Fortune*'s corporate hall of fame. *Fortune* paralleled Kaiser's achievements to those of other entrepreneurial giants over the past two centuries, including Carnegie, du Pont, Ford, McCormick, Morgan, Rockefeller, and Whitney.

In reviewing Kaiser's career, one is struck by the fact that, unlike Ford and Rockefeller, he achieved fame at a comparatively advanced age. Kaiser was sixty before his name was widely known in American households. His creativity and fame grew exponentially until his death. Kaiser was never a living relic. Ford and Rockefeller were less fortunate; the winters of their lives were marked by degrees of bitterness, seclusion, and strenuous efforts to overcome tarnished public images.

While Andrew Carnegie epitomizes the American image of a Horatio Alger tale, Kaiser's rise was nearly as dramatic. Although he was not an immigrant like Carnegie, Kaiser's family background was modest. In certain respects, Kaiser's achievements exceeded Carnegie's. Carnegie was a guiding force in several basic industries in the nineteenth century, including railroads, bridge-building, and steel. Kaiser's endeavors covered a far greater range of industries. In part, this reflected very different corporate cultures in their respective heydays. In the late nineteenth century, the nation was still forging its manufacturing base. Fifty years later, economic growth areas were dominated by consumer products. In public philanthropy, Carnegie and Kaiser revealed almost the reverse qualities. Kaiser concentrated his efforts in a single area: medicine. Although he was best known for his support of libraries and other quasi-public institutions, Carnegie demonstrated more breadth in the "stewardship" of his wealth. One reason was that after the sale of his steel company to the Morgan interests, Carnegie concentrated most of his energy in the last eighteen years of his life on philanthropy. Kaiser set up a family foundation, but he never retired. He delegated the task of giving away some of his fortune.

Most of this nation's great enterpreneurs paid their dues in years of hard work, including reversals, before they became rich. One common quality was the ability to perceive and fully exploit unusual opportunities. For fully half a century, from the rise of railroads to the emergence of the steel trust, Carnegie demonstrated an exquisite instinct for anticipating future trends. Rockefeller probed new frontiers in corporate innovation in personally organizing the petroleum industry down to fine details. To many social critics, Standard Oil epitomized malevolent monopolistic control; yet entrepreneurs in other fields adopted Rockefeller's techniques in vertical and horizontal integration. When Henry Ford developed his automobile company early in the next century, he copied many of Rockefeller's integration techniques, consciously or otherwise. Ford largely succeeded in vertically integrating his company, but his dominance of the automobile market ended in the mid-1920s.

Henry Kaiser never achieved the reputation as a corporate strategist that any of these men did. Kaiser was the big idea man, who led associates into ever-expanding new challenges; he left the details of day-to-day management to others. Whereas entrepreneurs such as Rockefeller, Alfred P. Sloan of General Motors, and others devoted much of their energy to "modernizing" their corporate structures, such matters held little fascination for Kaiser. He was an old-fashioned operator, who ran his companies and managed employees through sheer energy and the force of his enthusiasm. Corporate decisions about entering new industries were not always based on sophisticated market surveys. Kaiser often developed "gut feelings" about new opportunities, then sounded out his top men. On such occasions, his associates might develop sophisticated arguments for or against new initiatives. Kaiser earned a reputation as a good listener; but no amount of sound advice dissuaded him from pursuing opportunities once he made up his mind. The automobile venture was the best example. In hindsight, most long-time business associates claimed that they had opposed it all along. In that case, the doubters were right. But in following his instincts, Kaiser was usually right.

Kaiser's corporate empire has not survived in such easily identified form as those of the Fords, Rockefellers, and du Ponts, but important monuments to his greatness still stand. Although Kaiser's companies contributed to postwar industrial development around the world, their twentieth-century impact was most obvious and most concentrated in the American West. Barring natural or unnatural catastrophe, the dams he helped build should survive for centuries; their life-spans may ultimately dwarf those of some of the nation's great corporations. The Hoover, Bonneville, Grand Coulee, and Shasta dams have controlled flooding and helped irrigate millions of acres of new farmland. They have also provided cheap water and power for hundreds of new industries and millions of urbanites. Between World War II and the 1960s, job opportunities in Kaiser's shipyards, steel, aluminum, and other enterprises lured hundreds of thousands of newcomers to the West. His cement was used in new highways, bridges, office buildings, and many other types of installations.

Even given its more perishable nature, the Kaiser Permanente Medical Care Program remains his most notable contribution to American life. It has lasted half a century, and vital signs appear robust. Since Kaiser's death, membership has tripled and facilities have expanded proportionately. For these achievements, others also deserve large shares of credit. Yet Henry Kaiser's vision of developing corporate models for a national response to health care needs had profoundly important ripple effects far beyond the measurable results of his and Dr. Garfield's plan. Without Kaiser's leadership, Health Maintenance Organizations (HMOs) might not be as well developed in the United States as they are today.

In addition to his inveterate optimism and sense of urgency, two other qualities epitomized Kaiser. First, he was never satisfied that he and his men were reaching high enough. Kaiser constantly stressed his goal of creating "more things for more people," to make the quality of life "a little better for the little guy." A common thread joining most of his enterprises was an objective of producing vast quantities of goods at lower prices. Second, Kaiser's future vision was breathtaking. Where many of his corporate peers looked a year or two ahead, Kaiser's vision was measured in decades.

Kaiser's public relations department portrayed him as a cultured man, with a deep interest in poetry and philosophy. This was largely a fabrication. He had a phenomenal memory and recited poems by heart, but he was a man of action, not prone to brooding or deep reflection. As a famous industrialist and a highly sought-after public speaker, Kaiser gave hundreds of addresses. His staff wrote his speeches, but the boss provided the core ideas, which changed little over four decades. Kaiser never doubted that human ingenuity could overcome the most serious challenges. Through his own actions he demonstrated a rock-solid faith in capitalism, a sharing in the basic economic covenant which had shaped western civilization from the Enlightenment forward. In his unshakable optimism, Kaiser had far more in common with the majority of western intellectuals than his most ardent admirers suspected.

NOTES

INTRODUCTION

1. In this instance, Hughes' initial instincts were correct. Due largely to his own mismanagement, not until late in 1947 would one prototype, nicknamed the "Spruce Goose," be finished. The Kaiser-Hughes partnership had been terminated several years earlier. Donald L. Bartlett and James B. Steele, *Empire: The Life, Legend, and Madness of Howard Hughes* (New York: W. W. Norton, 1979), p. 116. For more detailed accounts of the Kaiser-Hughes partnership, see Charles Barton, *Howard Hughes and His Flying Boat* (Fallbrook, Calif.: Aero Publishers, 1982), and Mark S. Foster, "The Flying Lumber Yard: Henry J. Kaiser, Howard Hughes, and the Famous 'Spruce Goose' Caper," *Aerospace Historian* 33:2(June 1986):96–103.

2. I have so argued in two recent articles. See "Giant of the West: Henry J. Kaiser and Regional Industrialization, 1930–1950," *Business History Review* 59(Spring 1985):1–23, and "Five Decades of Development: Henry J. Kaiser and the Western Environment, 1917–1967," *Journal of the West* 26(July 1987):59–67. Other western historians share my view of Kaiser's impact on the region. See, for example, Gerald D. Nash, *The American West in the Twentieth Century: A Short History of an Urban Oasis* (Englewood Cliffs, N.J.: Prentice Hall, 1973), p. 205.

3. Alfred D. Chandler, Jr., *Strategy and Structure: Chapters in the History of American Industrial Enterprise* (Cambridge, Mass.: MIT Press, 1962); Chandler, *The Visible Hand: The Managerial Revolution in American Business* (Cambridge, Mass.: Harvard University Press, 1977); Louis Galambos, "Technology, Political Economy and Professionalization: Central Themes of the Organizational Synthesis," *Business History Review* 57(Winter 1983):471–493.

4. In fact, several such endeavors are already in print or in progress. Mimi Stein conducted numerous oral history interviews of prominent Kaiser executives and wrote *A Special Difference: A History of Kaiser Aluminum and Chemical Corporation* (Oakland: Kaiser Aluminum and Chemical Corporation, 1980). See also Richard M. Langworth, *Kaiser-Frazer: The Last Onslaught on Detroit* (Princeton, N.J.: Princeton Publishing, 1975); Rickey L. Hendricks, "A Necessary Revolution: The Origins of the Kaiser-Permanente Medical Care Program" (Ph.D. dissertation,

University of Denver, 1987); and Elizabeth A. Cobbs, "Good Works at a Profit: Private Development and U.S.-Brazil Relations, 1945–1960" (Ph.D. dissertation, Stanford University, 1988), draft Chapter 5.

CHAPTER I. ROOTS

1. Karl E. Demandt, *Geschichte des Landes Hessen* (Frankfurt: Kassel und Basel, 1972), pp. 562–563; Martina Sprengel and Norbert Finzsch, "The Origins of the Jobst and Kaiser Families," ms. (Cologne, 1985), p. 2; Leopold Ingram, *Geschichte der Stadt Steinheim*, Part 2, *Das ehemilage Gross-Steinheim* (Darmstadt, 1958), pp. 104, 148–157.

2. Sprengel and Finzsch, "Origins," pp. 2, 3, 5–7.

3. Staatsarchiv Darmstadt, (St.D.), CII, 448/343; Catholic parish in Steinheim St. John Baptist (St.J.B.) Records Marriage Register; Sprengel and Finzsch, "Origins," pp. 8–12; Stadtarchiv Hanau (Std.H.), E4, 557, 608.

4. Sprengel and Finzsch, "Origins," pp. 10–12; Henry J. Kaiser Papers, Bancroft Library, University of California, Berkeley: undated clipping from *Fort Plain* (N.Y.) *Standard*, carton 315; *Statistics of the Population of the United States at the Tenth Census, 1880*, vol. 1 (Washington, D.C., 1883), p. 267.

5. St.J.B. Birth Record; St.D., CII, 448/242, 142, 343, 244, 145, 147.

6. Std.H., E4, 534/1; Std.H., E4, 449; *Steinheimer Beobachter*, December 12, 1872 (this is a local Steinheim newspaper; John Yops and Frank Kaiser are mentioned as subscribers, and Kaiser's residence on the Yops farm is mentioned); Sprengel and Finzsch, "Origins," pp. 16–19.

7. "H. J. Kaiser Was a Schoolboy in Sprout Brook," *Fort Plain Standard*, n.d. (ca. March 1943).

8. Nelson Green, ed., *History of the Mohawk Valley: Gateway to the West, 1614–1825* (Chicago: S. J. Clarke, 1925), pp. 1481–1485; Nelson Greene, *The Old Mohawk Turnpike Book* (Fort Plain, N.Y.: Mohawk Valley Historical Association, 1924), pp. 256, 267–268; "Kaiser Was a Schoolboy." For a superb analysis of the development of family life in the region during the early years of settlement, see Mary P. Ryan, *Cradle of the Middle Class: The Family in Oneida County, New York, 1790–1865* (London and New York: Cambridge University Press, 1981).

9. Charles Luther interview by Irina Clark, May 16, 1984; Clark to author, June 7, 1984.

10. *Twelfth Census of the United States: Population*, vol. 1 (Washington, D.C., 1901), p. 281; Merrilyn R. O. O'Connell to Roy R. Kennedy, April 2, 1971, original in possession of Utica, N.Y., Chamber of Commerce.

11. Alyce Kaiser interview, December 5, 1983; Greene, *The Old Mohawk Turnpike Book*, p. 264; Samuel Durant, *History of Oneida County, New York* (Philadelphia: Everts and Fariss, 1878), pp. 622–623; Daniel E. Wager, ed., *Our Country and Its People: A Descriptive Work on Oneida County* (Boston: Boston History Co., 1896), p. 627.

12. Alyce Kaiser interview, December 5, 1983; "Kaiser Was a Schoolboy."

13. "Kaiser Was a Schoolboy"; Alyce Kaiser interviews, December 5 and 10, 1983; *Utica Observer-Dispatch*, April 4, 1948; "Henry J. Kaiser," *Fortune* 28 (October 1943): 147; *New York Times*, October 29, 1944. Kaiser Papers: Vance Fawcett to

Mary Ellen Weiss, August 16, 1946, carton 33; Margaret S. Holdredge to Kaiser, August 15, 1959, carton 275.

14. William J. Lederer, "Henry Kaiser's Seven Keys to Success," *Reader's Digest* 79 (November 1961): 142; *Facts about Henry J. Kaiser,* pamphlet (Oakland: Kaiser Co., September 19, 1946).

15. Alyce Kaiser, letter to author, n.d. (1984).

16. Kaiser Papers: Dr. Paul F. Cadman to Joseph A. Moore, August 5, 1944, carton 315. *Los Angeles Evening Express,* December 13, 1948.

17. *Spokane Spokesman-Review,* September 21, 1959; Alyce Kaiser interview, December 10, 1983.

18. *Twelfth Census, Population,* vol. 1, p. 281; John Gunther, *Inside U.S.A.* (New York and London: Harper and Brothers, 1947), p. 65; Alyce Kaiser, letter to author.

19. Kaiser Papers: Gunther, draft of Chapter 4, "Life and Works of Henry J. Kaiser," for *Inside U.S.A.,* n.p., and "History of the Kaiser Organization," mimeographed, n.d. (ca. 1946), n.p., both in carton 315.

20. *Utica Observer-Dispatch,* April 4, 1948.

21. Kaiser's recollection cited in a letter from his public relations director, Robert C. Elliott, to Robin Len, February 20, 1958, Kaiser Papers, carton 275. Of course, after Roosevelt's alleged "ride" up San Juan Hill and his election as governor of New York, a spate of pseudo-biographies appeared. Kaiser may well have read any one of a dozen books.

22. "History of the Kaiser Organization." Alyce Kaiser recalled her husband telling her that he was "about sixteen or seventeen" when he journeyed to New York in search of work (interview, December 10, 1983).

23. Kaiser Papers: Katherine Moerschler to Kaiser, February 23, 1958, carton 315.

24. *Utica Observer-Dispatch,* April 4, 1948; "History of the Kaiser Organization."

25. *Canajoharie Radii,* December 7, 1899.

26. "State of New York, Census 1900; Oneida County, Whitestown Township, Whitesboro Village," Enumeration District No. 101, p. 6.

27. "Henry J. Kaiser" (*Fortune*), p. 147.

28. *Utica Observer-Dispatch,* April 4, 1948.

CHAPTER 2. LAUNCHING A CAREER

1. For a brilliant analysis of genteel Americans' late-nineteenth-century quest for relief from overcivilization, see T. J. Jackson-Lears, *No Place of Grace: Antimodernism and the Transformation of American Culture, 1880–1920* (New York: Pantheon, 1981).

2. For samples of this account, see Clay P. Bedford interview by Mimi Stein, May 10, 1982, transcript, Oral History Associates, San Francisco, n.p.; Henry J. Kaiser Papers, Bancroft Library, University of California, Berkeley: "Notes of Meeting, June 22, 1943, between Henry J. Kaiser, Henry Kaiser, Jr., Chad Calhoun, and Mr. Murphy and Miss McEnany of *Fortune,*" carton 24. (The Kaiser Papers include several copies of notes of this meeting, with varying titles.)

3. Alyce Kaiser, letter to author, n.d. (1984); Kaiser Papers: Mrs. H. G. (Jill) Seim to Kaiser, n.d. (1958), carton 275.

4. Kaiser Papers: Vance Fawcett to Mary Ellen Weiss, August 16, 1946, carton 33.

5. "Notes of Meeting, June 22, 1943"; Fawcett to Weiss, August 16, 1946.

6. *Oakland Tribune,* October 7, 1951; Kaiser Papers: "Notes for Speech to Kaiser-Frazer Dealers, Willow Run, January 10, 1949," carton 61. Kaiser's criticism of railroad travel was extraordinary, considering the fact that he traveled in that fashion almost exclusively before the 1950s and had probably covered over 200,000 miles by train.

7. *Oakland Tribune,* October 7, 1951; Alyce Kaiser interview, December 10, 1983.

8. Bedford interview by Mimi Stein.

9. Kaiser Papers: John Gunther, draft of Chapter 4, "Life and Works of Henry J. Kaiser," for *Inside U.S.A.,* n.p., Kaiser Papers, carton 314. Alyce Kaiser interview, December 10, 1983.

10. "Chronology of Bess Kaiser's Early Life before Her Marriage," mimeographed summary of Mrs. [Paul F.] Cadman's conversations with Mrs. Kaiser, n.d. (ca. 1946), copy in possession of Alyce Kaiser.

11. Ibid.

12. These conditions were outlined in many corporate public relations releases and popular magazine articles about Kaiser. They are cited again in Mrs. Kaiser's conversations with Mrs. Cadman.

13. Alyce Kaiser interview, December 10, 1983. The late Dr. Sidney R. Garfield and his wife, Helen (Alyce Kaiser's sister), were extremely close to the Kaisers. The Garfields also recalled how Henry Kaiser had stated that he hated to "doctor" photographs (Sidney and Helen Garfield interview, January 18, 1984).

14. John T. Little, Sr., *Life at 80 and How I Got There* (Spokane: Artcraft Printing Co., 1970), p. 45; *Spokane Spokesman-Review,* August 30, 1942.

15. *Thirteenth Census of the United States, 1910, Population,* vol. 3 (Washington, D.C., 1913), p. 1004; Glenn C. Quiett, *They Built the West: An Epic of Rails and Cities* (New York: Cooper Square Publishers, 1965), p. 519.

16. Quiett, *They Built the West,* p. 519; Lucille F. Fargo, *Spokane Story* (New York: Columbia University Press, 1951), p. 258.

17. "Notes for Speech to Kaiser-Frazer Dealers."

18. Lambreth Hancock, untitled m.s., n.d. (ca. 1984), n.p., in possession of Hancock.

19. Bedford interview by Stein, May 10, 1982; *Spokane Spokesman-Review,* March 12, 1933.

20. "Notes of Meeting, June 22, 1943"; Little, *Life at 80,* p. 38.

21. R. L. Polk, *City Directory, Spokane,* 1907; 1908.

22. "Chronology of Bess Kaiser's Early Life"; *Boston Evening Transcript,* April 13, 1907.

23. "Chronology of Bess Kaiser's Early Life"; Little, *Life at 80,* p. 47.

24. The house at 418 Fourth Avenue has been torn down. The home built in 1908 at 1115 South Grand still stands, almost totally hidden from view by enormous fir trees. County of Spokane, *Mortgages Book 169,* p. 424; County of Spokane, *Deeds Book 213,* p. 448; *Spokane Spokesman-Review,* June 14, 1908.

25. *Spokane Spokesman-Review,* June 14, 1908.

26. Little, *Life at 80,* p. 47.

27. Mrs. Tom M. (Alice) Price interview, January 20, 1984. Eugene E. Trefethen,

Jr., who two decades later became one of Kaiser's closest business associates outside of the immediate family, knew Bess very well. He also remarked on her contributions to Henry's business decisions (Trefethen interview, September 22, 1983).

28. Little, *Life at 80*, p. 48.

29. *Spokane Spokesman-Review*, July 15, 1951; August 30, 1942; March 12, 1933.

30. Kaiser Papers: "History of the Kaiser Organization, vol. 1," mimeographed, n.d. (ca. 1946), n.p., carton 315. State of Washington, County of Spokane, Arthur Precinct, Enumeration Date April 22, 1910, Roll 216, sheet 11A; Bedford interview by Stein, May 10, 1982.

31. "History of the Kaiser Organization"; *Spokane Spokesman-Review*, August 30, 1942.

32. *Spokane Spokesman-Review*, March 12, 1933; August 4, 1911.

33. Kaiser Papers: Robert C. Elliott to Mr. Pollack, draft of letter, n.d., carton 295.

34. Ibid.

35. Kaiser Papers: Robert C. Elliott, "50 Year Book," m.s., n.d. (ca. 1964), carton 295.

36. Edgar F. Kaiser Papers, Bancroft Library, Berkeley: Edgar Kaiser to "Dad," n.d. (ca. 1935), temporary unnumbered carton.

CHAPTER 3. TAMING THE WILDERNESS—ROADS

1. Henry J. Kaiser Papers, Bancroft Library, University of California, Berkeley: "Notes of Meeting of Henry J. Kaiser, Henry Kaiser, Jr., Chad Calhoun, and Mr. Murphy and Miss McEnany of *Fortune*, June 22, 1943," carton 295. Lambreth Hancock, untitled ms., n.d. (ca. 1984), n.p., in possession of Hancock.

2. *Daily Building Record*, January 9, 1914; June 4, 1914.

3. Kaiser Papers: untitled ms., n.d. (ca. 1944), p. 3, carton 341.

4. A mimeographed copy of Kaiser's original corporate charter is in Kaiser Papers, carton 295. When the company filed its initial financial report in the spring of 1915, it listed assets and liabilities of just over $21,000. See Kaiser Papers: "Statement of Assets and Liabilities as [of] April 3, 1915, Henry K. Kaiser Co., Ltd.," mimeographed, carton 315.

5. "Warren Brothers Company," *America's Builders* (Los Angeles) 2:7 (1954): 6. Kaiser Papers: Ralph L. Warren to Paul S. Marrin, August 17, 1936, carton 2.

6. Kaiser Papers: "Nanaimo Paving Co., Ltd.: Summary of Contract," mimeographed, n.d., carton 319; "History of the Kaiser Organization, vol. 1" mimeographed, n.d. (ca. 1946), carton 315.

7. Mrs. Tom M. (Alice) Price interview, January 20, 1984.

8. There are dozens of first-rate books analyzing the emergence of the automobile in the early twentieth century and the public policy response. Two senior scholars with varying perspectives are John B. Rae, *The Road and Car in American Life* (Cambridge, Mass.: MIT Press, 1971), and James J. Flink, *The Car Culture* (Cambridge, Mass.: MIT Press, 1975).

9. Warren to Marrin, August 17, 1936; *Questions and Answers about Henry J. Kaiser*, pamphlet (Oakland: Kaiser Co., September 19, 1946), p. 48.

10. See *Portland Building Record*, April 29, 1916; *Seattle Bulletin*, May 3, 1916.

11. "Asphalt, Wheelbarrows, and Henry J.," *Western Construction,* October 1951, p. 79.

12. Kaiser Papers: Robert C. Elliott, "50 Year Book," m.s., n.d. (ca. 1964), n.p., and "Tom Price Anecdotes" (for "50 Year Book"), carton 295. *Oakland Tribune,* February 28, 1971; Alyce Kaiser interview, December 5, 1983.

13. *Spokane Spokesman-Review,* September 21, 1959.

14. Alyce Kaiser interview, December 5, 1983; Elliott, "50 Year Book"; Clay P. Bedford interview by Mimi Stein, May 10, 1982, transcript, Oral History Associates, San Francisco.

15. *Oakland Tribune,* February 28, 1971.

16. Elliott, "50 Year Book."

17. *Spokane Spokesman-Review,* September 25, 1958. Kaiser Papers: "Biographical Data: Key Kaiser Employees," mimeographed, n.d., carton 338; Elliott, "50 Year Book."

18. Kaiser Papers: Tom Price, "Man or Demi-God," April 27, 1950, in "Tom Price Anecdotes," carton 295.

19. Kaiser Papers: Tom Price, "Memories," in "Tom Price Anecdotes," carton 295.

20. For Ordway's detailed account, see *Oakland Tribune,* February 28, 1971; Elliott, "50 Year Book."

21. Kaiser Papers: interoffice memo, Alonzo B. Ordway to Pat Hoar, May 11, 1971, carton 316; Ordway to *Life,* March 24, 1943, carton 21; Elliott, "50 Year Book."

22. Ordway to *Life,* March 24, 1943; Clay P. Bedford interview by Mimi Stein, May 3, 1982, transcript, Oral History Associates, San Francisco. Contract figures were taken from Kaiser Papers: History of the Kaiser Organization," n.d. (ca. 1946), n.p., carton 349.

23. "Asphalt, Wheelbarrows, and Henry J.," p. 79; Kaiser Papers: "History of the Company," mimeographed, n.d., p. 1, carton 319; Gerard Piel, "No. 1 Shipbuilder," *Life,* June 29, 1942, pp. 81–89.

24. Le Tourneau worked for Kaiser off and on through the 1920s and 1930s, and on occasional jobs thereafter. However, he did not sell all of his patents to Kaiser. He maintained his own machine shop in Stockton. However, he supervised development of several shops for Kaiser and ran some of them. See Robert C. Elliott, "The Road," rough draft of chapter in "50 Year Book," in possession of Alex Troffey.

25. Kaiser Papers: unidentified newspaper clipping dated January 2, 1941, carton 295. Portland (Ore.) *Journal of Commerce,* August 26, 1942; "The Earth Mover: A New Power Scraper Developed by Contractor Used Efficiently on the Philbrook Dam," *Western Construction News,* December 10, 1926, p. 44.

26. Kaiser Papers: "Bob Le Tourneau's Book," page proofs, n.d., carton 295.

27. Technically, the Livermore gravel operation was not Kaiser's initial producing plant. That honor is reserved for a sand and gravel plant at Black Butte, near Mount Shasta, which was opened in 1921. The Black Butte facility yielded small amounts of gravel for commercial sale until 1930. If there was any difference between the opening of the two facilities, it was that Kaiser *anticipated* from the beginning that the Livermore facility would be a commercial venture. Elliott, "50 Year Book"; "History of the Company," p. 1; *Facts about Henry J. Kaiser,* pamphlet

(Oakland: Kaiser Co., September 19, 1946), p. 46; *Livermore Herald-News,* September 2, 1967.

28. Elliott, "50 Year Book."

29. Ibid.

30. For a good analysis of gasoline politics at various levels of government in the early twentieth century, see John C. Burnham, "The Gasoline Tax and the Automobile Revolution," *Mississippi Valley Historical Review* 68 (December 1961): 435–459. Kaiser Papers: Alonzo B. Ordway to Neal Fellom, January 31, 1967, carton 257.

31. *Facts about Henry J. Kaiser,* p. 45.

32. Ibid. Kaiser Papers: "Directors and Officers, Industrial Engineering Co.," mimeographed report, January 30, 1939, carton 3, listed Stephen D. Bechtel (Warren's son) as president. Kaiser was a major shareholder and a company director. See also interoffice memo, George G. Sherwood to Kaiser, January 7, 1939, carton 3; Mordecai Ezekiel to Kaiser, June 30, 1942, carton 17.

33. *Facts about Henry J. Kaiser,* p. 45; Bedford interview by Stein, May 3, 1982. By Bedford's account, Kaiser and his men perceived that limestone, of which there was an ample supply, could serve nicely. They rigged up a portable crushing plant, which they moved to outcroppings of limestone. The machinery, designed in consultation with Le Tourneau, could crush the rock and separate it into appropriate sizes of fine or coarse stone. See also Dr. Paul F. Cadman, "The Builder: the Life and Work of Henry J. Kaiser," ms., n.d. (ca. 1943), pp. 72–75, in possession of Donald A. Duffy.

34. Piel, "No. 1 Shipbuilder," pp. 82–83; *Oakland Tribune,* February 28, 1971.

35. *Oakland Tribune,* February 28, 1971; Bedford interview by Stein, May 3, 1982.

36. Bedford interview by Stein, May 3, 1982; Elliott, "50 Year Book."

37. Edward R. Ordway interview, January 13, 1984; Bedford interview by Stein, May 3, 1982; *Spokane Spokesman-Review,* September 21, 1959.

38. Elliott, "50 Year Book."

39. Bedford interview by Stein, May 3, 1982; presumably, Bedford excluded Kaiser's friends, Warren Brothers, when appraising the work of other contractors.

40. Ibid.; *Spokane Spokesman-Review,* September 21, 1959. In fact, Kaiser did accept $312,000 in Cuban bonds, which eventually defaulted. See "Financing," in "History of the Kaiser Corporation."

41. *Spokane Spokesman-Review,* September 21, 1959; Elliott, "50 Year Book." Kaiser Papers: "Kaiser Paving Company Cuba Account," mimeographed, December 31, 1930, unnumbered temporary carton.

CHAPTER 4. TAMING THE WILDERNESS—DAMS

1. Readers desiring deeper analysis of the planning and construction of Hoover Dam should consult U.S. Department of Interior, *Boulder Canyon Final Reports* (Boulder City, Nev.: Bureau of Reclamation, 1948); Joseph E. Stevens, *Hoover Dam: An American Adventure* (Norman: University of Oklahoma Press, 1988); and Paul Kleinsorge, *The Boulder Canyon Project* (Stanford: Stanford University Press, 1940).

2. Thomas D. Darlington, "Conquering the Colorado," *Explosives Engineer,* January–March 1931, pp. 1–7.

3. Ibid.; Imre Sutton, "Geographical Aspects of Construction Planning: Hoover Dam Revisited," *Journal of the West* 7 (July 1968): 301–344.

4. Kleinsorge, *Boulder Canyon Project,* pp. 84–85, 186–190; Sutton, "Hoover Dam Revisited," p. 307; Stevens, *Hoover Dam,* pp. 26–27.

5. Stevens, Hoover Dam, pp. 4–5, 48; Darlington, "Conquering the Colorado," pp. 4–5.

6. Kleinsorge, *Boulder Canyon Project,* pp. 66–74; Frederick Merk, *History of the Westward Movement* (New York: A. A. Knopf, 1978), pp. 513–522. Congress tried to appease Arizona by stipulating that California could never take more than 4.4 million of the 7.5 million acre-feet of water appropriated annually to the Lower Basin states. Arizona did not conditionally join the compact until 1944, and no final settlement was reached until 1963. For a deep analysis of the constitutionality of the water negotiations, see Norris Hundley, Jr., "Clio Nods: Arizona v. California and the Boulder Canyon Act," *Western Historical Quarterly* 3 (January 1972): 17–51.

7. Kleinsorge, *Boulder Canyon Project,* p. 53.

8. Henry J. Kaiser Papers, Bancroft Library, University of California, Berkeley: "Notes of Meeting, June 22, 1943, between Henry J. Kaiser, Chad F. Calhoun, Henry Kaiser, Jr., and Mr. Murphy and Miss McEnany of *Fortune,*" carbon copy of ms., pp. 21–22, carton 24. For other perspectives on the formation of Six Companies, see Leland W. Cutler, *America Is Good to a Country Boy* (Stanford: Stanford Univeristy Press, 1954), p. 153; "Six Companies, Inc.," *Western Construction News,* April 13, 1931, p. 173; Stevens, *Hoover Dam,* pp. 36–44.

9. Stevens, *Hoover Dam,* p. 41. Kaiser brought in Warren Brothers as a financial partner, although the eastern firm did not participate in the actual building. For particulars concerning the complex financial arrangements, see Kaiser Papers: Kaiser to Charles R. Gow, January 26, 1931, and Kaiser to Warren Brothers, July 2, 1931, both in carton 2. Joaquin F. "Joe" Reis claimed that Kaiser considered bidding alone, at least in 1929. The reason was that he and his men had more experience than most other contractors in assembling aggregates, a critical responsibility in building such a huge project (Reis interview by Alex Troffey, February 6, 1964, tape in possession of Troffey).

10. Kaiser Papers: Guy L. Stevick, "The Boulder Dam from a Surety Man's Standpoint," ms., n.d. (ca. 1954), carton 112. Cutler, *America Is Good to a Country Boy,* pp. 151–152; Stephen D. Bechtel interview, January 18, 1984. On the other hand, one noted scholar suggested that Kaiser persuaded Warren Bechtel to join him (see Stevens, *Hoover Dam,* p. 41).

11. Stevick, "Boulder Dam"; Stevens, *Hoover Dam,* pp. 36–45.

12. For sketches of backgrounds of Six Companies partners, see "Six Companies, Inc.," pp. 173–179; Cutler, *America Is Good to a Country Boy,* pp. 151–156; Stevens, *Hoover Dam,* pp. 36–45.

13. Stevick, "Boulder Dam."

14. Edward R. Ordway recalled his father, A. B. Ordway, describing such wild rides (interview, January 13, 1984). Ordway and other Kaiser executives recalled that Kaiser never returned to Hoover Dam after it was finished.

15. "Six Companies, Inc.," p. 173.

16. *Report on Hoover Dam Project and Present Status* (San Francisco: Associated General Contractors, December 1931), pp. 46–47; George Pettit, *So Hoover Was Built* (Berkeley, 1935), p. 33.

17. Sutton, "Hoover Dam Revisited," p. 311.

18. Kaiser Papers: unidentified, undated newspaper clippings, carton 112. Pettit, *So Hoover Was Built*, pp. 22, 25.

19. Pettit, *So Hoover Was Built*, pp. 23–24; Sutton, "Hoover Dam Revisited," pp. 336–337.

20. Edmund Wilson, *The American Earthquake* (Garden City, N.Y.: Doubleday, 1958), p. 373.

21. For a brief sketch of Crowe's background, see "Six Companies, Inc.," p. 177; for a more thorough account, see Stevens, *Hoover Dam*, pp. 36–39.

22. Sutton, "Hoover Dam Revisited," pp. 320–321; Theodore White, "Building the Big Dam," *Harper's* 171 (June 1935): 115.

23. Pettit, *So Hoover Was Built*, p. 32.

24. *Report on Hoover Dam*, p. 46.

25. Wilson, *American Earthquake*, p. 370; Stevens, *Hoover Dam*, pp. 62–63.

26. Kleinsorge, *Boulder Canyon Project*, pp. 219–223; White, "Building the Big Dam," pp. 115–116.

27. Pettit, *So Hoover Was Built*, p. 37.

28. *Report on Hoover Dam*, p. 68.

29. Kaiser Papers: Robert C. Elliott, "Men Grew Taller at Boulder," carbon copy of ms., n.d., p. 1, carton 294. Pettit, *So Hoover Was Built*, pp. 61–65; Stevens, *Hoover Dam*, p. 60.

30. Stevens, *Hoover Dam*, pp. 65–66.

31. Ibid., pp. 67–69.

32. Sutton, "Hoover Dam Revisited," p. 323. For a detailed account of the 1931 strike, see Stevens, *Hoover Dam*, pp. 65–79.

33. Accounts of the strike generally reflected extremes in opinion. A most unflattering picture of the Six Companies' response is presented in Wilson, *American Earthquake*, pp. 368–378. Stevens, *Hoover Dam*, pp. 65–79, is also quite critical. A third account, by Peter Wiley and Robert Gottlieb, *Empires in the Sun: The Rise of the New American West* (New York: G. P. Putnams Sons, 1982), pp. 17–19, is only slightly more forgiving of management's response. The Associated General Contractors' *Report on Hoover Dam*, and Pettit's *So Hoover Was Built*, pp. 38–39, essentially whitewash management's actions.

34. Stevens, *Hoover Dam*, pp. 84, 99–100.

35. Ibid., pp. 143, 207–213.

36. *U.S. Congressional Hearings, House Hearings* 630 (April 28, 1932): 18, 20, 60.

37. Elliott, "Men Grew Taller," p. 5.

38. U.S. Department of Interior, Bureau of Reclamation, *Hoover Dam*, pamphlet (Washington, D.C., 1968).

39. Tim A. Bedford interview, January 13, 1984.

40. *Report on Hoover Dam*, pp. 52–53.

41. Tim A. Bedford interview, January 13, 1984; Stevens, *Hoover Dam*, pp. 137–138.

42. *Report on Hoover Dam*, p. 61; Sutton, "Hoover Dam Revisited," p. 320.

43. White, "Building the Big Dam," pp. 118–119.

44. Ibid.; Sutton, "Hoover Dam Revisited," p. 337.

45. "The Earth Movers, I," *Fortune* 28 (August 1943): 212; Kaiser Papers: Robert C. Elliott, "The River Wrestlers" (chapter in "50 Year Book"), page proofs, n.p., carton 295.

46. Sydney Hyman, *Marriner S. Eccles: Private Enterprise and Public Servant* (Stanford: Stanford University Press, 1976), pp. 76–77; Stevens, *Hoover Dam,* p. 128.

47. Historian Richard N. Smith argues that in attacking the Bonus Expeditionary Force (BEF) marchers at Anacostia Flats, MacArthur not only shocked Hoover but acted in a blatantly insubordinate manner. But Hoover stoically accepted the blame. See Smith, *An Uncommon Man: The Triumph of Herbert Hoover* (New York: Simon and Schuster, 1984), pp. 139–140.

48. *U.S. Congressional Hearings, Senate Hearings* 387 (June 27, 1932): 11.

49. Stevens, *Hoover Dam,* p. 141.

50. Department of Interior Papers, National Archives, Washington, D.C.: Harold L. Ickes to Key Pittman, March 15, 1935, and Pittman to Ickes, March 19, 1935, both in Central Office File (COF), 1907–1937, box 1583.

51. Kaiser to Ickes, March 26, 1935, same file.

52. "Earth Movers, I," pp. 211–214. Kaiser Papers: A. B. Ordway, "Where We Have Been," mimeographed copy of address to Kaiser Company Public Relations Conference, Washington, April 30–May 4, 1954, carton 119.

53. Interior Papers: Kaiser to Ickes, June 27, 1935, COF, 1907–1937, box 1583; Stevens, *Hoover Dam,* pp. 233–234; "The Earth Movers, I," pp. 211–214.

54. Interior Papers: Ickes to Kaiser, March 23, 1936, COF, 1907–1937, box 1583.

55. Louis Glavis to Ickes, June 16, 1936, same file.

56. Ray L. Wilbur Papers, Herbert C. Hoover Presidential Library, West Branch, Iowa: Northcutt Ely to Ray L. Wilbur, July 22, 1936, file folder "Hoover Dam: Ely Correspondence, 1934–1936," box 13.

57. Stevens, Hoover Dam, p. 174; Kleinsorge, *Boulder Canyon Project,* p. 213.

58. Richard Neuberger, "The Biggest Thing on Earth," *Harper's* 174 (February 1937): 253, 256; Richard Lowitt, *The New Deal and the West* (Bloomington: Indiana University Press, 1984), pp. 159–171.

59. Neuberger, "Biggest Thing on Earth," p. 254. For background of motivation for damming the Columbia River, see also Murray Morgan, *The Dam* (New York: Viking Press, 1954), pp. 17–20.

60. Neuberger, "Biggest Thing on Earth," p. 257.

61. Kaiser Papers: Robert C. Elliott, "The Many Gabled House of Kaiser," ms., n.d., carton 305; see also "Chronology," n.d., carton 349.

62. Elliott, "The River Wrestlers."

63. George Sundborg, *Hail Columbia: The Thirty Year Struggle for Grand Coulee Dam* (New York: Macmillan, 1954), pp. ix, 187, 251, 262, 386, 397–400, 403, 435; Neuberger, "Biggest Thing on Earth," pp. 250, 254.

64. Sundborg, *Hail Columbia,* pp. 336–339.

65. Kaiser Papers: Robert C. Elliott, "50 Year Book," ms., n.d. (ca. 1964), n.p., carton 295.

66. George Kirov, *Shasta Dam,* pamphlet (San Francisco: Balakshin Publishing Co., 1941), pp. 7–19, 24–25.

67. Theodore A. Dungan interview, February 27, 1984.

68. Kaiser Papers: Kaiser to Henry Cowell Lime and Supply Co. et al., February 17, 1933, carton 4.

69. Kaiser Papers: George Gay to Kaiser, February 21, 1933, carton 4.

70. Kaiser Papers: R. F. Walter to Kaiser, December 20, 1938, and Kaiser to Walter, January 3, 1939, both in carton 4. Bureau of Reclamation Papers, National Archives: Kaiser to E. K. Burlew, December 19, 1938, Central Valley file .011, box 98.

71. Kaiser Papers, interoffice memos: "Comments of G. G. Sherwood on Cement Situation," March 14, 1938; Harry Morton to Kaiser, April 25, 1938, and May 7, 1938; all in carton 4.

72. "The Earth Movers, II," *Fortune* 28 (September 1943):220. Kaiser Papers: night letter, Kaiser to John Page, May 4, 1939, carton 4.

73. "Earth Movers, II," p. 222.

74. Kaiser Papers: Robert C. Elliott, "The Post War Gamble," ms., n.d., carton 295.

75. Bureau of Reclamation Papers: S. O. Harper to "Commissioner," July 24, 1942, Central Valley file .011, box 98.

76. W. W. Johnson to S. O. Harper, June 19, 1941, same file.

77. S. O. Harper to "Commissioner," July 24, 1942, same file.

CHAPTER 5. PATRIOT IN PINSTRIPES—SHIPBUILDING

1. *Facts about Henry J. Kaiser,* pamphlet (Oakland: Kaiser Co., September 19, 1946), p. 15.

2. Senate Special Committee for Defense Contracts, *Investigation of National Defense Program, July 30, 1942* (Washington, D.C., 1942), p. 4147.

3. "The Earth Movers, II," *Fortune* 28 (September 1943):17–18; Stephen D. Bechtel interview, January 18, 1984.

4. Henry J. Kaiser Papers, Bancroft Library, University of California, Berkeley: Kaiser to R. J. Lamont, October 14, 1938, carton 9. For more details on the connection between Kaiser and Seattle-Tacoma Shipbuilding Corporation, see C. Bradford Mitchell, *Every Kind of Shipwork: A History of Todd Shipyards Corporation* (New York, 1981), pp. 121–122.

5. "Earth Movers, II," p. 18.

6. Ibid.; in fact, the C-1 contract for five ships wound up costing $10,635,000. See Kaiser Papers: John W. Merryman to John A. McCone, July 17, 1940, carton 7.

7. Frederick C. Lane, *Ships for Victory: A History of Shipbuilding under the U.S. Maritime Commission in World War II* (Baltimore: Johns Hopkins University Press, 1951), pp. 50–53.

8. I. F. Stone, *Business as Usual: The First Year of Defense* (New York: Modern Age Books, 1941), p. 41.

9. U.S. Maritime Commission Papers, National Archives, Washington, D.C.: "Shipbuilding Memorandum," February 2, 1942–May 30, 1942, file 503:80, "Shipyards, Kaiser."

10. Frank J. Taylor, "Freighters from the Assembly Line," *National Gazette,* March 1942, p. 17.

11. "Earth Movers, II," p. 19. For a detailed description of the corporate dealings between Todd and the Six Companies, see "Shipbuilding Memorandum."

12. Taylor, "Freighters," p. 17; Tim A. Bedford interview, January 13, 1984.

13. Kaiser Papers: Katherine Hammill, rough draft of untitled ms., December 18, 1944, pp. 1–2, carton 27.

14. Ibid., p. 10.

15. Kaiser Papers: Alyce M. Kramer, "The Story of the Richmond Shipyards," ms., n.d., p. 57, carton 330.

16. Hammill, rough draft, pp. 6, 8.

17. Quotes are taken from captions on a remarkable set of photographs in the Kaiser Papers, "Richmond Shipyards, Housing," file 1983.19.

18. Ibid. Kaiser Papers: "Wartime Richmond," carbon copy of memo, n.d., carton 330; Federal Security Agency, Office of Defense Health and Welfare Services, "Data Respecting Manpower, Housing, Community, and Commercial Facilities at Richmond Shipyards," mimeographed report, April 15, 1943, carton 186.

19. Kramer, "Story of the Richmond Shipyards," p. 60.

20. Hammill, rough draft, p. 8.

21. Ibid., p. 5.

22. For background on general wartime conditions in Portland, see Carl Abbott, "Planning for the Home Front in Seattle and Portland, 1940–1945," in *The Martial Metropolis: U.S. Cities in War and Peace*, ed. Roger W. Lotchin (New York: Praeger Press, 1984), pp. 163–189; E. Kimbark MacColl, *The Growth of a City: Power and Politics in Portland, Oregon, 1915–1950* (Portland: Georgian Press, 1979), pp. 555–606 passim.

23. Abbott, "Planning for the Home Front," pp. 166–169.

24. Lane, *Ships for Victory*, pp. 248–249.

25. "Earth Movers, II," pp. 18–19.

26. Lane, *Ships for Victory*, p. 248.

27. Haughey Family Papers, Bentley Library, Ann Arbor, Mich.: "Mother" to "Dearest Children," December 31, 1941, and Phil and Fran Haughey to "Dear Family," July 12, 1942, both in box 2.

28. Abbott, "Planning for the Home Front," pp. 170–172, 175. During World War II Kaiser got into "home building" in a big way. Kaiser Company officials estimated that they built a total of $72.9 million worth of housing adjacent to the larger shipyards, all on a nonprofit basis. See *Facts about Henry J. Kaiser*, pp. 30–31.

29. *Bos'n's Whistle* 3:10 (May 20, 1943): 8; see also Lester Lynch, "Vanport, Oregon's Second Largest City," *Western Construction News*, August 1943, pp. 351–354.

30. *Bos'n's Whistle* 2:18 (September 27, 1942): 19–20.

31. *New York Times*, September 25, 1943; November 7, 1943. William M. Tuttle, Jr., shared information about child-care efforts in World War II boomtowns around the country. Reluctance to use centers run by professionals was widespread. See Tuttle, "America's Working Mothers and 'Latchkey Children,'" draft ms., in possession of Tuttle, Department of History, University of Kansas.

32. Franklin D. Roosevelt Papers, Franklin D. Roosevelt Library, Hyde Park, N.Y.: Edgar Kaiser to Harry Hopkins, July 1, 1943, Official File (OF) 2350–2361a. Kaiser Papers: Chauncey Del French, "Vancouver-Kaiser," ms., n.d. (ca. 1967), p. 61, carton 329.

33. MacColl, *Growth of a City*, p. 578; Del French, "Vancouver-Kaiser," p. 61.

34. For nostalgic accounts of wartime activities in Vancouver, see a series of columns by Bob Beck and Ted Van Arsdol in the *Vancouver Columbian*, October 18–31, 1981.

35. Lane, *Ships for Victory*, p. 296.

36. Ibid.

37. Ibid., p. 255. Kaiser Papers: INS release by Jack Vincent, March 22, 1943, copy in carton 22. International Association of Machinists Papers, Wisconsin State Historical Society, Madison: John Green to President Roosevelt, November 21, 1942, and John P. Fry to H. W. Brown, July 5, 1943, both on reel 550, box 378/2.

38. Kaiser Papers: Robert A. Lovett to Donald M. Nelson, November 8, 1942, carton 23. U.S. Maritime Commission Papers: Kaiser to Emory S. Land, July 6, 1942, in file 503:80, "Kaiser Co., Inc., June 1–July 31, 1942."

39. Westbrook Pegler Papers, Herbert C. Hoover Presidential Library, West Branch, Iowa: E. L. Sitton to Pegler, n.d. (ca. 1943); K. A. Breminstool to Pegler, November 21, 1943; and W. A. Detwiler to Pegler, November 27, 1943; all in box 78. *Special Committee Investigating the National Defense Program, March 9, 1943* (Washington, D.C., 1943), p. 721.

40. Fair Employment Practices Commission (FEPC) Papers, National Archives, RG 228: Cornelius Golightly to John A. Davis, August 15, 1944, and Rita Cowan to Franklin D. Roosevelt, March 22, 1943, both in box 99; "Percentage of Negroes to Total Work Force 3 Kaiser Yards, Portland and Vancouver," box 321C. Kaiser Papers: Edgar Kaiser to Henry J. Kaiser, July 12, 1944, carton 26. Karen Skold, "The Job He Left Behind," in *Women, War, and Revolution* ed. Carol R. Berkin and Clara M. Lovett (New York: Holmes and Meier, 1980), pp. 55, 58, 61, 67, 68. The only internal study of male versus female worker performance uncovered by the author revealed that in late 1942 female flat welders at the prefabrication plant at Richmond yard no. 3 welded 93 feet per hour, compared to an average of 98 feet by their male coworkers (see Kaiser Papers, oversized documents: "Women in Shipbuilding: A Graphic Portrayal of the First Six Months Experience of Women Employed in the Kaiser Shipyards" (Richmond, Calif.: Kaiser Co., January 1, 1943).

41. "The Shipyard Era," *Vancouver Columbian*, June 8, 1971; Del French, "Vancouver-Kaiser," p. 106; Bernard Taper, "Life with Kaiser," *Nation*, December 12, 1944, p. 646.

42. Quotation from press release attached to letter from Hal Babbitt to Henry Kaiser, n.d., carton 173, Kaiser Papers. Kaiser's "presentism" record was not distinguished. Early in 1943, of forty-one shipyards studied, four of the Kaiser yards (Swan Island, Oregonship, Richmond no. 1, and Richmond no. 3) were ranked twelfth, twentieth, thirty-third, and thirty-fifth respectively. See U.S. Maritime Commission Papers: "Absenteeism in Identical Shipyards," transmitted February 22, 1943, abstracted from Bureau of Labor Statistics, mimeographed, in "E. S. Land Misc. Files," box 3.

43. Kaiser Papers: "Shipbuilding," mimeographed memo, n.d., carton 323.

44. Kaiser Papers: interoffice memo, Chad F. Calhoun to Kaiser, February 22, 1941, and Kaiser to John D. Reilly, July 28, 1941, both in carton 149.

45. James F. McCloud to author, February 11, 1984.

46. Tim. A. Bedford interview, January 13, 1984; Stephen D. Bechtel interview, January 18, 1984.

47. Lane, *Ships for Victory*, pp. 227–229; John A. McCone to author, February 12, 1984.

48. Lane, *Ships for Victory*, pp. 238–239. I was disappointed at failing to find any evidence of workers' views, or Henry Kaiser's, on the excesses of standardization of tasks on assembly lines.

49. Kramer, "Story of the Richmond Shipyards," pp. 32–33; Joe Reis interview by Alex Troffey, February 6, 1964.

50. Pegler Papers: James Edmiston to Pegler, March 16, 1943, box 78. Clay P. Bedford interview by Mimi Stein, May 3, 1982, transcript, Oral History Associates, San Francisco.

51. *Joint Meeting of the Subcommittee on Technological Mobilization of the Senate Military Affairs Committee with the Subcommittee on Aviation of the Senate Committee Investigating the National Defense Program*, November 17, 1942, p. 4370. Washington, D.C., 1943.

52. Robert H. Connery, *The Navy and the Industrial Mobilization in World War II* (Princeton, N.J.: Princeton University Press, 1951), p. 327.

53. Kaiser Papers: Kaiser to W. A. Hauck, April 14, 1941, and Kaiser to President Roosevelt, April 21, 1941, both in carton 14. Roosevelt Papers: Kaiser to Benjamin F. Fairless, June 30, 1941, OF 5101.

54. "Omen for Kaiser," *Time*, September 7, 1942, p. 89.

55. War Production Board (WPB) Papers, RG 179, National Archives; Manly Fleischman and L. M. Lombard to Donald M. Nelson, April 19, 1943, and Emory S. Land to Nelson, January 25, 1943, both in container 1144.

56. Emory S. Land, *Winning the War with Ships* (New York: McBride and Co., 1958), p. 172.

57. Lane, *Ships for Victory*, pp. 112–113.

58. Ibid., p. 470. Kaiser Papers: Howard L. Vickery to Kaiser, May 1, 1941, carton 30; Vickery to Clay P. Bedford, n.d., carton 28.

59. Kaiser Papers: Vickery to Kaiser, April 16, 1943, carton 28; Kaiser to Vickery, August 8, 1945, carton 30.

60. Land, *Winning the War with Ships*, pp. 25, 171.

61. Donald H. Riddle, *The Truman Committee: A Study in Congressional Responsibility* (New Brunswick, N.J.: Rutgers University Press, 1964), pp. 26, 29, 30, 33.

62. "Wonder Man Hit," *Business Week*, March 27, 1943, pp. 30–32. Harry S. Truman Papers, Harry S. Truman Presidential Library, Independence, Mo.: "Senate Special Committee to Investigate the Defense Program, Hearings, March 28, 1944," pp. T-1396–T-1404, photocopied transcript in unnumbered box.

63. *New York Post*, September 24, 1946.

64. *New York Herald-Tribune*, September 25, 1946. The *New York Times* wholeheartedly agreed; see "We Got the Ships," editorial, September 26, 1946.

65. *Facts about Henry J. Kaiser*, pp. 14–20.

66. Lane, *Ships for Victory*, p. 808.

67. *Journal of Commerce*, June 11, 1964.

CHAPTER 6. MAN OF STEEL

1. Edgar F. Kaiser, Sr., Papers, Bancroft Library, University of California, Berkeley: Chad Calhoun to File memorandums, September 4, 1940; December 12, 1940; and December 24, 1940; all in temporary carton II-6-D. These internal cor-

porate memorandums summarize telephone conversations between Henry Kaiser and steel company and government officials.

2. For a brief overview of steel production in the West through the first half of the twentieth century, see Clifford Zierer, "Iron and Steel Production and Related Industries," in *California and the Southwest,* ed. Zierer (New York: John Wiley and Sons, 1956), pp. 298–301. For additional background on Edward H. Harriman's plans for southern California steel and the gradual emergence of related enterprises in the region, see C. Colcock Jones, "Los Angeles as an Iron and Steel Center," *Mining and Oil Bulletin* (Los Angeles, Chamber of Mining and Oil), May 1915, pp. 32–38; and *Southern California Business,* monthly issues between the world wars, particularly January issues. A comparatively recent work presenting the subject from the standpoint of competing regional interests is Kenneth Warren, *The American Steel Industry, 1850–1970* (Oxford: Oxford University Press, 1973).

3. Frederick C. Lane, *Ships for Victory: A History of Shipbuilding under the U.S. Maritime Commission in World War II* (Baltimore: Johns Hopkins University Press, 1951), pp. 50–53.

4. Leon Henderson Papers, Franklin D. Roosevelt Library, Hyde Park, N.Y.: Henry Morgenthau, Jr., to Roosevelt, December 18, 1940, box 35. For an excellent recent historical account of industry's reluctance to mobilize quickly, see Kim McQuaid, *Big Business and Presidential Power: From FDR to Reagan* (New York: William Morrow and Co., 1982), pp. 79–80.

5. Gano Dunn, *Report to the President of the U.S. on the Adequacy of the Steel Industry for National Defense* (Washington, D.C., February 22, 1941). Bruce Catton worked during the war for Don Nelson, head of the War Production Board (WPB), and was hardly an objective observer. Catton argued that FDR accepted the Dunn Report in good faith. See Catton, *The War Lords of Washington* (New York: Harcourt, Brace, and Co., 1948). Eliot Janeway basically describes FDR as a crafty manipulator, who set up scores of short-lived agencies to take the blame for inevitable fiascos during the buildup period. See Janeway, *The Struggle for Survival: A Chronicle of Economic Mobilization in World War II* (New Haven: Yale University Press, 1951).

6. Catton condemned management's ostrich-like mentality (*War Lords of Washington,* p. 100); Janeway had little praise for business in general, but argued that the President bore a large share of the blame for the slow buildup in steel (*Struggle for Survival,* pp. 97–98). With the advantage of forty years' perspective, historian Richard Lauderbaugh points out that steel producers, battered by the negative imagery wrought by the "merchants of death" tag stuck on them during the Nye Committee hearings in 1934, bent over backward to avoid appearing eager to expand production in 1940 and 1941. Lauderbaugh portrays the President as actively promoting rapid steel expansion. See Lauderbaugh, *American Steel Makers and the Coming of the Second World War* (Ann Arbor: University of Michigan Institute of Research, 1980). See also Henderson Papers: Richard V. Gilbert, "Comments on the Gano Dunn Report," n.d. (ca. March 1941), box 38; I. F. Stone, *Business as Usual: The First Year of Defense* (New York: Modern Age Books, 1941), pp. 149–152, 160, 259.

7. War Production Board (WPB) Papers, RG 179, National Archives, Washing-

ton, D.C.: "Supplement to Application for Certificate of Necessity West Coast Steel Project," Henry J. Kaiser Co., April 28, 1941, box 1410. For "pet project" comment, see "Kaiser Plans a Steel Plant," *Time,* April 28, 1941, pp. 77–78. Kaiser's "supplement" to his original proposal was presented one week after his initial meeting on the matter with the President. This suggests the strong likelihood of Roosevelt's encouragement.

8. WPB Papers: S. R. Fuller, "Memorandum for the President," May 15, 1941, box 1406.

9. Franklin D. Roosevelt Papers, Roosevelt Library: Kaiser to Ben Fairless, June 30, 1941, Official File (OF) 5101.

10. Ibid., and Kaiser to Gene Grace, same date, same file.

11. Henderson Papers: M. G. de Chazeau and R. G. Holden to Henderson, November 10, 1941, box 35.

12. Henderson Papers: de Chazeau to Henderson, November 28, 1941, box 35.

13. WPB Papers: Kaiser to W. A. Hauck, December 24, 1941, box 1134.

14. Warren, *American Steel Industry,* p. 245.

15. WPB Papers: Kaiser to Hauck, December 24, 1941, box 1134. On potential sites for the plant, see Henry J. Kaiser Papers, Bancroft Library: file memorandum, George Havas, February 11, 1942, carton 7. After the war, when Kaiser was attempting to renegotiate downward the loan received from the RFC, he frequently emphasized the inconvenience of the Fontana location.

16. "The Earth Movers, III," *Fortune* 28 (October 1943): 28.

17. Ibid. WPB Papers: Hauck to C. E. Adams, May 8, 1942, box 1412. *RFC Minutes* 121:1 (February 1–13, 1942): 348; 122:1 (March 1–14, 1942): 149.

18. Louis H. Oppenheim interview, January 17, 1984; Hauck to Adams, May 8, 1942; Peter Wiley and Robert Gottlieb, *Empires in the Sun: The Rise of the New American West* (New York: G. P. Putnams Sons, 1982), pp. 20–23.

19. Kaiser Papers: Henry J. Kaiser at the 'Blowing-In' of the Blast Furnace of the Kaiser Company, Inc., Iron and Steel Division at Fontana, California, December 30, 1942," mimeographed, carton 14.

20. For a description of the Utah coal situation and Kaiser's reaction, see Kaiser Papers: telegram from unnamed Kaiser Co. official to T[om] M. Price, January 7, 1943, carton 160. Although Kaiser overcame this particular supply problem, inadequate fuel sources became a chronic problem in the postwar years. Kaiser speech quoted in *San Francisco Examiner,* May 23, 1943.

21. For samplings of insults traded between Kaiser and the auto men, see Kaiser Papers: Kaiser to Fred Zeder, February 19, 1943, carton 174; *Detroit Free Press,* January 9, 1943; "Adventures of Henry and Joe in Autoland," *Fortune* 33 (March, 1946): 94. In aluminum, industry acceptance of Kaiser was quite routine. See "Aluminum Reborn," *Fortune* 33 (May 1946): 103–107; "Henry's in Aluminum," *Newsweek,* March 4, 1946, p. 68; "The Arrival of Henry Kaiser," *Fortune* 44 (July 1951): 150–152.

22. "Earth Movers, III," p. 28; "Kaiser, Steelmaker," *Newsweek,* January 11, 1943, pp. 50–53; Kaiser Papers: "Notes on Meeting, June 22, 1943, between Henry J. Kaiser, Henry Kaiser, Jr., Chad Calhoun, and Mr. Murphy and Miss McEnany of Fortune," mimeographed, carton 24.

23. Kaiser Papers: interoffice memo, Calhoun to Kaiser, November 17, 1943, carton 28.

24. Jack S. Ballard, *The Shock of Peace: Military and Industrial Demobilization after World War II* (Washington, D.C.: University Press of America, 1983), p. 159.

25. Kaiser Papers: "A Statement by Henry J. Kaiser apropos a Controversy Precipitated at the Inter-State Conference on Post-War Industrial Development of the West, Carson City, Nevada, February 12, 1944, by Mr. Benjamin F. Fairless, President of the U.S. Steel Corporation," carton 28. For data on the meeting itself, see Chad F. Calhoun, "Report on Meeting Held at Carson City, Nevada, February 11 and 12, 1944," carton 28. See also Mark S. Foster, "Giant of the West: Henry J. Kaiser and Regional Industrialization, 1930–1950," *Business History Review* 59: (Spring 1985): 1–23.

26. *New York Times*, February 7, 1945; "Maybe," *Time*, February 19, 1945, p. 77; Kaiser Papers: Paul F. Cadman to Kaiser, December 27, 1944, carton 28. For details on the Kaiser offer to lease Geneva and preliminary dealings with CF&I and Wickwire-Spencer, see Kaiser to DPC, July 13, 1945, carton 158, and "Steel for the West—and Kaiser?" *Business Week*, July 21, 1945, pp. 15–17. I am indebted to my colleague H. Lee Scamehorn, author of the definitive work on Colorado Fuel and Iron, for digging out newspaper clippings from Pueblo papers covering these negotiations. The *Pueblo Chieftain* reported that Colonel Edward H. Heller, a member of the Federal Surplus Property Board, suggested such a combine, including executive leadership from such respected westerners as former president Herbert Hoover, banker A. P. Giannini, and others. Heller suggested that Kaiser "might be selected to run the plants" (*Pueblo Chieftain*, July 12, 1945). Two days later, Kaiser announced formation of a western syndicate. Although these stories suggested that the idea originated with federal officials, Kaiser had been considering very similar initiatives for at least a year. Although Kaiser retained interest in the combine for several months, in late October 1945 he announced that financial constraints prevented his taking the plunge. See *Pueblo Chieftain*, October 24, 1945.

27. Kaiser Papers: interoffice memo, Calhoun to Kaiser, July 21–22, 1944, carton 25.

28. Hugh Fulton Papers, Harry S. Truman Presidential Library, Independence, Mo.: Calhoun to RFC, July 25, 1944, Kaiser File.

29. Hugh Fulton, "Suggestions RE: Fontana Project," November 27, 1944, mimeographed, same file.

30. Ballard, *The Shock of Peace*, p. 20; James M. Burns, *Roosevelt: The Soldier of Freedom, 1940–1945* (New York: Harcourt Brace and Jovanovich, 1970), pp. 534, 593–594; John M. Blum, *V Was for Victory* (New York: Harcourt Brace Jovanovich, 1977), passim.

31. Kaiser Papers: interoffice memo, Calhoun to Kaiser, November 17, 1943, carton 28.

32. Kaiser Papers: interoffice memo, Calhoun to Kaiser, July 22, 1944, carton 25.

33. Lester Velie, "The Truth about Henry Kaiser," *Colliers*, July 27, 1946, pp. 11–12; Morris Garnsey, "The Future of the Mountain States," *Harper's* 191 (October 1945): 333.

34. *New York Times*, September 4, 1945. Kaiser Papers: Sam H. Husbands to John S. McCullough, Jr., September 18, 1945, copy in carton 30.

35. *New York Times,* May 2, 1946.

36. *Facts about Henry J. Kaiser,* pamphlet (Oakland: Kaiser Co., September 19, 1946), pp. 6–7, 26–27, 37.

37. Kaiser Papers: interoffice memo, Calhoun to Kaiser, July 24, 1946, carton 31. Harry S. Truman Papers, Truman Library: Kaiser to Truman, January 25, 1947, and April 29, 1947, both in Official File (OF) box 796, folder 210-B, misc.

38. Truman Papers: President's Appointment File, Daily Sheets, June 16, 1945, and John A. Caskie, cover memo to John A. Steelman, n.d. (ca. February 1947), both in OF box 796, folder 210-B, misc.

39. For background on Kaiser's entry into automobiles and aluminum, see "The Arrival of Henry Kaiser," pp. 68–73, 131–154; Lawrence J. White, *The American Automobile Industry since 1945* (Cambridge, Mass.: Harvard University Press, 1971), p. 67; "Aluminum Reborn," pp. 103–108; *Facts about Henry J. Kaiser,* pp. 33–34; Mark S. Foster, "Challenger from the West: Henry J. Kaiser and the Detroit Automobile Industry, 1945–1955," *Michigan History* 70:1 (January–February 1986): 30–39.

40. Critics of Kaiser appeared in major newspapers around the country and in popular magazines. For a sampling of anti-Kaiser views, see John Fisher, "Kaiser Story: One Loan after Another," *Chicago Tribune,* April 6, 1946; "Help for Henry," *Time,* June 2, 1946, pp. 83–84.

41. Wiley and Gottlieb, *Empires in the Sun,* pp. 22–23; Robert Hine, *The American West: An Interpretive History,* 2d ed. (Boston: Little, Brown, 1984), pp. 343–344. Earl Pomeroy presents an interesting counterpoint to this view, observing that in the basic aluminum operations, Kaiser started in the West, but that after 1950 all of his major expansion was toward the East. See Pomeroy, *The Pacific Slope: A History of California, Oregon, Washington, Idaho, Utah, Nevada* (New York: A. A. Knopf, 1966), pp. 297–307.

42. Kaiser Papers: interoffice memo marked "Confidential," Calhoun to Kaiser, May 10, 1947, carton 34.

43. "Democrats Look West," *New Republic,* August 25, 1947, p. 3; Kaiser Papers: Kaiser to G. F. Ashby, January 18, 1947, carton 34; "Free Enterprise or Monopoly," *Christian Science Monitor,* June 21, 1948.

44. Kaiser Papers: "Press Release," September 8, 1948, mimeographed, carton 36; Kaiser to Paul G. Hoffman, February 25, 1949, carton 52. "Kaiser's Gamble at Fontana Defies Dire Predictions of Failure," *Iron Age,* October 7, 1948, p. 133.

45. *Outrage in Steel,* as told by Henry J. Kaiser (Oakland: Kaiser Steel Co., 1948), n.p.

46. Truman Papers: "Statement of RFC Chairman John D. Goodloe before Senate Banking and Currency Committee," January 23, 1948, OF 1396, folder 581.

47. Kaiser Papers: Kaiser to Hoffman, February 25, 1949, carton 52.

48. "The Arrival of Henry Kaiser," pp. 148–149.

49. C. H. Grattan, "The Future of the Pacific Coast," *Harper's* 191 (March 1945): 305–306; *Iron Age* 15 (February 1945): 88; both quoted in Warren, *American Steel Industry,* p. 263. For a typically optimistic view of Kaiser's prospects in western steel within his own ranks, see Kaiser Papers: George Havas to Kaiser, June 26, 1945, carton 333.

50. "Henry J. versus Big Ben," *Time,* March 10, 1947, pp. 90–92. Truman Papers: Kaiser to G. F. Ashby, January 18, 1947, OF box 796, folder 210-B, misc.

51. Steel figures from *Historical Statistics of the U.S.: Colonial Times to 1970,* vol. 2 (Washington, D.C., 1975), p. 698.

52. Truman Papers: "Radio Address of Henry J. Kaiser, Mutual Radio, August 9, 1947, prime time, 7:45," copy in OF box 1396, folder 581. The Bryan reference is to his "Cross of Gold" speech, delivered at the Democratic National Convention in 1896.

53. Peter Edson, "Bull and 13 Bears," *Washington News,* September 16, 1947; Gunther Stein, "Who Says We Can't Have More Steel?" *New Republic,* September 8, 1947, pp. 17–23. Kaiser overestimated 1949 demand significantly, but undoubtedly for "effect." By 1949 steel shortages were temporarily overcome, and output was 96.1 million tons. However, in a broader sense, he accurately anticipated future needs, and he was a leader in the industry's tremendous expansion during the 1950s. Production reached 125.8 million tons in 1955 and 148.6 million tons by 1960 (*Historical Statistics of the U.S.,* vol. 2, p. 698).

54. Kaiser Papers: interoffice memo, Calhoun to Henry J. Kaiser Co., April 3, 1950, carton 62.

55. Warren, *American Steel Industry,* pp. 267–268.

56. On rail rate discrimination charges, see Kaiser Papers: Kaiser to Fred G. Gurley, April 6, 1950, carton 62. Gurley was president of the Atchison, Topeka, and Santa Fe Railroad. Carton 62 also contains similar exchanges between Kaiser and other western railroad presidents: A. E. Stoddard of the Union Pacific and Wilson R. McCarthy of the Denver and Rio Grande. See also "Kaiser Gets His Coal," *Newsweek,* April 24, 1950, p. 75.

57. An account of the Kaiser-Pearson discussion is found in Kaiser Papers: interoffice memo, Calhoun to Kaiser, January 25, 1952, carton 82.

58. Robert J. Donovan, *Conflict and Crisis: The Presidency of Harry S. Truman, 1945–1948* (New York: W. W. Norton, 1977), pp. 116–126, 166–167; Barton J. Bernstein, "The Removal of War Production Controls on Business, 1944–1946," *Business History Review* 39 (Summer 1965): 243–260; Blum, *V Was for Victory,* passim.

59. Donovan, *Conflict and Crisis,* pp. 165–166.

60. *New York Times,* January 19 and 20, 1946; "The Biggest Strike," *Time,* January 28, 1946, p. 214.

61. Four weeks later, Big Steel settled for the $.18₅ figure. Management did pry a $5 per ton price increase from the government. See *New York Times,* February 16, 1946.

62. *New York Times,* April 3, 1952. The conflict grew more intense after Kaiser settled. With the strike, Truman seized the steel industry. Two months later, on June 12, 1952, the U.S. Supreme Court ruled the government's seizure illegal. The USWA struck again and stayed out until July 24. The final settlement was for very nearly what Kaiser had signed for almost four months earlier. For a review of the chronology of the strike, see *New York Times,* July 26, 1952.

63. *New York Times,* October 26, 1959; *Wall Street Journal,* October 27, 1959; *Newsweek,* November 9, 1959, pp. 104–106. Arthur Goldberg, former Associate Justice of the U.S. Supreme Court and Ambassador to the United Nations, was then a

leading labor lawyer, closely involved with the steel negotiations. Goldberg developed profound respect, even affection, for Kaiser. He remembered the westerner as an eminently fair, broad-minded man. According to Goldberg, the elder Kaiser did not really approve of Edgar's hobnobbing with the "fossils" in the steel industry and was relieved when his son pulled out of the combine (interview with Justice Goldberg, March 31, 1987).

64. "The Kaiser Plan: Pay for Peace and Prosperity," *Newsweek,* December 31, 1962, p. 45. Edgar Kaiser emphasized that the plan was not profit-sharing, but cost-saving (Edgar F. Kaiser interview by William Millman, January 18, 1965, tape in possession of Alex Troffey.

65. *Business Week,* March 14, 1964, p. 130.

66. Kaiser Papers: unidentified worker to Kaiser, n.d. (ca. March 1955); David Walton to Jack L. Ashby, October 3, 1955; and "Management-Labor Relations, January 1954–October 1955," mimeographed report, October 24, 1955; all in carton 120.

67. "Fruits of Kaiser Plan Sweet to All," *Business Week,* September 21, 1963, pp. 47–48; "New Slices for Kaiser's Melon?" *Business Week,* March 4, 1967, pp. 149–150. Unfortunately, enthusiasm for the plan tapered off in 1964 and 1965, along with the size of bonus checks. By the time of Kaiser's death in August 1967, both sides were grumbling, and the plan was dropped in favor of more conventional employee benefits a short time later.

68. For a sampling of commentary on the so-called Kaiser Steel smog problems, see *Los Angeles Times,* January 9 and January 14, 1959, and the *Rialto Record,* January 8, 1959.

69. Wiley and Gottlieb, *Empires in the Sun,* p. 32.

CHAPTER 7. CREATING AN IMAGE

1. Henry J. Kaiser Papers, Bancroft Library, University of California, Berkeley: "Henry J. Kaiser, Sr., Organizational Membership," mimeographed, October 15, 1951, carton 68.

2. Herbert C. Hoover Papers, Herbert C. Hoover Presidential Library, West Branch, Iowa: Hoover to Henry M. Robinson, August 25, 1932, Subject File, box 210. Ray L. Wilbur Papers, Hoover Library: Arthur S. Bent to Robinson, September 2, 1932, box 10.

3. Harold L. Ickes Papers, Library of Congress, Washington, D.C.: Ickes, "Diary," February 16, 1941, reel 4, p. 5224.

4. *Time,* March 3, 1941, p. 67; "Master Builder," *Business Week,* March 1, 1941, p. 28; Frank J. Taylor, "Builder No. 1," *Saturday Evening Post,* June 7, 1941, pp. 9–11, 120–124. Kaiser Papers: Chad Calhoun to Harry Morton, February 14, 1942, carton 13.

5. *Portland Oregonian,* July 20, 1942.

6. For a sample of the offers to Kaiser, see Kaiser Papers: Harry Cohn to Kaiser, July 13, 1942; Jason S. Joy to Kaiser, August 28, 1942; Edward F. Finney to Kaiser, September 9, 1942; and Abe Murdock to Kaiser, August 21, 1942; all in carton 15. In 1944 Republic Films released *Man from Frisco.* The protagonist was a West Coast shipbuilder whose hard-driving manner made it obvious to even the dull-witted that it was intended as the story of Henry Kaiser.

7. *Christian Science Monitor,* October 19, 1942.

8. Kaiser Papers: Paul F. Cadman to Kaiser, September 16, 1942, carton 13; Palmer Hoyt to Willard Chevalier, September 30, 1942, carton 14.

9. Kaiser Papers: Charles R. Gow to Kaiser, October 26, 1942, carton 17; Cadman to Kaiser, December 9, 1942, and Kaiser to Cadman, December 22, 1942, both in carton 13.

10. Kaiser Papers: Cadman to Kaiser, December 23, 1942, carton 13; mimeographed press release, *San Francisco Chronicle,* December 30, 1942, carton 22.

11. Kaiser Papers: Calhoun to Kaiser, June 28, 1943, carton 174; Carl R. Olson to E. E. Trefethen, Jr., August 24, 1943, carton 22; "Washington Office Expenses, August, 1943," mimeographed, carton 25; Cadman to Kaiser, November 27, 1943, carton 174.

12. Lawrence F. Davis, "Henry Kaiser Shows His Ships," *New York Times Magazine,* January 24, 1943, p. 6. Kaiser Papers: Nellie Bent to Kaiser, June 29, 1943, carton 18; Jenny L. Bothe to Kaiser, August 29, 1942, carton 12; Marta Czapiewska to Kaiser, December 6, 1943, carton 19.

13. Kaiser Papers: E. G. Burland to Kaiser, May 19, 1941, carton 7; John A. Adams to Kaiser, November 21, 1942, and Walter A. Wecker, undated handwritten reply to Kaiser at bottom of letter, Kaiser to Wecker, November 21, 1942, both in carton 17. Westbrook Pegler Papers, Hoover Library: James Edmiston to Pegler, March 16, 1943, in "Unions—Abuses and Rackets 1943" file, box 78.

14. Hoover Papers: "Excerpt from GE Broadcast, Saturday, May 8, 1943," carbon copy in post-Presidential papers, "Fellers, Bonner, 1940–1950" file, box 328.

15. Kaiser Papers: Kaiser to Eleanor Roosevelt, February 6, 1943, carton 25; Robert deRoos to Kaiser, February 8, 1943, and Corrine Thrasher to Edna Knuth, June 25, 1943, both in carton 24. *Chicago Times,* January 29, 1943.

16. Kaiser Papers: "Attitudes toward Kaiser in All Cities—Large and Small," mimeographed, n.d. (ca. 1943), carton 20.

17. Kaiser Papers: carton 15 contains a significant number of letters dated 1942; see also Dice Cowger to Kaiser, March 7, 1943, carton 18. *Portland Oregonian,* June 26, 1943.

18. *New York Times,* January 26, 1944; Kaiser Papers: Llewellyn White to Kaiser, February 28, 1944, carton 179. There are a large number of memos related to polling and advertising in early 1944 in carton 20. The ultimate purpose of the collected data is not entirely clear in the memos. Kaiser's executives may have been simply planning for postwar advertising for a number of his proposed consumer items. I make no ironclad claim that such inquiries were for ultimate political purposes, but the timing of these memos does create room for such speculation.

19. James M. Burns, *Roosevelt: The Soldier of Freedom, 1940–1945* (New York: Harcourt Brace Jovanovich, 1970), p. 503.

20. Eugene E. Trefethen, Jr., interview September 22, 1983.

21. Harry S. Truman Presidential Library, Independence, Mo., oral history interviews: no. 51, Samuel I. Rosenman, pp. 19–22; no. 69, Oscar Ewing, p. 103; no. 265, Robert G. Nixon, p. 62. Jack Smith quoted in *Spokane Spokesman-Review,* September 22, 1959. Franklin D. Roosevelt Papers, Franklin D. Roosevelt Library, Hyde Park, N.Y.: Rosenman, "Memorandum for the President," June 30, 1944, and FBI report, June 30, 1944, both in President's Secretary's File (PSF) 155. Ickes, "Diary," June 18, 1944, reel 6, p. 9012.

22. Ickes, "Diary," July 16, 1944, reel 6, pp. 9508, 9069.

23. Samuel I. Rosenman Papers, Roosevelt Library: memo, Edwin Pauley to Jonathan Daniels, n.d., box 14. John W. Partin, "Roosevelt, Byrnes, and the 1944 Vice-Presidential Nomination," *Historian* 42 (November 1979): 85–100.

24. *New York World-Telegram,* September 21, 1944.

25. Kaiser Papers: Stephen D. Bechtel to Kaiser, August 17, 1942, carton 13.

26. Kaiser Papers: "Notes of Meeting between Henry J. Kaiser, Henry Kaiser, Jr., Chad Calhoun, and Mr. Murphy and Miss McEnany of *Fortune,* June 22, 1943," pp. 25, 27, carbon copy in carton 24.

27. Ibid., p. 11. Kaiser Papers: telegram, Kaiser to R. D. Paine, December 23, 1944, carton 25; Paine to Kaiser, January 5, 1945, carton 30.

28. *Crow's Pacific Coast Lumber Digest,* editorial, May 15, 1945.

29. Kaiser Papers, H. F. Morton and William Marks, interoffice memo, July 20, 1945, carton 28.

30. Pegler quote from *Indianapolis Times,* May 31, 1945.

31. Kaiser Papers: Cadman to Kaiser, December 30, 1944, carton 174; A. A. Liveright to Kaiser, August 16, 1945, and interoffice memo, Cadman to Kaiser, August 29, 1945, both in carton 28.

32. Roosevelt Papers: Isador Lubin to the President, March 23, 1945, President's Personal File (PPF) 2924. Kaiser Papers: Gerard Piel to Kaiser, May 10, 1945, carton 30. Harry S. Truman Papers, Truman Library: President's Appointment File, Daily Sheets, June 16, 1945.

33. Kaiser Papers: Robert F. Wagner to Kaiser, May 24, 1945, carton 30; "Henry J. Kaiser, Sr., Organizational Membership," mimeographed, October 15, 1951, carton 68. Truman Papers: Walter White to Truman, May 10, 1946, OF 211, file 40, misc.; President's Appointment File, Daily Sheets, June 16, 1945.

34. Kaiser Papers: interoffice memo, Calhoun to Kaiser, February 19, 1946, carton 184.

35. Kaiser Papers: interoffice memo, Cadman to Kaiser, July 20, 1945, carton 28.

36. Kaiser Papers: Mrs. Karl Klein to Kaiser, December 2, 1946, carton 32; memo from Kaiser, n.d., concerning J. V. Murphy article in *Fortune,* carton 187; Calhoun to Kaiser, April 29, 1947, carton 34; Homer Hardesty to Kaiser, February 24 and May 9, 1948, both in carton 37; Elliott, handwritten addendum attached to Hardesty letter to Kaiser, May 9, 1948.

37. Kaiser Papers: Kenneth L. Maxwell to Kaiser, February 2, 1946, and John J. Phillips to Kaiser, January 21, 1946, both in carton 33; Kaiser to Frank A. Clarvor et al., October 24, 1947, carton 36.

38. *Questions and Answers about Henry J. Kaiser,* pamphlet (Oakland: Kaiser Co., September 19, 1946). See also Kaiser Papers: interoffice memo, A. B. Ordway to R. C. Elliott, October 18, 1949, carton 49.

39. Truman Papers: Linford E. Young to Truman, September 22, 1948, OF box 1033, file 345, misc.; for identical telegrams, see OF box 636, file 151.

40. Pegler Papers: Pegler to Kaiser, September 9, 1949, Kaiser, Henry J. file, box 44. Kaiser Papers: Henry Luce to Kaiser, April 17, 1950, carton 318.

41. Kaiser Papers: George D. Woods to R. C. Elliott, December 14, 1949, carton 51; Alex Troffey to Stub Stollery, February 6, 1951, carton 71.

42. Kaiser Papers: "Notes for Phone Talk with *Business Week*," September 1949, carbon copy in carton 51; Calhoun to Kaiser et al., December 3, 1953, carton 118.

43. "Kaiser Industries," in-house *Fortune* notes by Walter Guzzardi, January 31, 1963, mimeographed, p. 3, in possession of Alex Troffey.

CHAPTER 8. PLANNING FOR A POSTWAR WORLD

1. Otis L. Graham, Jr., *Toward a Planned Society: From Roosevelt to Nixon* (New York: Oxford University Press, 1977).

2. Mark S. Foster, "Giant of the West: Henry J. Kaiser and Regional Industrialization, 1930–1950," *Business History Review* 59 (Spring 1985): 1–23.

3. For Kaiser quote, see *New York Times*, December 5, 1942. In recent years, scholars have held varying perspectives on the responses to postwar planning. For example, William S. Hill, Jr., argued recently that by late 1942, with stabilization of battlefronts around the globe and American industry on a wartime footing, "public action on postwar planning became respectable and popular among businessmen." On the other hand, historian Bruce Catton, then serving Donald M. Nelson's War Production Board (WPB), recalled that "reconversion, when it came, came like a thief in the night." See William S. Hill, Jr., "The Business Community and National Defense, 1943–1950" (Ph.D. dissertation, Stanford University, 1979), p. 36; Bruce Catton, *The War Lords of Washington* (New York: Harcourt, Brace, and Co., 1948), p. 240. For other views on the politics of reconversion, see Jack S. Ballard, *The Shock of Peace: Military and Economic Demobilization after World War II* (Washington, D.C.: University Press of America, 1983), Ch. 2; Barton J. Bernstein, "The Debate on Industrial Reconversion: The Protection of Oligopoly and Military Control of the Economy," *American Journal of Economics and Sociology* 26 (April 1967): 159–172; Robert M. Collins, "American Corporatism: The Committee for Economic Development, 1942–1964," *Historian* 44 (February 1982):151–173; Roland Young, *Congressional Politics in the Second World War* (New York: Columbia University Press, 1956), passim.

4. Kaiser's speech quoted from the *Oakland Tribune*, September 30, 1942. For discussion on predictions of postwar unemployment in defense, see Catton, *War Lords of Washington*, p. 240; Hill, "Business Community and National Defense," pp. 69, 75. In fact, economists were split almost evenly in predicting depression or abundance. The most pessimistic was Leo M. Cherne, who estimated that postwar unemployment would reach a staggering nineteen million; see Cherne, *The Rest of Your Life* (New York: Doubleday and Co., 1944).

5. Barnard M. Baruch and John M. Hancock, *War and Postwar Adjustment Policies* (Washington, D.C.: Council on Public Affairs, 1944), pp. 9–13; *Post-War Planning: Hearings before the Committee on Public Building and Grounds, House of Representatives, 78th Congress, 2nd Session, February 3, 1944* (Washington, D.C., 1944), pp. 441–456. Henry J. Kaiser Papers, Bancroft Library, University of California, Berkeley: Kaiser to Paul G. Hoffman, June 12, 1940, carton 8. For a fine study of the interstate highway system, see Mark H. Rose, *Interstate: Express Highway Politics, 1940–1956* (Lawrence: Regents Press of Kansas, 1979). Kaiser's personal investigations into the possibilities of an interstate highway system actually went back at least as far as 1930. See Kaiser Papers: David H. Ryan to Kaiser, November 24, 1930, carton 341.

6. Franklin D. Roosevelt Papers, Franklin D. Roosevelt Library, Hyde Park, N.Y.: Bernard M. Baruch to Roosevelt, June 18, 1943, PPF 88. Kaiser Papers: Chad Calhoun to Kaiser, April 13, 1943, carton 174; "Notes of a Meeting, Henry J. Kaiser, Henry Kaiser, Jr., Chad Calhoun, and Mr. Murphy and Miss McEnany of *Fortune,* June 22, 1943," carton 24. "Henry Kaiser Plans for Peace," *Modern Industry,* September 15, 1943, reprinted.

7. Kaiser Papers: draft of letter from Kaiser to Tom Beck, n.d. (ca. November 5, 1943), carton 18. *New York Times,* December 19, 1943.

8. Kaiser Papers: interoffice memo, Llewellyn White to Kaiser, February 5, 1944, carton 25.

9. *New York Times,* March 10, 1944. Kaiser Papers: interoffice memo, White to Kaiser, April 17, 1944, carton 179; "Memorandum to President Roosevelt Setting Forth the Principles of Certain Post-War Proposals Designed to Strengthen and Enhance War-Time Morale among the Fighting Men and the War Workers," May 1944, carton 26. Kaiser, "America Can Win the Peace," *La Follette's Magazine* 8 : 22 (May 29, 1944): 1.

10. Kaiser Papers: "Henry J. Kaiser before the New York Financial Writers Association in New York City, October 5, 1944," carton 27. *New York Times,* October 21, 1944; S. J. Woolf, "Henry Kaiser Foresees Plenty of Jobs," *New York Times Magazine,* October 12, 1944, p. 41. Such an assessment of Kaiser's praise of woman's role is somewhat tempered by the fact that there was not a single woman in managerial ranks in his companies.

11. *Washington Post,* November 16, 1944.

12. Kaiser Papers: Norman Bel Geddes to Kaiser, December 15, 1942, carton 14; see also "Building the Future," address to the National Committee on Housing, mimeographed, March 9, 1944, pp. 4, 6–7, carton 28, and *New York Herald-Tribune,* December 12, 1942.

13. *New York Times,* May 10, 1945.

14. *San Francisco Chronicle,* May 10, 1945; *Chicago Sun,* May 10, 1945; "Greatest House Building Show on Earth," *Architectural Forum* 86 (March 1947): 105–113.

15. "Greatest House Building Show," pp. 105–113.

16. Kaiser Papers: H. V. Lindbergh to Kaiser, November 12, 1946, carton 33.

17. "The Bright New Hope of the Building Business: Industrialized Housing," *House Beautiful* 89 (April 1947): 194–196.

18. Steel was a notable exception. Because the Reconstruction Finance Corporation (RFC) demanded payment in full on wartime loans to build the Kaiser Steel plant at Fontana, California, Kaiser felt compelled to raise prices thirty dollars per ton over those of his competitors in 1948. He was able to charge those prices because of a severe shortage of the commodity. See "Kaiser's Gamble at Fontana Defies Dire Predictions of Failure," *Iron Age,* October 7, 1948, p. 133.

19. Kaiser Community Homes, *Annual Report, 1948;* U.S. Bureau of the Census, *Statistical Abstract of the U.S., 1952* (Washington, D.C., 1952), p. 726.

20. Kaiser Papers: "Champ" Pickens to Kaiser, June 19, 1943, carton 22.

21. Kaiser Papers: interoffice memos: Kaiser to E. E. Trefethen, Jr., et al., n.d., carton 174, and T. M. Price to Kaiser, August 7, 1944, carton 172.

22. *Facts about Henry J. Kaiser,* pamphlet (Oakland: Kaiser Co., September 19, 1946), pp. 23–24. Kaiser Papers: interoffice memo, H. V. Lindbergh to S. D.

Hackley, August 24, 1946, carton 170; "Program for 1952, Kaiser Metal Products, Inc.," mimeographed, n.d. (ca. December 1951), carton 79. (Soon after the war, Fleetwings' name was changed to Kaiser Metal Products.)

23. *San Francisco News,* July 1, 1946.

24. For negotiations, see Kaiser Papers: Edgar F. Kaiser to E. A. Charlton, December 7, 1944, and interoffice memo, Calhoun to Kaiser et al., May 17, 1945, both in carton 28; "E. A. Charlton Report," mimeographed, January 27, 1945, and Mike Miller to Kaiser, November 28, 1944, both in carton 321.

25. *New York Times,* May 21, 1943. Kaiser Papers: interoffice memo, R. E. Knight to Kaiser, August 25, 1943, carton 23; telegram, Trefethen to Kaiser, August 30, 1943, carton 24.

26. Kaiser Papers: telegram, Trefethen to Kaiser, August 30, 1943, carton 24; telegram, Kaiser to Julius Krug, May 3, 1945, carton 29.

27. The Kaiser Papers contain several hundred interoffice memos concerning shipbuilding; see in particular cartons 25, 33, 179, and 180. *New York Times,* September 12, 1943.

28. Kaiser Papers: interoffice memos, Louis H. Oppenheim to Trefethen, March 15, 1944, and Calhoun to Clay P. Bedford, May 19, 1944, both in carton 25. Tim A. Bedford interview, January 13, 1984.

29. Kaiser Papers: interoffice memo, Calhoun to Kaiser, August 19, 1944, carton 25.

30. Roosevelt Papers: Emory S. Land, "Personal and Confidential Memorandum for the President," September 8, 1944, and "FDR" to Jerry [Land], November 17, 1944, both in PSF 188. The reasons behind the decline of the U.S. Merchant Marine are considerably more complex than suggested here. They include international competition, labor costs, and many other factors.

31. Roosevelt Papers: Land, "Personal and Confidential Memorandum for the President," November 24, 1944; Harold Smith, "Memorandum for the President," November 25, 1944, PSF 188.

32. Kaiser Papers: R. G. Bowen to Kaiser, January 15, 1946, carton 33.

33. Kaiser Papers: Tim A. Bedford to Clarence Erickson and Richmond City Council, February 28, 1946, carton 31. John A. Steelman Papers, Harry S. Truman Presidential Library, Independence, Mo.: Chad Calhoun to Admiral W. W. Smith, July 30, 1946, box 3, Surplus Property File.

34. Kaiser Papers: Calhoun to Maritime Commission, April 2, 1947, carton 155. Steelman Papers: "Brief History—Swan Island," mimeographed, n.d., and telegram, L. C. Stoll et al. to Wayne Morse, April 18, 1947, both in box 3, Surplus Property File.

35. Kaiser Papers: Oscar Cox, "Memorandum; Subject: Richmond Yard No. 3," August 12, 1946, carton 183; Kaiser to Amos B. Hinckley et al., October 22, 1946, carton 33. Tim A. Bedford interview, January 13, 1984.

36. Kaiser Papers: Kaiser to E. S. Land, April 7, 1944, carton 173; D. E. Scoll to Calhoun, March 31, 1944, carton 178. Roosevelt Papers: "Summary of Jesse Jones Conversations with the President, Beginning April 12, 1944," OF 5101.

37. Kaiser Papers: Stephen D. Bechtel to Kaiser, March 5, 1944, carton 17.

38. Kaiser Papers: Paul F. Cadman, "Proposal for Far East Shipping Line," mimeographed, n.d. (1944), carton 320; Sterling Seagrave, *The Soong Dynasty* (New York: Harper and Row, 1985), pp. 368–369, 424–425.

39. Kaiser Papers: Dudley C. Lewis to James H. Verner, March 22, 1960, carton 194. By 1960, Kaiser Engineers performed hundreds of millions of dollars' worth of construction work overseas every year.

CHAPTER 9. DEBACLE IN DETROIT

1. *Automotive Daily News,* June 8, 1935, p. 4; for more detail on the car itself, see *Allgemeine Automobil-Zeitung,* March 1, 1935, p. 21. See also Mark S. Foster, "Challenger from the West: Henry J. Kaiser and the Detroit Auto Industry, 1945–1955," *Michigan History* 70:1 (January–February 1986): 30–39.

2. *New York Times,* December 6, 1942.

3. Henry J. Kaiser Papers, Bancroft Library, University of California, Berkeley: E. E. Trefethen, Jr., to R. Buckminster Fuller, December 18, 1942, carton 14. Kaiser's dealings with Fuller ended on an unsatisfactory note, as the men squabbled over both the design and Fuller's final fee (see Kaiser to Gerard Piel, May 21, 1943, carton 19). However, the two would join forces once again in Hawaii twenty years later, when Fuller designed a theater of the geodesic dome design. For details on Emeryville operation, see H. V. Lindbergh to Kaiser, February 6, 1943, carton 143.

4. *Portland* (Ore.) *Journal,* January 9, 1943; *Detroit Free Press,* October 16, 1943.

5. Kaiser Papers: Kaiser to Fred Zeder, February 19, 1943, carton 174. By 1943 and 1944, publicity concerning Kaiser's intentions of doing big things in the automobile industry was widespread. See "Mirrors of Motordom," *Steel,* July 5, 1943, p. 82; "Assembly Line," *Iron Age,* January 27, 1944, pp. 72–74; April 13, 1944, pp. 78–80.

6. Kaiser Papers: C. J. Reese to Kaiser, March 27, 1943, and Lindbergh to Kaiser, October 11, 1944, both in carton 143.

7. Kaiser Papers: R. E. Knight to Kaiser, May 10, 1943, carton 334; Knight to Kaiser, June 8, 1943, carton 20.

8. For a discussion of Ford's plans, see David L. Lewis, *The Public Image of Henry Ford* (Detroit: Wayne State University Press, 1976), pp. 391–392. Kaiser Papers: Kaiser to Harger and Probst, June 8, 1943, carton 143. *New York Times,* June 26, 1943.

9. Kaiser Papers: Knight to Trefethen, July 22, 1943, carton 143.

10. *Automotive News,* July 24, 1944; Lewis, *Public Image of Henry Ford,* pp. 391–392.

11. *Daily Worker,* June 8, 1945; Lewis, *Public Image of Henry Ford,* pp. 392–397. R. J. Thomas Papers, Walter Reuther Library, Wayne State University, Detroit: Thomas to Kaiser, June 11, 1945, box 26. Kaiser Papers: interoffice memo, Gerard Piel to Kaiser, carton 117.

12. "Adventures of Henry and Joe in Autoland," *Fortune* 33 (March 1946): 98. For a flattering portrait of Frazer, see Richard M. Langworth, *Kaiser-Frazer: The Last Onslaught on Detroit* (Princeton, N.J.: Princeton Publishing, 1975): pp. 8–21.

13. "Adventures of Henry and Joe," p. 98; Lawrence J. White, *The American Automobile Industry since 1945* (Cambridge, Mass.: Harvard University Press, 1971), pp. 66–67.

14. "Adventures of Henry and Joe," pp. 101–102; Langworth, *Kaiser-Frazer,* p. 20.

15. "Adventures of Henry and Joe," pp. 102–103.

16. Ibid., pp. 101, 103. Historian Lawrence J. White points out that the govern-

ment provided Kaiser these very generous terms, and that Kaiser-Frazer eventually purchased Willow Run for $15 million. But White also notes that other automobile manufacturers received equally favorable terms in buying or leasing surplus war plants and equipment. See White, *American Automobile Industry*, pp. 67–70.

17. William C. White, "Kaiser-Frazer," *Life*, December 31, 1945, pp. 72–79.

18. White, *American Automobile Industry*, p. 67; John B. Rae, *The Road and Car in American Life* (Cambridge, Mass.: MIT Press, 1971) passim.

19. "Birth of an Auto," *Newsweek*, January 26, 1946, p. 19.

20. "Henry and Joe in Autoland," p. 232; Langworth, *Kaiser-Frazer*, pp. 50–51.

21. Kaiser Papers: W. A. MacDonald to Charles R. Gow, October 24, 1945, carton 29. Kaiser had to turn Fitzgerald down, having already awarded a central Boston dealership to another investor.

22. Kaiser Papers: "Dealer Appointments as of April 1, 1946," mimeographed, carton 338. Langworth, *Kaiser-Frazer*, p. 233.

23. "A New Contract," *Survey* 82 (January 1946): 16.

24. Lester Velie, "The Truth about Henry Kaiser," *Colliers*, July 27, 1946, p. 24. In fact, none of the major auto producers' stock performed well in the immediate postwar period. Ford, of course, remained in the family's hands. In August 1945, Chrysler stock was hovering between $105 and $110 per share; its peak price in 1946 was $148, but it fell off rapidly in 1947 and 1948. On January 3, 1949, Chrysler sold for $58.125 per share. The fortunes of General Motors stock prices weren't much better. In August 1945, the price was $66 to $68 per share. Peak price in 1947 was $80.875. On January 3, 1949, it sold for $58.75 (figures from *Wall Street Journal*).

25. Langworth, *Kaiser-Frazer*, p. 266; Ed Cray, *Chrome Colossus: General Motors and Its Times* (New York: McGraw-Hill, 1980), p. 329; "Kaiser-Frazer Cashes In," *Fortune* 36 (December 1947): 94, *Kaiser-Frazer Annual Report*, 1947, pp. 3–4.

26. Langworth, *Kaiser-Frazer*, p. 264.

27. See Chapter 6 above.

28. Kaiser Papers: Joe Frazer, "Memorandum of a Conference with Officials of Republic Steel Corporation on the Morning of February 19, 1946 . . ." February 22, 1946, carton 182.

29. Kaiser Papers: telegram, Thomas to Truman, quoted in D. P. Connery to Gerard Piel, March 8, 1946, carton 182. Robert J. Donovan, *Conflict and Crisis: The Presidency of Harry S. Truman, 1945–1948* (New York: W. W. Norton, 1977), p. 168.

30. Kaiser Papers: Kaiser to Benjamin F. Fairless, September 25, 1947, carton 34. "Kaiser-Frazer Cashes In," p. 97.

31. Clay P. Bedford, a vice president at Willow Run, estimated that Kaiser-Frazer paid a 40 percent premium for steel. See "Kaiser-Frazer Cashes In," p. 97. Joaquin F. "Joe" Reis, another high-ranking executive at Willow Run, estimated that prices Kaiser-Frazer paid over and above those paid by competitors accounted for as much as *half* of the total losses sustained by the company in a decade of automobile production. (See Reis interview by Alex Troffey, February 6, 1964, tape in possession of Troffey).

32. *Kaiser-Frazer Annual Report*, 1947, 1948.

33. "Kaiser-Frazer Cashes In," p. 94; White, *American Automobile Industry*, p. 323; Langworth, *Kaiser-Frazer*, passim.

34. Kaiser Papers: Donald Magnuson to Kaiser, October 2, 1947, carton 36; Russell F. Blades to Kaiser, December 5, 1947, carton 34.

35. Kaiser Papers: Victor Hicks to Kaiser, May 25, 1948, and Harriet M. Smith to Kaiser, May 30, 1948, both in carton 39.

36. *Detroit News,* April 9, 1948; Clay P. Bedford interview by Mimi Stein, May 10, 1982, transcript, Oral History Associates, San Francisco; Tim A. Bedford interview, January 13, 1984; James F. McCloud to author, March 22, 1984; David Lamoreaux to author, n.d. (March 1984); Langworth, *Kaiser-Frazer,* p. 234; Peter S. Hass interview, January 10, 1984.

37. *Detroit Times,* June 8, 1946.

38. Kaiser Papers: two memos from Frazer to Edgar Kaiser, both dated November 25, 1946, carton 32; Edgar Kaiser to Frazer, March 16, 1949, carton 50. Langworth, *Kaiser-Frazer,* pp. 105–106.

39. Langworth, *Kaiser-Frazer,* pp. 105–106; Walston S. Brown, letter to author, April 19, 1984.

40. Cyrus Eaton Papers, Western Reserve Historical Society, Cleveland: Eaton to Harold Ruttenberg, August 16, 1947, box 258. "The Kaiser-Eaton Feud," *Fortune* 33 (October 1948): 88, 89, 162, 165; Walston Brown, "Kaiser and Eaton," ms., n.d., Ch. 9, p. 56.

41. For a general background, see "Kaiser-Eaton Feud," pp. 88–89, 162–165.

42. Ibid., p. 89.

43. Ibid., pp. 88–89. James F. Cocks Papers, Bentley Library, University of Michigan, Ann Arbor: Cocks, "Kaiser-Frazer Corporation, 1945–1953," ms., n.d., pp. 58–59. *Final Report of the Securities and Exchange Commission to the Committee on Interstate and Foreign Commerce Pursuant to Resolution of the Committee on Interstate and Foreign Commerce Dated August 22, 1951* (Washington, D.C., 1952), pp. 56, 57, 61.

44. "Kaiser-Frazer Slows Down," *Time,* March 8, 1948, p. 94.

45. The Eaton Papers contain significant files on Kaiser's dealings. See, in particular, boxes 195 and 196. See also Robert J. Bulkeley Papers, Western Reserve Historical Society, boxes 4, 25. Walston S. Brown, one of Kaiser's attorneys in the Eaton case, provided an interesting perspective on the outcome of the battle. If Kaiser received *any* benefit from the imbroglio, it was that many Wall Street financiers intensely disliked Eaton; this gained Kaiser indirect support from the eastern financial establishment: "One of the effects of Kaiser's fight with Eaton was to make Kaiser more acceptable to the investment banking community which disapproved of Eaton's tactics as an investment banker as well as his support of communism" (Brown to author, April 19, 1984).

46. I am particularly indebted to Mr. John P. Barden, a resident of Cleveland, who is working on a biography of Eaton, for pointing out Lewis' involvement in the settlement. Barden shared his extensive research notes on the stock fraud case with me. Notes accompanying letter from Barden to author, n.d., (ca. March 1984).

47. Figures taken from Langworth, *Kaiser-Frazer,* p. 266; and *Kaiser-Frazer Corporation History and Business,* pamphlet (Los Angeles and San Francisco: First California Co., December 31, 1951), p. 5.

48. Kaiser Papers: Mrs. Kenneth Cox to Joe Frazer, January 26, 1949, carton 48;

W. M. Guide to Kaiser, December 26, 1949, carton 42. Nina Kaiser interview, January 16, 1984; Clifford H. Keene interview, July 11, 1986.

49. Kaiser Papers: telegram, Kaiser to dealers, March 7, 1949, carton 41; interoffice memo, Frazer to Kaiser, February 3, 1949, carton 48. *Wall Street Journal,* March 30, 1949.

50. Kaiser Papers: "Henry J. Kaiser Talk over Closed Circuit to Kaiser-Frazer Dealers," typescript, May 11, 1949, and "SRC—First Draft, August 4, 1949, mimeographed, both in carton 48; Associated Automobile Company, Inc., to Edgar Kaiser, August 13, 1949, carton 42. *Wall Street Journal,* September 22, 1949.

51. Kaiser Papers: interoffice memo, Clay P. Bedford to Edgar Kaiser, May 28, 1949, carton 42.

52. "Kaiser-Frazer: The Roughest Thing We Ever Tackled," *Fortune* 44(July 1951): 161; *Wall Street Journal,* December 13, 1949; Langworth, *Kaiser-Fraser,* p. 109.

53. "Autos: The Big Gamble," *Time,* February 20, 1950, p. 79; Langworth, *Kaiser-Frazer,* p. 136.

54. Kaiser Papers: interoffice memo, Edgar Kaiser to Henry Kaiser and E. E. Trefethen, Jr., March 7, 1950, carton 58.

55. "Where Are They Now? What Ever Happened to Baby J?" *Newsweek,* April 6, 1970, p. 70.

56. Ibid.; White, *American Automobile Industry,* pp. 152, 342–344; Langworth, *Kaiser-Frazer,* p. 268.

57. *Consumer Reports,* September 1950, pp. 394–395; *Kaiser Motors Annual Report,* 1953, p. 5.

58. Langworth, *Kaiser-Frazer,* pp. 266, 268; "It's Too Good," *Washington Daily News,* March 3, 1954. Kaiser Papers: Howard A. "Dutch" Darrin to Edgar Kaiser, January 18, 1968, carton 172.

59. *Kaiser-Frazer Corporation History and Business,* p. 5; *Wall Street Journal,* January 31, 1956; Langworth, *Kaiser-Frazer,* p. 268.

60. *Kaiser-Frazer Annual Report,* 1953, p. 3; 1954, p. 3.

61. "Kaiser Deposed," *Business Week,* July 4, 1953, pp. 33–34; "Kaiser Headaches," *Newsweek,* July 6, 1954, pp. 60–62.

62. "Answering Some of the Questions behind the Kaiser-Willys Deal," *Finance,* April 15, 1953, pp. 43, 63.

63. Lambreth Hancock, a longtime aide to Henry Kaiser, emphasizes his shrewdness in foisting a white elephant onto General Motors (untitled ms., n.d. [ca. 1984], in possession of Hancock). Clay Bedford, on the other hand, argued that the Willow Run plant was worth at least $46 million and that Charlie Wilson, president of GM, knew it. But with no other decent offer, Kaiser had little choice but to accept $26 million. See Bedford interview by Stein.

64. *Wall Street Journal,* January 31, 1956. Kaiser Papers: Robert C. Elliott, "Years of Expansion," mimeographed chapter in "50 Year Book," n.d. (ca. 1964), p. 4, carton 295. Cocks, "Kaiser-Frazer Corporation," p. 192; Langworth, *Kaiser-Frazer,* pp. 266–269; White, *American Automobile Industry,* pp. 342–344; *Kaiser Industries Annual Report,* 1966, p. 18.

65. Hancock, untitled ms.

CHAPTER 10. VENTURING ABROAD

1. Henry J. Kaiser Papers, Bancroft Library, University of California, Berkeley: Robert C. Elliott, "50 Year Book," ms., n.d. (ca. 1964), carton 295. Between 1983 and 1985 I interviewed about thirty present and former executives and corresponded with almost one hundred others. Virtually to a man, those queried about Kaiser's overseas investments cited the bribery attempt in Cuba in the late 1920s as highly influential in delaying his involvement in such ventures.

2. For background on Kaiser's entry into cement, see Frank J. Taylor, "Builder No. 1," *Saturday Evening Post*, June 7, 1941, pp. 9–11, 120–124. Peter S. Hass interview, January 10, 1984.

3. Kaiser to S. O. Harper, June 27, 1941, box 98, RG 115, Bureau of Reclamation Papers, Project Correspondence File, Central Valley .011, National Archives, Washington, D.C.

4. As early as March 1940, when the Permanente Cement plant had been producing cement for less than three months, Kaiser was negotiating with the Dillingham interests in Hawaii concerning deliveries of bulk cement. See Kaiser Papers: Walter F. Dillingham to Kaiser, March 12, 1940, carton 6; Elliott, "50 Year Book"; Eugene E. Trefethen, Jr., to Walter Dillingham, September 30, 1941, carton 8; "Notes from Meeting between Henry J. Kaiser, Sr., Henry Kaiser, Jr., Chad Calhoun, and Mr. Murphy and Miss McEnany of *Fortune*," mimeographed, June 22, 1943, carton 24. Hugh Fulton Papers, Harry S. Truman Presidential Library, Independence, Mo.: "Permanente Cement Company Shipments Ready-Mix Concrete Company, Ltd.," box 3.

5. Kaiser was basically a "silent partner" on the Panama Canal job, but several managers and engineers were active participants on the $23.5 million contract. For details, see Kaiser Papers: T. M. Price, "Notes on Panama Locks Excavation," for A. Lindberger, 1946, carton 348.

6. Kaiser Papers: Horace W. Ash to Kaiser, November 19, 1942, carton 17; interoffice memo, Carl R. Olson to Trefethen, March 31, 1943, carton 22.

7. Kaiser Papers: interoffice memo, Kaiser to Trefethen, February 7, 1944, carton 27. *New York Times*, February 17, 1944; *New York Herald-Tribune*, March 28, 1944.

8. See Mark S. Foster, "Giant of the West: Henry J. Kaiser and Regional Industrialization, 1930–1950," *Business History Review* 59 (Spring 1985): 1–23; *Detroit Free Press*, March 29, 1944. Kaiser Papers: Kaiser to Isaias Medina A., President of the United States of Venezuela, June 10, 1944, carton 26.

9. Kaiser Papers: interoffice memo, Calhoun to Edgar Kaiser and Clay P. Bedford, March 28, 1945, carton 179; "Memorandum of Understanding," April 10, 1945, carton 160.

10. Kaiser Papers: interoffice memo, Calhoun to Kaiser, April 23, 1945, carton 28.

11. Kaiser Papers: Percy Chen to Kaiser, December 21, 1945, carton 30.

12. For conflict between Chen and Soong, and for a first-rate analysis of the slow decay of the Nationalists' interests, see Sterling Seagrave, *The Soong Dynasty* (New York: Harper and Row, 1985), p. 95 and passim.

13. Kaiser Papers: interoffice memos, Gerard Piel to Kaiser, December 22, 1945, and December 1945, both in carton 30.

14. Kaiser Papers: interoffice memo, Calhoun to Kaiser, December 29, 1945, carton 29.

15. *Automotive News,* October 4, 1948; *Detroit Times,* June 14, 1952; "The Rotterdam Story," *American Automobile,* February 1952, pp. 94–95; "The Mexico Story," *American Automobile,* April 1952, pp. 108–109; Elliott, "50 Year Book."

16. Kaiser Papers: Frazer to His Excellency Juan Perón, March 7, 1947, carton 179; interoffice memo, George Havas to Kaiser, July 15, 1947, and draft of letter outlining Kaiser's interest in Argentina, mimeographed, March 29, 1947, both in carton 35.

17. Lambreth Hancock, untitled ms., n.d. (ca. 1984), in possession of Hancock, n.p. For Morrison's view of the meeting, which closely paralleled this account, see Edward F. Haas, *De Lesseps S. Morrison and the Image of Reform* (Baton Rouge: Louisiana State University Press, 1986), pp. 156–157.

18. Quote from Hancock, untitled ms. For more authoritative background on Vargas, see John W. F. Dulles, *Vargas of Brazil: A Political Biography* (Austin: University of Texas Press, 1967), and Dulles, *Unrest in Brazil: Political-Military Crises, 1955–1964* (Austin: University of Texas Press, 1970), pp. 3–7.

19. Hancock, untitled ms.; Dulles, *Vargas of Brazil,* pp. 323–327. Elizabeth A. Cobbs presents convincing evidence that Kaiser's advance men had already made significant progress toward working out specific Brazilian investments before Kaiser met Vargas. See Cobbs, "Good Works at a Profit: Private Development and U.S.-Brazil Relations, 1945–1960" (Ph.D. dissertation, Stanford University, 1988), draft Chapter 5.

20. If the South American initiatives succeeded, New Orleans' import and export trade would expand by many millions of dollars' worth annually. Morrison's verbatim account of his conversations with Kaiser are attached to Elliott, "50 Year Book."

21. Hancock, untitled ms.

22. Elliott, "50 Year Book." Morrison provided only a slightly different account, but he, too, believed Antonio was "on the take." See DeLesseps S. Morrison, "Latin American Mission," mimeographed, n.d. (ca. 1964), in possession of Alex Troffey.

23. Kaiser Papers: "Confidential Inter-Office Memorandum," Robert C. Elliott and Henry J. Kaiser to Edgar F. Kaiser and E. E. Trefethen, Jr., August 28, 1954, and "Memorandum from Henry J. Kaiser (dictated) to Edgar F. Kaiser and E. E. Trefethen, Jr., in Flight from Caracas, Venezuela to New Orleans," August 26, 1954, both in carton 161.

24. James F. McCloud to author, February 11, 1984, and March 22, 1984, letters in possession of author.

25. McCloud to author, February 11, 1984. Tim A. Bedford, who accompanied Henry Kaiser on his second visit to Argentina in October 1954, recalled how Antonio distressed Kaiser by his attitude that supplies should be limited in order to maintain high prices and healthy profit margins (Tim A. Bedford interview, January 13, 1984).

26. *Washington Post,* October 6, 1954.

27. James F. Cocks Papers, Bentley Library, University of Michigan, Ann Arbor: Cocks, "Kaiser-Frazer Corporation," 1945–1953," ms., n.d., p. 190. Many additional

technical and financial details are set forth in a letter from Edgar Kaiser to Dr. Oscar L. Petliza and Santiago D. Bialet, December 14, 1954, Kaiser Papers, carton 161.

28. "Kaiser in Argentina" (editorial), *Washington Post,* October 10, 1954; *Wall Street Journal,* January 20, 1955; *New York Times,* April 10–13, 1955. Historian Elizabeth Cobbs observed that Kaiser was the first important American business leader to permit, let alone demand, majority foreign ownership: "Kaiser's recognition that foreign investment was intimately connected to questions of sovereignty placed him at the forefront of those seeking to better define the relationship of American business to the postwar developing world" (Cobbs, "Good Works at a Profit," draft Chapter 5, p. 24).

29. *Honolulu Star-Bulletin,* December 27, 1955.

30. Cocks, "Kaiser-Frazer Corporation," pp. 190–191. Kaiser Papers: clippings from *Resistencia Popular,* December 20, 1955, and *Nuestra Palabra,* December 20, 1955, carton 161.

31. Cocks, "Kaiser-Frazer Corporation," pp. 191–192.

32. "Argentina Opens Arms to Kaiser," *Business Week,* June 21, 1958, pp. 106–114; "Kaiser Hustles to Expand Its Diversified Empire," *Business Week,* August 22, 1959, pp. 52–54.

33. John D. Habron, "Kaiser's Argentine Gamble," *Executive,* July 1961, pp. 1–3; *New York Herald-Tribune,* March 9, 1964.

34. Bernard L. Collier, "One Firm's Formula for Latin Success," *New York Herald-Tribune,* March 9, 1964.

35. Thomas Aitkin, Jr., "The Double Image of American Business Abroad," *Harper's* 221 (August 1960): 8; David Smyth, "Kaiser: Model for Latin America," *Nation,* December 14, 1963, pp. 415–417; "Where Kaiser's Cars Lead the Pack," *Business Week,* November 5, 1966, pp. 114–120.

36. Habron, "Kaiser's Argentine Gamble," p. 3.

37. Kaiser Papers: interoffice memo, Henry Kaiser and Robert C. Elliott to Edgar F. Kaiser and E. E. Trefethen, Jr., August 25, 1954, carton 162; Elliott, "Brazil Steel Projects in Which Kaiser Engineers and/or Steel Might Participate," mimeographed, September 1954, carton 165.

38. Elliott, "50 Years Book." The size of the South American market was very significant in Henry Kaiser's overall automobile production; in fact, it rivaled total sales in the United States. During ten years in domestic sales, Kaiser-Frazer sold 745,928 vehicles; see Richard M. Langworth, *Kaiser-Frazer: The Last Onslaught on Detroit* (Princeton, N.J.: Princeton Publishing Co., 1975), Appendix C, p. 266.

39. Foster, "Giant of the West," pp. 1–23. Kaiser Papers: "Henry J. Kaiser on Industrial Development Tour Sees Vast Opportunities in Latin America," mimeographed, n.d. (ca. 1954), carton 164.

40. Kaiser Papers: "Proposal of Kaiser Motors Corporation to Establish Automotive Manufacturing Company in Mexico," mimeographed, 1954, carton 162; interoffice memo, George Havas to Kaiser, October 27, 1954, carton 163; Kaiser to Dr. Manuel Archila Monroy, November 16, 1954, carton 162; "Latin America and Its Importance for Kaiser Steel Corporation," mimeographed, July 28, 1954, carton 165; "Brief Summary of Incidents in Argentina," memo dictated by Henry Kaiser to Edgar F. Kaiser and E. E. Trefethen, Jr., August 26, 1954, carton 161. *Kaiser*

Facts, 1969 (Oakland: Kaiser Inter-Company Communication Services, 1969), p. 23; "The Kaiser Formula," editorial, *Cincinnati Enquirer*, July 5, 1960.

CHAPTER 11. CARGO PLANES AND GOVERNMENT INVESTIGATIONS

1. Mark S. Foster, "The Flying Lumber Yard: Henry J. Kaiser, Howard Hughes, and the Famous 'Spruce Goose' Caper," *Aerospace Historian* 33:2 (June 1986): 96-103. See also Charles Barton, *Howard Hughes and His Flying Boat* (Fallbrook, Calif.: Aero Publishers, 1982), p. 197; *U.S. Senate Report No. 440, Part 6: Report of the Special Committee Investigating the National Defense Program, 80th Congress, 2nd Session* (Washington, D.C., September 1947), passim.

2. Frank Friedel and Alan Brinkley, *America in the Twentieth Century*, 5th ed. (New York: Knopf, 1976), p. 328. In November 1942, Axis U-boats sank 119 Allied vessels. Thereafter, sinkings declined steadily, as merchantmen learned techniques of self-protection and the U.S. Navy expanded its fleet. See David D. Lewis, *The Fight for the Sea: The Past, Present, and Future of Submarine Warfare in the Atlantic* (Cleveland and New York: World Publishing Co., 1961), p. 230.

3. *Portland Oregonian*, July 20, 1942. In fact, Kaiser had been trying for many months prior to July 1942 to persuade federal officials to permit him to enter the aircraft business. See Edgar F. Kaiser, Sr., Papers, Bancroft Library, University of California, Berkeley: interoffice memo, Chad Calhoun to File memorandum, December 24, 1940, temporary carton II-6-D.

4. For the Joe Kennedy story, see *Washington Times-Herald*, August 10, 1942. De Seversky's ideas were presented in numerous articles in *American Mercury, Reader's Digest*, and other mass-circulation periodicals between mid-1941 and mid-1942. War Production Board (WPB) Papers, RG 179, National Archives, Washington, D.C.: Francis H. Hoge, Jr., to Chairman, Planning Committee, WPB, May 22, 1942, File 314.444, Aircraft, Cargo Production. For a detailed, if biased, account of the early months of negotiation concerning the entire cargo plane issue, see Franklin D. Roosevelt Papers, Franklin D. Roosevelt Library, Hyde Park, N.Y.: Donald M. Nelson to Senator Harry S. Truman, February 11, 1944, PSF 192.

5. "Who Can't?" *Time*, August 24, 1942, pp. 12-13; *New York Telegram*, September 2, 1942. Kaiser Papers: transcript of Boake Carter talk on radio, September 10, 1942, carton III.

Kaiser's rapid ascent as a public figure was assisted by publication of Frank J. Taylor's admiring article about him in 1941. See Taylor, "Builder No. 1," *Saturday Evening Post*, June 7, 1941, pp. 9-11, 120-124.

6. "Planes vs. Ships," *Business Week*, August 1, 1942, pp. 24-27; "Mr. Kaiser Goes to Washington," *Time*, August 10, 1942, pp. 22-23; "The Winner: Kaiser," *Time*, August 17, 1942, pp. 15-16.

7. Henry J. Kaiser Papers, Bancroft Library, Berkeley: mimeographed copy of "Senate Special Committee on Defense Contracts, Investigating the National Defense Program, Testimony of July 29, 1942," pp. 4144-4154, carton 148. Harold L. Ickes Papers, Manuscript Division, Library of Congress, Washington, D.C.: Ickes, "Diary," July 26, 1942, reel 5, p. 6902.

8. Gerald D. Nash, *The Great Depression and World War II* (New York: St. Mar-

tin's Press, 1979), p. 135, Table 1. In fact, established aircraft manufacturers even discussed ways to rid themselves of "the Kaiser problem." See Glenn L. Martin Papers, Library of Congress: Martin to Frank A. Garbutt, September 17, 1942, box 13.

9. Roosevelt Papers: William D. Leahy to Marvin McIntyre, August 1, 1942, OF 5101. "Kaiser's Plan," *San Francisco News,* August 7, 1942.

10. *New York Telegram,* September 1, 1942. Kaiser Papers: Boake Carter, transcript of radio broadcast over WOR network, September 10, 1942, carton 148. *Washington Times,* September 4, 1942.

11. Barton, *Howard Hughes,* pp. 16–17. See also *Los Angeles Times,* June 20, 1971; Clark Mollenhoff, "Howard Hughes' White House Connection," in *The Pentagon* (New York: Putnam, 1967), pp. 94–107; John B. Rae, *Climb to Greatness: The American Aircraft Industry, 1920–1960* (Cambridge, Mass.: MIT Press, 1968), pp. 216–217.

12. Eliot Janeway, "Trial and Errors," *Fortune* 26 (September 1942): 184; Raymond Clapper quoted in "Who Can't?" *Time,* August 24, 1942, pp. 12–13.

13. See, for example, WPB Papers: William L. Batt to Donald M. Nelson, August 14, 1943, File 313.202, Aircraft, Plant Expansion, Construction and Equipment Requirement, 1942–1946.

14. Kaiser Papers: Robert A. Lovett to Nelson, September 12, 1942, carton 23. Roosevelt Papers: Kaiser to U.S. Maritime Commission, November 30, 1942, OF 5101. It is noteworthy that when he and Hughes signed the contract, Kaiser clearly believed it would lead to far bigger things. Ickes reported Kaiser as being "exultantly happy" over the approval for three prototype planes. See Ickes, "Diary," reel 5, September 18, 1942, p. 7111.

15. For example, after his round-the-world flight in a twin engine Lockheed Model 14 Lodestar ending in July 1938, Hughes thoroughly enjoyed a ticker-tape parade in his honor in New York. A decade later he demonstrated his publicity skills again in demolishing his attackers at the Spruce Goose hearings. Despite strained working relations during the years of the partnership, the two men remained friends. Alyce Kaiser, Henry's second wife, recalled Hughes' frequent visits to the Kaiser estate in Hawaii in the 1950s and 1960s (Alyce Kaiser interview, December 5, 1983).

16. Kaiser Papers: E. E. Trefethen, Jr., to Howard Hughes, January 3, 1943, carton 20; interoffice memo, George G. Sherwood to Trefethen, February 2, 1943, carton 23; Kaiser to Hughes, April 10, 1943, carton 145.

17. WPB Papers: Ed Bern to Donald M. Nelson, August 30, 1943, File 314.44072, Aircraft Cargo Production.

18. Roosevelt Papers: Nelson to Truman, February 11, 1944, PSF 192.

19. Ibid.

20. Numerous documents reveal Kaiser's "departure" from the project several months before cancellation. See, for example, U.S. Maritime Commission Papers, National Archives: T. H. Lowry to Charles E. Wilson, October 4, 1943, RG 178, files of E. S. Land, box 3. The $7 million figure is taken from the *Los Angeles Times* story, June 20, 1971. John B. Rae provided the $17 million estimate in *Climb to Greatness,* p. 193.

21. *Kaiser Terminals: A Plan by Henry J. Kaiser* (Oakland: Kaiser Co., 1944); Kaiser Papers: Howard V. Lindbergh to Kaiser, July 12, 1944, carton 26 (Lindbergh is

unrelated to the famous flyer); Sherlock D. Hackley to Trefethen, March 14, 1946, carton 146; Otto B. Koppen to Kaiser, July 13, 1947, carton 35.

22. *New York Times*, March 17, 1943; *New York Herald-Tribune*, November 26, 1943.

23. *Investigation of the Progress of the War Effort: Hearings before a Subcommittee Appointed to Investigate Causes of Failures of Production of Brewster Aeronautical Corporation under Its Contract with the Navy, Committee on Naval Affairs, House of Representatives, 78th Congress*, October 22, 1943, pp. 2561–2598; November 4, 1943, pp. 2973–3121; November 30, 1943, pp. 3639–3748. Kaiser Papers: "Statement to Press by Henry J. Kaiser at Chicago, May 20, 1944," mimeographed, carton 26.

24. James F. Cocks Papers, Bentley Library, University of Michigan, Ann Arbor: Cocks, "Kaiser-Frazer Corporation, 1945–1953," mimeographed, n.d., pp. 104–105.

25. Ibid., pp. 105–106. Kaiser Papers: Kaiser Industries press release, December 5, 1950, carton 316. *Congressional Record, House*, May 21, 1952, pp. 5784–5785.

26. *Congressional Record, House*, May 21, 1952, p. 5785.

27. *American Aviation Daily of Washington, D.C.*, December 21, 1950. Kaiser Papers: "First Draft," Statement on Cargo Plane Contract, December 26, 1950, carton 57.

28. Cocks, "Kaiser-Frazer Corporation," pp. 110–111.

29. Ibid., pp. 146–149.

30. Kaiser Papers: "Munitions Board Report 3-C: 100 Companies Ranked by Volume of Military Prime Contracts in Fiscal Year 1951," mimeographed, n.d. (ca. 1952), p. 5, carton 55. Kaiser executives pointed out that unfavorable comparisons with Fairchild were based on skewed figures. Initial units produced in any plant would obviously be more expensive; once assembly lines ran more smoothly, costs declined. For O'Konski charges, see Cocks, "Kaiser-Frazer Corporation," p. 150; *Congressional Record, House*, May 21, 1952, pp. 5783–5787.

31. Kaiser Papers: Kaiser to Alvin E. O'Konski, May 26, 1952, carton 79.

32. Kaiser Papers: Calhoun, "Notes of Meeting with O'Konski in His Office, May 31, 1952," mimeographed, and Calhoun, memo, "Meeting with O'Konski in His Office, May 31, 1952," mimeographed, both in carton 80.

33. "New Kaiser Investigation?" *Aviation Week*, June 2, 1952, p. 12. Kaiser Papers: Walston S. Brown to Kaiser, June 2, 1952, carton 79.

34. Kaiser Papers: Calhoun to File memorandum, June 13, 1952, carton 79.

35. Kaiser Papers: "1 P.M. Official News Release from the Office of Alvin E. O'Konski," June 18, 1952, copy in carton 79. *Congressional Record*, June 19, 1952, p. A4060.

36. *Congressional Record*, July 5, 1952, pp. A5029–A5030; "O'Konski Renews Attack on Kaiser," *Aviation Week*, August 25, 1952, p. 18. Kaiser Papers: "News Release from Office of O'Konski," October 15, 1952, carton 79.

37. "Kaiser Faces the Music," *Reporter*, July 20, 1954, p. 16.

38. Kaiser Papers: Edgar Kaiser to Styles Bridges, November 13, 1952, carton 339.

39. "More Trouble for Kaiser," *Time*, November 24, 1952, pp. 104–105; "Leaps but Doesn't Look" (editorial), *Washington Post*, November 30, 1952. Kaiser Papers: interoffice memo, Calhoun to Edgar Kaiser, November 24, 1952, carton 81.

40. Kaiser Papers: Mark E. Bradley, Jr., to Kaiser Manufacturing Corporation, December 5, 1952, quoted in interoffice memo, W. Riggs to Edgar Kaiser, December 8, 1952, carton 81.

41. Cocks Papers: Edgar Kaiser to Bradley, December 18, 1952.

42. "Kaiser Deal Spurs New Drive on C-123," *Aviation Weekly,* May 21, 1954, pp. 13–14; "Willow Run Getting Ready to Roll," *Aviation Week,* September 10, 1951, pp. 19–20. Kaiser Papers: Clay Bedford to Mike Stroukoff, July 24, 1952; Edgar Kaiser to Stroukoff, February 9, 1953, and March 26, 1953; and Edgar Kaiser, "Notes of Meeting with Stroukoff, February 13, 1953," all in carton 95; interoffice memo, Calhoun to Harry F. Morton, March 13, 1953, carton 96.

43. Kaiser Papers: interoffice memo, Calhoun to Edgar Kaiser, May 17, 1953, carton 96. As early as March 1953, Eaton believed that Kaiser's C-119 contract was already dead in the water, and he was working to assure that the westerner would have no chance for future contracts for the C-123; see Cyrus Eaton Papers, Western Reserve Historical Society, Cleveland: "Memorandum for Mr. Lane," March 10, 1953, container 4553.

44. "C-119 Hearing," *Aviation Week,* June 8, 1953, pp. 17–18.

45. "Autopsy at Willow Run," *Fortune* 48 (August 1953): 76–80.

46. Dwight D. Eisenhower Papers, Dwight D. Eisenhower Library, Abilene, Kans.: Col. Harry Smith to Eisenhower, June 5, 1953, in Records as President, Alpha File, box 2901.

47. *Charlotte* (N.C.) *Observer,* June 14, 1953; "Air Power Is Sabotaged," *Aviation Week,* June 15, 1953, p. 94; *Washington Star,* June 14, 1953; "The Kaisers Face the Music," *Reporter,* July 20, 1953, p. 17.

48. *Washington Star,* June 14, 1953; *San Francisco News,* June 18, 1953.

49. Cocks, "Kaiser-Frazer Corporation," pp. 175–177; "Autopsy at Willow Run," pp. 78–80; "USAF Axes Kaiser Aircraft Role," *Aviation Week,* June 29, 1953, pp. 16–17; "Kaiser Cancellation," *Life,* July 6, 1953, p. 22.

50. *Wall Street Journal,* June 25, 1953.

51. Kaiser Papers: interoffice memo, Calhoun to File memorandum, July 9, 1953, carton 96.

52. Ibid.

53. *San Francisco News,* June 18, 1953.

CHAPTER 12. LIGHT METALS—HEAVY PROFITS

1. See Mimi Stein, *A Special Difference: A History of Kaiser Aluminum & Chemical Corporation* (Oakland: Kaiser Aluminum & Chemical Corporation, 1980). Although this is a sponsored history with a pro-company perspective, Stein points out ill-advised decisions too.

2. "Aluminum Reborn," *Fortune* 33 (May 1946): 103–108, 212–220; "The Arrival of Henry Kaiser," *Fortune* 44 (July 1951): 68–73, 141–154; Robert Sheehan, "Kaiser Aluminum: Henry J's Fabulous Mistake," *Fortune* 54 (July 1956): 78–84, 172–175. Henry J. Kaiser Papers, Bancroft Library, University of California, Berkeley: Robert C. Elliott, "50 Year Book," ms., n.d. (ca. 1964), carton 295; Kaiser to Harold L. Ickes, February 22, 1941, carton 7.

3. Department of Interior Papers, RG 48, National Archives, Washington, D.C.: Kaiser to Ickes, February 22, 1941, and Ickes to Frank Knox, February 24, 1941, both in Office of Secretary, Central Classified Files, 1937–1953, box 2791. Kaiser Papers: Ickes to Knox, n.d. (ca. March 1941), carton 7. Harold L. Ickes Papers,

Manuscript Division, Library of Congress, Washington, D.C.: Ickes, "Diary," February 22, 1941, reel 4, p. 5244.

Frank Knox, Secretary of the Navy, voiced skepticism concerning Kaiser's ability to handle such a big job, along with the start-up of magnesium operations and all his other projects. In essence, Kaiser's aluminum proposal got a "fast shuffle." See Interior Papers: Knox to Ickes, February 22, 1941, and Abe Fortas to Ferdinand Eberstadt, January 13, 1943, both in box 2791.

4. For overviews of magnesium, see Stein, *A Special Difference*, pp. 5–9; "The Earth Movers, III," *Fortune* 28 (October 1943): 21–22. The latter analysis is especially critical of Kaiser's government borrowing. When Chad Calhoun read preliminary drafts of the *Fortune* article, he objected heatedly and tried to persuade magazine editors that their criticisms were not based on facts. See Kaiser Papers: Calhoun to Janet McEnany, "Draft," August 16, 1943, carton 19. See also *Facts about Henry J. Kaiser*, pamphlet (Oakland: Kaiser Co., September 19, 1946), p. 22.

5. Franklin D. Roosevelt Papers, Franklin D. Roosevelt Library, Hyde Park, N.Y.: FBI Report, June 30, 1944, "Association with Dr. Fritz Hansgirg, Alien Enemy," PSF 155. Several Kaiser men commented on Hansgirg's large ego (Theodore A. Dungan interview, February 27, 1984; George Scheer interview, January 17, 1984; James E. Toomey interview, January 11, 1984).

6. War Production Board (WPB) Papers, RG 179, National Archives: National Academy of Sciences, National Research Council, "Report on the Hansgirg Magnesium Process, July 7, 1941," file 529.481, box 1640; "Report Given by Arthur H. Bunker at Staff Meeting, 8:30 A.M., August 12, 1941," Policy Documentation File, 529.422, box 1637.

7. WPB Papers: interoffice memo, Arthur H. Bunker to William L. Batt, March 24, 1942, and G. V. Hartwell to S. W. Anderson, June 16, 1942, both in Policy Documentation File, 529.481, box 1640. U.S. Maritime Commission Papers, National Archives: confidential memo, John M. Carmody to Admiral Emory S. Land, November 15, 1944, box 15. Carmody had a point; although Kaiser paid off loans from the RFC to build the plant, government agencies contracting for magnesium paid for development costs.

8. Kaiser Papers: "Permanente Magnesium," mimeographed, March 11, 1943, and Duncan Low to Permanente Metals, December 2, 1943, both in carton 153; "Products of Permanente Magnesium," mimeographed, July 1943, carton 256; interoffice memo, H. V. Lindbergh to Morton F. McCartney, September 20, 1943, carton 153. *Facts about Henry J. Kaiser*, p. 22.

9. *Facts about Henry J. Kaiser*, pp. 22–23; Kaiser Papers: "Speech by Captain G. E. Dawson, Chemical Warfare Service, U.S. Army "E" Award Ceremony, August 29, 1945, mimeographed, carton 180.

10. Philip F. Cashier, "Natural Resource Management during the Second World War" (Ph.D. dissertation, State University of New York at Binghamton, 1980), pp. 99–114. Kaiser Papers: Thurman Arnold to Kaiser, March 16, 1943, carton 19. Hugh Fulton Papers, Harry S. Truman Presidential Library, Independence, Mo.: Calhoun, interoffice memo, October 2, 1944, box 3.

11. Fulton Papers: "Preliminary Confidential Draft, Statement of Henry J. Kaiser before Senate Small Business Committee," February 28, 1945, box 3. *New York Times*, Marcy 7, 1945.

12. "Aluminum Reborn," p. 105; Sheehan, "Kaiser Aluminum," p. 82. Mimi Stein states that Don Browne and Thomas Ready shared Kaiser's vision in aluminum. See *A Special Difference,* p. 14.

13. "The Arrival of Henry Kaiser," p. 150; Sheehan, "Kaiser Aluminum," pp. 81–82. James F. McCloud recounted Eugene E. Trefethen's role in encouraging the boss to enter aluminum (McCloud to author, August 5, 1986).

14. "The Arrival of Henry Kaiser," p. 150; Sheehan, "Kaiser Aluminum," p. 82. For more details on the antritrust case by the Justice Department against Alcoa, see Irwin M. Stelzer, ed., *Selected Antitrust Cases* (Homewood, Ill., 1955), p. 19.

15. Clay P. Bedford interview by Mimi Stein, May 10, 1982, transcript, Oral History Associates, San Francisco, p. 108.

16. Elliott, "50 Year Book," Sheehan, "Kaiser Aluminum," p. 79; Stein, *A Special Difference,* p. 68.

17. Elliott, "50 Year Book," Sheehan, "Kaiser Aluminum," p. 80.

18. "Aluminum Reborn," p. 216.

19. Sheehan, "Kaiser Aluminum," pp. 82, 172; *Kaiser Aluminum & Chemical Annual Report,* 1952, p. 5. Kaiser Papers: interoffice memo, Calhoun to Kaiser, July 8, 1947, carton 302. Stein, *A Special Difference,* p. 42.

20. Kaiser Papers: Julius A. Krug to John A. Steelman, July 11, 1949, copy, carton 57; "Draft of Suggested Statement," November 7, 1949, carton 51.

21. Kaiser Papers: interoffice memo, Calhoun to Kaiser, July 8, 1947, carton 302; Kaiser to Emanuel Celler, October 10, 1949, carton 43; interoffice memos, Calhoun to Kaiser, February 14, 1950, carton 57, and March 7, 1951, carton 63.

22. Kaiser Papers: Kaiser to Roscoe Seybold, October 3, 1950, carton 57.

23. Stein, *A Special Difference,* pp. 44–45; Elliott, "50 Year Book," M. J. Robards, "Another Battle Comes to Chalmette," *L&N Employees' Magazine,* April 1952, pp. 4–17.

24. Kaiser Papers: telegram, Kaiser to Oscar L. Chapman, May 12, 1951, and "Conference with Secretary of Interior Oscar L. Chapman, May 21, 1951," p. 5, both in carton 63. *New York World-Telegram,* November 10, 1951.

25. Robards, "Another Battle," p. 6.

26. For an account of the severity of power shortages in the Pacific Northwest, see *New York Times,* September 30, 1951; for the Kaiser anecdote, see Leonard Lyon, "The Lyon's Den," *New York Post,* December 14, 1951.

27. "New Financing Program for Kaiser Aluminum," *Business Week,* February 3, 1951, p. 79; "The Arrival of Henry Kaiser," p. 14.

28. Sheehan, "Kaiser Aluminum," pp. 79–80; "Kaiser Aluminum Grows," *American Metal Market,* December 16, 1954, reprint; "Kaiser's Jamaica Bauxite Story," *Finance,* March 15, 1960, pp. 43–60.

29. Sheehan, "Kaiser Aluminum," p. 80.

30. For conflicting analyses of patterns of western industrial development in the twentieth century, see Gerald D. Nash, *The American West in the Twentieth Century: A Short History of an Urban Oasis* (Englewood Cliffs, N.J.: Prentice Hall, 1973), and Peter Wiley and Robert Gottlieb, *Empires in the Sun: The Rise of the New American West* (New York: G. P. Putnam's Sons, 1982).

31. Sheehan, "Kaiser Aluminum," pp. 79–80. Kaiser Papers: Kaiser to John L. Lewis, September 24, 1954, carton 101. "Kaiser Aluminum Grows."

32. *Parkersburg* (W. Va.) *News*, June 1, 1955; *Welch* (W.Va.) *Daily News*, June 1, 1955.

33. See two articles entitled "Aluminum" in *American Metal Markets*, June 15 and 16, 1955.

34. "Rebirth of the Ohio," *Time*, February 2, 1957, p. 81; "The Turning Point," *West Virginia School Journal* 92 (May 1964): reprint.

35. Sheehan, "Kaiser Aluminum," p. 175.

36. "The Turning Point"; *Kaiser Aluminum & Chemical Annual Report*, 1967, p. 22.

37. Kaiser Papers: Kaiser to Hans Eggers, June 4, 1954, carton 100; Robert C. Elliott, "Aluminum Potentials," mimeographed report, 1958, carton 121.

38. Carton 166 in the Kaiser Papers contains many of the original drawings and prototypes of Kaiser aluminum boats. The company started its own publication, *Aluminum Boats*, in the early 1960s in an effort to stimulate interest in its products.

39. "Two Days to Build a Dome," *Business Week*, February 2, 1957, pp. 75–76.

40. Ibid.; "Fuller's Dome Catches On at Last," *Business Week*, May 10, 1958, pp. 112, 116.

41. Lambreth Hancock, "He Could Sell Ice Boxes to Eskimos," mimeographed, in possession of Hancock. Kaiser Papers: Kaiser to E. E. Trefethen, Jr., interoffice memo, July 5, 1963, carton 224.

42. Milt Eisele to author, February 10, 1984. Kaiser Papers: interoffice memo, Kaiser to Donald A. Rhoades, March 4, 1955, carton 186.

43. *Kaiser Aluminum & Chemical Annual Report*, 1966, p. 22; *Kaiser Industries Annual Report*, 1966, pp. 2–26, passim.

CHAPTER 13. KAISER AND THE DOCTORS

1. Figures provided by Donald A. Duffy, Vice President, Public and Community Relations, Kaiser Foundation Health Plan, Inc., in letter to author, January 29, 1986. The legal history of the Kaiser Permanente Medical Care Program is quite complex, and the plan experienced numerous name changes and structural reorganizations. In this chapter, I will simplify matters by using the acronym KPMCP throughout.

2. *American Medical Association* (AMA), Commission on Medical Plans, "Report, Part 2," *Journal of the AMA*, January 17, 1959; Peter N. Grant, draft of Ph.D. dissertation in progress, Harvard University, prologue, p. 72; Jerome L. Schwartz, "Early History of Prepaid Medical Care Plans," *Bulletin of the History of Medicine* 39 (September/October 1965): 850–851, 856; Keith Sward, *The Legend of Henry Ford* (New York: Atheneum, 1968), pp. 136–140.

3. The best overview of the emergence of the medical profession is Paul Starr, *The Social Transformation of American Medicine* (New York: Basic Books, 1982); for more data on the rise of early prepaid health groups, see Keith L. Bryant and Henry C. Dethloff, *A History of American Business* (Englewood Cliffs, N.J.: Prentice Hall, 1983), p. 264. The definitive study of the KPMCP is Rickey L. Hendricks, "A Necessary Revolution: The Origins of the Kaiser-Permanente Medical Care Program" (Ph.D. dissertation, University of Denver, 1987).

4. Six Companies Papers, Bancroft Library, University of California, Berke-

ley: newspaper clipping from *San Francisco News,* February 2, 1932, in scrapbook, vol. 6.

5. Cecil C. Cutting, M.D., "Kaiser-Permanente Program History," final draft, mimeographed, July 15, 1983, pp. 4–5, in possession of Cutting. Experimentation with prepaid health insurance on remote construction jobs in southern California began long before the 1930s. When the Los Angeles Aqueduct was built between 1908 and 1913, contractors made very similar arrangements for medical care. See Doyce B. Nunis, ed., *Men, Medicine and Water: The Builders of the Los Angeles Aqueduct, 1908–1918; A Physician's Recollections by Raymond G. Taylor, M.D.* (Los Angeles: Friends of the Los Angeles County Medical Association and Los Angeles Department of Water and Power, 1982), p. 153.

6. Cutting, "Kaiser-Permanente Program History," pp. 5–6; Dr. Sidney R. Garfield interview, January 16, 1984. Henry J. Kaiser Papers, Bancroft Library: Robert C. Elliott, "The Hospital in the Desert," mimeographed, n.d. (ca. 1964), pp. 6–7, carton 295.

7. Garfield interview, January 16, 1984.

8. Paul de Kruif, *Kaiser Wakes the Doctors* (New York: Harcourt Brace, 1943), p. 21.

9. Garfield interview, January 16, 1984; Scott Fleming interview, January 10, 1984.

10. Cutting, "Kaiser-Permanente Program History," p. 8; Garfield interview, January 16, 1984; Dr. Cecil C. Cutting interview, January 12, 1984.

11. Garfield interview, January 16, 1984; Cutting interview, January 12, 1984.

12. Kaiser Papers: "Origin and Development of the Principles of the Kaiser Health Plan," mimeographed, n.d. (ca. 1945), carton 330.

13. Garfield interview, January 16, 1984.

14. Sidney R. Garfield, *Report on Permanente's First Ten Years,* pamphlet (Oakland: Kaiser Co., 1953), p. 1; "Origin and Development of the Principles of the Kaiser Health Plan," pp. 3–4; Cutting, "Kaiser-Permanente Program History," pp. 10–12; Duffy to author, January 29, 1986. For an "established physician" perspective on Garfield's efforts in the Bay Area, see Kaiser Papers: J. Philo Nelson to Kaiser, February 4, 1943, carton 330.

15. Kaiser Papers: Sidney R. Garfield, "First Annual Report of the Permanente Foundation Hospital," mimeographed, n.d. (ca. 1943), carton 330. Cutting, "Kaiser Permanente Program History," pp. 11–13; Elliott, "Hospital in the Desert," p. 12.

16. Kaiser Papers: Kaiser to Robert F. Wagner, December 30, 1944, carton 30; "Origin and Development of the Principles of the Kaiser Health Plan," p. 7.

17. Fleming interview, January 10, 1984. Kaiser Papers: Lloyd Kindall (M.D.) to John R. Green, December 21, 1943, and Sally Bolotin to Kindall, January 13, 1944, both in carton 309; Garfield to Kaiser, March 14, 1944, carton 175.

18. *Hearings before a Subcommittee of the Committee on Education and Labor, U.S. Senate, 77th Congress, Second Session, on Senate Resolution 291, Part I, November 6, 1942,* pp. 325–347; *New York Times,* November 14, 1942.

19. Milton Mayer, "The Rise and Fall of Dr. Fishbein," *Harper's* 199 (November 1949): 76–85. Kaiser Papers: Harold M. Landsman to Kaiser, November 17, 1942, carton 15. David R. Hyde and Payson Wolf, "The AMA: Power, Purpose, and Politics in Organized Medicine," *Yale Law School Journal* 63 : 7 (May 1954): 1011.

20. Kaiser Papers: "Health Plan Membership for Selected Years," mimeo-

graphed, n.d. (ca. 1969), carton 339; "Membership Growth," chart, n.d. (ca. 1956), carton 124.

21. Garfield interview, January 16, 1984; Cutting, "Kaiser Permanente Program History," p. 14.

22. "Health Plan Membership for Selected Years."

23. Fleming interview, January 10, 1984. Kaiser Papers: unidentified newspaper clipping, October 1947, carton 103.

24. Kaiser Papers: Horace R. Hansen to Garfield, November 25, 1947; Garfield to Hansen, December 15, 1947, both in carton 309; "Remarks Made by Henry J. Kaiser before Doctors' Group—St. Francis Hotel, June 9, 1948," mimeographed, carton 103.

25. Much of the analysis in this paragraph is borrowed from Hendricks, "A Necessary Revolution." Kaiser Papers: telegram, Eugene E. Trefethen, Jr., to Dr. Paul de Kruif, July 20, 1951, carton 67.

26. Kaiser Papers: interoffice memos, Robert C. Elliott to Kaiser, January 31, 1950, carton 56, and Trefethen to Dr. Richard Bullis, January 24, 1952, carton 77; Ernest Besig to Kaiser, October 8, 1951, carton 67.

27. Kaiser Papers: Chet Huntley, untitled, mimeographed copy of radio report, September 10, 1952, 5:30, over ABC network, Los Angeles, carton 78.

28. Duffy to author, January 29, 1986; de Kruif, *Kaiser Wakes the Doctors;* de Kruif, "How Can We Have Better Medicine?" *Alameda–Contra Costa California Medical Association Bulletin,* November 1952. Kaiser Papers: Paul de Kruif, "A Defense against Socialized Medicine?" *California Medicine* 78 : 1 (January 1953), mimeographed, carton 89.

29. Paul Foster, "Outlooks for Medicine, 1953," *Bulletin of the Los Angeles County Medical Association,* March 5, 1953. Kaiser Papers: Henry J. Kaiser, "AMA Declares War—The Challenge is Accepted," mimeographed, March 26, 1953, and telegram, Calhoun to Kaiser, March 27, 1953, both in carton 92; interoffice memo, Calhoun to Kaiser, March 27, 1953, carton 91.

30. Kaiser Papers: "Proposed Resolution for the Consideration of the Council," April 20, 1953, mimeographed, copy in carton 91. Dr. Raymond M. Kay interview, April 4, 1984; Kay, *Historical Review of the Southern California Permanente Medical Group* (Los Angeles: Southern California Permanente Medical Group, 1979), pp. 132–134.

31. "Sneak Attack Made on Kaiser Medical Plan," *Long Beach Labor News,* April 24, 1953. Kaiser Papers: William G. Riley to Paul Steil, May 14, 1953, carton 91; Foster, "Let's Get Practical," *Bulletin of the Los Angeles County Medical Association,* August 6, 1953, mimeographed, carton 92.

32. Kaiser Papers: unidentified newspaper clipping, November 6, 1945, carton 183.

33. Kaiser Papers: Kaiser to Northern California Advisory Committee to the Selective Service System, August 28, 1952; interoffice memo, Kaiser to Garfield, October 17, 1952; Kaiser to Vice Admiral L. T. DuBose, November 26, 1952; all in carton 77; interoffice memo, Charles Thomas to Kaiser, November 23, 1955, carton 116; Winnie C. Warren to Kaiser, February 15, 1957, carton 124.

34. Kaiser Papers: Kaiser to Selective Service System, Alameda County Local No. 49, April 13, 1954, carton 104; R. L. Black to Garfield, January 14, 1955, carton

77; "Confidential Memo, Record of Phone Call, March 18, 1955, between Kaiser and General Hershey," mimeographed, carton 116.

35. Joseph Garbarino, *Health Plans and Collective Bargaining* (Berkeley and Los Angeles: University of California Press, 1960), p. 96. Kaiser Papers: Kaiser to Dwight L. Wilbur, M.D., September 3, 1953, carton 92.

36. Kaiser Papers: "Essential Key Physician Executives, Summary Statement by Permanente Medical Groups, Kaiser Foundation Health Plan," mimeographed, December 6, 1955, carton 309.

37. Kay, *Historical Review,* pp. 3–12.

38. Garbarino, *Health Plans and Collective Bargaining,* pp. 162–166.

39. Ibid., pp. 184–187.

40. Ibid., pp. 195–196.

41. Ibid., p. 196.

42. Ibid., pp. 204–205, chart 9.1; Anne R. Somers, ed., *The Kaiser-Permanente Medical Group Program* (New York: Commonwealth Fund, 1971), pp. 47–48; Kay, *Historical Review,* pp. 3–12; Scott Fleming, "Chapter One—Kaiser Foundation Medical Care History," mimeographed (Oakland: Kaiser Foundation Health Plan, August 25, 1983), pp. 18–19.

43. Kay interview, April 4, 1984.

44. Kaiser Papers: Kaiser to Frank A. Carvor et al., October 24, 1947, carton 36.

45. Edward R. Weinerman Papers, Sterling Library, Yale University: Kay to Garfield, September 10, 1951, and Weinerman, untitled resignation speech, September 11, 1951, mimeographed, both in box 29, folder 86. Kay interview, April 4, 1984. See also Fleming, "Chapter One," p. 24.

46. Kaiser Papers: "Remarks of Henry J. Kaiser to be Given at Walnut Creek, May 15, 1953," mimeographed, carton 93; interoffice memos, Kaiser to Dr. Wallace J. Neighbor, September 16, 1953, carton 91, and Kaiser to J. F. Reis, December 15, 1953, carton 89. *San Francisco Chronicle,* December 15, 1953.

47. Kaiser Papers: interoffice memo, Kaiser to Trefethen, October 19, 1953, and Kaiser to Garfield, October 19, 1953, both in carton 89. Fleming interview, January 10, 1984.

48. For an excellent account of this dramatic and very divisive confrontation, see Hendricks, "A Necessary Revolution."

49. Garfield interview, January 16, 1984; Cutting interview, January 12, 1984; Fleming interview, January 10, 1984.

50. Dr. Clifford H. Keene interview, July 11, 1986; Garfield interview, January 16, 1984; Cutting interview, January 12, 1984; Fleming interview, January 10, 1984. See also *Oakland Tribune,* December 11, 1953; Kaiser Papers: Kaiser Foundation Hospital "Press Release," mimeographed, December 11, 1953, carton 98.

51. Kaiser Papers: Kaiser to Garfield, December 5, 1953, and Kaiser to Dr. Morris F. Collen, December 17, 1953, both in carton 89. In subsequent years, Kaiser occasionally became very impatient with Keene, accusing him of "balling up" several projects. See interoffice memo, Kaiser to Trefethen, February 27, 1959, carton 250; "Relationship between the Kaiser Foundation and Permanente Physicians," mimeographed, n.d. (ca. March 1, 1955), carton 116.

52. Kaiser Papers: interoffice memo, Dr. August L. Baritell et al., to Edgar F. Kaiser and E. E. Trefethen, Jr., May 12, 1955, and Henry J. Kaiser to "Dear Doctor,"

May 19, 1955, both in carton 116; untitled, mimeographed memo from Henry J. Kaiser, June 6, 1955, carton 117.

53. Garfield interview, January 16, 1984; Cutting interview, January 12, 1984; Fleming interview, January 10, 1984; Kay, *Historical Review,* p. 84, Appendix VII.

54. Kay, *Historical Review,* pp. 84, 86.

55. Kaiser Papers: telegrams, Kaiser to Garfield, February 6, 1958, and Garfield to Kaiser, February 7, 1958, both in carton 250.

56. Keene to author, August 15, 1986; "Health Plan Membership for Selected Years"; Fleming interview, January 10, 1984.

57. Kaiser Papers: A. C. Scott, M.D., to Henry A. Wallace, February 4, 1953, carton 309; Fiorello La Guardia to Kaiser, May 20, 1944, carton 37; Kaiser to Robert F. Wagner, December 30, 1944, carton 30; Kaiser to Claude Pepper, June 1, 1945, carton 185; Kaiser to Mrs. Albert D. Lasker, November 21, 1945, carton 29.

58. Monte Poen, *Harry S. Truman versus the Medical Lobby: The Genius of Medicare* (Columbia: University of Missouri Press, 1979); James M. Neill, M.D., "Does Medical Care Lengthen Life?" *New York Herald Tribune,* May 8, 1949. Kaiser Papers: "A National Health Plan by Henry J. Kaiser," mimeographed, n.d. (ca. 1948), carton 309.

59. Kaiser Papers: Kaiser, "Kaiser Medical Center Program," mimeographed, October 3, 1952, carton 77; "Henry J. Kaiser, President, the Kaiser Foundation, Introductory Statement for House Committee on Interstate and Foreign Commerce, Washington, D.C., January, 1953," mimeographed, carton 93.

60. Dwight D. Eisenhower Papers, Dwight D. Eisenhower Library, Abilene, Kans.: Calhoun, memo for Sherman Adams, Assistant to the President, January 27, 1953, Official File, box 598, "Health—1" file folder. Kaiser Papers: interoffice memo, Calhoun to Kaiser, January 23, 1953, carton 88.

61. Kaiser Papers, interoffice memos: Robert C. Elliott to Garfield et al., November 14, 1953, carton 88; Elliott to Calhoun, November 30, 1953, and Calhoun to Kaiser, December 16, 1953, both in carton 93.

62. Kaiser Papers: "From the President: State of the Union Message, January 7, 1954," mimeographed, and telegram, Calhoun to Kaiser, June 28, 1954, both in carton 107; interoffice memo, Kaiser to Calhoun, January 17, 1955, carton 117. *AMA Report on the Medical Sciences* (Washington, D.C., March 29, 1954).

63. Fleming interview, January 10, 1984; Kaiser Papers: interoffice memo, Elliott to Kaiser, March 5, 1962, carton 311.

64. Kaiser Papers: interoffice memo, Henry J. Kaiser to Edgar F. Kaiser, November 24, 1964, and Edgar F. Kaiser to Lyndon B. Johnson, February 1, 1965, both in carton 264.

65. In the mid-1960s the AFL-CIO presented Kaiser with its coveted Murray-Green Award, honoring him for making quality medical care more affordable for families of working-class Americans.

According to medical historian Paul Starr, in 1979 there were 217 HMOs nationwide, covering only 4 percent of the American public that year. Estimating growth of HMOs during the 1980s, health officials predicted 10 percent national coverage by 1990. See Starr, *The Social Transformation of American Medicine,* p. 415. Actual increases are running ahead of this prediction. The U.S. Bureau of the Census, *Statistical Abstract of the United States,* 108th ed. (Washington, D.C.: Department of

Commerce, 1987), p. 93, reports that at the end of 1986 there were 595 HMOs in the United States, with total enrollment of 23,664,000. In a letter dated December 19, 1988, Donald A. Duffy, Vice President of Public and Community Relations, Kaiser Foundation Health Plan, Inc., informed me that by mid-1988 there were 650 HMOs in the nation, with a total enrollment of 32 million; thus 13 percent of the U.S. population was covered by an HMO. Kaiser Permanente, with 5.5 million members, accounted for 17 percent of total HMO enrollment.

CHAPTER 14. BOSS

1. Thomas H. Peters and Robert H. Waterman, Jr., *In Search of Excellence* (New York: Warner Books, 1982).

2. Mrs. Tom M. (Alice) Price interview, January 20, 1984.

3. Gerard Piel, "No. 1 Shipbuilder," *Life,* June 29, 1942, pp. 81–89.

4. Henry J. Kaiser Papers, Bancroft Library, University of California, Berkeley: Henry J. Kaiser quoting Edgar in speech to Industrial Relations Conference, Claremont Hotel, Berkeley, April 6, 1956, mimeographed, carton 125.

5. "Kaiser-Frazer: The Roughest Thing We Ever Tackled," *Fortune* 44 (July 1951): 11.

6. Clay P. Bedford interview by Mimi Stein, May 3, 1982, transcript, Oral History Associates, San Francisco.

7. Kaiser Papers: George Sherwood to W. A. Bechtel Company, June 8, 1943, carton 18.

8. James F. McCloud to author, February 11, 1984.

9. For an excellent insight into how the process worked, see Kaiser Papers: interoffice memo, Chad Calhoun to Eugene E. Trefethen, Jr., October 27, 1942, carton 13.

10. Louis H. Oppenheim interview, January 17, 1984.

11. Kaiser Papers: interoffice memo, Kaiser to Trefethen, December 12, 1941, carton 9.

12. Kaiser Papers: "Quotes from Henry J. Kaiser's Speeches," mimeographed, n.d. (ca. 1962), carton 294. William Soule, prologue to ms., "Life with Kaiser," n.d. (ca. 1981).

13. Tudor A. Wall interview, January 12, 1984; Peter S. Hass interview, January 10, 1984.

14. *New Orleans Times-Picayune,* December 11, 1951. Several former company executives brought up the matter of infrequent divorces during extensive interviews in January 1984.

15. Kaiser Papers: "So What," mimeographed recollection of T. M. Price, April 27, 1950, carton 349. K. Tim Yee, interview, January 19, 1984; Wall interview, January 12, 1984.

16. Bedford interview by Stein, May 3, 1982.

17. Robert C. Elliott, "The Road," rough draft of chapter in "50 Year Book," in possession of Alex Troffey; Hass interview, January 10, 1984; Lambreth Hancock, untitled ms., n.d. (ca. 1984), in possession of Hancock. n.p.

18. Yee interview, January 19, 1984.

19. Tim A. Bedford interview, January 13, 1984.

20. Hancock, untitled ms. Kaiser Papers: interoffice memo, Calhoun to Kaiser, July 5, 1949, carton 40.

21. Hancock, untitled ms.; Wall interview, January 12, 1984.

22. Hass interview, January 10, 1984; Leonard Lyon, "The Lyon's Den," *New York Post*, September 21, 1944.

23. Hancock, untitled ms.; Tim A. Bedford interview, January 13, 1984; Doris Kearns, *Lyndon Johnson and the American Dream* (New York: Harper and Row, 1976), p. 253.

24. Hancock, untitled ms.

25. Henry Kaiser, Jr., quoted in "Henry J. Kaiser," *Fortune* 28 (October 1943): 249. Kaiser Papers: Leland Cutler, "Henry Kaiser," mimeographed tribute, n.d., carton 94.

26. Kaiser Papers: "Service Awards Celebration, December 17, 1952, Colonial Ballroom, St. Francis Hotel, San Francisco," mimeographed, carton 83.

27. Peters and Waterman, *In Search of Excellence,* passim.

28. Hancock, untitled ms.

29. Clay Bedford interview by Stein, May 3, 1982; Wall interview, Januar7 12, 1984.

30. Tim A. Bedford interview, January 13, 1984; Alyce Kaiser interview, December 5, 1983.

31. Hancock, untitled ms.

32. David C. Slipher interview, March 18, 1984.

33. Mansel G. Blackford and K. Austin Kerr, *Business Enterprise in American History* (Boston: Houghton Mifflin, 1986), pp. 278–279.

34. During the 1950s and early 1960s, when Detroit's products dominated domestic markets and sold well overseas, industry publications were extremely self-congratulatory concerning managerial development and innovation. Over the past quarter-century, however, historians have generally become more critical of the managerial performances of Big Three producers. The most sanguine scholarly account of the achievement of American producers is John B. Rae, *The Road and Car in American Life* (Cambridge, Mass.: MIT Press, 1971). With the "invasion" of foreign makes, concern over product safety, the energy crisis, and increasingly sophisticated inquiries into the impact of the automobile upon the quality of American life, historians have grown far more critical. See, for example, James J. Flink, *The Car Culture* (Cambridge, Mass.: MIT Press, 1975), and Lawrence J. White, *The American Automobile Industry since 1945* (Cambridge, Mass.: MIT Press, 1971). See also David Halberstam, *The Reckoning* (New York: Avon Books, 1986).

35. "Will Kaiser Reorganize?" *Business Week,* September 10, 1949, pp. 24–26; *Wall Street Journal,* January 30, 1956.

36. Almost every Kaiser executive I interviewed observed that overcoming the image of government favoritism was a crucial corporate objective after World War II.

37. *Wall Street Journal,* January 30, 1956; Donald A. Duffy to author, February 13, 1987; *Kaiser Industries Corporation, Annual Report,* 1955, p. 4.

38. *Kaiser Industries/Annual Report,* 1956, p. 4.

39. Numerous students of managerial development have emphasized these points. See Walter Bennis, *The Unconscious Conspiracy: Why Leaders Can't Manage* (New York: Amacon, 1976), p. 174; James M. Burns, *Leadership* (New York: Harper and

Row, 1978), p. 20; David McClelland, *Power: the Inner Experience* (New York: Irvington, 1975), pp. 259–260.

40. Hass interview, January 10, 1984; Wall interview, January 12, 1984. An astute critic of the conglomerate "fad" in the 1960s and early 1970s observed that the diversification worked best when corporations took over companies which performed tasks very close to their own primary functions. When they took over businesses in which they had little or no experience (typically for tax purposes), overall corporate effectiveness and profit ratios generally dropped off. Although Kaiser's companies were "internally developed," long-term corporate performance mirrored these tendencies. See Richard Rumelt, *Strategy, Structure, and Economic Performance* (Cambridge, Mass.: Harvard University Graduate School of Business Administration, 1974).

41. Kaiser Papers: Kaiser to James T. Nolan, June 28, 1965, carton 265. Several of Kaiser's men in Hawaii recounted the oxygen tent episode and similar stories. In Hawaii, I interviewed Tim Yee, David Slipher, Lambreth Hancock, and former Honolulu city planner Leighton S. C. Louis. Hancock recounted the "alumni association" story.

42. Kaiser Papers: Robert C. Elliott, "50 Year Book," ms., n.d. (ca. 1964), carton 295.

CHAPTER 15. GLOBAL DEVELOPMENT AND A PACIFIC PARADISE

1. Henry J. Kaiser Papers, Bancroft Library, University of California, Berkeley: "Description of Henry J. Kaiser Company Organization and Technical Qualifications," mimeographed, October 1958, carton 308. *Kaiser Industries Corporation Annual Report*, 1966, pp. 20–21. In "sponsoring" expansion of Armco Steel, Kaiser Engineers invited other firms to share the work; essentially, it was the Six Companies pattern of sharing work.

2. For a superb overview of the United States' rapid commitment to internationalism after World War II, see Paul Kennedy, *The Rise and Fall of the Great Powers: Economic Change and Military Commitment, 1500 to 2000* (New York: Random House, 1987), Chapter 7 and 8.

3. Kaiser Papers: interoffice memo, Chad Calhoun to Kaiser et al., September 4, 1947, carton 34.

4. "Victory in the Making," *Newsweek*, August 26, 1957, pp. 80–82; "Pride before a Fall?" *Newsweek*, March 3, 1958, p. 32; "The Kaiser Again," *Newsweek*, January 20, 1958, pp. 75–76.

5. Douglass Cater, "India: A Tale of Two Mills," *Reporter*, October 2, 1958, pp. 1–5.

6. "Ghana Gambles on Aluminum," *Business Week*, May 2, 1959, pp. 75–78; *Congressional Record, House* (vol. 106, no. 55), March 24, 1960; *Honolulu Advertiser*, October 23, 1961.

7. Kaiser Papers: Robert C. Elliott, "50 Year Book," ms., n.d. (ca. 1964), carton 295; Kaiser to Kwame Nkrumah, December 24, 1964, carton 202. "Ghana under Pressure" (editorial), *Honolulu Advertiser*, October 23, 1961; *Honolulu Star-Bulletin*, February 14, 1964.

8. Elliott, "50 Year Book."

9. "More Muscle for Henry," *Time,* June 4, 1956, p. 102; Elliott, "50 Year Book."

10. "Danger, Drama—Maybe Profit," *Newsweek,* November 1, 1966, pp. 75–78.

11. "Jeeps behind the Iron Curtain" (editorial), *Toledo Blade,* May 16, 1966; Dana L. Thomas, "What Henry Built: Kaiser Industries Has Become a Venturesome Global Conglomerate," *Barron's,* January 15, 1968, reprint.

12. *Hawaii 1983: Annual Economic Review* (Honolulu: Bank of Hawaii, 1984), p. 26.

13. Kaiser Papers: interoffice memo, D. E. Scoll to Chad F. Calhoun, March 31, 1944, carton 178; Kaiser to Admiral Emory S. Land, April 7, 1944, carton 173; Claude A. Jagger to Wallace Marsh, October 26, 1950, carton 70. Franklin D. Roosevelt Papers, Franklin D. Roosevelt Library, Hyde Park, N.Y.: "Abstract of Commerce Secretary Jesse H. Jones Dealings with Kaiser and President Roosevelt over Possible Sale of American President Lines," April 12, 1944, OF 5101. *Honolulu Star-Bulletin,* May 10, 1945.

14. Alyce Kaiser interview, December 5, 1983; Eugene E. Trefethen, Jr., interview, September 22, 1983. In addition to these two key interviews, I personally interviewed roughly thirty present and former Kaiser managers and corresponded with almost one hundred executives, friends, and family members who reflected various shades of opinion concerning their move in 1954.

15. Elliott, "50 Year Book."

16. Lambreth Hancock, untitled ms., n.d. (ca. 1984), in possession of Hancock; *Honolulu Advertiser,* April 23, 1955. Kaiser Papers: "Kaiser-Burns Hotel Development," mimeographed report, January 31, 1956, carton 235. Matson owned the Royal Hawaiian and Moana hotels; Roy Kelly owned Kelly hotels; and Kimball Brothers owned the Halekulani Hotel (Edward E. Carlson, "Recollections re Henry Kaiser," memo to author, 1984).

17. Kaiser Papers: Dudley Lewis to Chad Calhoun, May 3, 1955, carton 192. Hancock, untitled ms.; "Henry J. Kaiser: Pasha of the Pacific," *Parade Magazine* in *Oakland Tribune,* February 9, 1958, pp. 2–3.

18. Elliott, "50 Year Book." Kaiser Papers: "Report of John F. Child," mimeographed, July 1955, carton 233. Before Kaiser sold off his shares of the enterprise to Conrad Hilton in 1961, the complex boasted 641 rooms.

19. Hancock, untitled ms.

20. Carton 217 of the Kaiser Papers contains a flurry of letters between Kaiser and his subordinates and the planning offices and various Honolulu regulatory agencies, most dated in the late 1950s.

21. Hancock, untitled ms.

22. Ibid.

23. K. Tim Yee interview, January 19, 1984. Kaiser Papers: Donn Beach to Kaiser, September 26, 1955, and Kaiser to Stewart Fern, September 28, 1955, both in carton 115. For highly favorable statements of support for Kaiser from local union members, see "Testimony, AFL-CIO Musicians Union to Honolulu City Council and Planning Commission, November 22, 1957," mimeographed, p. 8, carton 217.

24. Hancock, untitled ms.; *Honolulu Advertiser,* November 5, 1956. Kaiser Papers: Fred Daily to Kaiser, July 11, 1957, and Kaiser to Fritz Burns, July 15, 1957, both in carton 233.

25. Kaiser Papers: interoffice memo, Mike Miller to Kaiser, December 1, 1955,

carton 236; Hancock to Kaiser and Burns, March 17, 1956, carton 214; "Hawaii Operations: Summary of Losses and Investment from Inception to November 30, 1959," mimeographed, January 12, 1960, carton 239.

26. Kaiser Papers: interoffice memos, Kaiser to Trefethen, November 29, 1956, carton 274, and James E. Durham to Calhoun, February 17, 1960, carton 215.

27. Kaiser Papers: interoffice memo, Edgar Kaiser to Henry Kaiser et al., June 25, 1956, carton 123; interoffice memos, Kaiser to Fritz Burns, July 16, 1957, and Kaiser to Trefethen, July 25, 1957, both in carton 214; Kaiser to William Shields, July 29, 1958, carton 215.

28. Carlson, "Recollections."

29. "He Believes in Hawaii" (editorial), *Honolulu Advertiser,* April 27, 1955. Kaiser Papers: "Outline of Proposal to Territory of Hawaii Senate Judiciary Committee," March 20, 1957, and John A. Burns to Kaiser, April 1, 1959, both in carton 210; interoffice memos, Kaiser to Chad Calhoun, July 17, 1957, carton 219, and Robert C. Elliott to Kaiser, February 3, 1958, carton 231.

30. Hancock, untitled ms. Kaiser Papers: Fritz Burns to Richard Wheeler, June 12, 1957, carton 216; "Henry J. Kaiser Talk to American Society of Newspaper Editors," July 16, 1957, carton 211.

31. *Honolulu Star-Bulletin,* January 29, 1960; *Hawaii 1983,* p. 26.

32. Carlson, "Recollections."

33. Kaiser Papers: Kaiser to Juan Trippe, February 19, 1958, carton 132.

34. For cost figures on Kaiser's own projected service, see Kaiser Papers: interoffice memo, Mike Miller to Trefethen, February 14, 1960, and Kaiser to "Our Friends in the Travel Industry," March 16, 1960, both in carton 194. Carlson, "Recollections"; "Kaiser's War with the Airlines: Statistical Bombardment" (editorial), *Honolulu Star Bulletin,* March 13, 1960.

35. Kaiser Papers: W. A. Patterson to Kaiser, May 4, 1960, and telegram, Lloyd Cutler to Kaiser et al., June 3, 1960, both in carton 194.

36. *Hawaii 1983,* p. 26. Kaiser Papers: telegram, Kaiser to W. A. Patterson et al., June 4, 1960, and Robert B. Murray, Jr., to Kaiser, August 18, 1960, both in carton 135. *Honolulu Star-Bulletin,* September 1, 1960.

37. "Hawaii Operations: Summary of Losses and Investment."

38. *Honolulu Star-Bulletin,* February 23, 1961; Carlson, "Recollections."

39. Yee interview, January 19, 1984; Lambreth Hancock interview, March 13, 1984.

40. *Honolulu Star-Bulletin,* February 23, 1961; Hancock, untitled ms. Kaiser Papers: Jim Stuart, "Press Release from Hilton Hawaiian Village," December 1, 1961, carton 198.

41. Lambreth Hancock, *Hawaii Kai: The First Twenty Years* (Hawaii Kai: Rotary Club of Hawaii Kai, 1983), pp. 2–3.

42. Ibid., pp. 1–4.

43. "Estate Exerts Huge Influence," *Honolulu Advertiser,* November 19, 1961; Hancock, *Hawaii Kai,* pp. 3–4; Yee interview, January 19, 1984.

44. For a charming account of the history and legends surrounding the Hawaii Kai area, see Jane Barr Stump, *Our Hawaii Kai: A History of Hawaii Kai and Maunalua,* Book I, Part I, *From 946 A.D. to the Kaiser Era* (Hawaii Kai, 1981); Hancock, *Hawaii Kai,* pp. 4–6.

45. Alyce Kaiser interview, December 5, 1983; Louis H. Oppenheim interview,

January 17, 1984; Yee interview, January 19, 1984. Kaiser Papers: John A. Havers to Kaiser, April 9, 1959, carton 196.

46. *Honolulu Advertiser,* August 5, 1959. Grant episode in Venice mentioned in William S. McFeely, *Grant: A Biography* (New York and London: W. W. Norton, 1981), p. 467. Alyce Kaiser interview, December 5, 1983.

47. For terms, see Kaiser Papers: Bishop Estate, "Open Letter," December 21, 1959, and interoffice memo, William Marks to Kaiser et al., February 12, 1960, both in carton 197; Kaiser Hawaii Kai Development Company press release, October 27, 1959, carton 266. *Hawaiian Reporter,* December 17, 1959.

48. Yee interview, January 19, 1984; Leighton S. C. Louis interview, March 13, 1984; Hancock, *Hawaii Kai,* pp. 12–14.

49. Three of his Hawaii men, David C. Slipher, Lambreth "Handy" Hancock, and K. Tim Yee, all volunteered this assessment separately.

50. For a sampling of comments, see Kaiser Papers: "Visit with Homeowners at Hawaii Kai, January 11, 1963," mimeographed, carton 223, identically titled memo, January 17, 1963, carton 209.

51. *Honolulu Star-Bulletin,* March 25, 1963. Kaiser Papers: interoffice memo, Kaiser to Richard C. Block, May 29, 1963, carton 266; Kaiser to the Trustees, Bernice Bishop Estate, February 22, 1964, carton 260; "Kaiser Hawaii Kai Development Co.," mimeographed, n.d. (ca. 1965), carton 266.

52. "The Changing Concept at Hawaii Kai," *Hawaii Business and Industry,* June 1964, pp. 53–56. Kaiser Papers: "Notes on Hawaii Kai," mimeographed, January 8, 1964, carton 197; Hawaii Kai Development Company press release, December 30, 1965, carton 269. Hancock, *Hawaii Kai,* p. 43.

53. Hancock, *Hawaii Kai,* p. 24.

54. Kaiser Papers, interoffice memos: Yee to Trefethen, April 18, 1967, carton 169; Yee to Kaiser, May 16, 1964, carton 260; Slipher to Kaiser, January 31, 1962, carton 267.

55. Hancock, *Hawaii Kai,* p. 36.

56. Kaiser Papers: "Dope Sheet, Alfred Apaka," mimeographed, n.d. (ca. 1965), carton 115; Kaiser to Milt Gabler, August 16, 1956, carton 124; Kaiser to Gabler, November 19, 1956, carton 196; Hawaiian Village Record Company press release, January 28, 1957, carton 218; interoffice memo, Elliott to H. V. Lindbergh, April 8, 1957, carton 219; Mort Werner to Kaiser, May 16, 1957, carton 230; Michael H. Goldsen to Kaiser, July 1, 1957, carton 218; "Hawaii Operations: Summary of Losses and Investment." Hancock untitled ms.

57. Hancock, untitled ms.

58. Ibid.

59. Ibid.; *Honolulu Star-Bulletin,* September 21, 1956. Kaiser Papers: "*Honolulu Advertiser* Press Release," June 10, 1958, carton 229; "Memo on KHVH Radio Conference, Agreements Adopted on Wednesday, September 11, 1957," carton 226; interoffice memo, Mort Werner to Dick Block et al., October 6, 1958, carton 229; Block to Hal Lewis, November 10, 1960, carton 229. *Honolulu Advertiser,* November 6, 1960; *Hawaiian Reporter,* February 16, 1961.

60. Kaiser Papers: Hancock to Herbert C. Richek, December 10, 1957, and Benjamin Draper, "Top Television in Hawaii, KHVH-TV," mimeographed, n.d. (ca. December 1960), both in carton 230.

61. "Switch Man," *Time,* July 20, 1956, p. 43. Kaiser Papers: Publicity Release, Kaiser Aluminum, June 28, 1956, and telegram, Merle S. Jones to Kaiser, May 22, 1957, both in carton 226; T. Mukiada to Kaiser, June 3, 1957, carton 230.

62. Elliott, "50 Year Book." Kaiser Papers: Kaiser Aluminum Press Release, July 2, 1957, carton 131; Al Heiner, "Proposed Comments on Television Advertising, Kaiser Steel Board of Directors Meeting, August 23, 1957," mimeographed, carton 258.

63. Al Heiner, "Proposed Comments." Kaiser Papers: Arthur Hays Sulzberger to Kaiser, March 11, 1958, and Pat Weaver to Robert C. Elliott, April 15, 1958, both in carton 258.

64. Kaiser Papers: telegram, Kaiser to Jack Warner and Bill Orr, October 13, 1960, carton 258.

65. Kaiser Papers: interoffice memo, Chandler Young to Kaiser, October 3, 1960, Young to Kaiser, October 27, 1960, Richard C. Block to "Friend of Hong Kong," n.d. (ca. November 1960), and Kaiser to Rod Taylor, March 21, 1961, all in carton 258.

66. Kaiser Papers: Marion Hargrove to Kaiser, September 21, 1961, carton 256; Kaiser to Trefethen, February 22, 1962, Fred Drewes, "Distribution List," February 19, 1962, and Kaiser to Thomas J. McDermott, November 29, 1962, all in carton 258. Hollywood *Variety,* December 4, 1961; *Honolulu Star-Bulletin,* December 26, 1961; *Kaiser Industries Annual Report,* 1966, p. 26.

CHAPTER 16. THE SUNSET YEARS

1. Eugene E. Trefethen interview, September 22, 1983; Edward R. Ordway interview, January 13, 1984; Stephen D. Bechtel interview, January 18, 1984.

2. Mrs. George D. Woods interview, December 9, 1983; Ordway interview, January 13, 1984; Ordway to author, February 16, 1984.

3. Henry J. Kaiser Papers, Bancroft Library, University of California, Berkeley: "Denby" Fawcett to Alyce Kaiser, September 5, 1967, carton 294; Kaiser to Mario Bermudez, November 23, 1954, and March 24, 1955, and Bermudez to Kaiser, May 9, 1955, all in carton 192; Bermudez to Kaiser, June 28, 1955, carton 114.

4. Todd Woodell, letter to author, June 5, 1984.

5. Mrs. Tom M. (Alice) Price interview, January 20, 1984; Herb Caen, *Baghdad by the Bay* (New York: Doubleday, 1953), p. 92; *Sacramento Union,* February 23, 1956.

6. Kaiser Papers: "Market Value Report on Fleur du Lac, Tahoe Pines," mimeographed, December 1960, carton 324. Lambreth Hancock, untitled ms., n.d. (ca. 1984), in possession of Hancock.

7. Hancock, untitled ms.; Tudor A. Wall interview, January 12, 1984; Louis H. Oppenheim interview, January 17, 1984.

8. Kaiser Papers: "Information for Press Release," mimeographed, n.d. (1948), carton 37.

9. Kaiser Papers: interoffice memo, Frank Hewlett to Kaiser, April 6, 1949, and Hewlett to Harold D. Leslie, May 16, 1949, both in carton 44.

10. Hancock, untitled ms. Kaiser Papers: Robert C. Elliott to Phiroze Nazir, October 21, 1963, carton 273; Dean B. Hammond to Skip Young, May 5, 1971, carton 67.

11. Alyce Kaiser interview, December 10, 1983; Hancock, untitled ms.

12. "The Arrival of Henry Kaiser," *Fortune* 44 (July 1951): 141-143.

13. Alyce Kaiser, letter to author, n.d. (February 1984).

14. Over thirty years after the match, virtually all persons interviewed still had very strong feelings about it. Some still haven't "forgiven" Alyce for "usurping Bess's place." Others believe that the rudeness and hostility expressed toward her were unconscionable and admire her for the manner in which she handled the situation.

15. *New Orleans Times-Picayune,* December 11, 1951.

16. Details about life at the Kaiser home were obtained from Alyce Kaiser interview, December 5, 1983, and Hancock, untitled ms.

17. Hancock, untitled ms.; Alyce Kaiser interview, December 5, 1983.

18. Hancock, untitled ms.

19. Sale of the Lafayette estate is mentioned in Kaiser Papers: press release from Henry J. Kaiser Company, May 17, 1956, carton 316; Henry J. Kaiser, "Portlock Estate, Summary of Costs to June 30, 1961," mimeographed, carton 295.

20. Hancock, untitled ms.; Carlyn Stark, letter to author, February 9, 1984.

21. Hancock, untitled ms.; Alyce Kaiser interview, December 5, 1983; July 16, 1951, p. 43.

22. *Honolulu Star-Bulletin,* September 4, 1960; *Honolulu Advertiser,* September 4, 1960.

23. *Honolulu Star-Bulletin,* April 16, 1961.

24. Alyce Kaiser interview, December 10, 1983; Dr. Sidney R. Garfield interview, January 16, 1984. Kaiser Papers: UPI Press Release, September 3, 1961, carton 295. The Athletics did not move to Oakland until the 1968 season.

25. Address to Marshall College graduates quoted verbatim in *Huntington* (W.Va.) *Herald-Dispatch,* May 31, 1955. Kaiser Papers: "Address to St. Mary's College Commencement," mimeographed, carton 126; Kaiser to Gardner Cowles, December 5, 1958, carton 296. Lorna Elliott, "Henry Kaiser: You May Live to be 100," *Science Digest* 53 (May 1963): 59–65.

26. Kaiser Papers: "Medical Record, Henry J. Kaiser, 1944," mimeographed, carton 296. Garfield interview, January 16, 1984; Alyce Kaiser interview, December 5, 1983.

27. Garfield interview, January 16, 1984. Kaiser Papers: interoffice memo, Garfield to Kaiser, May 29, 1945, carton 29.

28. Kaiser Papers: Permanente Hospitals Progress Record, Kaiser, Henry J., February 16, 1951, and March 21, 1956, both in carton 296; Kaiser to Harry W. Morrison, January 16, 1963, carton 136.

29. In mid-1948 tax consultant B. B. Robinson, president of Motion Pictures Enterprises in Beverly Hills, informed Kaiser that his inheritance tax situation was "about as dangerous as it possibly could be." Kaiser Papers: Robinson to Kaiser, August 3, 1948, carton 40. C. Ted Perry to Bernard E. Etcheverry, April 2, 1984; "The Henry J. Kaiser Family Foundation: History," mimeographed, n.d. (ca. 1981).

30. Hancock, untitled ms. Kaiser Papers: Kaiser to James T. Nolan, June 28, 1965, carton 265.

31. Unidentified newspaper clipping, n.d. (ca. 1966). K. Tim Yee interview, January 19, 1984.

32. James F. McCloud to author, February 11, 1984; Alyce Kaiser interview, December 10, 1983.

33. Edgar F. Kaiser, Jr., interview, May 24, 1983.

34. Hancock, untitled ms.

35. Henry Kaiser, Jr., had contracted multiple sclerosis in 1944 and suffered declining health until his death in 1961, at age forty-four.

36. Kaiser Papers: telegram, Lyndon Johnson to Edgar F. Kaiser, August 25, 1967, dozens of other condolence letters and telegrams, Kaiser Jeep Corporation release "To All Employees," and Dr. Jimmie B. Smith to Alyce Kaiser, August 28, 1967, all in carton 294.

BIBLIOGRAPHIC NOTE

During the course of any multi-year research project, authors encounter a number of dead ends along with their rich lodes of information. Since a key purpose of any bibliographic section is to assist future researchers in closely related subjects, I will discuss both.

When I discovered in 1981 that no biography of Henry J. Kaiser had yet been written, my interest in filling the void developed steadily, and I spent several months combing secondary sources. I read several dozen books and hundreds of articles; since I assessed the most useful and challenging interpretations in the text and chapter endnotes, I will not review them again here. As I began research, the *New York Times Index* helped me compile an almost daily chronology of the last thirty years of Kaiser's public career. The *Guide to Periodicals* index led me to hundreds of contemporary assessments of Kaiser's activities. I read every article recounting Kaiser's activities in *Aviation Week, Business Week, Colliers, Fortune, Life, Nation, New Republic, Newsweek, Saturday Evening Post, Time,* and *U.S. News and World Report*. Collectively, these journalistic accounts alerted me to the fact that Kaiser was highly controversial from the time he became a personage. I also became aware that Kaiser's public image vacillated considerably from month to month. Primary source materials revealed that he and his corporate advisors were very sensitive to public opinion, so the articles helped me better understand many of Kaiser's decisions.

Once I possessed basic knowledge of the broad outlines of Kaiser's career, I began the job of uncovering primary sources. Corporate contracts informed me that Kaiser's personal and business papers were being donated to the Bancroft Library at the University of California, Berkeley. Historians dream of being at the head of the line when important new collections become available to researchers. Scholars usually try to present their subjects "warts and all," and I hoped that family members and corporate personnel would not examine the papers too closely and confiscate any intimate or potentially embarassing materials. On the other hand, in the interests of efficient use of my own time, I hoped that archivists at the Bancroft Library would index the papers thoroughly and intelligently. When I examined the collection, I sensed that family members or corporate personnel had studied the documents carefully; almost no correspondence of an intimate nature remained. Corporate officials had far more material to examine; they left behind a good deal of correspondence revealing Kaiser's fighting qualities. Surviving records revealed his magnanimity; on occasion they also showed peevishness and exasperation.

I knew in advance that the Kaiser collection was massive, about seven hundred linear feet. Naturally, it was the first stop on my research trip. I spent several months in the summer and fall of 1983 examining the collection. The vast majority of the materials documented Kaiser's business career from the 1930s forward. Fortunately, secretaries and managers kept correspondence and carbon copies of replies between corporate headquarters and numerous government agencies. Interoffice memorandums between headquarters and the various Kaiser companies provided fascinating details on how Kaiser and his top managers ran his rapidly growing enterprises. There was considerably less correspondence between Kaiser and his peers in American business. Much of the collection documented interchanges between Kaiser's publicists and outsiders; hence Kaiser's activities and opinions were often conveyed secondhand. Yet I quickly identified "the Boss's" own handwriting; his cryptic instructions on how to respond to bureaucratic meddling, or a gentle remonstrance to a misguided subordinate, were often very revealing. Kaiser did most of his direct business by telephone; fortunately, his large office staff frequently wrote detailed memos which revealed clearly the nature of Kaiser's decisionmaking. The papers were so rich in source material that I spent much of the remaining year on the road attempting to fill in comparatively narrow, but important gaps in my information.

In addition to Kaiser's papers, the Bancroft Library held two other collections of interest. Kaiser's son Edgar worked as an executive in the organization from the late 1920s until his death in 1981. His papers were nearly twice as voluminous as his father's. However, most of the material either duplicated what I had found earlier in his father's papers, or pertained to projects not involving the senior man. The Six Companies Papers provided minutes of the Hoover Dam partners' organizational meetings and some useful insights into how responsibilities were divided up, plus some nuggets concerning their attitudes toward labor unions.

Official correspondence and internal memorandums provided a clear picture of how Kaiser organized and ran his enterprise, but they rarely yielded revealing glimpses of the inner man. Personal interviews with family members and former business associates helped me fill some of the gaps. Alyce Kaiser, Henry's second wife, provided fascinating stories in two interviews. Grandson Edgar F. Kaiser, Jr., spent a great deal of time with Kaiser in his last years, and he shared deep insights into his grandfather's philosophy of business and life. Nina Kaiser, Edgar's second wife, discussed her husband's later years. Former business associates provided revealing accounts of life with "the Boss." I interviewed Stephen D. Bechtel, Tim A. Bedford, Dr. Cecil C. Cutting (M.D.), Donald A. Duffy, Theodore A. Dungan, Scott Fleming, Dr. Sidney R. Garfield (M.D.), Sherlock D. Hackley, Lambreth Hancock, Peter S. Hass, Stanley Hiller, Jr., Dr. Raymond M. Kay (M.D.), Dr. Clifford H. Keene (M.D.), Leighton S. C. Louis, Louis H. Oppenheim, Edward R. Ordway, Gerard Piel, Mrs. Tom M. (Alice) Price, George and Ruth Scheer, David C. Slipher, William Soule, James E. Toomey, Eugene E. Trefethen, Jr., Tudor A. Wall, and K. Tim Yee. I corresponded with several dozen other business associates, many of whom provided useful additional insights.

Detailed exchanges between Kaiser executives and many federal agencies provided a reasonably detailed picture of how Kaiser did business with the government even before I visited Washington. Much of the documentation I uncovered at the National Archives, Library of Congress, and other depositories duplicated materials I had discovered earlier in the Kaiser Papers. This largely explains my heavy reliance on the Kaiser Papers; when citing primary sources, I credited the collection in which I first discovered them.

All told, I spent approximately six weeks in Washington, uncovering the most useful material at the National Archives. Without question, the War Production Board (WPB) Papers were my best "discovery." Detailed negotiations between Kaiser and government officials concerning aircraft, aluminum, and steel production yielded fascinating insights into Kaiser's thoughts and decisions. My high hopes that Bureau of Reclamation Papers would further detail Kaiser's maneuvering to keep funds flowing into dam projects in the 1930s were largely disappointed; most of these records are detailed engineering studies or technical exchanges between engineers and government inspectors. The Fair Employment Practices Commission (FEPC) Papers contained "Tension Files," which documented racial discrimination and other workers' problems in war production areas; this collection yielded little on Kaiser himself, but provided good insights into life in the shipyards in Portland/Vancouver.

Several other collections at the National Archives were useful, to varying degrees. The War Assets Administration (WAA) Papers contained some interesting exchanges between Kaiser's representatives and federal decisionmakers concerning the disposition of government-owned production facilities after World War II. Three other collections yielded less fruit.

The Senate Special Committee to Investigate the National Defense Program, 1941–1948, investigated Kaiser's enterprises on several occasions, but little beyond official testimony survived. According to several secondary sources, the Federal Trade Commission encouraged competitors against Alcoa; its papers provided few insights into the regulators' perceptions of Kaiser. Kaiser's papers were far more useful on that score. The western industrialist was periodically involved in national highway planning and politics from the mid-1930s until mid-century. Unfortunately, the records of the Bureau of Public Roads (BPR) yielded little information about Kaiser's role, or those of his partners in construction.

Surprisingly, promising-appearing collections at the Library of Congress yielded less than I anticipated. An exception was the Harold L. Ickes Papers. The self-proclaimed "Old Curmudgeon" compiled detailed diaries in which he recorded pungent opinions and anecdotes about many luminaries of the New Deal and World War II era. He had unusually strong likes and dislikes; while he generally admired Kaiser, he penned some revealing criticisms. For a time in the mid-1930s Kaiser worked closely with Thomas G. Corcoran, a noted Washington insider. If "Tommy the Cork" ever recorded details of his work for Kaiser, the evidence was destroyed; his papers were a major disappointment. The same assessment applies to the Jesse Jones collection; evidently, the shrewd Texan removed any revealing memos before presenting his papers to the library. I discovered occasional nuggets in the following collections; Raymond L. Clapper, Benjamin V. Cohen, Alexander P. de Seversky, Julius A. Krug, Grover Loening, Glenn L. Martin, Robert Patterson, and Henry A. Wallace. I had hoped that the Vannevar Bush Papers would provide more details of Kaiser's involvement in magnesium production during World War II; but the Kaiser Papers provided almost all of my information.

I visited four presidential libraries; three yielded fair harvests. At the Herbert C. Hoover Presidential Library, West Branch, Iowa, I found the Ray L. Wilbur Papers disappointing for material on the early politics of dam building. On the other hand, columnist Westbrook Pegler was an inveterate gossip; his papers contained rich files of letters from American praising, or, more often, condemning wartime contractors, including Kaiser.

At the Franklin D. Roosevelt Library, Hyde Park, New York, I found that most of the surviving exchanges between Kaiser and the President involved little more than conventional pleasantries. This was disappointing, as Kaiser was much closer to Roosevelt than any other president. Scattered references to Kaiser in the President's official and personal files were not particularly illuminating. Yet Roosevelt was renowned for his ever-changing masks, and several individuals in his inner circle assessed his relationship with the famous industrialist. I used the following papers: Adolf Berle, John M. Carmody, Leon Henderson, Harley Kilgore, Herbert Marks,

Leland Olds, Samuel Rosenman, and the United States Council on National Defense. Kaiser irked John Carmody of the U.S. Maritime Commission; White House aides Isador Lubin and Sam Rosenman revered Kaiser. The latter was Kaiser's most powerful supporter in the 1944 vice presidential nomination sweepstakes. One of my most interesting discoveries was an FBI background check on Kaiser, before candidates were chosen. It was a remarkably superficial and inaccurate piece of work.

At the Harry S. Truman Presidential Library, Independence, Missouri, I found little material in the collections of Attorney Generals Tom C. Clark and Howard McGrath, or in the collections of Will Clayton, John W. Snyder, and the records of the National Aircraft War Production Council. Comments about Kaiser in Truman's White House Files (especially OF 581) and the John R. Steelman Papers were more revealing. Steelman was an aide to the President during the postwar years when Kaiser was very actively seeking government property and reduction of his huge debt to the Reconstruction Finance Corporation (RFC). A good source for Kaiser anecdotes was the oral history collection, which included memoirs of numerous Truman Cabinet members, White House aides, secretaries, and other functionaries. Several individuals provided revealing comments on Kaiser's activities.

On my return trip to Colorado from Independence, Missouri, I stopped at the Dwight D. Eisenhower Library in Abilene, Kansas. I hoped to find primary source material further illuminating Kaiser's involvement in national health insurance initiatives, plus further insights into the political ramifications of the C-119 cargo plane investigation in 1953. However, voluminous White House files and personal papers yielded little new information.

Fortunately, a research trip to the East in late winter 1984 yielded additional useful material. At the Western Reserve Historical Society in Cleveland I concentrated on the Cyrus Eaton and Robert J. Bulkeley papers. The Eaton Papers did not enable me to fully resolve all the complexities of the Kaiser-Eaton stock fraud litigation between 1948 and an out-of-court settlement in 1954, but they provided a few additional insights. Equally useful were the Bulkeley Papers; he was a Republican senator from Ohio who was involved in the controversy. At Wayne State University, the Walter Reuther, Richard T. Gosser, and R. J. Thomas Papers yielded useful background information on the United Auto Workers' (UAW) efforts to help Kaiser-Frazer challenge the Big Three. Reuther and Thomas in particular admired Kaiser. Once the company briefly achieved fourth place in the field, lower-level union officers were considerably less helpful. The Bentley Library at the University of Michigan yielded a totally unexpected treasure. The Haughey Family Papers contained dozens of long letters "home" from two successful young engineers employed at Kaiser's Portland/Vancouver shipyards. These letters enriched my sense of life in these yards in the early years of the war.

I discovered only occasional items of interest in the Donald M. Nelson Papers at the Huntington Library in San Marino, California. The Robert F. Wagner Papers at Georgetown University yielded several letters between the New York senator and Kaiser concerning federal health care legislation in the postwar period. At Yale University, the Edward P. Weinerman Papers contained several letters and reports by a top-level administrator and troubleshooter in the Kaiser Permanente Medical Care Program in the 1950s; these provided a close look at interpersonal conflict between corporate administrators and many doctors.

INDEX

CPSIA information can be obtained at www.ICGtesting.com
Printed in the USA
LVOW08s2006010614

388126LV00001B/46/P